Sixty Miles
from
Contentment

Sixty Miles *from* Contentment

Traveling the Nineteenth-Century American Interior

M. H. DUNLOP

BasicBooks
A Division of HarperCollinsPublishers

Designed by Kathryn Parisee

Library of Congress Cataloging-in-Publication Data
Dunlop, Mary Helen, 1941–
    Sixty miles from contentment : traveling the nineteenth-century American
interior / M.H. Dunlop.
        p.   cm.
    Includes bibliographical references and index.
    ISBN 0–465–03365–2
    1. United States—Description and travel.   2. Travelers' writings—American
history and criticism.   3. United States—Social life and customs—19th century.
I. Title.
E.161.5.D86   1995
917.304´8—dc20   94–34240
                                                                            CIP

95 96 97 98 ◆/HC 9 8 7 6 5 4 3 2

For Donald, Amy, Meg,
and Ray

Contents

Preface

Nearly twenty years ago, I was beginning a search for early narratives about the region now called the Midwest when I came upon Reuben Gold Thwaites's *Early Western Travels*, a twenty-six-volume collection of narratives. I remember thinking how convenient it was for me that Thwaites had collected all the available material in such beautifully edited volumes that were such a pleasure to handle. I did not then know the extent of travel literature about nineteenth-century America, and in fact neither I nor anyone else knows it now; I have searched for, borrowed, bought, and scrolled through hundreds of nineteenth-century travel books, and still the field expands before me. Each book is a delight; many are very long, many are tediously detailed, none has any suspense—and as a result each is a series of surprises. The books are predictable on just one count: there is scarcely a travel writer in this rich literature who does not open the book with a brief preface asserting that he or she never intended to write a book and most definitely did not intend to write well. They were in a hurry, they said, and had more important matters to attend to than the niceties of style. Out of their conventional disclaimer comes their very freshness today. Most did not work over or organize their impressions of America; instead they rushed their books into print before the upheavals of change in America rendered them out of date. Their voices—asserting, complaining, laughing, questioning, marveling—dominate books that otherwise display, in many cases, no ordering devices whatever.

Their challenges for me lay not in reading them but in finding them, forgotten as most of them are, and most of all in discovering a way of working with them, writing about what they wrote about without pushing them into the background, and rendering their collective excitement over the old interior—Ohio, Indiana, Illinois, Missouri, Michigan, Iowa, Wisconsin, and Minnesota—an area whose interest has, since they left it, been too often blurred, forgotten, ignored, sentimentalized, and erased. Because I wanted my readers to be able both to hear them speak and to listen to what they spoke about, this book is an effort to bring a clamor of voices to the page and to reveal the subjects over which they clamored. I made no exclusions: every travel writer I could locate who visited and described a region that was to each of them entirely distinctive is included here, no matter the form of the book; the social and cultural matters they tackled I tackle here, taking care not to avoid or gloss over the disgusting, embarrassing, and painful and not to miss the surprising, puzzling, and wonderful. The region, during the century that they traveled it, was unsettled while being settled, and no one of the travelers said the final word on the interior. Nor do I.

For their aid, support, and interest in my project, I wish to thank Dale Ross, Ted Nostwich, and Jamie Stanesa of the Iowa State University English Department; Ed Goedeken, humanities librarian at Iowa State's Parks Library, for his prompt and knowledgeable help; and my editor, Steve Fraser, for his vision of what I could do with the material I had and for the extraordinary sharpness of his organizational eye. I owe more than I can express to my mother, who furnished me with a lifelong example of the indefatigable reader, to my father, whose excellent memory and fund of railroad knowledge I tapped again and again, and to my husband, Donald, without whose imagination, expertise, knowledge of American culture, and attention to detail this book would not have come to be.

Chapter 1

Secrets of the Interior

The American interior, in the first half of the nineteenth century, was the place to be. Five centuries of exploration and encounter had left only the North and South poles and continental interiors unvisited; early in the nineteenth century, a few explorers aimed for the poles, but ordinary travelers set out for the Ohio and Mississippi valleys, the expanse that was the focus of intense international interest. Uncounted thousands of travelers—American, French, English, Irish, Welsh, Scots, Spanish, Italian, German, Scandinavian, Russian, Austrian, Mexican, Australian; women, men, and children; persons of nearly every social attitude and political persuasion, every level of education and privilege—roamed the interior, and uncounted hundreds of them rushed into print accounts of their travels and observations. Of these texts a few are still read; some are lost; three hundred of them are the meat of this study. Together these travel books brought to visibility for readers around the world the daily life of the American interior.

There was no specific point of arrival in the interior, no single port of entry, no certain jumping-off place. The interior had no center and no set destinations that could mark either the end or the goal of a journey through it. Travel writers circled and wandered and roamed, never certain of exactly what they ought to see in three weeks, three months, or three years on a landscape unlike any other: for them, travel writing became a matter of framing observations and narratives that would somehow assess an expanse of barely differentiated landscape features on which everything was changing hourly and across which nearly everyone was moving. From their books, the interior emerged as the most important locale for the most detailed examination of landscape ever conducted in North America and the vantage point from which to inform an intensely listening and watching audience of the greatest and most rapid experiments in social equality and landscape alteration that had ever occurred anywhere on the globe.[1]

The heyday of travel in and description of the interior was intense but limited. Late in the eighteenth century the French traveler Constantin François Chasseboeuf Volney climbed a ridge in the Alleghenies just to "taste how the wind blew" from the interior; nearly every succeeding traveler descended the western side of the ridge and set out, on foot, on horseback, or by coach, to see it. By 1850, however, travelers were beginning to look farther west, across the Missouri, for new material, and by 1880, in their rush from the East Coast to the Rockies, travelers ceased even to glance at what lay between. Never again would so many observant eyes be trained so closely on the expanse of the interior.

The area travelers scrutinized during those decades stretched from Ohio in the east to the Missouri River in the west, bounded on the south by the Ohio River and southern Missouri and on the north by the border with Canada, an area now encompassing eight states— Ohio, Indiana, Illinois, Missouri, Michigan, Iowa, Wisconsin, and Minnesota—and a half million square miles. No traveler then called it *the Midwest*, no one thought that it extended into any southern state, and everyone experienced the area as distinctive—full of internal differences and variations, but nonetheless distinctively different from the East Coast and the South.[2]

Many claimed they had not seen America until they reached the interior: it defied their expectations, and its very unexpectedness often eluded characterization. Most found that, in the words of James Leander Scott, it "expanded amazingly upon reaching it," and some very American phenomena, though not necessarily peculiar to the interior, seemed peculiarly intense in the interior and more observable there than elsewhere. Its very newness and distinctiveness challenged even the most experienced travelers. When English travelers went to Greece, for example, they conceived of themselves as traveling in space but also as traveling back in time, to antiquity; likewise, Americans who traveled to Europe saw themselves as going back in time to the Old World, to society as it had been before America came into being. But travelers to the American interior before 1860 found themselves in the novel situation of traveling into the future, to a society emerging on an unfamiliar landscape aswirl with a mobile population. Many travelers underwent shock: if half the international travelers thought they had met their "kindred" in America, the other half thought they had visited an "entirely foreign" people. If some British travelers made efforts to see Americans as "brothers and cousins," Americans in the interior saw those same British as backward strangers embodying what Americans had rejected. Travel forward in time meant meeting a way of life and a set of attitudes invigorating to some and completely alarming to others. Locals displayed none of the characteristics of colonial powerlessness familiar to experienced travelers: they did not smile, sing, appear happy-go-lucky, offer gifts, or attempt to ingratiate themselves with the visitors; they displayed neither colorful native costumes nor curious but remote rituals. The locals that travelers encountered in the interior were not simple, were not peasants, and were not the folk, and their customs and practices were, though never exotic, often mysterious. The tension for travelers of expecting familiarity and not finding it—of having everything from table manners to nature itself defamiliarized—was never restful and at times was explosive. Caroline Kirkland pronounced the scene to be inexhaustible by observers: "It is," she wrote in 1845, "like nothing else in the wide world, and so various that successive travelers may continue to give their views of it for years to come, without fear of exhausting its peculiarities. Language, ideas, manners, customs—all are new."[3]

Travelers were further challenged by the effort to describe a landscape in flux. Between 1835 and 1837 alone, 38 million acres of public land in the United States were sold, with perhaps 29 million of those acres bought as speculative investment; between 1810 and 1870 the population of the United States increased from 5.3 million to 35 million, and a sizable segment of that population was on the move. The massive movements of life and property across a landscape in such flux of ownership, speculation, and alteration demanded that travelers revise old ideas. When every section of the landscape was either under alteration or available for alteration at a dollar and a quarter per acre, who was doing what to the landscape of the interior—altering it, disturbing it, eradicating its native cover—became a question of the most intense interest. What was "natural" was not the question. Nor was it to the point to apply familiar town-and-country divisions to a landscape where many towns were imaginary, or where within weeks tactics of rapid landscape alteration could be applied to a section and lo! a bank, a church, and a grid of numbered streets replaced the prairie. In observing that rapid alteration process, travelers recorded the near disappearance, within a fifty-year span, of the prairie landscape unique to the North American interior.

Travelers' individual motives were of far less moment to their accounts than were their distinctive capabilities as observers. From the earliest encounters with America—whether those of Leif Eriksson, Prince Madoc, or Christopher Columbus—travelers of course bore motives with them to America. They came for gold, for fishing grounds, for access to persons they might press into servitude, for valuable artifacts, for botanical and geographical knowledge, for personal profit, for a place to live, for an affirmation of cultural superiority. Travelers to the American interior in the nineteenth century revealed themselves motivated by desires to escape debts, hunt, gain asylum, do missionary work, visit friends and relatives, collect bones, rocks, and wildflowers, settle, dig for treasure, act as land agents, spy, promote rutabaga culture, demolish other travelers' reputations, analyze the American experiment, and see for themselves what America was all about on the expanse most available for seeing exactly that. Some appear to have traveled only because they had read the novels of James Fenimore Cooper, and they hoped to encounter a simulacrum of the noble Uncas. It was not, however, their motives that mattered; it was their personal equipment for observing that made a difference. The many pairs of traveling eyes that scanned the antebellum landscape belonged to persons who joined a powerful interest in landscape features with some highly developed abilities for describing it. Many among them were devoted botanizers, interested in the taxonomy of bugs and birds, eager to know the details of geology, and fascinated by the beginnings of archaeology; none of these fields of knowledge had yet been taken out of their hands by professionals. Their interests should not, however, be read as innocent, and the interior that was ripe for the exercise of such interests should not be seen as a source of innocence. Travelers' knowledge of natural history fed sharp-eyed appraisal and assessment more often than it indicated an interest in landscape aesthetics, and appraisal was not driven by an innocent interest in natural beauty. Instead, travelers' knowledge of and interest in landscape features allowed them to glimpse the costs of the settling, "improvement," and landscape alteration going forward in the interior—costs that will emerge throughout this book.[4]

Between 1810 and 1870, movement was the central experience of life in the American interior. Both the local population and crowds of international travelers and potential settlers were on the move; travel writers sped their observations into print and many Americans just as speedily wrote back and constructed their own views of the rapidly changing interior. Everyone who wrote was new to the landscape, there were few old settlers to serve as local informants, and there was little lore; everyone traveled in the same storm of rumors, speculation, and interpretation. When the population was not performing movement, it was reading about the movements of others, and travel books furnished the most popular and widely discussed general reading of the time, outstripping even the novel in popularity. In the interior, residents kept abreast of who was bringing out a book and when; they subscribed to it before publication or they rushed the bookstores on the day it was delivered. The harsher the book's judgment of the American scene, the better it sold: when the German traveler Francis Lieber approached a publisher about writing a sympathetic book on his American travels, the publisher said, "Anyone who writes on this country ought to know that the severer he is the better his book will sell."[5] Books by the alpha wolves of the traveling pack—a Basil Hall or a Frances Trollope—caused regional uproars and furnished the materials of daily conversation in the interior. In a cultural climate in which travel books were eagerly received, read with critical attention to every detail, searched for mention of the reader's own current habitation, collected, compared, discussed, toted about, and consulted in planning the reader's next move, these books became a household literature. No one, least of all angry local reviewers, thought that the American interior had given up its meanings to the travel writer easily, if at all. Although travel literature had no more of a center than did the interior itself, as a body of detailed description it nonetheless functioned to assemble the interior, shape it, people it, interpret it, and create lasting representations of it that readers could actually occupy.

Travel literature constitutes a literature of public life and the visible landscape. Even though traveling women had greater access to private domestic spaces than did traveling men, in fact most travel books focused on public life in the interior. Nonetheless, travelers had unparalleled access to daily life because, with nearly everyone on the move, much of the private and personal was carried on in public in the nineteenth-century interior—at meals taken in great public halls, in rooms and even beds shared with strangers on the road, in the public sleeping arrangements on steamboats, in the public combs dangling over public washbasins at public inns, and in public spitting. Furthermore, through repeated description, travel literature created a public agenda of notable sites and items on the visible landscape: the banks of the Ohio, the English Prairie settlement in Illinois, old French villages along the Mississippi, mounds, earthworks, Indian tribes, the confluence of the Ohio and the Mississippi, the 1811 earthquake damage at

New Madrid, worm fences, girdled trees, Cincinnati, steamboats and steamboat luxury, squirrel behavior, hunting, prairie fires, prairie flowers, the prairie itself. Most travel books had much less to say about presidents, states, political events, and local conflicts than they did about the dailiness of life, the sweep and the details of landscape, the tensions of mobility, and the irritations of manners. The events they ignored or missed occur and fade, and the noted personages they failed to meet pass into myth or oblivion, but the dailiness they observed persists, shifting, looping, backtracking, leaping forward, reappearing.

The books that came of their efforts tend to thicken around certain subjects they believed their international audience expected to hear about, and around those that defined what was distinctive about the area they were visiting: the landscape of the American interior—its features, its cover, its weather, and the behavior of its horizon; its unexplained prehistoric remains that dotted the landscape; its aboriginal population; and the effects of its sale, settlement, and "improvement" at the hands of white settlers. Also under continual interpretive contest were the features of the culture evolving while the landscape was being altered—the habits of mobility, the position of women, and the local views of food and eating, animals, sport, amusement, health. From travelers' books emerge the potential interactions between the landscape and the dailiness of the lives being lived on a shifting landscape, and finally, an interior far more interesting and strange than many have since chosen to believe. Many of their observations thicken even further around one question that was for them a very great one: the question of comfort—a matter of daily life and a topic of near obsession to nineteenth-century travelers, especially to the British among them—and how comfort was to be defined in and by the interior. To speak of comfort is to speak of the objects that fill and the attitudes that govern everyday life, and of these matters in the interior travelers spoke constantly. The subjects that troubled travelers continue to be troublesome; they suggest the uneasiness of a living past that is in no way comfortably disconnected from the present.

To tease out the texts' living contemporaneity and bring them into collision with the present, I went to their only contemporary equivalent—the literature of tourism issued by the eight states of the old interior—to see how and where in that literature nineteenth-century travel literature's subjects might emerge. Leading the tourist-literature barrage are state agencies that issue four-color photography on slick paper; local areas follow with newsprint pages stapled inside slick covers; bringing up the rear are hand-addressed mailings and photo-copied sheets of local history from towns with populations of only two hundred. As I read through the materials I had accumulated, the interior washed over me in waves of food, lodging, and attitudes toward the weather. In the southernmost parts of the interior, travelers are invited to see Civil War battles reenacted, to eat barbecue, and to venture outdoors at any season. Northward across the dairy belt appear the cheese shops and the dozens of festivals dedicated to single fruits or vegetables, each with its accompanying craft fair. Fast-food shops and chain motels are everywhere. In the middle latitudes, travelers are assured protection from the weather and the outdoors, summer and winter, in the form of skywalks, domed facilities, and enclosed malls. Moving farther north, travelers pass through a fudge belt, a sausage belt, and a walleye belt. Everywhere up to this point in the interior, there is an explosion of bed-and-breakfast establishments, everywhere food is fried, everywhere there is pie, and everywhere towns compete for travelers with numbers of Christmas lights—a quarter million lights here, a half million lights there, finally 625,000 lights illuminating Holly, Michigan. Tribally owned casinos dot the map. Still farther north, bait shops appear and, in the face of eight months of winter, fast-food outlets and golf courses diminish in number. Specifics about a tourist site's distance from "the blacktop" or "the groomed trail" become common. Then farthest north of all, in the forests and bogs, in the guide-service belt, even the previously ubiquitous bed-and-breakfasts disappear. At 249 days of winter, the outdoors is once again made available year-round.[6]

In the paper deluge of contemporary tourism I searched for patterns in the interior's current construction of itself for travelers, for hints of discoveries yet to be made, for experiences to be had there and not elsewhere, and for intimations of the curious and hidden. As I read, many subjects around which the commentary of travelers in the interior once clustered reappeared before me, some reshaped, some partially submerged, some unaltered. Just as in the nineteenth century, the landscape of the contemporary interior is continually implied to be without risk or danger to the traveler, and a certain warm and homey welcome is claimed to be ubiquitous. Few nineteenth-century travelers regardless of gender or age perceived the interior as a physically risky or dangerous place; they claimed they could wander it "armed with a pocket knife and a reporter's notebook."[7] They discovered its dangers only when they risked solitude on the landscape. Nineteenth-century travelers in the interior liked to represent themselves as lone explorers, though few actually were such; they suppressed information about the numbers of their companions and

cherished fantasies of being first and only at a given site. But the actuality of traveling alone (or even with a guide whose language a traveler did not speak) was for those who tried it such an agony of
monotony and silence that halfway through their solitary itineraries
they changed their plans and sought the society of the steamboat or
the stagecoach. Although certain locals apparently knew how to be
alone on the landscape, they did not open that secret to travelers. Neither the photographs nor the text of contemporary tourist literature
suggests that the interior is even now a place to be alone or to seek
solitude: couples, families, and groups populate all photos, and in isolated areas where, according to the brochures, "the silence is so absolute that you can hear the wing beats of the birds flying over," offers
of six-person packages and four-bedroom cabins subtly encourage
travelers to visit in groups. The other major source of risk perceived
by nineteenth-century travelers came from the interior's weather, but
the veering, extreme, and unpredictable weather that astonished and
even terrified travelers has been repackaged in tourist literature and is
rarely a subject except in the far north, where it is handled matter-of-
factly by resort owners who declare, for example, that they "have unpredictable weather. It can be cool, hot, rainy, or dry. Occasionally all
four within a 24-hour period." Tourist literature never offers the
weather as spectacle: there are no photos of floods, ice storms, or tor-
nadoes, and Cape Girardeau's brochure never mentions its historic
standing near the epicenter of the 1811 earthquake that rang church
bells as far away as the state of Virginia. Nonetheless the climate that
nineteeth-century travelers encountered is still in effect, even if some
tourist literature likes to attend to the seasons only as recreational possibilities. No tourist brochure from any state in the interior speaks of
"normal" weather; there may be averages but there are no norms.
Some resist the subject openly: the state of Michigan, under a heading
"Tips for International Visitors," tries to persuade those innocents that
Michigan is exempt from ferocious weather because it has "a moderate climate that is unique to the Midwest—a coastal climate in the
heart of a continent." Other well-known weather theaters avoid the
direct lie but tend to offer information without attention to its consequences: Minneapolis offers without comment a table of average daily
highs and suppresses information on average daily lows. Walker, Minnesota, just above the 47th parallel, says flatly that it experiences 116
days between hard frosts, leaving it to the traveler to guess what that
means. Detroit Lakes, west and slightly south of Walker, says, in a tone
of lyrical wonderment, "Seemingly overnight the brilliant colors of
fall are replaced by a blanket of dazzling white snow," but goes on at
once to note that many businesses nonetheless prepare to "greet the

hardy visitors." Farthest north of all, where January and April can strongly resemble each other, the weather becomes a travel destination: "We have snow when no one else does," says Ely, Minnesota, near the 48th parallel. The dense and busy insect population of the interior, a much-discussed torment to nineteenth-century travelers, is today even less often mentioned than the climate. Only two of the hundreds of local festivals in the interior celebrate an insect: the Mosquito Fest in Zoar, Indiana, and the Boxelder Bug Festival in Minneota, Minnesota.

If the twentieth-century interior often fails to be candid about physically felt features that startled nineteenth-century travelers, those matters are as nothing compared to its great secrets, its near-total silence about matters of the first notice not only to nineteenth-century travelers but to anyone who enters the interior today. Foremost among these is the look of the landscape. Today's tourist literature represents the interior as a landscape of lakes, forests, waterfalls, and gorges. Tourist booklets reaching for the picturesque and scenic try to supply what the past notably lacked. Nineteenth-century travelers, many of whom loved and desired picturesque views and traveled in search of them, now and again located a picturesque scene in the interior but always complained that the picturesque's rare appearances were separated by hundreds of miles of something else. That something else is utterly concealed in contemporary tourist literature; although distances between picturesque sites are just as great as they were 150 years ago, what lies between one waterfall and the next is now entirely squeezed out of view, never mentioned, erased, secret. If travelers to the interior do not already know they are entering an eight-state area in which 185 million acres are under cultivation, tourist literature is not divulging that secret to them; furthermore, in a full season's stack of travel brochures from eight states, there appeared not one telltale aerial view of the grid. On the cover of the Western Illinois booklet appears the only photo of a cultivated field, and the lone visible combine in all of the interior is at work in that lone cornfield. Inside the booklet a traveler may learn that the pictured $120,000 air-conditioned combine belongs to no particular farmer and the field to no particular farm: the photo advertises John Deere Headquarters in Moline, Illinois. All else tourist literature suppresses: the photogenic landscape judged suitable for luring late-twentieth-century travelers to the interior holds, across its half-million-square-mile expanse, not a single visible silo, machine shed, feedlot, confinement house, or grain elevator. Of 657,000 farms on this expanse, the only farms pictured belong to Amish farmers who, wherever possible, have been snapped driving something antiquated and horse-drawn, and who constitute the complete picture of agriculture in the interior. These Amish farmers resemble the farmers that nine-teenth-century travelers might have seen; here tourist literature opts for the past and refuses the present. Occasionally agriculture draws mention in the text as a concealment of what travelers must want to see, as a feature they will have to ignore; if on the landscape itself cul-tivation conceals fun, in tourist literature the fun landscape utterly submerges the cultivated grid.

When tourist literature sank the farm, the livestock went under with it. In all of the interior's current tourist literature not a single cow, calf, or hog appears in a photograph. In the nineteenth-century interior, travelers dodged pigs on the road, stepped around pigs in the city streets, and wrote at length of pig behavior that they found amus-ing, instructive, or irritating, but in the late twentieth century, the pigs of the interior have entirely lost their public presence. Iowa is home to one of every four pigs in the United States—16,400,000 in one state alone, or 5.19 porcine residents to every one human resident. But apparently not one of these pigs is photogenic—no Blue Boy, no half-ton State Fair prizewinner—for the state tourist guide pictures only a doe in captivity, a giraffe in a zoo, and two draft horses. Nearly four million head of cattle in the state of Wisconsin are anthropomor-phized into just one photo of a mechanical cow—Chatty Belle, the World's Largest Talking Cow, on view in Neillsville, Wisconsin. Some tourist sites suggest that farm animals may be suitable for viewing by children: Cosley's Animal Farm in Wheaton, Illinois, offers "a chil-dren's zoo containing farm animals and wildlife found in and around farms," and Fond du Lac, Wisconsin's Autumn Harvest Days Festival has a Little Farmer Event that allows children to view "geese, ducks, sheep" and (in the small print) "other farm animals" unnamed. In the Indiana Bed and Breakfast Association's alphabet-coding of its 112 ap-proved B&Bs, Type F, which describes just 7 of the 112, stands for "Farm house. Located on a working farm," and, the brochure warns, "Animals and implements may be present." The livestock that travelers are not invited to see have, however, been transformed into art and can be purchased. A traveler will find those same concealed domestic animals, represented realistically or in caricature, done up in jigsawed wood, plaster of paris, ceramic, and T-shirt form at arts and crafts shows and in shops in the interior, and a buyer can carry home sou-venir representations of the animals whose real presence on the land-scape tourist literature refuses to recognize. Furthermore, certain entertaining public activities involving livestock are never pictured or described. Many local festivals listed in tour booklets name among festive activities Kiss-the-Pig contests and games called Cowpie Bingo and Sow Bingo, but the rules of the games are not elucidated for travelers. The latter games involve painting a field into rectangles on which sporting locals then place cash bets. A well-fed sow or cow is then let loose in the field, and the local on whose rectangle of choice the animal first defecates is the winner.

The visible animal of the moment, as far as contemporary tourist literature is concerned, is the American bison, and the secret is how few of them actually reside in the interior. Even the earliest travelers to the area could locate little remaining large animal life there; the animals they did see and describe—chipmunks, gophers, squirrels, raccoons, and the unfamiliar skunks—are not considered tourist draws. Around 1787, the bison, said to be escaping the sound of cowbells, departed the scene for the West, only to be, after the Civil War, ruthlessly slaughtered on the western plains in the move to deprive Plains Indians of their food supply. Now, however, each and every state in the interior offers large photographs of bison, often in closeup so a reader can discern neither their actual numbers nor the nature of their captivity. The text may claim, as it does at Little Falls, Minnesota, that its bison "herd . . . roams next to a small-animal zoo," but an actual roaming herd would be unavailable for view by humans, of whom bison are not fond. And although buffaloburgers are offered for sale at Pioneer Days festivals even in such states as Indiana, where no early settler or traveler ever glimpsed the animal itself, no suggestion that bison can be a food source is made in the text near the photos of the noble animal. The appeal of the once nearly extinct bison is so great and the animals themselves so photogenic that bison have become a requirement of the tourist booklet even if, as is the case with the Iowa booklet, the bison are so thoroughly absent from the state that the Visitors Guide has resorted to a photograph of three dusty taxidermized specimens roaming a diorama in the State Historical Building in Des Moines.[8]

When tourist literature turns to wildlife in the interior, sport and recreation confront preservation, a confrontation which in itself embodies a difficult connection between the past and the present. Just as certain livestock can be used for entertainment, so some fish and amphibians, in the contemporary view, can be caught, laughed at, and played with. Plenty of photos show happy visitors displaying great strings of fish or single lunkers, and it is clear that the lakes of the interior have been amply and deliberately stocked for this purpose. Travelers are invited to acquire a turtle and race it down Main Street in Longville, Minnesota, population 200, where 400 turtles may race on a given Wednesday afternoon during the season, or to attend the International Eelpout Festival in February at Walker, Minnesota, and attempt to hook through a hole in the ice the eelpout, an inedible item billed as the world's ugliest fish. No wild bird or quadruped, however, is treated as a joke item. Some threatened species are kept at a distance from travelers, who are advised that they "might be lucky" to see a white egret, or told to tote binoculars in hopes of spotting a blue heron, or are admitted to a "controlled winter view" of bald eagles. When state departments of natural resources want to display some scenery but keep travelers out of it, they insert in the brochure a closeup of a timber rattlesnake sunning itself on a rock at the site the traveler might have been too interested in. Numerous nineteenth-century sportshooting travelers arrived in the interior equipped for the hunt, and many were disappointed; even while they failed, market hunters were stripping the landscape of its edible wildlife. Contemporary tourist literature makes abundant reference to hunting, shooting, game laws, and guide services, but the hunter's specific relationship to animals is never pictured. There are no photos of hunters, carcasses, or dogs tracking prey. The presence of taxidermists' advertisements throughout tourist literature suggests that they must be busy with something more than freeze-drying chipmunks for sale at souvenir shops, but all visual representations of the racks and trophy heads cherished in the nineteenth century are gone. It is rare even to come upon such an advertised tourist site as the Wildlife Museum at Bagley, Minnesota, which offers "780 wild animals on display (preserved by taxidermy)." Late-twentieth-century tourist literature looks away from hunters and the results of what they do, while nonetheless making available to travelers all the services necessary to those activities.

Both food production on the cultivated landscape and the fact that wildlife can be eaten are kept secret by tourist literature, but these sizable suppressions do not indicate that the interior is troubling itself over food. Food and eating in the interior interested nineteenth-century travelers deeply: they spent many pages describing and detailing the array of foods made available to them, the problems of limited access to that array, and their astonishment at locals' combination of avidity for and lack of interest in food. Food may still trouble travelers, but in tourist literature it does not trouble locals, no matter how much it may confuse them. Contemporary tourist literature caters to neither a strong interest in nor a knowledge of food on the part of the traveler: it does not detail the food, apologize for it, boast of it, torture itself over it, or connect it to health. A Peoria, Illinois, restaurant sums up a great deal about food in the interior when it offers "American cuisine, healthy alternatives available." But no one who stops to eat will go hungry, because the interior does not understand hunger; food is not a troubled subject so long as it can be produced in quantity, served in quantity, and consumed in quantity. A staggering array of food items is as much admired as it was 150 years ago at the long dining tables of the steamboats and hotels; casinos lure customers with buffets of a hundred or more food items, and it is more common to find the numbers of available menu items advertised than it is to find the items described or the style of preparation specified. The sizes of some foods enlarge drastically: muffins grow to six-inch diameters, cinnamon rolls to dinner-plate and shoebox size, and steaks to two pounds apiece, all following the path blazed perhaps by the giant sculpted food items—enormous corncobs, trout, and ducks—that appear here and there on the landscape. And while corn items—relishes and breads—have lost the power position they held on the nineteenth-century menu, other local specialties continue to be just as rare as they were 150 years ago. Across the interior, there are local festivals devoted to forty-nine different food items, often many festivals per item, but few of these foods are mentioned or featured in descriptions of local eating options.

In the nineteenth century, travelers perceived locals as interested in stoking themselves up rapidly but as inarticulate about what they ate. Names of individual foods and dishes tended to go wildly astray or to be collapsed into categories. The interior of tourist literature still chooses to locate eating in categories and then to struggle with modifying and combining those categories: tourist literature names among its categories, for example, country cooking, fun food, family dining, elegant dining, gracious dining, eclectic gourmet, eclectic American, and country food with gourmet flair. In Illinois's Heritage Corridor Visitors Guide, a local food writer struggles with categories for the eatery he is describing to travelers: "It's not a stuffy 'fine dining' experience," he writes, "but it's not in the category with taverns that serve burgers too. It's fun. It's relaxed." Some brochures pare—or enlarge—the eating categories to just three: fast food, homestyle eateries, and fine dining. Any traveler who reaches the interior has, without doubt, already learned the nature of fast food; "home-cooked" and "homestyle" mean a menu of items familiar to locals, with no surprises and often no liquor license; fine dining is both more and less elusive. In St. Joseph, Missouri, a traveler can eat steak, fried chicken, and seafood under the headings of both *family dining* and *gracious dining;* in East Peoria, Illinois, a traveler can eat those same items under the heading of *continental fare;* the identical foods ingested at Lake of the Woods, Minnesota, are called *gourmet dining.*

The rate at which Americans ingested anything they ate astonished nineteenth-century travelers, who were forced to speed up their own intake or go hungry; they insisted that the speed of eating increased as they moved westward through the interior. That competitive speed-eating is now so culturally enshrined that numerous local festivals feature eating competitions and award prizes; moreover, at the United States Watermelon Seed–Spitting and Speed-Eating Championship at Pardeeville, Wisconsin, speed-eating is combined with a sanitized version of the public spitting that nineteenth-century travelers loathed.

If food and eating in the contemporary interior suggest considerable continuity with the past, on the subject of the landscape of the past there is forced discontinuity. The traveler today has access to neither of the two landscapes that once acted as a major lure, that impressed nineteenth-century travelers into writing volumes of description, and that were unlike anything else on the face of the globe: the oak savanna—oak openings in nineteenth-century parlance—and the prairie. The oak savanna, a landscape of nicely spaced mature bur oaks with an understory of prairie grasses and no scrub between, is gone, and is never mentioned in the tourist literature of Michigan and Illinois, once its primary location. The term *prairie,* never used loosely in the interior, refers to land covered by the prairie association of grasses and forbs (broad-leaved herbs) whose dense and tangled root system can extend to a depth of fifteen feet. When the prairie association is burned, it makes a rapid recovery, but once it has been plowed, it is gone, and no one in the interior refers to plowed land as prairie. The extensive mixed-grass prairies of Indiana, Wisconsin, Michigan, southern Illinois, and eastern Minnesota, and the tallgrass prairies of central and northern Illinois, western Minnesota, and all of Iowa are gone except for patches in old cemeteries, along railroad rights-of-way, and in county parks.[9]

Contemporary tourist literature comes nearly empty-handed to confront the prairie past. It rarely offers a photograph of a surviving patch of prairie; because the prairie thrived on being an expanse, surviving remnants have neither the variety, the health, nor the visual effect of expanse. Furthermore, prairie does not photograph well, is never picturesque, and refuses to compose into scenery. Because individual prairie flowers that look stunning in extreme closeup tend to blur en masse and to become, from a distance, nearly invisible, nineteenth-century travelers lured by extravagant claims about great natural gardens of showy flowers were always disappointed with the reality of the prairie, and it is rare today to find any of those old claims repeated in tourist literature. When the state of Minnesota claims that a traveler can drive a twenty-mile Wildflower Route on U.S. Highway 218 from south of Owatonna to Blooming Prairie and "see hundreds of species of beautiful and fragrant prairie wild flowers," it meets the past by repeating one of its most questionable claims. The seasonal nature of such a promised display is not mentioned, nor are the facts that individual members of the prairie association bloom at different times within the season itself and that there is no moment when everything is on show. The possibility of differentiating species and inhaling fragrances from the vantage point of an automobile is dim.

Nineteenth-century travelers found the prairie to be a down-in experience of delicate detail. Some walked the interior, and many, walking or not, got lost. Many learned the interior's great paradox: that it is not a walker's landscape, though much of it can be seen only by a walker. This paradox remains in force; it was not eradicated along with the original prairie cover. Contemporary tourist literature, however, rarely suggests a walk in the interior, and it often submerges, muddies, or fails to mention distances that are very great. Only one of its travel arenas, the moundscape, refuses to cater to the automobile.

For nineteenth-century travelers, the mounds were invisible from the trains and rarely glimpsed from the steamboats; only to foot and horseback travelers were the mounds a compelling landscape feature. Every antebellum traveler wanted to see the lines, rings, and groups of mounds and earthworks that dotted the Ohio and Mississippi valleys; most wanted also to offer a theory about their builders; and many wanted to dig into them and carry off a souvenir. Because the moundscape was unprotected, nineteenth-century travelers excavated it at will; many would not cease raiding it until they acquired desirable display objects to carry off with them. Antebellum locals, in contrast, viewed the land as their resource and saw the moundscape neither as a repository of history nor as capable of yielding knowledge about a past of any interest to them. They did not respect the mounds, and often leveled them.

Today tourist literature mentions the landscape of prehistory to travelers but does not quite open it to them. The remaining moundscape has become a very quiet place: the thunder of nineteenth-century interpretive efforts has died, and no tourist literature today suggests that explanations of the mounds and earthworks are readily available: "Archaeological surveys" of Mounds State Park near Anderson, Indiana, "seem to indicate it was used as a gathering place for religious ceremonies," according to the brochure; at the Jeffers Petroglyph site near Renville, Minnesota, an exhibit shelter offers "clues to the meanings of the carvings"; and the literature on the astonishing Serpent Mound, an uncoiling snake a quarter-mile long and twenty feet wide near Locust Grove, Ohio, says of the serpent's architects, "No one knows exactly why they did it." While some prehistoric moundsites continue to be attacked by developers, those offered by tourist literature are aggressively protected—and not for nothing:

the desire to raid the moundscape is as alive as it was in the nineteenth century. Unlike most tourist sites, moundsites make demands on the tourist. Some require travelers to walk and to climb, some can be seen only by appointment, and park systems that control such sites may offer exhibits and interpretive programs but rarely cabins, picnic areas, marinas, or concessions. At Effigy Mounds National Monument near Marquette, Iowa, twenty-nine effigies of birds and bears survive; some nineteenth-century foot travelers found the effigy shapes so difficult to perceive from ground level that they refused outright to believe in their existence. Today the effigies are no easier to see; the extraordinary ten Marching Bears are a good two-mile walk along an unmarked trail from the nearest road and must be circled on foot if a traveler seeks to glimpse their shapes. No souvenirs can be taken away from such a site—no rock or flower is to be disturbed—and the brochure suggests that although rattlesnakes are rare, a traveler must "be alert for poisonous plants." The key invocation in tourist literature of the rattlesnake, whether present or not, signals sites that are not to be touched by travelers—and that, perhaps, travelers are better off not visiting at all.

When contemporary tourist literature displays for travelers the interior's Indian population—proportionally very small, just as it was very small 150 years ago—it plays its most complex cultural game of give-and-take with the past. Nineteenth-century travelers wanted to wonder at, if not fear, Indians, wanted to see them in paint and tribal costume, wanted them to perform, wanted to buy at the lowest possible price everything they carried or wore, and then wanted to flee them. Many travelers sought to immobilize Indians in sketches and to imagine them as statues, moves that allowed the traveler's gaze to rest uninterrupted on its object. Contemporary tourist literature continues to picture the Indian immobilized in statue form—in Cincinnati's booklet, a bronze statue of a half-naked male accoutred for the hunt gazes across the Ohio at Riverfront Stadium, and the Northern Illinois brochure offers Lorado Taft's forty-eight-foot concrete statue of Black Hawk in Lowden State Park.[10] But the Indian in tribal dress constitutes tourist literature's favored mode of representation just as it did in the nineteenth century, and any area that holds a tribal population offers four-color photos (never black and white) of Indian men and children (almost never women) in tribal dress. Indian men are regularly pictured talking to groups of white children or to white families who kneel or squat between the Indian and the camera, and who appear in profile so their pleased and intent expressions are visible. Tribal dress was in itself a tourist sight in the nineteenth century and is still considered such, but travelers can no longer demand performances as they once did, and brochures that list dates and places of powwows a traveler might attend also make it clear that not every representation can be appropriated. The Mille Lacs Band of Chippewa advises that at its powwow "picture taking is allowed, but a wise visitor will observe the courtesy requested by the tribe. A tribal member will guide you, explaining certain objects and rituals that should not be photographed." The body of fakelore-and-legend about Indians that nineteenth-century travelers wrote and rewrote makes only rare appearances now, though a few remnants of the pageant craze of the 1920s continue to dramatize, for the entertainment of whites, stories about Indians dying.

When contemporary tourist literature tackles the related subjects of the Indian population, the past, and land ownership, its language is a mix of the delicate, the abrupt, and the foggy. Norway, Wisconsin, both invokes and resists the subject of Indian land ownership when it asserts: "Before white settlers *invaded* the area, several Indian tribes *called* this area home." Possibly there is an equality of insult in the statement. The Fort Ridgely Festival at Fairfax, Minnesota, denies historical ownership to Indians by insisting that it commemorates "a time when the land belonged to no one and was nurtured by all." Warren County, Ohio, pushes Indians into nature when it invites travelers to stop and see "woods, water, and Indians"; Mankato, Minnesota, invites Indians to "return to their ceremonial grounds in Land of Memories Park," and thereby simultaneously acknowledges ownership and constitutes it as a "memory." A Treaty Site Museum proposed for St. Peter, Minnesota, "will celebrate the lives of all who have lived in this valley, and the stories we create in the present," says the brochure, in the apparent hope of simultaneously commemorating the past and erasing its conflicts.

The relentlessly celebratory tone of most tourist literature makes greater precision and acknowledgment of both past and present hard to come by. Only the state of Wisconsin issues a brochure that describes factually and precisely the size, location, and enterprises of each of the eleven tribes resident in the state; it is also the only brochure to contain a photo of an Indian woman, a member of the Lac Courte Oreilles Band of Lake Superior Chippewa. When tribes themselves control the tourist literature, the nature of major Indian enterprise on the landscape of the contemporary interior—the casinos—comes into view while its owners move out of sight. Some casino brochures make it difficult even to discern on whose tribal land the casino sits; and some, in a letter accompanying the brochure, use only one quiet line to announce that, for example, "The Bois Forte Band of Ojibwe would like to invite you to Fortune Bay

Casino." The brochure for Mesquaki Bingo in Iowa separates its photos of tribal-member callers and of all-white patrons, but then remixes the scene by putting an "Indian Taco" on the menu. The Shakopee Mdewakanton Sioux in Minnesota choose not to picture themselves but to play to the still ongoing nineteenth-century desire for legends: "At Mystic Lake," the brochure reads, "the legend is told of the wise, old eagle who carried his people's wishes to the Great Spirit. Some people believe that if the lake is still you can hear the eagle fly over the water carrying good fortune and prosperity on his wings. Perhaps one night it will be yours." The "legend" is satisfyingly obscure, but it is clear enough to whom casinos bring prosperity and which people's wishes are being borne aloft to the Great Spirit. Finally, late in the twentieth century, at these casinos, non-Indians can get from Indians the entertainment they continue to crave while tribes can move into control of their privacy and firmly position themselves, for the first time, in an appropriative relationship that reverses the past.

Tourist literature's tangled representation of the tribal populations of the interior is intensified when it turns to the construction of a visitable past, that same past that nineteenth-century travel literature so fully offers. The interior's landscape as it looks today cannot be a direct guide to the past, since its distinctive nineteenth-century natural covers have all but vanished. In the nineteenth century, settlement meant erasure, and erasure became a habit. Settlers took the ground cover, took the mounds, took the trees, took every acre for use, in some areas took nature entirely, and left the interior with a special problem: how to respond to a past that occurred on a landscape that, aside from some of its contours and the behavior of its horizon, is no longer visible. Tourist literature, however, is so little in the business of making travelers uneasy about the past that it rarely uses the word *past,* employs *history* only when followed by *buff* and thus reduces it to a personal quirk, and instead favors *heritage.* The tourist literature of the interior tortures itself, however, with a further effort to interpret the remains of the past as simpler than the present, to read the past as an expanse dotted with simple people enjoying simple times, and then, even though no one today may wish to reinhabit that simple scene, to mourn the simplicity as lost. This dominant reading of the past has two effects: on the one hand, lamentations over lost simplicity create a gulf between past and present, and thus deny contemporaneity to the past; on the other hand, they directly connect the contemporary interior to its past, for the interior's simplicity has always been a lost simplicity. What nineteenth-century travelers usually read as the interior's utter lack of simplicity, nineteenth-century locals often insisted on lamenting as a loss. In 1888 Charlotte Van Cleve, for example, was already "looking back regretfully at the days when we [local settlers] seemed like one large family, with common interests, and we involuntarily breathe a sigh for those simple primitive pleasures that will be ours nevermore."[11]

Tourist literature continues to breathe that historic sigh, which becomes an even greater torture when the lost simplicity is embellished with tourist literature's vocabulary for the past, a vocabulary loaded with such terms as *easy, warm, quaint, cozy, carefree,* and *charming.* Nineteenth-century travel literature suggests a different vocabulary for characterizing the interior: complex, hurried, cool, detached, mobile, unpredictable, ideology-driven, and public; its interior emerges as an expanse on which objects were lightly owned and just as lightly abandoned, an expanding space that made no clear suggestions about the size or placement of objects and structures, and an arena in which persons were best addressed as "stranger" because they found "friend" offensive. To note these divergent interpretations is not in any way to claim that one of them constitutes an authentic reality denied by the other; indeed, the mentalities of both the present and the nineteenth century are identical in lamenting an absence of simplicity. What matters here is how present-day tourist literature struggles to compose something visible out of the difficult past that it reads as simple, to impose patterns on it, and to deploy on it "authentic reconstructions" that can be, in tourist literature's favored term, "experienced" by the traveler.[12]

Tourist literature performs a not unusual division of the nineteenth century into two pasts, with the Civil War as a rough demarcation between them; the division is significant because the two pasts are handled differently. Antebellum sites are treasured, and accessibility to them is controlled; postbellum sites, in contrast, may be on display, in use, available for adaptation, or all three at the same time. A few antebellum sites are full-scale on-site survivals: Madison, Indiana, for example, is an architectural museum whose entire downtown is on the National Register. Others are collections: Naper Settlement Museum Village near Chicago, for example, holds a mix of pre- and postwar buildings transported to a single thirteen-acre site. Although the Naper brochure labels its two-part nineteenth century "Pioneer" and "Victorian," that division is a convenience only; in tourist literature, the artificial pioneer/Victorian disjunction signals no more than how a site will be presented, whether or not it is protected, and whether it is an indoor or outdoor tourist experience. On occasion it also indicates the intensity of the shopping opportunity available to the tourist at the site. The division itself illuminates nothing about the interior's nineteenth-century past.

Both the reproduction past and the museum past of the antebellum interior are created and controlled by an expertise that meets problems when it attempts to reconstruct not only the structures but the people and activities of the antebellum interior. Some once-standard patterns of interpretation have, in the late twentieth century, lost their force or have been revealed as uncomfortably exclusionary, and the stock of images available for peopling a visitable past has dwindled: invocation of the *pioneer* is now infrequent in tourist literature, and invocation of *the frontier* is even more rare.[13] Since nineteenth-century travelers rarely invoked either term—in their vocabulary, for example, locals were not *pioneers* but *movers*—the dwindling set of references to *pioneer* and *frontier* in tourist literature may indicate a new potential of connection with the past. *Pioneer* is a loaded word; it denotes not a fact but an ideology of land ownership and landscape alteration, and it casts an aura of purpose and nobility over compulsive movement; it is used to invoke incompatible visions of individual hardihood on the one hand and social cooperation in the form of barn-raisings on the other. Furthermore, invoking the *pioneer* creates an unbridgeable gulf between past and present; both present and future emerge as disappointing retreats from an imagined wholesome past. In tourist literature, some remaining mentions of *the pioneer* are only that: Portage, Wisconsin, for example, claims that "Wisconsin's pioneer heritage thrives," and there and then drops the subject. Occasionally the mention grows into a narrative. Sauder Farm and Craft Village near Archbold, Ohio, for example, offers a pioneer story: "In the mid-1830s some poor but hearty souls entered the Great Black Swamp of the Northwest Ohio wilderness. They sweat. They became ill. Many even died. But together they drained the swamp. And today Northwest Ohio boasts some of the nation's very finest farmland." Sauder Village, it is claimed, "pays tribute to those forefathers who tamed the wilderness." The narrative's many problems zoom into view: the story withholds mention of any preceding populations, and it can present landscape alteration as a sacrifice only for those who performed the alteration. As is usual in the *pioneer* narrative, what was nature to the Indian inhabitants emerges as wilderness to the white male erasers and tramplers, whose employment of Indian trails and sites is also entirely suppressed. Furthermore, the *pioneer* narrative without fail either imposes sharp gender division or erases women altogether: its regular invocation of "forefathers" includes only white male behavior and attitudes.

Because tourist sites cannot bring to visibility the historical activities of landscape alteration and restless mobility that nineteenth-century travelers observed in detail, their pioneer past is visible only in a very limited way through artifacts of production, old tools and old machinery, and through what visible and sanitized in-place craft activities they can muster: at Hale Farm and Village in Bath, Ohio, travelers can watch carpentry, blacksmithing, glassblowing, pottery-making, spinning, and weaving; Conner Prairie in Fishers, Indiana, offers candle-dipping and soap-making as observable antebellum activities; and the John Deere Historic Site at Grand Detour, Illinois, celebrates the self-scouring steel plow used to eradicate the prairie association but does not show it in operation on the "two acres of natural prairie" the site also offers for view.

The post–Civil War past of the nineteenth-century interior, in contrast, is assembled and constructed not by research and expertise but by individual and community fantasy. No traveler ever saw anything resembling it except when that traveler, in the final two decades of the century, stepped aboard a Pullman Palace Car. This past is located today on dozens of surviving Main Streets, in abandoned railroad depots, and in the heavily built houses once occupied by late-nineteenth-century money. Its name for itself is *Victorian*. If the recreated "pioneer" past is forced to ignore the landscape-alteration activities and intense mobility that constituted the core of that past, the urban "Victorian" past, whose decades of choice are the 1880s and 1890s, must both turn its back on the landscape and erase the documented social pain suffered by locals during those decades, when conditions on the land were so bad that a farmer spent more to put in a crop than he or she could possibly earn by harvesting and marketing it. The "Victorian" vision of the postbellum interior has, however, a stunning advantage over the "pioneer" past; where that past struggles and fails to show its populace, the "Victorian" past bypasses the problem by inviting contemporary travelers to act as the populace, and to be—albeit briefly—occupants of shops, houses, and eateries done up in Victorian Revival style, brilliantly lit, riotously scented, swagged, draped, and stuffed full of "crafts," teddy bears, doilies, candy, and Christmas decorations.

The consumer emphasis of the Victorian past reaches its zenith at Christmas. The nineteenth-century interior had no Christmas of its own that anyone nowadays wishes to repeat; there were no evergreens on the prairie or in the cornfield, and no fuss even in the homes of the wealthy. Tourist literature, however, offers a version of Christmas past that plays to desires long held in the region: Christmas authorizes heavy consumption of sugar, it can be seen from a moving car, it revives the red-and-gold splendor of the antebellum steamboats, it reauthorizes the interior's historic disregard of privacy by inviting open inspection of the houses of others, and it plays to the religion of abundance. Despite its gaudy consumer advantage, however, the "Victorian" past experiences even greater difficulties than the "pioneer" past in defining or even suggesting activities to be performed by its temporary residents, and its politics and covert expressions of ideology bring it into direct conflict with the ideology that dominated the antebellum interior.[14]

The interior, in tourist literature, offers little apparent resistance to the term *Victorian,* or perhaps can no longer remember the grounds for resistance to a term that nineteenth-century locals would have scorned. It is worth noting that Victoria ruled not the United States but a remote island and an enormous empire, resistance to the social and political conditions of which sent hundreds of thousands of immigrants to the interior. There they not only perpetuated their resistance through very different social practices and politics, but also expressed that resistance daily, to the discomfort of class-conscious travelers, by denying all efforts at class division and by directing expressions of scorn and pity at those same travelers. Nonetheless, the "Victorian" past that tourist literature of the interior invites travelers to visit is a phenomenon of astonishing range, whose language, more than any other element in tourist literature, works to cut itself off from the past it is speaking about.

Tourist literature's vocabulary for the Victorian past is extensive: *romantic, exquisite, cozy, charming, warm, tasteful, elegant, rich, quaint, majestic, lavish, grand, stately, gracious, plush, opulent,* and *exclusive.* The verbal vision explodes into life in the many hundreds of bookable bed-and-breakfast lodgings that dot the landscape of the interior, and that occupy not only structures described by their owners as stately homes, mansions, manors, museum homes, and country estates, but also such structures as barns, schoolhouses, rectories, sod-house reconstructions, poorhouses, bunkhouses, jails, and churches. The Victorian vision is powerful enough to transform the 1869 Fillmore County Jail in Preston, Minnesota, into an "Italianate" B&B and its cells into "rooms furnished in Victorian motif in individual styles and named after old-time sheriffs," and because the vision operates without reference to the landscape, it can transform a twentieth-century farm owned by a Minnesota highway patrolman into a "Victorian gentleman's country estate." *Victorian* is an experience not of time or place but of architectural detail and interior decoration; it is sold to the traveler with a detailed vocabulary of antiques, wood floors, tin ceilings, lace curtains, heirlooms, nooks and crannies, quilts, wicker, stenciling, stained glass, Tiffany chandeliers, verandas, balconies, turrets, cupolas, and suitor's windows. The nineteenth-century urban style it seeks to reinhabit worked at blocking the sun and excluding the out-of-doors with a half dozen layers of fabric over the windows; preferring nature dead, perpetrators of the style transported it into the domestic interior in the form of taxidermy and dried flowers. It is the style emulated by Pullman Palace Cars in the final two decades of the nineteenth century. The Pullman cars, however, combined their decor with the most advanced technology and the best service; the Victorian B&B, in contrast, strips the Pullman of two of its three meals, its service, and its inspired gadgetry, and offers the traveler only the same faded decor which, on its previous trip through the interior, operated to conceal the landscape from visibility.

On the landscape of the interior, the Victorian vision of the past excludes some matters and rewrites others. The contemporary edition of the *Victorian* keeps the nineteenth century's dried flowers but replaces its taxidermy with stuffed teddy bears; it allows none of the spittoons and spring-loaded under-chair spit-drawers familiar to the nineteenth century, and it forbids smoking everywhere. Other everyday and inexpensive elements of Victorian decor it refashions into contemporary treasures: the fact that post–Civil War urban decor was machine-made, cheap, and easily reproducible has been suppressed, allowing the products of the fret saw, the metal template, the rubber mold, the stamping die, the lacemaking machine and the printing press to be transformed into the antique, the unique, and even the handmade, and inducing individual restorers to labor at reproducing by hand the machine-made effects of a hundred years ago. An accurate name for the style—Later Nineteenth-Century American Industrial—lacks the romance and the cherished anglophilic sentiments evoked for some by the very word *Victorian,* a term that, in its current usage, constructs the interior's past as a brilliantly lit, seriously cluttered, and elaborately festooned domestic interior—and then, significantly, defines that interior as comfort itself.[15]

Few concepts were under heavier contest in the interior, from the point of view of travelers, than that of comfort. In the nineteenth century, Americans in the interior lived so differently from any previously known version of either urban or rural wealth or poverty that every observer found himself or herself struggling to define the difference. Locals looked to be favoring a combination of bare private spaces more or less open to the out-of-doors and glittering public spaces that, though much admired, were often treated with disdain, and spat upon. The mobile population of the nineteenth-century interior seemed to have taught itself to disdain objects; if taste is what persons make room for in their lives, the antebellum interior preferred not to make room. Comfort seemed to run on a principle of some comfort for all, rather than the principle more familiar to international travelers of perfect comfort for the few and none for others. But the new principle sometimes meant no comfort for anyone. Furthermore, locals seemed to find their comfort not in the home but in ideology and in public mobility—in the dazzling Mississippi River steamboats whose heyday lasted fewer than ten years but whose vision of luxury lived on, in plush-covered hotel lobbies, and in the Pullman Palace Cars of the last decades of the century.

The interior's version of comfort may have been a challenge and a mystery to many travelers, but efforts to import other versions of comfort from other cultures failed to displace it, and the imports themselves failed, in their isolation, to survive on their own. In the 1820s, Morris Birkbeck and Richard Flower, two Englishmen seduced by a resemblance between Illinois's uncultivated landscape and the grounds of certain English country estates, set out to build themselves English country houses at Albion, Illinois, and to live a lordly life that had been unavailable to them in their native England. Their fantasy of the country gentleman required the collusion of their American neighbors, but those persons refused to play their assigned roles of underpaid servants and cap-tipping rustics. Because no one else would do his work for him, Birkbeck's crops were fantasies, he was cut off from the life around him, and his vision of leisure emerged as a precious and brooding idleness. He never understood how different a meaning the word *country* acquired when it crossed the Atlantic.

Although the landscape that once suggested the carefully maintained grounds of an English country house is gone, efforts to stabilize in the interior a saleable version of English country life continue everywhere on the B&Bscape. Dozens of "Victorian" B&Bs denominate themselves Victoria Manor and Victoria Arms, and invite travelers to "experience English hospitality" and sleep in "English country style" in rooms that "evoke images of King Arthur with suit of armor and hand-hewn woodwork." The planned and tidy gardens that no nineteenth-century traveler ever found in the interior—because sheer space denied visual point to that type of garden—appear, finally, and are offered by the B&Bs as "period courtyard gardens" that "recapture the majesty of history" or, failing such an effort, as "an English garden seat in the pines." A meal that no one in the interior ever ate is shifted back eight hours to be sold as an "English Tea Breakfast." Numerous nineteenth-century international travelers would have read the boast of "English hospitality" as not a lure but a warning. "I have frequently traveled in England, both by coach and on foot," wrote James Logan in 1838, "but I never met with any hospitality there." In 1856, Ida Pfeiffer dismissed "that English comfort of which we hear so much" with the assertion that nowhere in the world had she suffered so much inconvenience as in England.[16]

The Victorian B&B vision replicates Morris Birkbeck's project at the English Prairie—but Birkbeck's problems are inseparable from his project. Like Birkbeck's English Prairie vision, the Victorian B&B has a servant problem. Across the nineteenth century, travelers never ceased discussing the interior's "servant problem," and never stopped concocting plans for luring girls and women into domestic service; servants, however, remained simply unavailable, and anyone who, in the face of so much opportunity, chose to work as a bodyservant or a domestic was pitied. The country-house vision is still difficult to activate in the interior because no one—least of all the B&B owners—wants to play some of the roles necessary to that vision. B&B owners try to avert the question of who is serving whom by defining the lodging house as "our home" and confining the guests to the bedrooms, but the uneasiness of the situation persists. Morris Birkbeck's vision of the gentleman's leisure life was transformed into an appalling idleness when he performed that life on what was and is essentially a landscape of work; the B&Bs also struggle with the question of what travelers can do in the vision of the past that they have bought entry to. Most B&B rooms contain neither telephone, nor radio, nor television: the owners' rigorous exercise of the antiquarian point of view excludes communication between the past and the present. Travelers will not have the run of the house; the advertised fireplaces seem pointless in a nation devoted to central heating for the past 150 years; smoking, pets, and children are not allowed. Just as Birkbeck learned that what passed for comfort in England became uncomfortable in the interior, so the B&B version of "English comfort," marketable as a concept, is uncomfortable in performance.

From another angle, the Victorian B&B phenomenon could be said to meet antebellum discomfort head-on by replicating it: B&Bs answer to needs exactly as basic as those answered to by antebellum inns in the interior, which also were lodged in private homes, also offered a bed and a breakfast, and also forced travelers to share the washing-up facilities. Like contemporary B&Bs, the nineteenth-century inns put the traveler under the control of a dictatorial innkeeper, brought domestic animals—live as opposed to ceramic—indoors, and seriously reduced the privacy level for all concerned. The same unease and tension over whose space was whose obtained then as now, along perhaps with the intense relief travelers might feel on departing after eating a breakfast whose contents they did not select. From this point of view, only the decor differentiates the nineteenth-century inn from the twentieth-century B&B. The B&B's shadowy replication of a past that it furiously rejects does not, however, mitigate that rejection, that expressed longing to be elsewhere, that characterizes the phenomenon. Any re-creation of English country life in the interior speaks directly not only of class-based distinctions but also of America's recurrent enchantment with titles and hereditary privilege. Numerous B&Bs even title the guest rooms "Sir Thomas's Room" or "Queen Anne's Chambers" because they cannot title the guests. The vision of class-based exclusivity and privilege collapses, however, before the fact that hundreds of B&Bs offer the vision in identical form: the egalitarian undertow of the interior allows nothing to be rare or unique.

Numerous towns in the interior also engage in Victorianism's genteel project and offer "Victorian Fairs" to "celebrate the elegant past," but that fantasy past is in continual collision with other pasts. In Chillicothe, Ohio, Victoria Manor coexists on the landscape with some great remains of Hopewell culture, twenty-three mounds on a thirteen-acre site marked by an earth wall. In Granville, Ohio, Victoria's Parlour jostles with Moundbuilder Antiques; in Mendota, Illinois, Lord Stockings B&B with English garden is, the owners note, "close to Starved Rock," where in the eighteenth century a band of Illinois Indians under siege perished slowly of thirst and starvation. These juxtapositions suggest that after sleeping and eating breakfast in the English country-house fantasy provided by the Victorian B&B, the traveler will step outside onto a landscape that bears no visible relation whatever to fantasy, and whose points of interest are utterly disconnected from flowered chintz and teddy bears. Only in the interior's far north is the Victorian vision rejected. At Two Harbors, Minnesota, near the Canadian border, the Lodging Directory forthrightly rejects "boutique-bottled quaintness" and the motel listings are equally forthright about such individual local conveniences as hot-water heads, telephones, and in-room coffee.[17]

Although the beckoned flight to the Victorian interior performs the service of pointing out that comfort—which was seriously disarranged in the nineteenth-century interior—is as much under contest as it was 170 years ago, in every other sense the confection called *Victorian* is a set of idle fabrications barring entry to the past. The interior's past, whether pre— or post—Civil War, is too unruly to be contained by the narrowness of the Victorian phenomenon: outside the fantasy manors, on the slippery and deceptive landscape of the interior, there exist more interesting versions of discomfort, revisions of perception, and actual confrontations to be had with the past. In the tourist literature just examined, the paths on which past and present cross are those of colliding interpretations. Tourist literature interprets as simple an arena that did not see itself as simple, often sentimentalizes a past that was unsentimental about everything, conceals the dailiness of a landscape whose cover was erased in service of dailiness, and in the delicate ideological dance of democracy occasionally stumbles toward genteel class division—but at the same time tourist literature answers to the interior's love of mobility, repetition, and universal availability of every desirable, and it sketches the continuing struggle of the present with its continually contemporaneous past.

Nineteenth-century travelers found the interior free of danger but difficult to locate themselves on comfortably. Local life on it was neither simple nor slow, everyone was a stranger, everyone loved innovation, and the rate of visible change probably surpassed anything known today. The locals who roamed the interior in a state of self-controlled egalitarian public detachment were working on the subject of comfort, trying it out, testing it, paying to visit and lounge about in its arenas of public luxury. They opened the subject of comfort but did not close it; how to live on the landscape of the interior remained in question. The landscape on which their search went forward has lost its cover but not its shape: the interior continues to be easy to enter, easy to get lost in because of its lack of markers, stranger, funnier, and more deceptive than either insiders or outsiders usually think, still an area of great monotony and great subtlety, its rimmed horizon still delimiting travelers' vision and offering only the pale distance of the sky as a release, still challenging perceptual habits formed by built or scenic landscapes, still pulling objects out of shape, still deranged by space. On the interior's landscape, nineteenth-century travelers felt certain that they were in the presence of meanings under construction in highly volatile ways, and the travelers' three hundred surviving texts open that volatile contest now.

Chapter 2

The Derangement of Comfort

In 1828, the English traveler Frances Trollope, who had been living in Cincinnati, was pleased to be able to move her family a mile and a half outside town to "a very pretty cottage" offering "all the privileges of rusticity." From Trollope's English point of view, true gentry were to live not in the city but in the country, where they could enjoy a suitable life of privilege and leisure. Determined to make the landscape of the interior supply experiences she valued, Trollope equipped herself and company with books, sketchpads, pencils, and sandwiches, and set out from the cottage on a bucolic excursion. The day was very hot. In search of cooling breezes and a prospect to sketch, the group struggled up what they took to be a hill, but a hill so steep that they could have leaned against it while climbing. Nonetheless, Trollope wrote, "We were determined to enjoy ourselves, and forward we went, crunching knee deep through aboriginal leaves."

Eventually the climb exhausted and the landscape frustrated the party: they were unable either to emerge from the heavy tree cover or to locate a sketchable prospect. When the group decided to "repose awhile on the trunk of a fallen tree, the whole party sank together through its treacherous surface into a mass of rotten rubbish. Frogs, lizards, locusts, katydids, beetles, and hornets had the whole of their various tenements disturbed ... we were bit, we were stung ... a cloud of mosquitoes gathered round. We lost all patience." The landscape gave up to them one secret when the hill they had climbed ultimately revealed itself to be a ridge, more thickly wooded at the top than at the bottom. Unable to capture any "views" of the landscape below them, the party got turned around in the effort, slid and scrambled down the far side of the ridge, and ended their descent a full three miles away from the "pretty cottage" where their excursion had begun. Trollope wrote: "We shall none of us ever forget that walk. It was painful to tread, it was painful to breathe, it was painful to look round ... we promised each other faithfully never to propose any more parties of pleasure in the grim stove-like forests of Ohio."

Trollope lost her battle with a landscape that never struck travelers, once they were in it, as simple, easily readable, or accommodating. It rarely presented itself for conventional scenic interpretations, it did not readily yield up its history, and it posed stiff resistance to travelers' efforts to make it accommodate imported, culture-bound demands. In the case of Trollope's adventure, the landscape's features prevented access to the vista she desired, offered no place to sit, and refused themselves to the artist. The landscape was not rustic, pastoral, bucolic, or even rural; the insects owned it and let on that they did. It did not intend itself for the "repose" of humans, and it would not aid in Frances Trollope's gentrification project.[1]

Travel writers, whether or not any so intended, acted as landscape assessors and evaluators for readers around the world who used their books as guides to the possibilities of emigration, but they could not assess the interior without plunging into it, its weather, its weeds, its swarms of insects. Unable to both see the landscape and be artificially sheltered from it, travelers were made to experience the interior much as the local settlers did, and that experience was less visual than it was intensely physical. The ordinary landscape of the American interior refused to suit itself to such popular visual categories as the sublime and the picturesque, it offered few vistas or prospects for a traveler to assemble into panoramic description, and its immense sameness from one mile to the next refused to compose into "views." After the initial novelties of Ohio River scenery and the prairie landscape—scenes that all travelers exclaimed over with delight—had dissipated, the peculiar monotony of the American interior became "alike fatiguing to the eye and the fancy." The unchanging continuous level of the prairie horizon moved with the traveler, eliminating sensations of forward progress and leaving travelers to slosh in a silent and humid landscape bowl.

Pleasures that travelers associated with nature did not always present themselves in the interior: Constantin François Chasseboeuf Volney complained that he had traveled in July of 1804 from Louisville to Vincennes "without hearing the song of a single bird." Travelers who wanted to admire colorful and unthreatening chirpers were instead assaulted bodily by the interior's formidable insect population. In 1843, William Oliver described in detail a traveler's battle with the interior's dominant population: "Among the novel discomforts of the west, that of insects is one of no trifling character," he wrote. "The whole earth and air seems teeming with them, and mosquitos, gallinippers, bugs, ticks, sandflies, sweat-flies, house-flies, ants, cockroaches, etc., join in one continued attack against one's ease. No sooner do those who wage war during the day retire, than their place is filled with others, laboring with equal effect through the night, whilst the indefatigable mosquito heads the attack at all times." Despite such a range of unfamiliar discomforts, travelers were determined to render the value and quality of a landscape whose look was elusive and whose feel was at times a torture.[2]

Between 1790 and 1870 the landscape of the interior was being rapidly altered in service of production and a local style of daily living. No travelers, regardless of their national origin, could adjust their aesthetic categories to make acceptable the alterations that locals, under the headings of cultivation and improvement, were effecting on the landscape of the interior. The earliest of nineteenth-century travelers in Ohio claimed that locals were so devoted to stag and bear hunting that they did nothing whatever to "meliorate their new possessions" of two or three hundred acres of land. By the 1820s both stags and bears had retreated from the scene of cultivation, locals had laid hands on the landscape, and travelers spent the next twenty-five years agonizing over the look of the land that had passed under the "meliorating" and "improving" hands of its owners. The landscape of improvement shocked the eye of the traveler with its ugliness: half-rotted tree stumps, skeletons of trees notched and left to die, straggling worm fences, fields like gashes in the prairie, doorless cabins daubed with clay, and towns like mere heaps of shacks dropped on mud. The interior was, no one doubted, a rich country, but after improvement its richness was as visually unreadable as were its comforts.

Cross-cultural commentary on American-style improvement was angry, disgusted, even appalled, never less than sharply disapproving. "American settlers' 'improvements,' as they are called, are what an English farmer would call by any other name," asserted William Amphlett, but many who held no brief for English farming methods had the same difficulty with accepting the look of "improvement." Locals' methodical destruction of the trees, whether few or many, diverged so sharply from travelers' valuation of trees as to be a source of pain: no traveler felt comfortable in the presence of a tree being slowly and deliberately made to die. In 1824 an angry William Blane charged that "an American has no idea that anyone can admire trees or wooded ground. To him a country well cleared, that is where every stick is cut down, seems the only one that is beautiful or worthy of admiration." Timothy Flint, an experienced resident of the interior, assented to the charge—though exempting himself from it—that settlers disliked trees: to the eye of some American improvers, Flint wrote, "the lofty skeletons of dead trees, the huge stumps that remain after cultivation has commenced, are pleasant circumstances." In Michigan, Caroline Kirkland observed settlers who classified "the fine remnants of the original forest" as nothing but "heavy timber" and dreamed both day and night of wiping the landscape bare; "not one tree, not so much as a bush, of natural growth, must be suffered to cumber the ground, or he fancies his work incomplete." When the Kirklands insisted on preserving the oaks surrounding their house in Michigan, a neighbor said, "Well! I *should* think there was oak-trees enough without keeping 'em in a body's dooryard! Jus' like the woods!"[3]

The scenes of improvement signaled travelers that land, labor, and comfort had undergone complex revaluation; travel writers determined to render exact assessments of life in the interior to their international audiences of potential emigrants laid out the revaluations concisely. "Rich country," wrote James Flint, "signifies fertility of soil, and not the opulence of its inhabitants. It would be vain to search [the interior] for a rich district, according to the European acceptation of the term. Fine houses are brick ones of two stories high, covered with shingles, and frequently unfinished within; and where the work is completed, it is usually in a bad style; the windows often broken; and the adjoining grounds perhaps studded with the stumps of trees, overgrown with rank weeds, or rutted by hogs. Gardening is performed in the most slovenly manner imaginable." S. H. Collins in his *Emigrant's Guide* (1829) explained that Americans lacked no skill in agriculture; their "slovenly" style arose instead from the nature of a situation in which land was plentiful and cheap while people were few and hired labor was unavailable. American farmers, Collins explained, could not afford to manicure the landscape and "raise great crops from a small portion of soil" when profit lay in "turning over negligently, with as little toil as possible, a large portion of it." In the same year, Gottfried Duden coached his German readers step by step through the procedures for killing the trees on their potential sections in Missouri, and Harriet Martineau noted that the English farmer who hoped to succeed in the interior had to learn "to spend land to save labor; the reverse of his experience in England; and he soon becomes as slovenly a farmer as the American, and begins immediately to grow rich."[4]

Travelers, on the one hand, found the landscape of the interior, unpeopled and uncultivated, to be, in its own unpicturesque but overwhelming way, beautiful; its cultivation and improvement, on the other hand, produced landscape effects of jarring and depressing ugliness. The landscape attitude that drove improvement was defined by Thomas Hamilton in 1833 as "exerting the privilege to deface," by Margaret Fuller in 1844 as "a Gothic progress" bent on "obliterating the natural expression of the country," and by Joseph Featherston-haugh in 1847 as settlers'"determination to proclaim that one of their privileges was to set all comfort at defiance." Studying the face of improvement, Fuller hoped "to woo the mighty meaning of the scene, perhaps to foresee the law by which a new order, a new poetry, is to be evolved from this chaos." If "mighty meaning" is construed as power, the meaning of the scene is relatively clear; many travelers, however, searched for emotional meanings. Anthony Trollope wooed the scene into meaning that "the western American has no love for his own soil, or his own house," whereas Charles Fenno Hoffman wooed Michigan settlers into being "pleased with the country, and I may almost say attached to its soil."[5]

Most travelers assumed that, unlike European peasants, no one living on the vast cheap and abundant landscape of the interior was either poor or deprived and thus that living conditions they observed in the interior were matters of daily choice for the settlers streaming over the landscape. That daily life was so startling a divergence from anything travelers had seen elsewhere as to erase the presumption that they would observe in the interior people they liked to call "our brothers and cousins." Some early travelers suggested that the population of the interior, though temporarily backsliding from established notions of comfort, would reestablish that cousinly ideal as soon as more available goods allowed them to "catch up," but that view did not survive the 1820s, by which time it became apparent that in the interior a different standard, a different definition of comfort, was going to prevail, and that practicing the "old ways" had, in the interior, some connection to failure. Travelers attempting to read the local text of comfort were challenged to reread their own views of the subject.

Some could spot comfort only in its absence. In 1839, the French traveler Michel Chevalier described comfort in the American interior as "almost absolutely wanting. Whoever is neither operative nor domestic, whoever, especially, has tasted and enjoyed the life of the cultivated classes in Europe will find the actual practical life in America, the mere bone and muscle, as it were, of life, to consist of a series of jars, disappointments, mortifications—I had almost said, of humiliations. When the force of innovation, acting without check or balance, operates with an excess of energy, all classes suffer equally from the derangement. The whole social machine gets out of order, discomfort becomes general." Across eight decades of intense travel and travel writing in the interior, both international travelers and travelers from the American East Coast examined the "derangement" of comfort experienced by Chevalier.[6]

Many travelers operated on the general assumptions that a house should be a comfortable refuge from surprising weather and that closing out the climate and the landscape constituted a step forward to comfort. Locals in the interior seemed to define housing differently: they did not engage in defending themselves against the unpredictable, extreme, and often violent climate of the interior, and they drew little distinction between indoors and outdoors. Without a sharp division between indoor and outdoor life, the pleasant foray Frances Trollope tried to take from the cozy home interior to the bucolic outdoor scene was unavailable. In all of the interior almost no space locatable by travelers could be denominated "cozy." In 1796, Francis Baily advised new settlers to build at once a gristmill, a sawmill, and a log house; later, Baily suggested, they might construct frame houses if they had not been by then "rendered indifferent to the comforts and conveniences of life." In 1805, François Michaux followed Baily into Ohio to observe that the settler had indeed built the mill, showed signs of owning other valuables, but had not yet built the house. Any settler, Michaux asserted, could "live in the greatest comfort; yet he resides in a miserable log house about twenty feet long, subject to the inclemency of the weather." Michaux did not think that the "miserable log house" signaled poverty; the settler had plenty of food, and more than one horse; the settler calibrated his status not by the quality of his house but by his vehicles and "not having to go on foot to see his neighbor." In the interior, coziness and comfort took leave of each other, and the house was not defined as an enclosure against the weather. Late on a cold night in 1815, John Melish arrived at an inn at Tinker's Creek, Ohio, and, finding the kitchen chilly, "retired to bed in an adjoining room. I threw my own clothes over the bed-clothes and, noticing a pane out of one of the windows, I shoved an empty bag into it. I awoke early, shivering with cold, and wished that it might soon be daylight, that I might depart from this uncomfortable place. There was an opening close by my bed-side that would have let in a horse. I could not but laugh at my precaution of last night, in stopping up the broken window." In fact, the gaping hole that Melish saw at dawn may have been intended for a horse. In 1854, Friedrich Gerstacker spotted an Illinois farmer "leading his horse by the bridle into the sitting-room, which I should have taken for the stable, had I not seen smoke issuing from the chimney. Full of curiosity, I followed my host into his little dwelling, and here the riddle was explained. He had been hauling wood, and he had fastened his horse to a log about eight feet long, to draw it into the house; then he rolled it to the fireplace, which took up nearly one whole side of the little blockhouse, and as he could not conveniently turn the horse on account of tables, chairs, and beds, he had made an opening on the side opposite the door, in order to lead him out again."[7]

International travelers were not alone in detecting difference in these living arrangements; American travelers from the East Coast, especially those traveling missionaries whose stays in private homes enlarged their opportunities to experience the interior's everyday life, were equally astonished. In 1831, Hannah Backhouse described a cabin at Jericho, Ohio, as "a very new world" to her. There was a great plenty to eat, "a succession of chickens running about one half hour and in the pot the next," very good bread, "apples cooked in many forms," and clean sheets upon the bed, but Backhouse and her husband, in order to sleep, had to remove the blanket from the bed and tack it "against the wall to keep out air from the many holes in the wall." James Leander Scott, a missionary from upstate New York, remarked in 1843 that he had slept in "rooms where the snow, rain, and sleet would sift through the crevices" and that during heavy storms he had sat indoors under his raised umbrella. In 1829, Gottfried Duden observed among his Missouri neighbors a family life built on accommodation to rather than protection against the out-of-doors: "In every season one sees the children run half-naked into the open from their beds or from the heat of the hearth. Some houses are open to the wind on all sides, and the householders do not take the trouble to guard against the penetration of the cold northwest winds by using a little clay. Every day they would rather drag a cartload of wood to the hearth, around which the whole family gather." Duden observed that "this manner of living, which is the common one here, would very soon kill half the population in Germany." In Ohio in 1835, D. Griffiths could not understand how the contents of domestic interiors and the style of domestic life could lag so far behind the propriety, intelligent conversation, and behavioral tone of the locals. Those locals themselves did not necessarily like the dominant conditions. In 1832, on the Rock River in Wisconsin, Juliette Magill Kinzie met a miner who advised her to backtrail as soon as possible and never return, "for comfort *never touched* this western country."[8]

Connected as closely to comfort as the house itself, in the view of most travelers, were domestic objects—furniture, carpets, pianos, vases, bookcases, curtains, china, shades, upholstery, pier glasses, lamps, pictures. If locals persisted in allowing the veering and violent climate of the interior to rush through holes small and large in their houses, then the objects constituting the domestic interior would also have to undergo accommodation to those circumstances. Early travelers did not expect to see many such objects in the interior. In the 1820s, travelers such as Adlard Welby suggested that domestic life in the interior would for a time require "a certain sacrifice of many of the little comforts they can possess and have been used to enjoy at a moderate cost in England." Welby predicted, however, that once settled in the interior, a hardworking person who "avoided habits of drinking" would eventually amass all such "little comforts"; James Flint, who also defined comfort as a variety of household objects, thought that several seasons might pass before a settler could "raise a quantity of produce sufficient to procure in exchange such foreign luxuries as they formerly consumed, and such articles of imported dress as they have been accustomed to wear." From Flint's point of view, emigrants left behind their European-style "comforts" in order to go to the American interior, plant, harvest, and then exchange their produce for the same comforts they had owned before emigrating. Flint's assumption that comfort meant a variety of objects and that settlers in the interior would view their crops as a medium of exchange for those objects found very little support in the observed life of the interior, where few if any settlers counted their emigration, their work, and their produce on one side of a ledger to be balanced by the acquisition of teacups and upholstery on the other side.[9]

In the 1830s, the objects travelers associated with comfort were still failing to appear. Travelers who immersed themselves in the life of the interior to a degree not attempted by the wary and defensive travelers of the 1820s had their imported notions of comfort deranged by the experience of a life without domestic furniture. During six weeks of wandering the interior in 1835, Patrick Shirreff wrote, he "had not seen a sofa, or a chair with a stuffed bottom, nor a window-curtain, or carpet. The walls of the rooms did not support a painting or print of any description, and in all domestic arrangements there was a total absence of the elegances of life. I had become so much habituated to the state of things around me, that for the remainder of my days I would have been satisfied with bare walls and wooden-bottomed chairs, and regarded the gewgaws of refined society with contempt." On returning to New York City, however, Shirreff readopted its refinements with such "facility" that he felt "ashamed of his weakness." Similarly, Charles Augustus Murray, after a full summer of travel in the interior, felt awkward when he entered a dining room and had difficulty sitting on a chair. Neither Shirreff nor Murray thought that life with sofas was better than life without; they saw each as a difference in style appropriate to its landscape. It was in the texts of American women travelers, however, that the subject of comfort was most fully examined. In 1836, Caroline Kirkland moved from New York to Michigan with her family; she and her husband had expected to start a school there, but William Kirkland instead caught the fever of town-planting and Caroline Kirkland turned to writing books of travel and description. Kirkland never disguised the fact that she was a city-bred person of cultivated tastes, wit, and extensive knowledge, thus making even more compelling her reassessment of what constituted her own and others' comfort in the interior. Kirkland herself carried to Michigan many fancy articles whose uselessness she realized immediately upon unpacking them; the interior narrowed her ideas of comfort "down to a well-swept room with a bed in one corner, and cooking apparatus in another." Both her own experience and her observations of others convinced Kirkland that in the interior the usual list of objects suggesting comfort had to be redrawn in the service of a new comfort. "No settlers," she wrote, "are so uncomfortable as those who, coming with abundant means, as they suppose, to be comfortable, set out with a determination to live as they have been accustomed to live." Comfort in the interior, Kirkland found, required abandoning city-style ideas about the gendered division of labor; a man "too proud or too indolent" to pitch in on all kinds of work, too bound by adherence to early habits acquired elsewhere, would, according to Kirkland, experience a mortifying loss of daily comfort. Kirkland recorded several stunning observations of object-laden gender-divided discomfort among locals who refused to adjust to the interior: while out walking one day, she chanced to lose her shoes in six inches of mud and sought help at a house surrounded by flowerbeds, a most unusual sight in the 1830s interior, which did not honor cultivated flowers. The interior of the house was furnished in contradictions. A harp, French chintz drapes, large looking glasses, a French pier table, vases, pictures, and two young women seated on a sofa doing fancywork collided visually with "two great dirty dogs," a floor stained with tobacco juice "although a great box filled with sand stood near the hearth, melancholy and fruitless provision against this filthy visitation," and a rocking chair occupied by a man on whose face Kirkland read "reckless self-indulgence and fierce discontent and determined indolence." The owners of all these domestic comforts were revealed to be living in a state of extreme deprivation; there was no scrap of food of any kind in the house.[10]

From Kirkland's observations, imported objects of comfort not only prevented comfort in the interior but also interfered with adaptation to the landscape, and came in the end to serve as no more than a decaying veneer over deprivation and misery. If James Flint believed in 1822 that settlers would exchange their produce for the objects of comfort, Kirkland saw in 1839 that where these objects were honored there would be no produce. "Many things," she wrote in 1842, "which are considered essential to comfort among those who make modes of life a study and a science, appeared to us absolutely cumbersome and harassing." To reproduce urban refinement, she observed, meant the loss of the real comforts and advantages of "solitude and freedom." The real refinement of country life, she believed, differed from what passed for refinement in the cities of the East Coast; the interior exposed imitations of city life as hollow and made the imitators themselves appear boorish. In 1844, Margaret Fuller, thinking over the same subject, suggested that urban comforts were too small for the interior and that their scale was wrong: she suggested abandoning "miniature improvements which a chicken could run over in ten minutes," in favor of thinking on a larger scale about how humans might carry out their own plans on the landscape "without obliterating those of Nature."[11]

Both Kirkland and Fuller were certain that in the interior they were observing a new version of comfort connected to—if not dictated by—a landscape that made its own demands and certainly its own refusals. To them, life in the interior was not a barer or more backward version of life on the East Coast, life in England, or life in Europe, not a stripped-down version of comfort waiting to amass the objects validated by an older world, but a version so different as to require either revaluation of what constituted comfort or perhaps utter rejection of comfort as a goal. To Kirkland and Fuller, society in the interior was not looking to reanimate habits of the past but was rushing into the future; they asked, in effect, whether society advanced by providing and honoring ever-increasing numbers of objects or by stripping itself of old comforts and habits and moving on toward something quite other. They were certain that in the interior a settler unwilling to sacrifice the old comforts would thereby be sacrificed to them.

Nonetheless, for familiar luxuries many travelers and some denizens of the interior longed. James Hall, though a longtime Illinois resident and booster, always wrote with an envious eye fixed on the East Coast and in 1836 complained delicately that in Illinois "but few expenditures have been made for ornament or luxury." Some travelers offered remedies: in 1839 Frederick Marryat claimed that the goods composing his British view of home luxury—"marble chimney-pieces, pier-glasses, pianos, lamps, candelabra"—were available everywhere in America, even in Cleveland, and that he had often spotted such luxury items in "mean-looking" log houses. He thought this was good. Luxury of the tufted-red-velvet chandelier-lit variety made its major antebellum appearances in the hotels of Cincinnati and St. Louis and amid the jigsaw work on the gorgeous but potentially explosive riverboats of which many travelers had experience.

The interior, however, had its own plans for the upholstered version of luxury. In 1832 Cincinnati, Godfrey Vigne stayed in two luxury hotels claimed to be excellent, "both of which gave promise of every comfort. The table was very good," he wrote, "but my rest was destroyed by the worst of vermin." The twelve-year-old travel writer Victoria Welby-Gregory, so attuned to luxury everywhere that she rated the shininess of hotel silver all across the interior and finally awarded the palm to a hotel in St. Louis, exclaimed over the lavishly draped and upholstered ladies' cabin on an Ohio River steamboat until she discovered that every fold of the draperies and each tuck in the upholstery harbored cockroaches. Where it appeared, upholstered luxury not only deteriorated under the assault of the weather, but also made too great an appeal to a huge and various insect population always on the lookout for new housing. Where insects intervened—in the area of upholstery—residents backed off, and allowed the insects to dictate what the residents could comfortably call their own. The antebellum interior placed a high value on mobility and on accommodation to both the weather and the nonhuman population, resulting in an attitude toward objects classifiable as neither materialist nor utilitarian. Locals called what they considered a comfortless life "hard doings," whereas a sufficiency of comfort was defined in the phrase "getting along." The suggestion of mobility in the latter phrase reveals how low a valuation was placed on elaborate immobile objects.[12]

For over fifty years, between 1818 and 1870, a certain landscape cover seen in the interior evoked among travelers of many national origins a very specific dream of comfort; the dream was generated by a landscape view that, for once at least, elicited enthusiastic aesthetic response from travelers. Generating both the response and its accompanying fantasy was the oak savanna, often called "oak openings," gently rolling expanses dotted with trees of considerable size, found primarily in Illinois, Wisconsin, and Michigan. On this landscape international travelers imagined themselves transported to a far more familiar and conventionally admired landscape: the extensive and expensively planned park attached to the English country house. In order to evoke the English-park fantasy, however, the oak savanna had to be untouched and uncultivated, if not completely uninhabited; only in that state could it suggest to travelers the careful artificial improvement, planning, and assembled order of the English park. To travelers, the oak openings resembled a scene they were accustomed to admiring, a scene that—unlike most of the American interior—had long been validated as beautiful in a correct, tasteful, and comprehensible style. In its presence, Charles Augustus Murray described its trees as "tastefully disposed" about the prairie landscape, "so regularly and carefully grouped as to remind me of Windsor and other noble English parks." Frederick Marryat instructed his English readers to imagine "an inland country covered with splendid trees, about as thickly planted as in our English parks; in fact, it *is* English park scenery. Nature here having spontaneously produced what it has been the care and labor of centuries in our own country to effect." As a landscape aesthetic, the English-park illusion was not disinterested, but it constituted a comfort for travelers; momentarily a viewer could feel permanence in a land where everyone seemed to be on the move, where familiar social distinctions were generally absent or uncomfortably upended, and where so few other scenes had ever "composed." Furthermore, the English-park illusion domesticated the prairie, made it cozy, familiar, and intimate, all the while implying social differentiation, status, privilege, and ease.[13]

At the very core of the English-park fantasy, however, lay deep trouble: the scale of social differentiation it connoted was unobservable in the interior, where there were neither gentlemen to exercise their taste on the landscape nor peasants to make the taste of the gentlemen possible. The English-park image was so fragile that any evidence of inhabitation threatened to shatter it: in 1835 Charles Fenno Hoffman complained that even where no tree stumps damaged the fantasy, the "rude shantees which indicated recent settlement" interfered with a viewer's sustaining the illusion of being in a "cultivated old country." In the interior, only uncultivated, unimproved, and uninhabited land could be imagined into the high degree of cultivation that fed the travelers' fantasy. Moreover, the dream of a "noble English park" on the Illinois prairie was incomplete without a country house, and in all the interior there was no house to feed the illusion. In 1819, Edwin James wrote: "The unaccustomed eye, in roving over these extensive undulating prairies, is beguiled by the alternation of forests and meadows, arranged with an appearance of order, as if by the labor of men, and seeks in vain to repose upon some cottage or mansion embosomed in the copses of trees, or in the edge of the forest, which margins the small streams and ravines in the distance." The only housing, however, to be seen on the landscape—cabins, frame houses, "rude shantees"—carried inappropriate connotations of work and indistinct social status, and no grouping of tidy cottages suggested social subservience to any country-house life of ease and privilege.[14]

In 1817, however, a large-scale effort was launched to force the landscape illusion to fulfill its promise of social and domestic comfort when Morris Birkbeck announced in a series of letters published in England that he and his friend George Flower were settling on two "estates" of fifteen hundred acres each on the English-park landscape of Edwards County, Illinois. "On these estates," wrote Birkbeck, "we hope to live much as we have been accustomed to live in England," although he immediately noted that the unavailability of servants in the interior meant that "to be easy and comfortable here, a man should know how to wait upon himself." Birkbeck invited prospective English settlers to make application to him for a section or quarter-section, and promised each settler that there would be in readiness for him "a cabin, an enclosed garden, a cow, and a hog, with an appropriation of land for summer and winter food for cows." Speculators were discouraged; Birkbeck requested English residents only for his self-sustaining settlement, thereafter known among travelers as the English Prairie.[15]

Although Morris Birkbeck described himself as "an American proprietor" and claimed to be fully Americanized, he was critical of American farming methods and of Americans in general, finding them insensitive to the "charms of distant and various prospect" in nature, lazy, dirty, ignorant of the agricultural value of manure, potentially violent, and "strangers to rural simplicity." "America," Morris Birkbeck wrote in his most famous six words, "was bred in a cabin." Of those same despised locals, however, Birkbeck said, "It is surprising how comfortable they seem," signaling the observable but to him incomprehensible difference between the interior's going definition of comfort and his own. Stretches of unbroken prairie in his chosen part of Illinois reminded Birkbeck of "some open, well-cultivated vale in Europe," but in that vale established owners of prairie "estates" that Birkbeck considered beautiful mystified him by living as "remote from comfort as the settler of one year." Although Birkbeck at times found the landscape of the interior oppressive and the winter "doleful," he nonetheless pronounced his part of the interior to afford "all that nature has decreed for the comfort of man," indicating a relationship between the landscape and human comfort that was neither accommodating nor destructive but appropriative, as if he were ready to receive the gifts that the landscape had been holding in store for him.[16]

Richard Flower, one of Birkbeck's partners in the English Prairie enterprise, insisted even more strongly than did Birkbeck on transplanting a fully and specifically English version of comfort to Illinois; Flower came out firmly against the log house, then the interior's only native architecture, and wrote glowingly of his settlement's English social circle, of unbroken prairies that his vision transformed into "natural parks already stocked with deer" and laid out with taste, of the store he and Birkbeck had established to supply them with luxuries, and of the English-style Christmas celebration he had arranged after which "the company were pleased to say I had transferred old England and its comforts to Illinois." Both Birkbeck and Flower insisted that the prairies could be cultivated with ease: "Nothing but fencing and providing water for stock is wanted to reduce a prairie into the condition of useful grass land; and from that state, as we all know, the transition to arable land is through a simple process, easy to perform, and profitable as it goes on." Cultivation, according to Birkbeck, even "altered the character of the soil: where the plough goes it is no longer a marsh, but dry sandy arable." As a final touch, Richard Flower invited his transoceanic readers to imagine him at the English Prairie, "quite at home again, and writing to you surrounded by the same library standing in the same relative situation, in my large easy chair, and enjoying every earthly comfort."[17]

"Oh, God! What delusion!" cried the English traveler William Cobbett in 1818 in response to Birkbeck's claims. Cobbett characterized Birkbeck's promotional letters as fantasies "calculated to produce great disappointment, not to say misery and ruin," in that Birkbeck's settlement vision took no account of the needed equipment, workers, storage, or building materials. "How can a sane mind lead an English farmer into this expedition?" demanded Cobbett. Birkbeck's letters had by then, however, created a sensation in England, and for several years travelers, especially the English among them, felt obligated to visit and evaluate the Edwards County "estates" and the new town of Albion. Although Birkbeck and Flower's plan to acquire 23,400 acres in Illinois faded when their application to Congress for a land grant was refused, both men continued to promote their vision. Birkbeck announced in January of 1818 that he planned to put in one hundred acres of corn that spring, but when the English farmer Thomas Hulme arrived in the fall of 1818, he found Birkbeck living in a "little hutch," having directed all his energies into the proprietary gesture of fencing. He had cultivated only a garden, and he was buying his staples from the

German settlement of Harmony, in Indiana, about twenty miles away. The Illinois landscape, however, served its fantasy function even for the aristocracy-hating Hulme by reminding him of "immense noblemen's parks in England," and when Hulme remarked on the size and peskiness of the flies infesting that park, Birkbeck assured him that the flies "go away altogether as soon as cultivation begins."[18]

Those travelers who assented to Birkbeck's vision of fenced and hedged proprietary comfort also assented to his and Flower's notions that local farmers were lazy and that potentially violent ruffians made up a fair proportion of the local population; according to Emanuel Howitt, when Birkbeck's servants deserted him in the interior, they too adopted the local habit of criminal behavior. The charge that Americans were idle and indolent maintained a good head of steam among certain English travelers throughout the first quarter of the century; around 1825, it abruptly vanished and was replaced by complaints that male Americans in the interior devoted their every conscious moment to hard and profitable work. Birkbeck and Flower's insistence on American laziness might possibly be read as a function of the English Prairie's servant problem. Although Birkbeck announced his recognition that servants were not available in the interior, Flower tended to complain of their absence: "It ought not to be concealed that we are much in want of farming laborers. . . . We are also destitute of female servants," wrote Flower; "although I have hitherto been well off, yet I am fearful we may be as others are, inconvenienced for want of servants. How much I regret that more of the overflowing population of England cannot find their way here, exchanging their poverty for plenty of employment and good fare." Flower's transforming his feared loss of ease into a social salvage operation for the English poor does not disguise the fact that the English Prairie's mode of settlement and farming required extensive cheap labor; that requirement could not be met in an area where land of one's own could be bought for under two dollars per acre. Neither Flower nor Birkbeck ever admitted in print to what other travelers saw as the case: local settlers refused to redesign themselves to work in service of the English vision of comfort. Birkbeck and Flower might choose to practice the manners of the patron and benefactor, but the settlers surrounding them in Illinois refused to adopt the corresponding manners of the English rustic. In 1833, Simon O'Ferrall remarked that a local settler in the vicinity of the English Prairie "would rather have died like a cock on a dunghill than be patronized after the English fashion."[19]

By 1821, rumors began to circulate in the travel-book network that Birkbeck was mired in difficulties, that his land was spongy, that the site of the English Prairie was malarial, that the best land actually lay just seventy miles north of Albion, that Birkbeck had lost track of the location of his own acres, and that the English-park landscape illusion presented itself for viewing only in summer and even then only if one "looked at the country through the windows of Messrs. Flower's and Birkbeck's houses." When Adlard Welby arrived at Albion's English-style tavern in 1820, both food and water were scarce; the English Prairie's cows had strayed in search of water some days before Welby's arrival, and a wheelwright confided in Welby that the settlement had "no comforts whatever." Welby found Birkbeck "living in a two-room log cabin, unfinished except for the library," the last cozy refuge of the nonworking gentleman. Even though Birkbeck had recently made the newspapers with his claim that seven hundred acres of corn had been sown, Welby's persistent questioning failed to elicit from Birkbeck any information whatever about the English Prairie's actual crops. In 1823, William Faux found Albion's tavern even worse than Welby had described it—"a hog-sty of a room . . . three in one bed, all filthy, no comfort, and yet this is an English tavern." Birkbeck, however, had by 1823, according to Faux and Adam Hodgson, "a very comfortable house, excellent fences, and from sixty to eighty acres of Indian corn." Faux claimed that Birkbeck, known roundabout as "the emperor of the prairies," denied that he had ever intended to farm: "I came here to rest," he told Faux. The rumor grew that Birkbeck was surviving by selling off his acres—once intended to be the life and sustenance of the settlement—at twice what he had paid for them.[20]

Numerous travel books enumerated the details of Birkbeck's and Flower's efforts to transplant English country life to Illinois: flower gardens, hedges, fences, a porter's lodge, roast beef, mutton, plum pudding, mince pie, pianos, books, upholstery, and cricket matches. James Stuart remarked that Flower's was "the only house in America where I saw egg-cups." Birkbeck and Flower also, however, carried on internecine quarrels and lodged lawsuits against each other, the bitterness of which was heightened by their chosen isolation. Without servants to support a mode of life that required them, the settlement's design suffered enormously, and since its proprietors could not or would not do for themselves what the servants would have done, their lives and persons deteriorated oddly amid their imported comforts. Eventually their quarrels split them and their resources into efforts to build competing towns. In 1825, Morris Birkbeck, returning from a day's dealings with the German settlement at Harmony, whose produce had supported his vision of comfort during the short life that it had, drowned in the Fox River. Of his four children, one returned to England and three went to Mexico; over subsequent years, the English

Prairie settlement gradually disappeared into the great landscape sur-rounding it.[21]

For forty-five years after Morris Birkbeck's death, travelers of many nationalities were teased by the interior into glimpsing his vision of a landscape of ease, comfort, and class division, though no one again tried to inhabit that vision on a similar scale. In 1837, Harriet Mar-tineau was struck by the "park-like air" of Michigan; in 1839 Charles Augustus Murray glimpsed Windsor park near Fort Leavenworth, Kansas, and Frederick Marryat saw English park scenery at Fond du Lac, Wisconsin; John Newhall saw the "extensive parks, the copse and lawn" in Iowa in 1844, and in the 1850s several travelers experienced the English-park fantasy in Minnesota. In 1870, however, the English-park landscape was no longer visible. Newman Hall, traveling through Michigan in that year, found in its scenery "nothing very interesting." The oak trees essential to the English-park illusion had been deliber-ately burned and left to rot. Hall saw "the same succession of belts of forest and partial clearings, and farms and villages, everything looking very new. The parts which were cleared had been cleared a great deal too much, denuded of trees, and without so much as a hedge." In 1873, Julius Medley, traveling from Michigan into Illinois, "almost fancied [him]self in the plains of the Punjab." The English-park vision, after nearly fifty years of skittering westward and northward from Edwards County, Illinois, finally disappeared among the burned trees that were the signposts of cultivation and improvement in the interior.[22]

Between 1822 and 1862, dozens of travel writers analyzed emigrants' adaptation to the design of the interior, the adaptation that Birkbeck and Flower had refused because they believed the landscape was invit-ing them to refuse it. John Woods, an illusion-free farmer who spent two years at the English Prairie, wrote in 1822 that "the American settlers understand the culture of this country better than the Euro-peans, and I mean generally to follow the rules of the former." One after another, travelers lined up behind Timothy Flint's views that it was "folly" for emigrants to "select associates according to their coun-try," and that group emigration to the interior was bound to fail. "No one," wrote James Stuart in 1833, "should emigrate from his own country, even to this land of milk and honey, who has not sufficient firmness of character to enable him entirely to change his mode of life, and conform to that of the people with whom he is in future to live." In 1835, Charles Latrobe reconfigured the subject slightly and advised prospective British emigrants to stay at home because, unlike persons of other national origins, they were unable to make do without their accustomed comforts.[23]

The degree of adaptation required of an emigrant by the American interior—even aside from the still unsettled question of which objects constituted comfort—became the focus of a travelers' conversation conducted across decades of travel literature; the conversation suggested that the interior required a range of revaluations. To farm in the interior, for example, did not lower personal status; many international travelers were surprised to meet a judge or a doctor who cultivated a section without undergoing any change of status in the eyes of his neighbors. No domestic animal bore higher status than another: observation of life in Cincinnati, for example, forced Anthony Trollope to revalue hogs. In England, he wrote, "a trade in hogs and pigs is subject to some contumely. There is a feeling that these animals are not so honorable in their bearing as sheep and oxen. It is a prejudice which by no means exists in Cincinnati." The relative status of city life and country life required revaluation: notions of aristocratic country life, the country estate, and what Frances Trollope called "the privileges of rusticity" had no place in the interior's conceptual apparatus. No "gentleman farmer" in the interior could buy or steal the general assent to the country-estate illusion of comfort that its sustenance required. Without proprietary and decorative attitudes toward the landscape to support it, the garden, a feature of landscape endeavor treasured by some travelers, also withered in the interior; a planned and manicured garden looked out of scale surrounded by acres of corn or stretches of uncultivated prairie. Although Isabella Trotter wrote in 1859 that "Americans have not the slightest idea of a garden," the great expanse of landscape itself forced revaluations of land and labor from which the garden emerged as a precious piece of self-indulgence, a sign not of comfort but of misguided effort and possibly even of deprivation. At the English Prairie, after all, Morris Birkbeck had a garden but his crops were a fantasy that he enlarged each spring; in his case, the garden signaled an inhabitant who did not understand the landscape. These numerous revaluations required by the interior were closely tied to its redefinition of comfort, a subject that travel literature also addressed under the heading "improvement." So many settlers appeared to have made identical choices that travelers could not doubt that they were being presented with a new design of life, landscape, and comfort. Attempts to measure the phenomenon by degrees of private and individual attachment to specific private pieces of land in the interior regularly came up empty; but travelers were also baffled when they turned from examining the interior as a scene of private ownership to viewing it as a public space occupied by residents constructing themselves as public persons and constructing a public definition of comfort.[24]

Just as settlers seemed to observe no sharp division between indoors and outdoors, so they also seemed to draw little distinction between the public and the private. In the antebellum interior, one person's private facilities were often reconstructed into public accommodations. Well into the 1830s, it was customary for complete strangers to double up in beds at inns, taverns, and even hotels; the practice, familiar and apparently not troublesome to locals, appalled travelers. Edouard de Montule could not understand how it was that American travelers who hardly ever talked to each other made no objection to sleeping in the same bed. Patrick Shirreff, offered half a bed at a crowded hotel in Alton, Illinois, hit upon the expedient of telling the landlord that he "was a foreigner, and not likely to make the most agreeable companion to a native," and thus succeeded in obtaining a whole bed for himself. In 1857, at a Missouri inn, Aleksandr Lakier felt he had no choice but to take the half bed assigned to him. Once in the bed he realized that its other occupant was feverish, but not until morning did he actually see "the yellow, worn-out, terribly sick stranger" with whom he had shared the bed. "I couldn't get out of there fast enough," wrote Lakier. "For a long time afterward it seemed that death itself was pursuing me." A traveler might succeed in getting a private bed and still not find privacy. Godfrey Vigne noted that in spite of the prevailing custom of doubling up in a bed, he seldom failed in his "application for a room with a single bed—some of them containing as many as four or five. The Americans think nothing of this." Occasionally landlords construed Vigne's request for a single room to mean that he was ill.[25]

If Americans' private at-home arrangements for comfort in the interior puzzled travelers, their public arrangements for comfort—or derangements of comfort, to adopt Michel Chevalier's term—closely touched travelers' lives; they lost the safety of the observer's distance when they were faced with public arrangements and, as public persons themselves, were invited to engage in them. In 1821, Adlard Welby was disgusted at being directed toward a communal washstand lodged "under the shed of the house" at an Ohio inn. In 1833, Thomas Hamilton claimed to have seen on every steamboat plying the rivers of the interior "a public comb and hairbrush, suspended by a string from the ceiling of the cabin. These utensils are used by the whole body of the passengers, and their condition the pen of Swift could alone adequately describe. There is no toothbrush simply, I believe, because the article is entirely unknown to the American toilet. A common towel, however, passes from hand to hand." Not only were the grooming objects hanging there, but travelers were also expected to use them. In 1842, Charles Dickens, aboard an Ohio River steamboat, noted that every other male passenger used the communal comb and brush while staring at Dickens, who was using his own. Two or three of the men, he wrote, seemed "strongly disposed to banter me on my prejudices, but didn't." By 1851 the toothbrush Hamilton had claimed to be nonexistent had arrived in the interior, and Arthur Cunynghame claimed that a single public toothbrush was used by all aboard a riverboat headed for St. Louis. These public grooming tools were unrelated to any notions of communal life or property, for the same travelers who observed communal objects claimed to miss communal feeling; on the same boat where Cunynghame saw the solitary toothbrush in general use, he also saw a man fall overboard and vanish under the wheel without generating any excitement among the surviving passengers. Cunynghame read the apparent callousness of his fellow passengers as a function of emigration, which he thought had "blunted that brotherly feeling which exists among old established communities." Rather than being a gesture at communal life, the public comb and brush and towel and toothbrush might be read as gestures at providing creature necessities and comforts, gestures of awareness that such items might be needed—but also indicators that in the public life and public sleeping cabins of the riverboat such items could not be individually provided. Richard Levinge claimed that Americans were so accustomed to traveling so light—with no more than a "change of fronts" carried in a small valise—that the public grooming utensils were a necessity and were expected. The public comb was not a comfort but a convenience in a possibly desperate public moment. Along the same lines, hotels in the interior made certain gestures toward providing comfort that failed to satisfy demanding travelers like Frances Trollope, who complained of "queer comfortless hotels" and of large but uncarpeted rooms darkened with "uncomfortable" paper shades that required hand-rolling.[26]

Great—certainly vast—hotels appeared all across the interior, in small towns and large, from the 1820s onward; to the astonishment of travelers, the hotels were populated by entire local families who took up residence in them and ate all their meals at the long tables in the hotels' public dining rooms. Charles Dickens remarked on "that comfortless custom, so very prevalent in country towns, of married persons living in hotels, having no fireside of their own, and seldom meeting from early morning until late at night, but at the hasty public meals." Dickens assigned the custom not to any housing shortage—since no traveler presumed shortages in the interior—but to the interior's dominant business atmosphere. In 1855, Marie Grandfort speculated that families might choose hotel residence because they were unable to afford the expense of housekeeping, but then remembered that a family had to be "possessed of a certain revenue" in order to afford hotel residence; she settled finally on the explanation that hotel life "was naturally attractive for a people who find amusement only in noise, tumult, and animation." In 1873, Joseph Alexander, after noting numbers of families resident in Chicago's hotels, set down the cross-culturally mysterious custom to mobility, speculating that the families were in transition from one town to another. Possibly the cultural meaning of hotel residence is connected to the porous log houses whose meaning travelers also wondered over. In 1853 Alfred Bunn explained the practice of families' boarding at hotels by noting that "the Americans live more out of their private houses than in them." To locate domestic comfort in public places rather than in the uncozy private home constituted a revaluation of domestic comfort as complete as the redefinition of *improvement* constituted by the ubiquitous field of stumps. Americans in the interior were constructing their comfort in public—and to many travelers, the public vision of American comfort was the one most readily available for study. Public comfort was disconnected from personally owned objects and unrelated to feelings of proprietorship. Furthermore, public comfort was neither communal in feeling nor dependent on others' goodwill: hotel residency seemed to epitomize a readily purchasable version of public independence, of a free, detached, and possibly solitary life conducted not at Walden Pond but in a bustling lobby thronged with equally comfortable strangers. Hotel residence was a version of comfort that most travelers could see but almost none could experience as comfortable. It was very like the conditions of their own lives as travelers.[27]

The busy public comfort of the interior's hotels and riverboats proposed to test class attitudes as they had perhaps never before been tested anywhere on the face of the globe. Two possible mental comforts of public life elsewhere—status and anonymity—were both erased by the interior, resulting in painful status collisions for those travelers determined to perform their accustomed or desired status in life. After crossing the Alleghenies in 1809, John Bradbury noticed that a certain "species of hauteur which one class of society in some countries shows in their intercourse with the other, is here utterly unknown." Bradbury's observation held true for at least the next fifty years; the social phenomenon he defined was especially troubling to British travelers who, as James Stuart noted, had "more difficulty in accommodating themselves to the manners of the Americans than any other people. No people consider it so great a hardship to be obliged to eat or associate with those whom they consider to be their inferior in point of station, as the British." British reaction against American manners was severe; Patrick Shirreff believed the British to be so "trained in habits of arrogance or servility" as to be disqualified as observers of American manners. The exquisite sensitivity of an Arthur Cunynghame, who complained of being "forced to share a riverboat cabin with a man without a coat," the agony of a Frances Trollope when she was addressed as "honey" in a Cincinnati shop, the astonishment of a Charles Weld at being addressed as "man," made the interior a torment of social discomfort for certain British travelers, to say nothing of the social pain they in turn inflicted on locals who had to put up with them. The American assumption of equality that caused so much cross-cultural discomfort rose in the interior to an intensity that was unmatched anywhere on the East Coast. "No one who has visited only the Atlantic cities," wrote Charles Augustus Murray in 1839, "can believe in the social republicanism of America." In the East, Murray saw "distinctions of wealth and family" making an appearance, accompanied by coats of arms; but "the equality existing elsewhere in theory, exists here [in the interior] in fact." William Oliver found the population of the interior to be "as unlike that of the eastern states as if they were of different nations." "In the west," wrote Anthony Trollope, "there are no distinctions whatever." The interior confronted international travelers with the most advanced ideas about human equality they had ever met. Some had assumed that they could travel in the social atmosphere created by those ideas but continue nonetheless to act out their individual social superiority; they had thought that locals would apply democratic ideas among themselves while exempting outsiders from their pressure. These travelers were mistaken, and they hated their resultant situation. Some felt certain that class divisions had to exist in the interior but believed they could not hear them: "It is the accent," wrote Emily Pfeiffer, "which makes the difficulty" in discerning class distinction. Many represented democracy as an epidemic, a ghastly and infectious disease raging through the interior.[28]

The interior's presumption of social equality was only a little more painful to many travelers than its corollary: the astonishingly uncomfortable—to them—quality of a daily life constructed in the almost complete absence of servants, who were not to be had on any terms in most areas, who were "a berry that don't grow on these bushes" in Michigan, who were never to be called *servants* or they would leave their place at once, who required to be treated "as one of the family, and eat at the same table, and at the same time," and who might *hire out* briefly but only for "a special reason, never as a regular calling, or with an acknowledgment of inferior station." Harriet Martineau described young women in the interior who had briefly "hired out for a special reason" as behaving like "captive princesses." Most residents of the interior read the position of servant as class-bound and as requiring the servant not only to work under the direction of another but also to conspire in the illusion that the employer was obscurely superior to the servant. The resulting employment situation was desperately uncomfortable for both the employer and the employee; in Michigan, Caroline Kirkland came to dread any occasion that required hiring help, for each such occasion multiplied the "vexations of the proprietor much more rapidly than his enjoyments." Kirkland knew that in the interior there existed no class of persons somehow culturally or socially intended to be servants, but many international travelers believed that somewhere on the prairies there had to be such persons obstinately refusing to fill their intended place in life. James Flint thought there was a class of idle white females whose "repugnance to support themselves, by the earnings of hired labor, induces them to lead a life of profligacy and ruin," and Frances Trollope asserted that "the whole class of young women are taught to believe that the most abject poverty is preferable to domestic service." William Faux predicted social retrogression in the absence of class-bound servitors: "Having no servants to do that for us which was once daily done, we become too idle in time to do anything but that which nature and necessity require; pride and all stimuli forsake us, for we find ourselves surrounded only by men of similar manners; hence, the face is seldom shaved, or washed, or the linen changed except on washing days. The shoes are cleaned, perhaps, never; for if, indeed, a servant from England is kept, he or she is on a happy equality, rising up last and lying down first, and eating at the same time and table."[29]

As is apparent, no one could talk about servants without talking about class, and in the interior no conversation about class—except the one against it—could be conducted. No matter who one was or where one had come from, the keeping of a servant in the interior was uncomfortable; a situation elsewhere intended to aid personal comfort produced in the interior intense ideological discomfort. Aboard the riverboats, English and European travelers, acting on advice offered by earlier travelers, disguised their servants as companions or secretaries in order to avert the attention of earnest residents ready to conduct an anticlass conversation with the servant and point out to him the easy freedom to be gained by his simply walking away from his employer; travelers reported that many took that walk. In 1833, when Thomas Hamilton set out from Wheeling, West Virginia, into the interior, he instructed his bodyservant to designate himself to the other steamboat passengers as Hamilton's clerk or secretary, and to "ensconce himself behind a curtain" while cleaning Hamilton's clothes and boots. Had Hamilton not taken these steps, both he and his servant would have been subjected to round-the-clock interrogation of their social ideas, and Hamilton's servant would shortly have left the boat to buy a section and commence life as a free man. A traveler's dream of being "served properly" could be fulfilled only below the Mason–Dixon line where, as Anthony Trollope noted, "the difference in comfort is very great." Travelers who enjoyed in the South a "comfort level" unattainable in the North found themselves in an embarrassing position; most travelers opposed slavery and thus experienced ideological discomfort engendered by awareness that their excellent southern servitors were "symbols of the luxury of the white men who own them, and as such are signs of decay."[30]

Travelers' claims about the discomfort of manners in the interior frequently invite rereading. The do-it-yourself approach to life dominant in the interior pained the British traveler Basil Hall because, in the absence of what he called "the spontaneous desire to be civil and useful" among the settlers, he was required to ask for the personal services he wanted. Hall predicted that many dangers, including "augmented ideas of self-importance" on the part of inhabitants, would arise from their having to be "prompted" to oblige a person like himself. Inhabitants whose work put them in the public arena of the interior were more likely to be judged "not obliging" by travelers than were inhabitants who worked the land. The farmers that Fortescue Cuming met in Ohio in 1809 he judged to be friendly, while the traders he judged not to be so. Likewise in 1824 William Blane found the interior's tavernkeepers "sordid" but its settlers "open-hearted and hospitable" even though, he wrote with regret, "it is true they always treated me as their equal." The division Cuming and Blane drew between the manners of private settlers and those of public men widened over the next decades. In 1835, Charles Latrobe contrasted the "honest bearing" of settlers to the "consummate vulgarity" displayed by the steamboat-traveling "scum of the population," to which class belonged many Americans traveling on business. They, Latrobe asserted, "have apparently no thought, no reading, no information, no speculation but about their gains—dollar is the word most frequently in their mouths. The proportion of men with money and without manners would appear to be greater in this part of the globe than elsewhere." Although Latrobe professed himself ready to be comfortable with—and amused by—"rusticity" and to find in it "virtue in disguise," he was not ready to be ignored by a population busy being prosperous. When "rural simplicity" refused, as it always did in the interior, to rise before him, he reacted with anger and disgust. Thomas

Hamilton also longed to meet the simple cap-tipping peasantry, and when he wrote that "there is nothing *rustic* about any American," he was not intending to flatter Americans.[31]

Throughout travel literature, discussions framed in terms of *rural, rustic, simple,* and *class* express not only loss and discomfort on the part of travelers, but also their keen sense of exclusion from an unfamiliar arena of behavior in which apparently thousands of others were operating comfortably. By contrast, when travelers were not feeling excluded—when they were directly approached in public by residents of the interior—the hypersensitive among them claimed that locals were unbearably inquisitive, pelting them with "curious questions" and reacting in "anger because we could not satisfactorily answer." When the questions stopped, travelers labeled the settlers "self-centered, uncommunicative, and distrustful," and "absolutely indifferent as to who or what you are." Across a class divide desired by a given traveler but not perceived by residents there could be no comfortable conversation, and as a result travelers whose allegiance was sworn to class division and whose comfort depended on it often read the interior's indistinct social divisions as filth and dirt. Now in a literal sense the American interior was obviously not Holland; the interior was far too large to scrub. But if read under the anthropologist Mary Douglas's definition of dirt as "matter out of place," travelers' remarks on dirt emerge as statements about class. The traveling English farmer William Faux, whose 1823 book is an uproar of loathing for all things American, pronounced Americans in the interior to be "filthy, bordering on beastly," unredeemed for Faux even by his notice of their fine teeth; Basil Hall, who composed his observations on America into an argument in favor of class distinctions, monarchy, an established church, aristocracy, and permanent leadership, concurred; and Anthony Trollope, who suffered gloomily through many painful status collisions presented to him by the interior, judged the inhabitants to be "essentially a dirty people. Dirt, untidiness, and noise, seem in nowise to afflict them. I have, as it were, been educated to dirt, and taken out my degree in outward abominations. But my education had not reached a point which would enable me to live at my ease in the western states." At supper one evening in a Lexington hotel, Trollope watched seventy-five teamsters "summoned into the common eating-room by a loud gong to sit down to their meal at the public table. They were very dirty; I doubt whether I ever saw dirtier men; but they were orderly and well-behaved and but for their extreme dirt might have passed as the ordinary occupants of a well-filled hotel in the West. Such men, in the States, are less clumsy with their knives and forks, less astray in an unused position, more intelligent to adapting themselves to a new life than are Englishmen of the same rank." If "dirt" constitutes a judgment of "matter out of place," then the seventy-five teamsters first struck Trollope as persons out of place, as dirt in the hotel dining room; but their manner and manners gradually transformed them into persons "less astray" until Trollope admitted that he "conceived rather an affection for those dirty teamsters; they answered me civilly when I spoke to them, and sat in quietness, smoking their pipes, with a dull and dirty, but orderly demeanor." The *order* that appears at the end of Trollope's narrative is an ordering of comfort new to him: civil, quiet, adaptable, and public.[32]

The dullness that, according to Trollope, prevailed among the teamsters was amplified in other scenes by many international travelers even when no language barrier existed to encourage the judgment; almost no American travelers, however, saw it. Alone among British travelers, Harriet Martineau wrote frequently of the humor which she found "one of the chief characteristics of Americans." At tea on one occasion, Martineau's American escort "dropped some drolleries so new to me, and so intense, that I was perplexed what to do with my laughter." Visiting a "merry household," Martineau recorded three hours of "wit in full flow; by which time we were all begging for mercy, for we could laugh no longer with any safety. I cannot conceive how it is that so little has been heard in England of the mirth of the Americans; for certainly nothing in their manner struck and pleased me more. One of the rarest characters among them, and a great treasure to all his sportive neighbors, is a man who cannot take a joke." The comfort of humor—at times genuinely physically uncomfortable for Martineau—was apparently inaccessible to most international travelers, especially those who claimed that Americans in the interior spoke only in monosyllables or spoke not a single word to anyone except under duress.[33]

If comfort in the interior was publicly conducted without reference to the weather and without the aid of servants, it was also mobile, and devoted neither to creature comforts nor to the exercise of a normative aesthetic. Comfort in the interior had a style that did not announce itself as a style; at times it was so unreadable that travelers dismissed it as having no style at all. The comfortable style, when it emerged into view, seemed to be a quite sturdy mode of even-humored public detachment, uncomplaining, amusing itself with the newspapers, and not looking at the landscape; as such it constituted an image at the furthest remove from that of the gentleman sequestered in his library, the vision of comfort that Birkbeck and Flower attempted to realize in the interior with distinctly hollow results. In hotel lobbies, on riverboat decks, and in their homes, settlers read newspapers; newsprint was apparently the only incarnation of a tree that some settlers appreciated. Godfrey Vigne, who traveled through Ohio on a coach that paused to drop off newspapers at one solitary log house after another, claimed that not one in five hundred settlers was illiterate, and that all were well informed about events in Europe and England. When Frances Trollope remarked sarcastically to her milkman in Cincinnati that he spent "a good deal of time in reading the newspapers," he came back at her with a challenge: "And I'd like you to tell me how we can spend it better. How should free men spend their time, but looking after their government, and watching that them fellers as we gives offices to, doos their duty, and gives themselves no airs?" The newspapers engendered "all manner of disputes about the presidential election, the tariff, the banks" that in 1846 the German traveler Erich von Raumer enjoyed listening to aboard an Ohio riverboat: "Notwithstanding the zeal and vivacity of the disputants, uninterrupted good humor prevailed, and not a single bitter or discourteous word was uttered. This is the consequence of daily, all-composing habit. Here is displayed a self-control to which the constrained and irritable literati and non-literati of our fatherland have not yet attained." Travelers were, furthermore, astonished by the self-critical nature of such discussions. Lawrence Oliphant advised English travelers to condemn or sneer at nothing in America but to listen to Americans themselves condemn the faults in their own system, which, he said, they regularly did in "unmeasured terms."[34]

The public manner of the interior—a controlled, class-denying, good-humored public detachment—was understood by the French traveler Michel Chevalier to be both a philosophical satisfaction and an ideological comfort. It was not without threat and not without critics. Such longtime resident writers as Timothy Flint and James Hall, always looking to the east and always nervous about difference, liked to assure their readers that the interior would soon become "a more polished" society "recognizing all the ordinary rules of decorum," but Charles Fenno Hoffman, who dreaded and despised the society in which "the mode of eating an egg is the test of good breeding," confuted James Hall's notions about the gradual arrival of "polish" when he argued that there were "no gradations in society long tolerable between the raw material as you find it on the frontier and the thoroughly manufactured article as one occasionally meets with it elsewhere," in that vulgarity, affectation, and pretension had no place in either. Anthony Trollope, for all the social suffering he underwent in the interior, came to admire the settler who "has worked out his independence, and shows it in every easy movement of his body. He tells you of it unconsciously in every tone of his voice. You will always find in his cabin some newspaper, some book, some token of advance in education. When he questions you about the old country he astonishes you by the extent of his knowledge. I defy you not to feel that he is superior to the race from whence he has sprung in England or in Ireland. He is dirty and perhaps squalid."[35]

Caroline Kirkland, however, pressed hard on the unapologetic grace of independence that Anthony Trollope saw in the interior and made it show its other side: "The absolute democracy which prevails in country places imposes as heavy restraints upon one's free-will in some particulars as do the overbearing pride and haughty distinctions of the old world in others." Kirkland saw that the public nature of comfort in the interior meant that persons who exhibited any desire for privacy were labeled, at the least, proud, and that any public display of difference was punished in a social arena consumed by "a burning, restless desire to subject all habits and manners to one procrustean rule. Whoever ventures to differ essentially from the mass is sure to become the object of unkind feeling, even without supposing any bitter personal animosity." Unobservable to most travelers in the interior, the uncomfortable pressures exerted on difference exposed a fragility in ideological comfort and highlighted the dangers of a social misstep: as Kirkland observed, "Of all places in the world in which to live on the shady side of public opinion, an American backwoods settlement is the very worst." Erich von Raumer had noted on his 1846 riverboat journey that ideological comfort was a "daily, all-composing habit," but it carried a price. The search for comfort on the landscape of the interior did not—and has not—ended, and the struggle for comfort can still veer toward the disastrous English models that failed in the nineteenth century. The interior's version of comfort was never settled but always mobile, and an examination of the daily workings of mobility casts another light on the never-settled connections between the landscape and the life lived on it.[36]

Chapter 3

Dreaming on the Run

In 1842, the Scots traveler William Thomson recorded, in *A Trades-man's Travels,* his search for "the very best land" in America. As an observer, Thomson had no sense of scene and no interest in describing landscape; he chose to measure and calculate his way across the interior. When he was on a steamboat, he noted precisely its fare structure and described its dimensions; when on land, he inquired diligently after bushels per acre and the standard of local health, in order to locate exactly in the interior the "very best land" for the price. His measurement project, however, defeated him, and he eventually advised prospective emigrants to alter their attitudes toward land values, as he had his, and to abandon the search for the "very best land." On the great expanses of the interior, that land, Thomson had determined, was eternally elsewhere. "Wherever I have been," he wrote, "on inquiring if the land was good, I found there was far superior locations somewhere else—at some place where nobody had ever been: some, indeed, have got within sixty miles of what they consider first-rate land and a healthy climate; and this is, probably, as near an approach to contentment as can be arrived at in any country." The shifting slippery dream of a landscape's perfect spot, the dream that

Thomson, jotting figures in his little notebook, pursued until he realized it had not one but many locations, all of them always up ahead, suggests how great a contribution the landscape of the interior itself made to the mobility of those, both travelers and potential settlers, who entered it. Throughout the century, travelers struggled with describing a landscape whose major features might always be elsewhere and whose present features so often failed to allow them to distinguish one spot from another. To many travelers, all spots seemed similar and all spots seemed unfamiliar.[1]

In remarking on "the problematic air of American nature for the early reporters," David Wilson observed that "it was not a matter simply of an unfamiliar plant here, a slightly different snake there. The whole design of American nature seemed unsettling." Travelers, remarking on a series of unfamiliar aspects of climate and landscape, noted that landscape variations across the interior were rarely drastic: bands of trees alternated with strips and expanses of prairie, gently rolling land alternated with flat land, and the variations themselves occurred in a rhythm unfamiliar and unpredictable to travelers whose eyes had been trained in western Europe or on America's East Coast. To some, the interior, furthermore, seemed to have two seasons rather than four, and those two might alternate with each other day by day. There was no period of twilight—at one moment the sun was on the prairie horizon and at the next moment the sun vanished, plunging the prairie traveler into darkness. Moreover, on the open prairie, travelers often felt paradoxically constrained in empty space, an effect caused by the nature and behavior of the prairie horizon; they stood as if in the center of a shallow bowl whose rim was the not-too-distant and slightly raised prairie horizon. The rimmed landscape fostered the dismal illusion of movement without progress; after a day's travel, the grove ahead often seemed no nearer than it had in the morning, and the grove behind seemed no more distant. The prairie bowl seemed to move with the travelers, and to their eyes the horizon appeared always nearer than it was but at the same time less accessible, close but continually receding. "The heart of a European," wrote Simon O'Ferrall in 1832, "sickens at the sameness of the scene, and he cannot get rid of the idea of imprisonment, when the visible horizon is never more distant than five or six hundred yards." It was not only European eyes that felt the horizon's effect: "The eye," wrote the easterner James Leander Scott in 1843, "stretches from one undulation to another, in its native velocity, and view succeeds to view, until the power of vision fails, and yet there is nothing on which to rest the sight."[2]

Travelers whose eyes had appraised mountains, waterfalls, cathedrals, ruins, scenic variety, and the geometrical environments of cities found the landscape of the interior an agony of monotony. It was a monotony of coarseness when categorized as mere expanse, and a monotony of delicacy when viewed in close detail by a traveler on foot. The monotony made any new detail a gift to the eyes: "The slightest changes in the features of the country, or in the complexion of the soil," wrote Henry Rowe Schoolcraft in 1825, "become interesting. The sudden starting of a prairie-hen or a whirring pheasant are circumstances which the memory seizes upon, in the common dearth of local interest." Certainly the interior was without such assertive landscape features as mountains, gorges, and canyons; its very ridges were smoothed by vegetation, and its color spectrum was narrow. Considered in quantity, there was, as Harriet Martineau put it, "probably too much" of the landscape. The rapid scenic variations that smaller-scale countries offered were persistently missing in the interior: travelers found their first few river bluffs beautiful, but many miles of bluffs were wearisome; their first glimpse of an uncultivated prairie was stunning, an experience every traveler wanted, but hundreds of miles of prairie were desolating. Some travelers praised the landscapes of the interior before launching into complaint about their repetitions; others on first view began to wish for variety, or mountains, or home; and still others expressed passions of loathing and contempt for what they saw.[3]

On their first day out from Pittsburgh down the Ohio River into the interior, most travelers were enchanted by the scenery. In 1833 Thomas Hamilton "remained on deck for several hours, gazing on a character of scenery to which I had seen nothing similar in Europe." The enchantment did not last. "On the second day, something of the charm was gone," wrote Hamilton, "and at length its monotony became almost tedious. A thousand miles of any scenery, with one definite and unchanging character, will generally be found too much." Prairie scenery underwent the same shift. The prairie's beauty, though "very agreeable" to D. Griffiths in 1835, was so uniform that after riding all day across the prairie, he felt himself to be exactly where he had started in the morning. In 1843, woods and low hills grew tedious to Charles Daubeny, who required something more bold and striking to keep him alert, and in 1852 Hugh Tremenheere complained that in an expanse as large as the interior, scenes of great beauty were too widely spaced and too few in number. Nor could the bluffs of the upper Mississippi sustain interest: in 1855 Laurence Oliphant found that bluffs "which appeared so fantastic in shape at first, lost their interest in a great measure from the great similarity which subsists between them, and it was quite a relief to come upon a stretch of prairie land."

For Frederick Goddard in 1869, Iowa's "very beauty and fertility were so monotonous as to be tiresome."[4]

Under the weight of travelers' complaints, the landscape flattened. In Ohio in 1818, Henry Fearon saw scarcely a single elevation that he cared to denominate a hill, and in 1865 northern Illinois was judged by George Borrett to hold "nothing which the wildest imagination, or the purest disregard for accuracy, could designate as a tenth-rate hill." David Macrae, having arrived at the Mississippi in 1870, announced that "the main features of American scenery are two, namely flat forest land and flat prairie land." The sharper the traveler's pen, the sharper the landscape derogation—and the smaller the prairies became. To Charles Dickens in 1842, the prairie was "the great blank"; in 1859 John MacGregor cut the prairie down to "a field of rank grass, two hundred miles between the fences"; in 1892, Robert Louis Stevenson reduced the landscape of the interior to "a billiard-board" and then to "wallpaper with a vengeance," and for Oscar Wilde in 1895 the prairies were "a piece of blotting-paper." Miniaturized, the great landscape seemed about to shrink to pinhead size and disappear altogether.[5]

The indescribable scale of the interior seems to have troubled travelers into rejecting it, as did its insistent repetitions of landscape forms, and not least its mood, the state of mind that the interior suggested to—or even promoted in—its observers. A great many travelers seemed to sense that something momentous would happen to them if they gave themselves over to the expanses of the interior and, seeking to preserve themselves from whatever that momentous change might be, they held back. In 1842 Charles Dickens took a planned and controlled excursion to view a prairie. Although the excursion was hedged round with such safety devices as timetables, chartered vehicles, and elaborate picnic baskets, Dickens nonetheless experienced fear and impatience on the prairie. He found the view to be "oppressive in its barren monotony. I felt that, in traversing the prairies, I could never abandon myself to the scene, forgetful of all else, but should often glance towards the distant and frequently receding line of the horizon, and wish it gained and passed. It is not a scene to be forgotten, but it is scarcely one to remember with much pleasure, or to covet the looking on again in after life." Dickens thought that the prairie "left nothing to the imagination, tamed it down and cramped its interest"; Harriet Martineau, who in 1838 likewise found the landscape of the interior oppressive to the imagination, resisted the idea of "the spirit growing into harmony with the scene, wild and solemn as the objects around it." Travelers were further troubled when the prairie disarranged familiar sense impressions: Thomas Farnham complained that his "eyes ached as [he] endeavored to embrace the view," and James Hall thought his eyes were failing him when he stood on a bare and windy Illinois prairie in winter and felt a blast of wind rushing over him while around him no visible object was seen to stir. Not only did the eye fail, but the ear was similarly deprived. In Ohio in 1824, William Blane heard no sound of any living thing except for the occasional hawk or eagle wheeling above him. Although Blane had experienced similar silence and solitude in forests, he was more struck by it on the open space of the prairie. On the Mississippi above St. Louis, Giacomo Beltrami was struck by "the death-like silence which pervades this vast solitude," and in Ohio in 1843 William Oliver surmised that the landscape's powerful silence had overcome the settlers themselves. Oliver stopped at a prairie house for a meal and "during the short time we sat, before and after supper, there were scarcely half a dozen words of conversation. The silence of the woods is not half so oppressive. A pin can't fall without being heard, and the jaws of those who yawn through sheer weariness are heard cracking right and left." The interior refused to give itself over to the senses but seemed to James Leander Scott in Illinois to require "a stretch of thought, like contemplating infinity," only then to defeat that stretch by refusing to delimit it. "Like the vanishing lines in prospect," wrote Scott, "so is contemplation lost in this expanded prairie."[6]

Some travelers claimed to have discovered a new happiness on the landscape of the interior, while others experienced extreme melancholy or abrupt shifts and drops of mood. Patrick Shirreff, a traveler who claimed a special "fellowship with the vegetable kingdom," had been warned that he might become low-spirited in the interior, but instead he came to regard his wanderings on the prairie as the most pleasant and instructive period in his existence. Charles Fenno Hoffman, who traveled alone through the interior in winter, "felt amid some scenes a kind of selfish pleasure, a wild delight, that the spot so lovely and so lonely was, as it were, all my own," but the prairie solitude that allowed Hoffman his possessive fantasy induced in Charles Augustus Murray "an attack of the blue devils." On first view of the prairie, Fredrika Bremer felt "peculiarly cheerful and expansive," as if she wanted to stretch out her arms and fly, but a moment later she shifted into feeling stupid and strange because she was unable to do so. Many travelers experienced, like Bremer, landscape reactions that shifted uncomfortably from the pleasant to something other and less definable. In 1842 James Silk Buckingham joined a sizable excursion party of men on a planned three-hour tour of an Illinois prairie under the protective cover of daylight. Buckingham was looking forward to enjoying the novelty of the excursion, and once on the prairie he drew pleasure from imagining the uncultivated tallgrass prairie domesticated into a lawn adorned with flowers; then he projected excitement onto the scene by transforming the prairie into a rich green sea. When his fantasies were exhausted, however, he glimpsed the expanse for itself and was struck with fear because he saw on it no visible shelter from potential danger, not a single tree, shrub, house, or shed. He began to list his worries: a horse might be disabled, the coach might break down, the driver might miss the track and lose his way, fog might roll in, night might fall. He tried to draw solace from feeling part of the group of travelers, but all social feeling leaked away and left him captive of the most powerful surge of loneliness he had ever experienced. The excursion party, he reasoned, had but one vehicle, and all would be equally helpless if it broke down on the prairie. Were that to occur, he thought, each man in the party of strangers would become "a solitary individual without the power to aid another." A landscape that could act to fragment an excursion group into solitary, endangered, helpless individuals was a powerful one indeed, and its rapid agency on the imagination is measured here by Buckingham's equally rapid succession of prairie fears. In 1824, William Blane, a plucky and practical solitary traveler who busied himself with assessing depth of soil and quality of resources as he traveled west into the interior, nonetheless chose to alter his itinerary by the time he arrived in St. Louis. Blane had planned to ascend the Mississippi alone and cross the Great Lakes on his return east, but his tolerance of solitude on the landscape of the interior collapsed. "I had no companion," he wrote, "and could not even hear of anyone wishing to make the same journey. I had already felt that traveling by oneself in these vast solitudes is but a very melancholy pleasure; and I was confident that I should not be able to endure being alone in so great a tract of uninhabited country as I should have to pass through between St. Louis and Canada."[7]

Some travelers developed tactics for coping with prairie-induced moods. For relief from the "solitude and monotony of the prairie," Charles Augustus Murray tried to call up "the ghosts of remembered social enjoyments—a walk, a word, a smile," and Francesco Arese carried with him objects given him by his friends in the hope that handling them might sustain his morale. Nonetheless, Arese confessed, "I came to passing whole days in reveries; and toward evening my imagination was so worn out and my thoughts so confused that I realized that that is how people go crazy." Even an exceptionally tough solitary traveler in good control of his mood could trip over a fearsome demonstration of his solitude. In December of 1854, Friedrich Gerstacker was walking across Ohio at a good pace when darkness fell. Thinking he glimpsed a light through the trees ahead, he made for it in hopes of a warm bed and a cup of hot coffee. Another half mile's walk through the night brought him within sight of a house that appeared to be lighted. He approached and, he wrote, "knocked at the low door; all was silent as the grave. I pushed it open in rather ill humor and found—a deserted house, with all as still as death. The stars shone through a hole in the roof, the chimney had fallen in." Suddenly struck with fear, Gerstacker closed the door and was surprised to find himself running, springing over the fence, and "leaving the building to its mournful solitude." Women travelers especially wondered how anyone bore life on the expanses of the interior; to Harriet Martineau settlers seemed to be "lost in space," and to Frances Trollope to lead lives of awful and unnatural loneliness. Some degree of cultivated detachment allowed locals to live "lost in space" on the same landscape that made some travelers shrink, run, shorten their itineraries, and backtrail, and led others to seek the dream-view, the special vision, the new category that might transform the interior into something less alien and more comfortable, organized, describable, and bearable.[8]

Travelers' attempts to locate on the landscape of the interior scenes that fit such European aesthetic categories as the *picturesque* always failed. Twelve hundred miles of travel through the interior might yield up one decayed mill that a traveler could read as a picturesque ruin, whereas the remainder of the trip offered not a single natural or built scene to be appreciated by a devotee of picturesque travel. The picturesque was too entirely visual a category to suit the interior, which offered itself to physical entry but regularly refused aesthetic viewing: the walker on the prairie physically experienced enclosure, insects, dust, pollen, faint smells, and the crackling of low dense vegetation, while the viewer saw only space. Furthermore, the interior was too expansive, undifferentiated, and unpredictable to serve as "soft" nature, to be a stage for bucolic interludes, or to furnish a refreshing retreat from urban pressures. The picturesque belonged to Europe, and travelers' efforts to find it in the interior lapsed into dead assertion that bleached the landscape of its detail: "Exceedingly picturesque," wrote Paul Wilhelm, "were the various colors with which nature adorned the different kinds of trees in America during the autumn." In Illinois, Eliza Farnham found the picturesque indoors, in illustrated volumes of travels; she regularly leafed through books of Italian and Swiss scenery in order to preserve her love of the "picturesque and rugged in nature," but outside her cabin, on the actual Illinois landscape, there lay something else. Godfrey Vigne claimed that the picturesque was absent because Americans did not value it. "The English and American ideas of the picturesque are widely different," he wrote. "The

Englishman travels to other lands in search of wilder scenery. The American would readily dispense with the romantic, and wonders that everybody is not like himself, an admirer, by preference, of a railroad, a canal, or a piece of newly cleared ground . . . the *ne plus ultra* of the beautiful." Vigne's remarks, however, say more about the uselessness of his visual categories to the scale of the interior than about American tastes in landscape or art, and more about class than about aesthetics. The railroads and canals that Vigne scorned expressed to some travelers not an aesthetic but a certain ideological beauty. In Michel Chevalier's view, the railroads and canals themselves established equality and democracy, and "extended to all the members of the human family the power of moving about and using the world which has been given to all as a common patrimony. The effect of the most perfect system of transportation is to reduce the distance not only between different places, but between different classes. Where the rich and the great travel only with a pompous retinue, while the poor man who goes to the next village travels painfully alone over mud and sand and rocks and through thickets, the word equality is a mockery and a falsehood, and aristocracy stares you in the face."[9]

In their struggle to describe the landscape of the interior, many travelers set aside the miniaturizing effects of the picturesque in favor of the vast, and named the interior after another global surface of expansive undifferentiated blankness—the ocean. The earliest adventurers and explorers who glimpsed the American interior had described it as a sea of grass, and every explorer, traveler, and observer who followed them into the interior throughout the eighteenth and nineteenth centuries repeated the metaphor: it became the dominant landscape-organizing vision, and was regularly embroidered with such other seascape elements as billows, swells, and islands. The sea metaphor became a theory when travelers claimed that great stretches of the sea of grass were treeless because they had until quite recently been under water, and the theory led to speculation that occasional groves of trees must once have been islands in a great inland sea. In the 1830s many labeled the underwater theories preposterous, and pointed out not only that groves often appeared in low-lying areas but also that, for example, Illinois's highest points were its central prairies. In 1838, however, Edmund Flagg could sweep away such factual objections to assert that "the *idea* strikes the spectator at once, and with much force, that the whole plain was once a sheet of water." For most observers, landscape facts were overridden by the sea idea, and the idea had consequences. Embroidering the sea metaphor allowed Basil Hall, who was invariably unhappy in the interior, to "almost forget where [he] was"; it allowed William Blane to erase the landscape from aesthetic consideration by claiming that "the large prairies, from their size, almost entirely lose their beauty, and present nothing but an immense sea of grass"; it allowed Charles Dickens to drain the prairie into "a tranquil sea or lake without water"; and it allowed John Francis Campbell to crush it flat when he wrote, "Except in the middle of the Atlantic in a dead calm, such another dead flat landscape is hard to find." The sea metaphor expressed travelers' difficulties with the scale of nature in the interior and, moreover, constituted an outsider's view: though plenty of insiders have since repeated the metaphor, a landlocked native of the interior would not have invented it. Immensity is not the sea metaphor's sole effect, for travelers regularly applied it to prairies of all sizes, many of them not even faintly oceanic in extent. If and when the sea metaphor expressed immensity, it expressed it specifically as a traveler's frustrating inability to measure distances accurately, a traveler's weariness with moving through apparently empty space, and a traveler's desire for a destination that promised life, habitation, and variety. "When the grand, gloomy, misty magnificence of old ocean presents itself on every side," wrote Charles Fenno Hoffman of the prairie landscape, "the relief to the picture afforded by the discovery of man's habitation can hardly be described." Furthermore, visual effects that on the ocean could be described as grand and sublime became, when transferred to the prairie, "nothing but monotonous swells to catch the eye wherever its glances roamed."[10]

Application of the sea metaphor to the landscape served to erase what few landmarks there were in the interior and to create instead an unmarked, undifferentiated space whose effects were those of oppression, loneliness, and dreary monotony. The metaphor had the power to survive the eradication of the original prairie landscape that had given rise to it: in 1879, Newman Hall still saw "small clumps of trees, standing alone, like islets in the vast ocean" even though the surrounding landscape was composed no longer of shoulder-high grass but of "nothing but corn—corn to the right of us, corn to the left of us, corn in the front of us—as far as the eye could reach, without hedge or visible fence"; and the metaphor could incorporate the railroad: in 1864, near Joliet, John Francis Campbell wrote, "The iron horse gallops over a sea of green grass, which has no apparent limit but the horizon." Certainly the sea metaphor derived some of its staying power from its capacity to express great fear. In 1837, Henry Ellsworth set out to cross an Illinois prairie in a snowstorm. He had left his compass behind, and the heavy snow obscured the stars.

Now, I was on a broad sea without chart or compass, and without one stray light in the heavens whereby to direct my course. The mariner, when tossed upon the billows of the stormy ocean, has at least the satisfaction of knowing where he is, for the needle will always point to the pole, and his chart will tell him of the dangers in his path—but the weary traveler who has lost his way on a prairie is on a boundless sea, where he cannot even tell the direction he is pursuing, for oft-times he will travel hour after hour, and still remain at nearly the same point from which he started. Had even one accommodating star beamed in the heavens, I should not have been the least disconcerted, for then I could have some objects whereby to guide my steps. But all the elements combined against me.

Lost in snowy space, Ellsworth revealed the prairie and its heavy weather as even less suited to human travel than was the ocean. In other writers' hands, the sea metaphor continually revealed the prairie as uninhabitable; the sea, after all, is neither a place nor an idea of place that humans can inhabit. The sea is a mover's surface to be crossed on the way to a real landscape, to society, to elsewhere. In Ellsworth's hands, the prairie became an uncrossable sea, a conspiracy of elements against human life, and an effective thief of any aid from equipment, printed information, the galaxy, or the human eye.[11]

Nonetheless across this landscape everyone—whether traveler or settler—moved. The greatest number of travelers wandered the American interior during exactly those decades—1820 to 1850—when settlers' mobility throughout the area was also most intense. Although it is not easy to distinguish between traveling mobility and mobile settling, mobile travelers insisted on seeing the settlers' mobility as different in kind from their own. Travelers called themselves *travelers* or *observers;* everyone called mobile settlers *movers.* Between 1830 and 1850 movers surged into the old northwest; by 1850 they were streaming into the upper Mississippi River valley, and in 1855 they were rushing through Iowa on their way to Nebraska. Settlers practiced regular short-distance movement among similar spots: they arrived, they "improved," they moved on west. It might be said that they practiced interrupted mobility as opposed to travelers' uninterrupted mobility.

Although some extraordinary travelers walked across the interior, settlers did not choose to walk. In 1822, James Flint claimed to have seen not a single pedestrian in any twenty-five miles of traveling, and in 1833 James Stuart, stopping at a country church in Ohio, wrote: "No one who does not live in the village walks to church on foot. All have conveyances of some sort or other, and come in them. Indeed, such a thing as a human being walking anywhere on the public roads out of the villages is rarely seen. The custom of the country is for all to ride in some sort of carriage." Some travelers suggested that the interior was not a walker's landscape: Margaret Fuller, in Wisconsin in 1844, complained that "to come to this monotony of land, with all around a limitless horizon—to walk, and walk, and run, but never climb, oh! it was too dreary for any but a Hollander to bear." Moreover, travelers viewed distance differently from locals who, making no discrimination between distances, chose to ride everywhere. Adaptable emigrants quickly picked up local habits of mobility: in 1822, John Woods said he had traveled more than he ever had during the same span of time in England, and local observers accepted mobility as a central feature of life in the interior. Daniel Drake, a longtime resident of Cincinnati, pointed out that emigrants moved, itinerant preachers moved, and politicians moved about to debate each other and address the populace; James Hall reported from Illinois in 1833 that "few men can be found who have not traveled beyond the limits of their own state; indeed, few are found residing in the state in which they were born. They are a migratory and an inquisitive people." International observers assented: "Here all the world travels," wrote Francis Lieber in 1837, and in 1850, Thomas Mooney described traveling in the interior as having achieved the level of a mania.[12]

Moving across—and around in—the interior was represented by travelers as easy. In 1832 the National Highway extended from Wheeling, West Virginia, to Zanesville, Ohio, and in 1839 an ascent of the Mississippi that, according to Frederick Marryat, had once required six or seven months was being performed in fifteen days. James Stuart in 1833 thought the scenery of the rivers dull, but gleaned "a great deal of pleasure from penetrating into the very heart of an immense continent by so easy, and, in many respects, luxurious a mode of conveyance" as the steamboat. Even travelers who dwelt more on steamboats' tendency to explode than on their ease and luxury nonetheless admitted that "all that does not bother the Americans, so long as you can go and go quickly." In 1826, Timothy Flint represented continual movement as a sociable erasure of distance: "A family in Pittsburgh," he wrote, "wishes to make a social visit to a kindred family on Red River. The trip is but two thousand miles. They all go together: servants, baggage or 'plunder,' as the phrase is, to any amount. In twelve days they reach the point proposed. Even the return is but a short voyage. Surely the people of this country will have to resist strong temptations, if they do not become a social people. You are invited to a breakfast, at seventy miles' distance. You go on board the passing steamboat and awake in the morning in season for your appointment." Flint's happy vision of long-distance sociability, though apparently about connection, is, from another point of view, about disconnection by distance; very little other commentary on the scene of mobility supports his particular vision. The fuel of mobility was not the desire to visit relatives, and mobility pushed past desire into ideology, with travel literature and settlers' devoted reading of it as a further spur to movement. So many places to go, such easy access.[13]

For nearly six decades, travelers discussed mobility in the interior; the discussion ended, without resolution, only when they stopped noticing the subject. In 1805, François André Michaux pitched into the subject with his assertion that locals in Ohio who could not bring themselves to settle on the soil they had cleared invented various pretenses—"better land, more wholesome country, a greater abundance of game"—to explain their desire to push on west where, according to Michaux, they seized the chance to fulfill their truest desire: that of treating Indians badly. From early on, travelers noted but failed to understand why backtrailing did not constitute a choice. In 1819, John Stillman Wright claimed that most settlers longed to return to wherever they had come from, but could not afford to; thus, feeling restless and uneasy where they were, they determined to go farther west. In the same year, William Amphlett guessed that Americans who failed to achieve instant success in the interior tended to attribute their failure to some local disadvantage, whereupon they picked up and left to try another spot. In 1823, William Faux counted up numbers of deserted houses and lots in Chillicothe, Ohio, and concluded that "the American has always something better in his eye, further west; he therefore lives and dies on hope, a mere gypsy in this particular." The gloomy Tocqueville thought mobility was accelerated by Americans "forever brooding over advantages they do not possess," but his countryman Michel Chevalier reversed that mood when he asserted that "in general the American is little disposed to be contented." In 1842 Caroline Kirkland saw her Michigan neighbors "bit with the strange madness of ceaseless transit, flitting westward like ghosts that shun the coming day. Some of them—not a few indeed—are now living on their third or fourth Western farm—successive purchases and residences in scarcely more than a corresponding number of years." Kirkland read their mobility as "a blundering search after happiness."[14]

In 1843 James Leander Scott defined mobility as a problem and offered his diagnosis: the landscape of the interior itself, he thought, caused mobility because "on reaching its borders, [the interior] expands astonishingly." In St. Paul in the spring of 1856, Christopher Columbus Andrews thought mobility formed the stuff of the national conversation in the interior. Eavesdropping on conversations in crowded hotel lobbies, Andrews noticed that everyone was seeking bits of information about "some place where he thinks somebody has been or is going, and so a great many new acquaintances are made without ceremony or delay." Meditating on mobility, Timothy Flint ascribed the phenomenon to the emigrant's imaginative awareness of the possibilities:

> They arrive, after long and diversified, but generally painful journies, painful, especially if they have young and helpless members in their families, in the region for which they started. The first difficulty, and it is not a small one, is, among an infinite variety of choices, where to fix. The speculator, the surveyor, the different circles, all propose different places, and each vaunts the exclusive excellence of his choice. If the emigrant is a reader, he betakes himself to the papers, and in the infinity of advertisements, his uncertainty is increased. *Some, under these circumstances, try all places.* I lodged at the house of a Baptist exhorter, a very aged man, who had made seven distant removes in less than three hundred miles, each being too short a distance to give him a new trial. After the long uncertainty of choice is finally fixed—which is not till after the expenses and the lapse of a year—a few weeks' familiar acquaintance with the scene dispels the charms and the illusions of the imagination. The earth, the water, and the wood of these distant lands, are found to be the same well-known realities of his own country. Hunting, though the game be plenty, is a laborious and unproductive business, and everything visionary and unreal gradually gives way to truth and reality . . . the immigrant experiences not only the gloom of seeing himself among strangers to himself, to his country, to his opinions, and habits, but he is even in the midst of a nature that looks upon him as an intruder.

Thus, in Flint's view, each new location sustained the emigrant's dream for a time; when the dream dissipated, the dreamer moved on to "intrude" elsewhere, always a stranger, inevitably discontented.[15]

Dreaming, punctuated by successive intrusions upon nature and controlled by the mover's being always a stranger among strangers, affected, travelers guessed, identity, longevity, and society in general. Travelers found nothing in the interior that could be called a folk culture, and the restlessly jostling human particles that spun across the landscape could by no wishful effort be made to congeal into "the folk." Furthermore, as Frederick Marryat noted in 1829, mobility made anonymity unavailable in the interior, and no one could successfully "attempt the incognito" until he or she was west of the Mississippi. In 1855, Charles Weld was sure that mobility shortened lives: "The entire want of rest and peace must be fatal to longevity." Across the decades, travelers claimed that attachments both to other people and to specific locales were weakened or erased by mobility: in 1832 Simon O'Ferrall claimed that personal connections in the interior never went beyond the level of ordinary acquaintance, and Charles Augustus Murray noted that an American, though always proud of his state of origin, nonetheless readily left his childhood home without either effort or regret. George Holyoake asserted in 1881 that the mover no longer remembered even the location of that childhood home: he said he had "met with men who had been in so many places that they seemed to have forgotten where they were born." Observing the effects of nearly one hundred years of accelerating mobility since the Revolution, Joseph Alexander concluded in 1874 that "in this country men seem to be made of different stuff. Broken in to endure every kind of fatigue, always hurried, even in their everyday life, accustomed to think nothing of distances, to take their meals in ten minutes, to rush about here, there, and everywhere, the American may be called the very essence of locomotion." In 1842, change and mobility, according to Caroline Kirkland, pervaded all of life in the interior: "Horses, oxen, wagons, carts, are equally subject to mutation. Some people scarce ever have the same for six months at a time . . . they never seem to doubt that each change is for the better." Moreover, nonmobile landscape features such as hedges and permanent fences rarely appeared in the interior; instead the easily movable worm fence—a zigzag construct of loose logs—was the boundary marker of choice. In Cincinnati there was brisk business in prefabricated houses packed in crates that movers bought for a few hundred dollars before setting out for Kansas and Nebraska, and the house-moving concerns that sprang up in the cities of the interior performed their maneuvers unnoticed, according to Aleksandr Lakier, by the house's occupants whose "style of life is in no way disturbed by this move; the owner continues to read his newspapers, to argue, and to carry on his trade." Finally, if no other form of movement was available, a local used a rocking chair or chose simply to "stretch his limbs and keep his muscles in play, " according to Charles Dickens. "When his feet are not in motion, his fingers must be in action; he must be whittling a piece of wood, or notching the edge of a table, or his jaws must be at work grinding tobacco." Michel Chevalier, taking a distinctly French view of the phenomenon, thought that mobility took the place of absent pleasures of the senses, since "public opinion and the pulpit forbid sensual gratifications, wine, women, and the display of a princely luxury; cards and dice are equally prohibited." And so, without games or gratifications, movement constituted life itself: "An irresistible current," wrote Chevalier, "sweeps everything away, grinds everything to powder, and deposits it again under new forms.

Men change their houses, their climate, their trade, their condition, their party, their sect; the states change their laws, their officers, their constitutions. The soil itself, or at least the houses, partakes in the universal instability."[16]

Mobility's effect on the landscape and on local attitudes both civic and personal was analyzed from the eighteenth century onward by travelers. While Caroline Kirkland favored the mobility that removed from her Michigan neighborhood in 1839 the restless rowdies who amused themselves by dropping dead pigs down wells, hanging pet dogs from gateposts, and forming mobs to dunk traveling entertainers who charged admission, she nonetheless also noted that mobility reduced local interest in public improvements. Timothy Flint regularly agonized over the "result of the mobile spirit upon the face of the country" and how mobility turned the landscape into "naked wastes" bare of the improvements and accumulations of durable buildings, plantings, and institutions. Mobility rewrote the nature of work, according to Michel Chevalier, by transforming the mobile American of the interior into a migratory worker "fit for all sorts of work except those which require a careful slowness. Those fill him with horror; it is his idea of hell."[17]

Most of the commentary just examined has been by and about men, and phrased in terms of masculine pronouns only; mobility's other face, however, is that of an unhappy woman. If men in the interior were discontented when not moving, women differed, and their roles in mobility reveal its social asymmetry. In 1780 the Marquis de Chastellux, staying at an inn near Virginia's Natural Bridge, fell into conversation with a young family on their way from Philadelphia to Kentucky. Their equipment for the move seemed to consist of nothing but a horse, and Chastellux, studying the young man, was "astonished at the easy manner with which he proceeded on his expedition." While the young woman remained silent, holding her baby, the enthusiastic young man told Chastellux that he had plenty of money, expected to want for nothing, and planned to purchase a thousand acres of land upon his arrival in Kentucky. Chastellux, though taken with the young man's spirit, secretly "doubted not but that his wife was in despair at the sacrifice she had made." He attempted to "discover in her features and looks the secret sentiments of her soul" but he failed, and could only see that she was "admirably disposed to increase and multiply," a matter that he did not read in her face. At Carondelet in 1842, Charles Dickens met a very old innkeeping couple who might have been Chastellux's young couple sixty years later. The old man "had all his life been restless and locomotive," and indicated to Dickens, with a jerk of his thumb toward his wife, that were it not for her, he would be off and moving again that very day; the old woman told Dickens that she had come with her husband from Philadelphia and in the West had seen her children die one by one of fever. "Her heart was sore, she said, to think of them." When Aleksandr Lakier met another version of this couple at Portsmouth, Ohio, in 1857, they were on their way from Pennsylvania to Kansas. The male mover's elderly mother and young wife told Lakier that they "did not know why or where the restless head of the family was dragging them," but the young man "defended himself cleverly and boldly" with a rapid stream of talk about land, wealth, and permanent security, all to be had in the interior. James Leander Scott, a minister who stayed at private homes throughout his travels in the interior, thought that, in contrast to their happy husbands, most of the women he met were lonely and homesick. The consequences of such differing and gendered attitudes—especially when acted upon by social isolation—were only infrequently glimpsed by travelers. In 1855 John Oldmixon was awaiting the arrival of a Mississippi River steamboat when out of the woods near the jetty "a wounded woman came limping along in search of a constable to look for her husband who 'had cut her to pieces and run off into the bush with their two children.' This woman," wrote Oldmixon, "was the picture of famine and misery as she sat on a log. On being asked if she lived far off, she exclaimed, 'Oh, I live nowhere. He never would settle in no place, but keeps moving about.'" Scenes like this one paint the asymmetrical consequences awaiting a population "living nowhere" on a complex and detailed landscape where, as Timothy Flint wrote, "everything shifts under your eye." These gendered glimpses suggest that many locals were not managing life on the slippery and shifting landscape of the interior any more effectively than were travelers, and travelers' landscape frustrations were continual.[18]

Travelers of both genders experienced the interior as expanse rendered incalculable by the constant presence of the slightly raised horizon. Because travelers were rarely positioned above the landscape but more usually down in it, the landscape nurtured in them a variety of dreams, deceptions, illusions, and fantasies. Travelers knew that their eyes were deceiving them, but women travelers were far more likely to admit that they could not correct for the deception. In Kansas in 1856, when Sara Robinson drove out to visit a friend living at two miles' distance, she "saw the house, or more properly the flume, a long time before reaching it, while constantly expecting to be at the door; but we have to learn what everyone else does in these prairies, that eyes unaccustomed cannot judge correctly of distances. Getting lost on the prairie in the darkness is an easy matter; and it has happened here, several times, that persons have wandered around nearly all night, trying to find the town, when at no time were they more than half a mile from it." Male travelers were less accepting of a perceptual situation that their eyes were untrained to handle. Near Decatur, Illinois, in 1859, James Caird and his party decided to leave the road and strike out across an unbroken prairie whose tall grasses overtopped the horses' heads. Caird, however, was one Englishman who knew what he was doing: he fixed his eye on a distant grove and for an hour drove directly toward it. The grove disappeared. Deciding he had got into a hollow, for two more hours Caird drove on, seeing "nothing but the long grass and the endless prairie, which seemed to rise slightly all around us." Exasperated, he fixed his eye on a cloud directly ahead and drove for it; half an hour later, the grove reappeared on the horizon, but Caird was no closer to it than he had been three and a half hours earlier. Humiliated, Caird blamed the horses. "We had got into a flat prairie about five miles square," he wrote. "One of the horses stepped a little quicker than the other, and we had been diligently driving in a circle for the last two hours." The prairie landscape altered both distance and size, an effect Harriet Martineau found "bewildering . . . a man walking near looks like a Goliath a mile off," and its few sharply delineated forms, mostly the stumps and skeletons of burned trees, frightened lonely travelers with their dubious shapes and their effect of forcing themselves on the traveler. According to a disgusted Frances Trollope, nature in the interior took "a thousand fantastic forms" to eyes unaccustomed to it but on investigation the forms were rarely anything more than "a mass of rotten leaves, or a fragment of fallen rock."[19]

To regain control over their perceptions and render the interior intelligible to their readers elsewhere, many travelers pounced on the organizing potential of prairie flowers. Numerous travelers were natural-history enthusiasts who identified and labeled their finds and who knew their flowers, ferns, birds, insects, moths, and butterflies. The earliest reports of prairie flora were extravagant enough to raise serious expectations among these travelers. In Dayton, Ohio, in 1808, Thomas Ashe claimed that "the uncultivated portion of the prairies abounds in flowers of such luxuriance and height that in riding through, it is often necessary to turn them from the face with the whip; and the general herbage, plants, and flowers rise to the saddle skirts." But it was Edmund Dana in 1819 who fired off the major volley of flower fantasy when he claimed that prairies produced "a numerous variety of flowers of every hue which blossom and decay in succession from spring to the winter months." Across the succeeding decades, Dana's orderly succession of flowers was increasingly specified: the flowers, travelers claimed, were all purple in spring, all red in summer, all yellow in autumn—or they were red in spring and blue in summer and yellow in autumn. The color succession was both created and confused by the fact that no one had seen it, no traveler stayed five months on any prairie to see it, and it could never be available for viewing on the single prairie visit many travelers made. In 1836 James Hall labeled the color-succession claim "one of the *notions* that people get who study nature by the fireside," but the notion's value to travelers lay in its imposing visual order on a landscape whose order was otherwise indiscernible and in its suggesting sensual pleasures otherwise notably absent from the interior. Since familiar and desirable flowers had scents, Timothy Flint in 1826 filled a prairie near St. Charles, Missouri, with "millions of flowers of every scent and hue," and travelers who followed him—and who had all read him—went on to describe prairies that even at some distance "wafted toward [them] the fragrance of many flowers" and enveloped them with "sweetest fragrance." What flowers in what numbers these travelers saw cannot be recovered, but the prairie flowers that most travelers actually saw tended to be small, pale, and scentless in the spring, and tall, coarse, and rank in late summer. When prairie experience collided with expectations raised by floral fantasy, travelers eager to experience the sensual spectacle of the great prairie flower garden were disappointed. Charles Dickens saw a few "poor and scanty" flowers in Illinois, and all of Charles Augustus Murray's experience of the prairie disappointed his expectations in regard to flowers. William Oliver disparaged Flint's "every scent and hue" flower description; it was Oliver's experience that "while yellow is the prevailing *hue,* the word *scent,* if it mean anything fine, must be taken as a poetical license." The floral extravaganza was, however, so appealing a fantasy that travelers resisted relinquishing it; some kept it alive by expressing their regrets at having missed seeing it. The prairie that Isabella Bird visited in 1856 offered few flowers to view, so she reported that "of the most gorgeous flowers, nothing remained but the withered stalks," and Isabella Trotter, who in 1859 saw on her prairie visit only "long brown grass," described it as "the dark remains of what must have been such a rich parterre of flowers."[20]

As a further disappointment, what prairie flowers there were refused to become garden stock: in Kansas in 1856, Sara Robinson and friend set out, shovels in hand, to obtain for transplanting some beautiful straw-colored flowers that a dinner guest had reported seeing nearby. Determined on possession, they began to dig down into the three-foot-deep root system that underlay the prairie association and met there complete resistance, no matter which of the "beautiful bunches" they attacked with their shovels. Finally, Robinson reported, they were obliged to leave the flowers in place, "their firmly-set roots still clinging to the soil." After the floral fantasies collapsed, prairie flowers became to travelers only a rumored decoration of an often desolate and empty landscape. Not only did the flowers refuse transplant, but once picked, they wilted rapidly and were unsuited to interior decoration. To see the flowers at all required seeking them out and viewing them in their own habitat and in their own season. Without prairie flowers, there were no flowers. Avid traveling gardeners met no likeminded flower-loving locals in the interior. Frances Trollope claimed that no local ever "dreamed of an attempt at garden scenery." Cultivated flowers in the interior were so rare, and settlers were so uninterested in them, that when in 1819 Thomas Hulme saw cultivated flowers at the German settlement of Harmony in Indiana, he read them ethnically as "a symptom of simplicity and ignorance, if not a badge of their German slavery." In Michigan, Caroline Kirkland's neighbors sneered at her tulips when they were not doing worse; one man "coolly broke off a spike of [her] finest hyacinths and after putting it to his undiscriminating nose, threw it on the ground with a 'pah!' as contemptuous as Hamlet's." The gulf between travelers' cherished floral fantasies and the attitudes of locals toward cultivated flowers was immense; the landscape of mobility made nonsense of the idea of cultivating perennials when the likelihood of seeing them bloom was so slight. Locals' contempt for Kirkland's perennials expressed indifference toward rootedness to place, aesthetic improvement, and the stoop labor required by gardening, while her cultivated flowers, which were neither profitable nor edible, expressed resistance to a life conducted on the run. Kirkland's neighbors refused proffered plant cuttings, saying that they "never know'd nobody make nothin' by raisin' sich things."[21]

When the dream of the great fragrant orderly domestic flower garden of the interior collapsed, travelers were left with two nightmare landscapes of the interior, one of which was the prairie afire, reported to be a grand spectacle of great bodies of flame "leaping and plunging like the waves of the sea . . . emitting a continued roar like that of a heavy surf." When the fire had passed, all that remained was "one uniform black surface" littered with the bones of horses and cattle. Travelers were uncertain about who fired the prairies in the fall and to what end. In 1805, François Michaux claimed that Indians fired prairies in order to better spot stags and bison that would be lured to the burned areas. In 1819 members of the Long expedition up the Missouri filled out Michaux's surmise by explaining that it was the "growth of tender and nutritious herbage which springs up soon after the burning" that lured large animals. In the 1820s and 1830s, travelers who saw no large animals anywhere in the interior came to believe that fire itself had created the prairies, and that prairies were "artificial," owed their existence as land forms to fire, and would be forested were it not for the annual burning. When knowledgeable locals debunked these notions, travelers turned to terror tactics: Adlard Welby claimed that prairie fires, which he had not seen, "advanced so quickly that the speed of a horse has sometimes proved unavailing" in escaping them. In displays of prairiecraft, travelers advised readers trapped by prairie fires to "take the precaution of also setting fire to the grass, and retreating upon the burnt spot, which of course the original fire can never reach for want of fuel." Timothy Flint asserted that many travelers had perished in prairie fires, and Paul Wilhelm claimed to have saved himself from death only by escaping in a boat from the burning banks of the Missouri. By the 1830s, scenes of men and animals racing ahead of prairie fires embellished children's books and school geographies. In 1836 James Hall wrote, "There is not an authenticated case on record or in tradition, in which a man or an animal has been burned by these fires, unless he was drunk or wounded." Nonetheless, fire was the prairies' only spectacle, and thrill seekers like the crazed Italian traveler Francesco Arese set the prairie afire every evening for "diversion and the enjoyment of a fine spectacle."[22]

In the 1850s, after state laws and the spread of cultivation had erased most possibilities of prairie fires in the interior, travelers' fire descriptions grew more fanciful. One night in 1852, Daniel Curtiss, driving his buggy from Platteville to Mineral Point, Wisconsin, saw "miles of fire" ahead of him. He drove to the top of a nearby mound "which lay rolled up and shrouded in smoke, handsome as an apple-dumpling all steaming from the kettle," to survey the "enchanting panorama" of a fire that "screamed for victims." The flames threatened to surround the apple-dumpling mound, even to creep up its side: Curtiss thought of "the spot on the banks of the bright Kankakee where, some years ago, two young persons—betrothed lovers—perished in the prairie flames; their crisped forms, near their horse, being found next day by a hunter." Luckily Curtiss's reverie was interrupted by his recalling that he had in his pocket a match, a piece of equipment that he advised other travelers to bear in mind. He fired the grass on the mound, the fire burned a clear path ahead of him, and he, his horse, and his buggy followed the little path to safety. Curtiss's melodramatic narrative, organized around cooking images of apple dumplings and crisped people, signaled the limits of fire fantasies about the interior. By 1870, no traveler had witnessed any such scene, and all furiously debunked prairie fire descriptions. "Bombast," John White called such stories: "After having seen some hundreds of lines of fire licking up the prairie grass, I have yet to see one which it would be hard to jump across." "Preposterous," wrote W. M. Stewart, who asserted that the prairie fires were so small that he had seen boys jump through them for sport, or stand astraddle them. "A prairie fire," observed David Macrae, "was a miserable exhibition that nobody would give two cents to see again."[23]

With the prairie fires extinguished, the landscape drama of the interior had but one remaining location, one scene waiting to disappoint travelers who, searching their maps for scenes of potential grandeur in the interior, picked the confluence of the Ohio and Mississippi Rivers as the scene of choice. The scene itself did not live up to the map. Travelers learned on arrival that there was no prospect at the confluence of the two rivers, no vista, no scenic overlook, nothing but "low muddy bottom lands and the unrelieved, unvaried gloom of the forest." In 1838, Edmund Flagg, who had expected to see "vastness and sublimity," found instead "the dullest, dreariest, most uninviting region imaginable." William Oliver called it a scene of "solitary desolation" and melancholy, Frederick Marryat found it "a vile sewer," and Charles Dickens labeled it "slimy" and "intolerable." George Rose, who traveled the interior wrapped in a black cloud of disgust, allowed of the confluence that "DeSoto might as well have kept his discovery to himself; but this remark will also apply to Columbus." To Rose, the scene epitomized all the failings of scenery in the interior.[24]

The confluence of the two great rivers, in effect, looked better and more impressive on a map than it did in actuality. It failed to be scenery in the composed sense, and it sprawled in a pattern that even eyes keen for panorama could not grasp. In 1870 the Scots traveler David Macrae, ruminating on the scenery of the interior, told a story of "a plaid-weaver [who] projected a tartan of so vast a check that it would have required four Highland regiments to be dressed in it to let the entire pattern be seen. American scenery is on that kind of scale. You sometimes travel hundreds of miles before you see any change or get a glimmering of the general pattern." Lost in space—or unable to locate themselves in a spatial pattern too large to grasp visually—both locals and travelers kept moving. The landscape features capable of bringing every antebellum traveler to a halt, however, were the prehistoric mounds and earthworks, and to pause over them, as many did, was to become enmeshed in a web of speculation, misreading, fantasy, and theory that no other feature of the interior had been so capable of engendering.[25]

Chapter 4
Marvels and Wonders

In 1846, George Featherstonhaugh and his party stepped ashore on Round Island in Lake Huron where they had spotted a number of burial mounds—the remains, their guide told them, of an ancient Indian settlement. Excited to see that the mounds appeared previously undisturbed, Featherstonhaugh "selected a very antique-looking mound" and began to dig into it. He obtained from the mound a "noble skull with a remarkably fine set of teeth" and, choosing to excuse his actions by enclosing them in a scientific framework, told himself that he "destined the skull for some learned craniologist" to study. But he felt he wanted more, something for himself. When others in the party noticed his "anxiety to secure a number of Indian relics," they began to present him with items they had dug out of the several other mounds on the island; Featherstonhaugh stuffed his pockets with these items and wrapped the skull in his pocket handkerchief.

The party returned late to their lodgings on the lakeshore, and there the change of scene functioned to make Featherstonhaugh suddenly and acutely aware that he, his clothing, and his effects were imbued with the odor of death: "Disencumbering my pockets hastily, to go to a dinner which was to conclude the day," he wrote, "I found my hands and my clothes so infected with charnel-house nastiness that I could not endure myself." Sickened and alarmed, Featherstonhaugh stripped off his clothes and began to scrub, spending more than half an hour on his hands alone, but he was unable to rid his person of the odor. At dinner, the "horrid stench" was "in [his] nostrils all the evening," reminding him of how he had spent his afternoon; the evening, he wrote, was the most uncomfortable of his life. The next day, seeking to cleanse himself of the incident, Featherstonhaugh had the bones and relics packed into a bag and, attempting to assure himself that the items would not merely be tossed on the ground somewhere, he "sent them to one of the party who seemed to value them very highly." He himself did not touch the objects again nor did he record any consideration of returning them to Round Island. He knew he had behaved like a graverobber and chose to dispose of the goods rather than have to, as he put it, "pass for a resurrection-man" wherever he went.[1]

Although George Featherstonhaugh was unusual in recording the troubling personal consequences of his digging on Round Island, the digging itself was a common activity among travelers in the interior. The landscape that travelers entered—while empty of the castles and ruins that many favored seeing and often fantasized about—displayed its past in the form of thousands of grass-covered mounds and earthworks spread across the Ohio and Mississippi river valleys in lines, rings, and groups. Not scarce (in Ohio they were often two or three to a farm), the mounds and earthworks occupied not only notable scenic overlooks but also the most desirable farm and town sites. Of the cultures that had built them, only their burial practices remained; or at least to the prearchaeological eyes of antebellum travelers nothing of the everyday lives of their builders was discernible. Looking at the mounds and earthworks elicited from some travelers melancholy sentiments on the subject of mortality, but others desired more: a history, a legend, an explanation, something wonderful to report, something valuable, a souvenir. Travelers who had found in the interior no picturesque sites and even less exotica looked to the mysterious moundscape for gratification; they glimpsed on it the opportunity to produce the story about the past that would explain just enough to make them comfortable.

As a landscape the interior was notably stingy with souvenirs; great expanses offered not even a shell or an interesting rock to pick up, nothing but the faded wisp of a dried wildflower to add to a collector's cabinet. Many travelers were collectors; the collector's desire to carry away display objects overwhelmed George Featherstonhaugh on

Round Island and touched many other travelers also. No woman traveler, however, exhibited strong interest in the moundscape, and many had no interest whatever. In 1841, Eliza Steele grew so weary of hearing marvelous claims about the moundscape that she mashed all prehistoric sites into one that she called "Big Bloody Bone Buffalo Lick," and thereby dismissed the moundscape from consideration. Many male travelers, in contrast, were consumed with dreams of buried valuables; for most of them, however, value meant precious metals, ivory, and intact objets d'art, and in that context not a single traveler, after opening a mound, ever recorded coming away with an object he considered valuable. There was a moment in 1808 near Zanesville, Ohio, when Thomas Ashe—a traveler devoted to reporting the marvelous—excavated several mounds and found a number of metal balls that his companions believed to be gold. Ashe, however, threw one of the balls into the fire, whereon it "filled the room with sulphurous smoke," proving itself to be, he said, spirite. In 1817 Samuel Brown opened several mounds in Athens County, Ohio, to find "nothing except stone axes, arrows, and bones," and in 1824 William Blane and his party opened mound after mound in Missouri to find "nothing but a little sunbaked pottery and a few stone axes, which sadly disappointed the searchers." Not every traveler liked to do the work himself: Charles Fenno Hoffman "superintended the opening of some ancient Indian graves" in a "search after relics" near St. Louis in 1835, but there a day's digging yielded up nothing, "neither bones nor weapons." Travelers defined their disappointment with the contents of the mounds, but they did not put a name to the activity of tearing them open, and when it became apparent that the interior was not going to reveal itself as a vast underground treasure vault, travelers did not necessarily turn to recognizing it as a vast graveyard.[2]

Travelers regularly represented their own "search after relics" on the moundscape as a kind of connoisseurship different from local settlers' activities on the moundscape—those activities travelers often represented as a wholesale destruction that they mourned over everywhere they went in the two great river valleys of the interior. Some mounds, travelers reported, settlers converted to practical use: in Ohio in 1805, Thaddeus Mason Harris saw a mound excavated to make an icehouse, and at St. Louis in 1838 Edmund Flagg saw a great mound converted into a public reservoir with similar civic plans under way for conversion of another. Flagg found the St. Louis locals to be so "busy" with the mounds that, he predicted, "in a few years the mounds will quite have disappeared. The practical utility of which they are available appears the only circumstance which has attracted attention to them . . . such indifference of feeling to the only relics of a bygone race which our land can boast is not well in the citizens of St. Louis, and should exist no longer." Throughout the first half of the nineteenth century, successive travel books reported on the gradual disappearance of such notable landscape markers as the great complex of earthworks in Pickaway County, Ohio, over which the town of Circleville was planted in 1806. According to Samuel Brown in 1817, the earthworks at Circleville covered twenty acres and consisted of earth walls fifteen feet high, shaped into two concentric circles—the larger of the two a thousand feet in diameter—and a rectangle nine hundred feet on a side. By the time David Thomas arrived at Circleville in 1819, an octagonal brick Pickaway County Courthouse had been constructed at the center of the two circles; when Bernhard Saxe-Weimar Eisenach saw Circleville in 1828, the concentric walls had been partly demolished in order to open street traffic through the town, and Circleville's residents were gradually removing the clay walls of the rectangle and making bricks of the clay. In 1833, Caleb Atwater, Circleville's postmaster and a writer on antiquities much resorted to by travelers, noted that the town of Circleville had spread to cover "all the round and the western half of the square fort. These fortifications where the town stands will entirely disappear in a few years." When James Silk Buckingham saw Circleville in 1842, the circular street patterns that had once observed the forms of the earthworks had given way to a grid, and the central courthouse, which had burned in 1841, was set to be replaced by a row of stores. By 1878, every trace of the concentric circles was gone; the earthworks had been so extensive that, it was reported, "it took the citizens months and years to remove what would now be one of the greatest curiosities of the country."[3]

Travelers themselves were often more interested in the potential contents of mounds and earthworks than in the earthforms themselves, and they represented the settlers as interested in neither. At Cincinnati, two circular earthworks and seven large mounds were gradually removed to clear traffic patterns and erect houses. In 1842 James Silk Buckingham watched the last of the Cincinnati mounds demolished; the contractor and workmen, reported Buckingham, were astonished when he inquired whether "anything of interest" had been found in the mounds. In 1869, in the neighborhood of the great Mississippian temple mounds at Cahokia, Illinois, six miles below St. Louis, Greville Chester "sought in vain to purchase some of the stone implements" that frequently came to light in the area, but locals told him that when they found any such items they "invariably buried them again." So much alteration had been practiced on the mounds in St. Louis proper that Chester judged "American taste . . . not yet sufficiently educated to disapprove such vandalism." Aleksandr Lakier, fascinated by the moundscape, found no corresponding interest among locals he quizzed about earthworks in their vicinity. Americans, he wrote, "take pride in the newness of their country and do not pursue archaeological research and excavations." Settlers' treatment of the moundscape brought travelers to define settlers not as persons who settled down for a stay on a given plot of land but as persons who, no matter where they stopped or for how short a time, immediately put the landscape to use without regard for anything that was already on it. The moundscape, in the context of this definition, received no more special handling from settlers than did any other landform in the interior. The effects of travelers' desire to obtain souvenirs and settlers' desire to clear the landscape were, nonetheless, identical: destruction and eradication of the moundscape.[4]

Travelers wishing to describe the moundscape in detail were further frustrated by a simple physical inability to see some of its most artful features; they lacked both the aerial point of view necessary for some sites and the special expertise necessary to all. In 1839 in Wisconsin, whose landscape held five thousand effigy mounds, Frederick Marryat twice went out to view effigy mounds near Prairie du Chien but was, at ground level, unable to discern the animal shapes he had been told of: "It required more imagination than I possess to make out the form of any animal in the mounds," wrote Marryat. Because he could not see them, Marryat rejected the concept of effigies and created his own theory: "I should rather suppose the mounds to be the remains of tenements . . . formerly built of mud or earth. Desertion and time have crumbled them into these mounds." Other travelers unable to see the effigies settled for reporting their presence. In 1852 Lauchlan Mackinnon wrote that his companion called his "attention to some earth-mounds in the shape of prostrate animals such as beavers, bears, deer, squirrels, etc. These were of gigantic proportion, very distinctly marked and discriminated." Mackinnon's "et cetera" and his quick disposal of the subject suggest how little he actually saw of the earthforms.[5]

To the further disappointment of travelers, digging in the moundscape produced no written materials. Although there was from early on in the interior a brisk business in the sale of inscribed stones said to have been excavated from mounds—a business that answered to collectors' desires of the time—all such stones were fakes. Travelers accustomed to drawing on both written material and local informants for explanations of interesting sites were continually disappointed by the absence of such materials about the mounds that they might bend to interpretive use. "Neither documents nor traditions," mourned

Saxe-Weimar, existed to explain the mounds. "Why can't one inquire among contemporary Indians as to why their ancestors built these mounds, or do they themselves no longer remember what was happening here a century ago?" demanded Aleksandr Lakier, underestimating, as many travelers did, the age of the moundscape. "Are there no legends or tales?"[6]

Frustrated travelers who were unable to discern the shapes of earthworks, find treasure, record legends, or reach sites before they were demolished found an alternative when they plunged into the antebellum debate raging over the mounds' origins. Here travelers glimpsed the possibility of creating for the interior the readable past they thought it lacked. The origins debate did not require the continued presence of the mounds on the landscape and seemed at times even to suggest their destruction; consequently, travelers could effectively combine origins theories with complaints about locals who were wiping the traces of the past from the actual physical landscape. Using as starting points the absence of legends and the reports that local Indians had no traditions explanatory of the mounds, travelers reiterated popular assertions that the mounds were the work of a superior, and probably white, race called Moundbuilders who had emigrated to the American interior from, variously, Wales, Asia, Mexico, and Israel. Travelers repeated and discussed popular theories that the Moundbuilders had been wiped out by the Iroquois, or had been destroyed by flood and pestilence, or had been erased in a great daylong battle that had left only twelve warriors alive at sunset. Unverifiable claims—such as the claim that the earth composing the mounds was "entirely distinct from earth in the vicinity of the mounds"—moved from one traveler's book to the next and promoted the view that Moundbuilders had brought with them from elsewhere not only their skills but also their building materials. Some travelers argued for the existence of the Moundbuilders from the evidence of a single "celebrated piece of pottery—a small vase formed by three perfect heads blended in one, the features being marked, and wholly dissimilar from those of any existing race of Indians," which vase was on display in 1835 at William Clark's St. Louis museum. In the 1830s the debate over how to name the earthworks' architects—and the implications of that name for contemporary Indians, the age of the earth, the history of the interior, and the authority of biblical accounts of creation—so consumed a traveler like Paul Wilhelm as to make him suggest slicing in two, down to its base, the great temple mound at Cahokia in order to "settle the question" of who was buried there and who had built the moundscape.[7]

Although nothing in the origins debate seemed to some travelers quite to account for the mounds' bulky and silent presence on the landscape of the interior, or their occupation of the choicest sites, or settlers' indifference to them in a country where everything was supposed to be new, the Moundbuilder arguments advanced by some travelers smoothly fit the uses of those wishing to justify extermination or removal of contemporary Indian tribes; these propagandists for genocide could claim that the land had never belonged to the Indians, that they were mere temporary occupants of it, that they had only recently seized it from the vanished and superior Moundbuilders. The racial underpinnings of the Moundbuilder controversy are clearly available in the work of many travelers who suggested that an infusion of energy and skill from a transatlantic elsewhere had created the mounds, an infusion so different and so superior that it had not deigned even to build with local dirt. Every aspect of the origins argument could be—and was—used to disconnect the moundscape from its surviving native inhabitants who, traveler after traveler claimed, had not even the ability to construct such earthforms.

In 1849, archaeology arrived in the interior when Ephraim Squier and E. H. Davis made their survey of the moundscape; the burial and temple and effigy mounds were reclassified as archaeological sites requiring expertise to examine. Some sites were thus saved, but for travelers the arrival of archaeology did less to reconnect the mounds to the present native population than it did to reduce the appeal of Moundbuilder theory and erase the mounds as a subject. Some travelers driven by a succession of desires, all unfulfilled by the moundscape, and especially by a desire to refuse history to the Indians, responded to the shift by denying outright the built nature of the moundscape and claiming that the mounds were nothing but nature's own "alluvial deposits." In travel books after 1849, the mounds began to slide out of the categories of history and architecture and into the category of nature, grouped with "Sinkholes and Other Natural Curiosities." Longstanding confusions between built and natural landscape features were resolved on the side of nature: Mount Joliet, for example, situated on the west bank of the Des Plaines River in Illinois, long thought by travelers to be "probably the largest mound in the United States," was reclassified as nature and then disassembled by the locals in order to build the Illinois and Michigan canal.[8]

Neither origin theory nor professional archaeology ever constituted, for many travelers, a satisfactory approach to the moundscape: they wanted objects, secrets, mystery, history, and art. Furthermore, art to them was portable, not site-specific; and items of artistic value were made not of stone but of gold, silver, and ivory. Most of the grave goods travelers saw in the interior—and they actually saw very little—fit none of their categories of meaningful objects. The hoax objects they were occasionally offered for purchase were, moreover, always very bad art. The stunning locations of many of the mound groups, commanding as they did the richest soils and the finest scenic views, did not constitute a subject; most travelers recognized these scenic qualities but barely discussed them, perhaps because they wished to evade complex and suggestive questions of the Native American landscape aesthetic raised by actual examination of the sites' locations.

Travelers' desire for stories to tell and secrets to unveil remained strong, but local history and legend related to white habitation of the interior were everywhere weak, often consisting of no more than a rumor of a "hermit's haystack" in Michigan, a Wizard's Island in the Missouri whose resident wizard always disappeared at the approach of people, or a sycamore tree in Ohio said to be sixty feet in circumference "into the hollow of which thirteen men rode on horseback, in June, 1806, and the fourteenth was only prevented by the skittishness of his horse." Julien Dubuque (1762–1810), a Quebecois miner who had crossed into Iowa when it was still part of Spanish Louisiana and who had been buried, by the Indians he had lived among, on a bluff overlooking what later became known as Dubuque, Iowa, was one of the few historical subjects of some notice in the interior, and even then it was only his burial that drew travelers' attention to him. In 1828 Giacomo Beltrami had Dubuque reposing "with royal state in a leaden chest contained in a mausoleum of wood, which the Indians erected to him upon the summit of a small hill." By 1838 Edmund Flagg could not recall Dubuque's name but elaborated his burial site into an iron coffin suspended between two crags along the Mississippi. A year later Charles Augustus Murray claimed to have clambered up a high bluff at Galena (on the opposite bank of the Mississippi) to visit the grave of Dubuque, whom he identified as a Spaniard. Although no Indians figured in Murray's version, he said he had seen Dubuque's actual skull lying on the ground near a brick grave "bearing a simple Latin inscription." In 1854, Henry Lewis's version reinstated the Indians but erased their agency in Dubuque's burial: Lewis said that Dubuque, before his death, had charged local Indians with making a lead casket for him, and had himself prepared a stone monument decorated with a cross to hold that casket. "In the monument," wrote Lewis, "was a window with an iron grating. The Indians often visited the grave, and for many years kept a lamp burning there. The casket no longer exists, for visitors to the grave carried it off, bit by bit, by cutting off little pieces for souvenirs." Filling out the story—or emptying it out—by accounting for the apparent absence of artifacts related to Dubuque, Charles Lanman explained in 1856 that the Indians, after burying Julien Dubuque, had "destroyed every vestige of his property."[9]

The line followed by the Dubuque material furnishes a fair example of how successive travel books historicized the interior. As pieces of material moved from book to book, the identities of the participants became blurred, agency shifted from hand to hand, sites and objects were displaced or altogether lost, and the role of contemporary Indians—if they had a role in the material—grew psychologically elusive, until finally travelers' interest dissipated. Amid the mobile population of the vast interior, hurriedly written and published travel books often constituted the major printed repositories of information, and travelers' very mobility made fact-checking and investigation on their part a near impossibility. Travel writers who wanted material about the mysterious past were willing to repeat the details, no matter how dubious, of another traveler's marvelous find. Repeating a few oddments about the burial of one eighteenth-century Quebecois was, however, hardly enough for an army of travelers to work with. More of the marvelous was required.

From the beginnings of travel literature, reports of marvels had been a staple of its contents; for centuries monsters and physical grotesques had been reported in volumes of voyages and travels, and images of them had appeared in the margins of maps and prints. Furthermore, a fascination with the grotesque—which had swept Europe and England during the eighteenth century—was making itself felt in the museums and traveling shows of nineteenth-century America. Travel writers knew what their readers wanted and, perhaps wanting it themselves also, they opened old volumes of voyages and in effect shook out their marvelous leaves over the weeds and bugs of the American interior. No pictures were necessary: travelers' marvelmaking in prose was aided by the fact that the staggering popularity of their accounts of America was not matched by any corresponding demand for visual images. Relieved, by audience lack of interest, from the burden of producing drawings or photographs of the claimed marvels of the interior, travel writers could move at greater ease to unveil in prose the wonders of the American past.[10]

In travelers' reports of the Americas, claims of the existence of giants went back to 1525, when Antonio Pigafetta, a survivor of Ferdinand Magellan's voyage around the world, described the hairless giants of Patagonia, who were able to swallow and regurgitate arrows without doing themselves bodily harm; the Patagonian giants became not only legend but also a touchstone of both marvel-reporting and marvel-debunking over the following centuries. Evidence for the giants was scarce: in the eighteenth century, the skeleton of a Patagonian giant twelve to thirteen feet tall was reportedly on its way to France when sailors tossed its bones overboard in the belief that their presence aboard ship was causing a storm. Numerous living giants—male persons over seven feet tall—were on display in England at the end of the eighteenth century as curiosities, catering to an intense popular interest in the physical grotesque. Giants first appeared in the American interior in 1808, in the form of a rumored tooth: Thomas Ashe, raiding a burial mound at Cincinnati, was tantalized by reports of a molar found in the vicinity whose size indicated "a man four times the size of the modern human race." Ashe did not see the molar. In 1817 at Prairie du Chien, Wisconsin, Stephen Harriman Long did not see the bones he heard about from a Mr. Brisbois who, in digging a cellar, had unearthed "the skeletons of eight persons lying side by side. They were of gigantic size, measuring about eight feet from head to foot. He remarked that he took a leg bone of one of them and placed it by the side of his own leg in order to compare the length of the two. The bone of the skeleton extended six inches above his knee. None of these bones could be preserved as they crumbled to dust soon after they were exposed to the atmosphere." In the same year, Samuel Brown dismantled a group of twenty mounds near Harrison, Ohio, and claimed to have found skulls and thigh bones "which plainly indicated that their possessors were men of gigantic stature." The interior was reported to contain other outsize features suitable to a giant population: in Ohio, John Melish saw fruit for a giant's table, including apples measuring seventeen and a half inches in circumference, and Godfrey Vigne heard from William Bullock reports of a "gigantic horse that could not have been less than twenty-four hands high" whose bones had been destroyed by fire just three weeks before Vigne's arrival in Cincinnati.[11]

In 1825 Henry Rowe Schoolcraft suggested exercising "no ordinary degree of vigilance" over continuing reports of giants, noting that the giant bones, when investigated, invariably turned out to be "the more elongated joints of certain quadrupeds." After 1825, the giants continued in rumor only; the bones themselves were always inaccessible. In 1827, near Detroit, Thomas McKenney was touring the farm of the territorial governor when he stopped to pick up bits of bone near a deteriorating burial mound; the bones crumbled under his touch, but he was told that a certain Major F. had taken from the same mound a "skull of enormous dimensions" that would be McKenney's to study if it could be found. Locals in the interior seem to have accurately perceived the nature of the material travelers wanted to hear about. In Illinois in 1854, Friedrich Gerstacker heard reports of a human lower jaw whose size indicated an original owner nine feet tall, but the bone itself had been disposed of. Like other travelers in such a situation, Gerstacker chose not to doubt the jawbone's existence but to criticize careless local attitudes that resulted in the loss of such extraordinary finds. "These people," remarked Gerstacker, "have no regard for anything that does not offer some immediate prospect of gain." Reports of giants remained current in 1860, but their locations had become increasingly distant. In 1861, the English sportsman George Charles Grantley Fitzhardinge Berkeley hired a prairie guide whom he soon came to loathe as an "unmitigated prevaricator who really knew no more of the prairies than pertained to the beaten path"—or who at least would not show Berkeley anything off the beaten path unless offered extra money for it. On one occasion, however, when Berkeley judged the guide to have nothing to gain by lying, the guide told Berkeley of a hunter, the guide's good friend, who lived in the Rockies and who had stumbled into a cave containing *"the largest print of the foot of man that he had ever seen in his life,"* plus numerous "great bones." Berkeley grew excited about seeing these items, no matter how distant they might be, and offered his guide the customary extra cash to take him to the cave, at which point the guide uncustomarily backed off, murmuring that "his friend was dead, and had not described to him the exact position of the cave, and indeed at the time he had taken very little heed of the matter," and so on. Berkeley, seeing that he had to abandon his desire, labeled the incident "a hasty view of the wonders of buried worlds."[12]

Fossil bones of extinct megafauna, no matter how large, interested most travelers far less than did reports of giant humans; even less were they interested in whether humans and mammoths, as they called them, had coexisted on the landscape of the interior. Knowledge was not, for any but a few travelers, the point of marvel-reporting; focusing on marvels was a way of suggesting a past that was so strange and lost that it did not have to be understood, that connected to no vexing questions that might be aroused by a past that had continuity with the present. To focus on physical marvels of grotesquerie allowed a traveler not only to elude the religious, historical, and scientific questions aroused by the origins-of-the-mounds debate, but also to evade troubling matters of race, of ownership of the land, of the ethics of grave robbery, and of the ownership of artifacts. In the human-grotesque arena, race rarely mattered, all artifacts were always lost, all sites inaccessible, and all problems eluded. The grotesques had such overriding appeal to some travel writers that a given writer might report in the same paragraph both the marvel itself and the evidence denying its existence, and then go on to promote the marvel.[13]

On 6 November 1818, the *Missouri Gazette* published a report of a site at Fenton, Missouri, south of St. Louis, where a Mr. Long had opened several graves in a burial ground of unspecified size. In each of the graves he found six pieces of stone arranged in a coffin shape, with headstones and footstones, uninscribed, sometimes projecting slightly above the surface of the ground. The stone coffin shapes measured twenty-three to fifty inches in length; a few of the burial spaces contained bones while the rest held dust. Almost at once the site was transformed into a widely circulated rumor that Missouri had once been populated by a race of pygmies. Debunkers weighed in at once: in 1819, in his *View of the Lead Mines of Missouri,* Henry Rowe Schoolcraft reproduced the *Missouri Gazette* item and explained that the graves' size was evidence not of pygmies but of either seated interment or disarticulated interment. In the same year, Thomas Say and Titian Ramsay Peale, both attached to Long's Yellowstone expedition, took a side trip to Fenton—which a local real-estate developer and town-planter was by then trying to rename Lilliput—examined the site, and "satisfied themselves that all the bones found there were those of men of the common size." But Schoolcraft, Say, and Peale could not kill a story as appealing to travelers as that of the pygmy population of the interior, and in the 1820s the story received two big boosts. In 1823, Lewis Beck in his *Gazetteer of the States of Illinois and Missouri,* a text many travelers carried with them, redescribed the Fenton burial site; although Beck punctiliously repeated knowledgeable explanations of the interment practices that had produced such tiny graves, he also referred throughout the *Gazetteer* to the pygmies of Missouri and thereby gave the rumor a life unaltered by its factual explanation. In 1826, Timothy Flint, whose *Recollections* was also in every traveler's library, expressed regret at being unable to visit the Fenton site, but went on to offer descriptions of numerous graves at Fenton and of stone coffins said to contain nearly entire skeletons that "could not have been more than from $3^1/2$ to 4 feet in length. Thus, it should seem, that the generations of the past in this region were mammoths and pygmies," concluded Flint. In 1838, by which year the growth of Fenton had obliterated the original burial site, Edmund Flagg reported from Fenton on an "immense cemetery" containing thousands of pygmy graves whose headstones bore "unintelligible hieroglyphical inscriptions." Later, after pillaging several graves elsewhere and noting the size of the bones they contained, Flagg renounced belief in pygmies, but renunciations never seemed to reduce the force of the original report. In 1842 James Silk Buckingham repeated the pygmy story, again in the standard context not of doubt but of regret over the American carelessness that had destroyed the valuable pygmy site at Fenton. In 1843, in William Oliver's hands, the pygmy population briefly backtrailed to a site on the banks of the Scioto, in Ohio, but failed to seize the imagination there in anything resembling the way it had at Fenton.[14]

Although Tyrone Power wrote in 1836 that it was not prehistoric Americans but Power's fellow company of travelers who constituted the pygmy population of the interior, the trail taken by the pygmy material may indicate how the sheer space and sprawl of the interior rendered credible to observers any size of early inhabitant. Since the interior held no built cityscapes or ruins to suggest the measurements of persons suited to the landscape, the measurable length of stone-lined graves became compelling hard evidence for some travelers. In their desire to make the past speak, they put inscriptions on the head-stones, while their ignorance of what the past might have to communicate made those inscriptions unintelligible. On one hand, no other marvels in the interior ever spoke as strongly to travelers' desires for the marvelous or spoke as strongly for their perceptual difficulties with space in the interior as did the rumored pygmies and giants; on the other hand, many travelers who repeated descriptions of pygmy burial sites refused to repeat available knowledge of burial practices—whether flexed or disarticulated—that differed from their familiar standard of extended burial and that would have served to connect the Fenton site to the contemporary Indian population.

Throughout the antebellum decades, assorted marvels slipped off the landscape of the interior into traveling shows and into the museums of the time where they took up their places in the company of wax figures, three-headed calves, Fejee mermaids, and damnation shows. Some items travelers stole before they vanished. The traveler Thomas Ashe, masquerading as a Frenchman named D'Arville, in 1804 duped Dr. Samuel Goforth of Cincinnati out of seventeen chests filled with mammoth bones that Goforth had collected at Big Bone Lick in Kentucky. The bones were destroyed in a warehouse confla-gration in New Orleans before Ashe could raise enough money to transport them to England, but the resourceful Ashe wrote a book—*Memoirs of Mammoth* (1806)—that reassembled the bones and revivi-fied their presence on the landscape of the interior. Compilers of books about American antiquities seized on any and all marvels ru-mored and reported by travelers and moved them into compendia of theory and fantasy that were sold door to door in the interior. In Josiah Priest's *American Antiquities and Discoveries in the West* (1833) the Prairie du Chien giants were transformed into Scotsmen or Welsh-men said to have been exterminated by local Indians. Ira Hill's *Antiq-uities of America* (1831) described tiny graves at Fenton that were cased with marble and held the "sacred remains" of a colony of royal monkeys worshiped at prehistoric Fenton; and Edward Wood's *Giants and Dwarfs* (1868) shrank Fenton's pygmy graves to eighteen inches in length and fifteen inches in depth, and reported that the tiny graves held tiny intact skeletons.[15]

In their search for the marvelous, travelers reported on items they did not have time to see or that no one could see: in 1829, Gottfried Duden reported a wall nine thousand feet long and fourteen feet high at Chillicothe, Ohio; in 1839, Frederick Marryat reported on the invisible subsurface remains of a great city on the Rock River in Illinois; and in 1843, James Leander Scott claimed that miles of tile-paved streets ran below the surface of Beloit, Wisconsin. Travelers described objects that had crumbled on exposure to the air, or had disappeared, or were in the hands of a person whom the local informant could not reach before the traveler had to move on. Locals pointed out to travelers items that were no longer there: in 1839, on the rocky banks of the Missouri, near the mouth of the Osage, Charles Augustus Murray was told of "representations of strange figures . . . originally red, but time and the weather have so worn out the color that they were not distinguishable from the part of the river where we passed, so that I was obliged to take the word of the passengers and other persons well acquainted with the neighborhood." Sometimes a great and irreplaceable collection of fossils, bones, and artifacts burned, as did that of William Bullock at Cincinnati; in 1843 Charles Daubeny, hoping for a look, had to settle for hearing about them while viewing nothing but Bullock's Italian paintings.

In reporting on what they did not or could not see, travelers kept reports alive, allowing the next traveler to repeat the report while dropping the fact that the marvel could not be seen. The invisible marvels moved from one travel book to the next, and travelers in effect mapped in the interior a tour of the invisible across a landscape whose markers were either buried or set at inaccessible heights. In passing the marvels from book to book, plucking invisible marvels from one text and replanting them in their own, many travelers violated their own claims to truth, the trust they asked readers to place in them as eyewitnesses, and the value they placed on "seeing with their own eyes." On its visible surfaces, the interior, except for the mounds and earthworks, did not look like an expanse of marvels, and its actual artifacts of bone and stone did not correspond to travelers' ideas of value; across the marvelous bookscape of travel literature, however, the interior resonated with the odd and the merely possible, though never with the valuable or precious. No souvenirs came to the surface, leaving the travel book itself the only souvenir of the marvelous landscape of the interior.[16]

The actual landscape of the interior, meanwhile, lost more mounds, gained no large marvels, yielded no precious objects, and insisted on producing only small-scale unfamiliarities. In 1820, Daniel Drake, fully aware of what travelers wanted in the way of marvels, recommended that traveling collectors in the interior focus on "the lower classes in the animal kingdom—to reward the inquisitive student of zoology with a rich and varied cabinet." Some few travelers in search of re-portable oddities chose that small-scale approach to the interior, and, still searching for marvels to report, took a close look at the lower—and numerous—members of the interior's animal kingdom. In 1805 François Michaux, for example, reported squirrels infesting the Ohio Valley in such numbers that "several times a day the children are sent round the fields to frighten them away." The squirrels had some appeal for travel writers: by 1811, according to Charles Latrobe's fanciful ac-count of the New Madrid, Missouri, earthquake—a cataclysmic event that very few had been present to experience at its epicenter—"a spirit of change and restlessness seemed to pervade the very inhabitants of the forest. A countless multitude of squirrels, obeying some great and universal impulse, left their reckless and gambolling life, and their an-cient places of retreat in the north, and were seen pressing forward by tens of thousands in a deep and sober phalanx to the South. No obsta-cles seemed to check this extraordinary and concerted movement: the word had been given them to go forth, and they obeyed it, though multitudes perished in the broad Ohio, which lay in their path." But many survived, enough for the intensely practical Gottfried Duden to advise prospective German emigrants to Missouri that they should ex-pect to harvest squirrels before they might hope to harvest corn, and enough for William Blane to report in 1824 on a plague of ravenous squirrels in Ohio, squirrels who, hunters told him, were castrating each other. "I myself thought the circumstance so unlikely," wrote Blane, "that I did not believe them until, upon examining the squirrels I shot, I found to my great surprise that many had apparently suffered the above-mentioned deprivation." In 1857, Elisha Lewis, though fully aware that squirrels hated water, nonetheless repeated rumors about squirrels moving through the interior in "immense droves" and never hesitating to "swim the widest rivers." Lewis said that such circum-stances proved the "indomitable energy of character that these active little creatures possess."[17]

Small animals might behave strangely, but they were certainly not rare; they were no substitute for the desired exotica of the moundscape, and, like much in the interior, they did not accommodate traveling humans, lend themselves directly to human designs, or consent to be souvenirs. Very early one morning in 1824, William Blane was riding across a small prairie forty miles from Carmi, Ohio, when he saw coming toward him on the prairie path the most beautiful little animal he had ever seen, "about two feet long, of a dark color, with longitudinal white stripes down its back, a bushy tail, and very short legs." Intending to capture and make a souvenir of the animal, Blane galloped forward and was astonished when the beautiful animal "did not attempt to run away, but stopped in the middle of the road, as if it had been tame." Tantalized by the thought that the animal was already domesticated for his use, Blane drew so close to it that his horse's forefeet almost touched it; the beautiful animal drew up its back and looked at him but still did not move. Something in its very immobility, its failure to "offer to escape," made Blane reconsider capturing it for a souvenir. Considering that he could do nothing with it, and that it might bite him, he "determined to leave it alone, and content [him]self with admiring it." Having thoroughly looked it over, however, Blane was prompted, he wrote, by some "spirit of mischief . . . to lean forward on my horse, and strike it over the back with a small whip I had in my hand. Scarcely had the whip touched the animal's back when, turning its posteriors towards me and lifting up its hind leg, it discharged a Stygian liquor, the odor of which I shall recollect till my dying day. In an instant, the whole prairie seemed to be filled with a stench that is beyond all description. It was so powerful, pungent, and sickening that at first it nearly made me faint, and I galloped away from the brute with all possible expedition. I had previously supposed that I had, in the course of my life, smelt very bad odors; but they were all perfumes compared to this."

Blane was too sickened by the odor to eat breakfast and too ashamed to enter any house; he rode his horse into a river and "had him washed with soap and water, but nothing would do." By evening, hungry and tired, Blane stopped at an inn whose proprietor "immediately observed the offensive odor," forcing Blane to tell of his intent to catch the rare and beautiful animal; the proprietor, laughing "most heartily," informed Blane that skunks were extremely common in Ohio. Like George Featherstonhaugh raiding the mounds on Round Island for souvenirs, Blane carried off with him only an ineradicable odor. For a week afterward, he wrote, he could not get upon his horse "without perceiving, in a most disagreeable degree, the stench of my little enemy." Resistant to easy removal, the unfamiliar beauties, wonders, and marvels of the interior effectively marked the traveler but left him empty-handed.[18]

Much of what those travelers who were in search of the marvelous had done on the moundscape—excavate, theorize, invent, steal—had depended on their denying all connection between the mounds and the contemporary Indian population of the interior. To make their activities tolerable to themselves, they insisted that they were opening the graves of—and tinkering with the history of—a vanished population. When they moved on to meet the actual living descendants of the Moundbuilders, few among them could, without indicting themselves, suggest any ties between the architects of the mounds and the tribes they visited. They could, however, and did, continue their hunt for desirable souvenirs of the interior.

Chapter 5

Still Life

In 1822, after a residence of one year in Illinois, John Woods wrote, "I have not seen one Indian." Passage of the Indian Removal Act in 1830 further decreased the likelihood that a traveler in the interior would encounter any Indian: by 1838 only 26,700 Indians remained resident east of the Mississippi. Travelers who entered the interior after 1830 had seen more Indians immobilized in murals and marble in the United States Capitol than they would see in the flesh on the landscape of the interior, and they had read more ornate metaphors spoken by Indians on the pages of James Fenimore Cooper's novels than they would hear syllables uttered by Indians. Fully aware, however, that their worldwide reading audience expected descriptions of so famous a North American fact as its Indian population, travelers wrote in answer to that expectation—and if they were writing as much about Horatio Greenough's sculpted Indians as about any real persons, they could nonetheless cling to the peculiar confidence that arises from presuming that their subjects were unlikely ever to hear of what travelers said or wrote about them.

Sometimes they were wrong in their presumption. In 1856, Sara Robinson and her friends freely discussed the looks of a group of

Shawnee women they saw at a general store. The Shawnee women "listened gravely" while the white women "talked of their dress and ornaments, not supposing," wrote Robinson, "that they could understand us." Then, to Robinson's surprise, the women repeated in Shawnee to the Shawnee store proprietor everything Robinson had said, and the proprietor repeated all of it in English back to Robinson. All the Shawnee "seemed much amused and laughed heartily," while Robinson, shamed, could only murmur that "they had the advantage of us."

Few travelers experienced similar shocks. As non-Indians they sent to other non-Indians protected communications about Indians; difficulties of understanding they evaded or hedged round with legends and with continual reference to what other non-Indians had written earlier, and the cultural views they expressed were those shared by other non-Indians. Travelers who met and observed Indians were often in no better position to render them on paper than were those travelers who had no contact; no traveler could exercise unmediated clarity of vision, and all struggled. The explanatory confidence travelers had exercised on white movers in the interior often collapsed, before the Indians, into fear, uncertainty, and mystification. That travelers wrote about Indians they did not encounter—or wrote in ignorance of those they did—should not be taken to mean that what they wrote was unimportant. Thousands of readers, after all, received travelers' descriptions as information. No subject was more difficult for travelers to write about than America's Indian population—but write about it they did, and I write about it here because the attitudes travelers passed on to their readers, the avenues of wish and desire they followed, the fears they accepted from their informants, and the beliefs they perpetuated had long cultural lives and are fully expressive of painful cultural collisions.[1]

Before meeting the native population, most antebellum travelers, both American and international, lodged open and loud objection to official government policies toward Indians, and expressed their sympathy with the Indian population. When they actually met or even glimpsed Indians in the interior, however, their expressions of sympathy became at once inadequate. Suddenly they did not know at what point to enter the national debate over Indian policy; they felt a guilt so diffused as to be impossible to dispel; and they could not let go of their desire to engage in that longtime staple of travel literature, the description of colorful and exotic native customs. Meanwhile, to their horror and fascination, local informants stuffed them with tales of massacre and butchery that they were unequipped to counter. Not only did travelers in the interior know with how little knowledge they were working, but they also, in an abrupt reversal of their standard position, became listeners rather than tellers. They searched for ideological frames to contain the awful stories they were told, but then they retailed the stories anyway. They repeated, for example, statements that Indians did not rape and then they retailed rape narratives told them by locals. They ransacked art and literature, retreated into the fictional worlds of James Fenimore Cooper and Walter Scott, took refuge in scholarly comparisons between living Indians and Greek statuary, and fled into a dreamworld of white-concocted narratives masquerading as Indian legends. On the subject of Indians—more than on any other that they took up—travelers openly deployed other travelers' books, filled out their own scanty observations with surveys of others' reports, and actually named the travelers whose texts they were using so as to pin on that writer responsibility for the often dubious material they were repeating. In the world of travel literature, where there is much borrowing and little attribution, such care with sources is most unusual and shows a heightened anxiety about the validity of the views offered.

Travelers who saw no one but white movers in the interior nonetheless regularly invoked the presence of an unseen Indian population. In 1856 Isabella Bird, on whose railroad tour Davenport, Iowa, was the westernmost point, saw movers, oxen, and loaded wagons, but no Indians. Nonetheless she represented Davenport as the "*far West*—the land of Wild Indians and buffaloes . . . the land of adventure and romance," and told her readers how savagely her *train* made its return into Chicago: "With a whoop like an Indian war-whoop, the cars ran into a shed." In 1870, on David Macrae's railway journey through Iowa, a region associated in his mind with "the Red Indian and the buffalo," Macrae saw nothing but farms, towns, and—most remarkable in his view—a farmer running a buggy-plough whose seat was shielded by an umbrella. Fear, however, moved west: in 1875, W. S. Rusling, who also saw no Indians, was continually told that the Indians were not only just ahead but were also feeling "moody and hostile." In 1867, Henry Morton Stanley encountered aboard a train a troop of Kansas volunteers bound for Fort Harker who spent the trip whooping and yelling about scalps, skulls, and the devastation they planned to wreak on any Indian they met; at midnight two of the volunteers, worked into a frenzy, disembarked from the train and attacked a telegraph pole that they called "Mr. Injun." The pole was victorious. Other travelers promoted fears of Indian footsteps too muffled to hear, Indian personages too stealthy to glimpse, and midnight murder scenes too distant to witness but fearsome enough to be fled by any sensible traveler. In these stories that were not quite stories, these tales in which perpetrator, victim, and location all remained unspecified, Indian absence was pumped up into thrills of fear that the interior's daylit landscape of farms and weeds and small animals utterly refused to validate.[2]

Travelers in Ohio, Indiana, and Illinois experienced no contact with Indians; and even travelers' firsthand reports of Indian life from Michigan, Wisconsin, and Minnesota had the quality of heavily managed sightseers' glimpses, the view across the velvet rope: like the three-hour "prairie visits" set up by excursion outfits, the "visit to the wigwam" was thoroughly controlled by local authorities, and was often available to only the most heralded of international travelers. Such special visitors might be shepherded here and there by the governor, and afforded "peeps" at Indian life rendered all the more mysterious by the lack of any common language among the viewers, the viewed, and the view-managers. Neither the concocted adventure stories nor the "peeps" at mysterious realities were enough for some travelers. Fredrika Bremer, the Swedish traveler whose fame as a novelist made her the recipient of an official wigwam-peeping tour with Alexander Ramsey, the governor of Minnesota, knew she had missed seeing what she wanted to see. "I am not quite satisfied about leaving this part of the country," she wrote in 1848. "I wish to see more of the Indians and their way of life, and feel something like a hungry person who is obliged to leave a meal which he has just commenced. I wish to see more of the country and the aborigines, but do not see exactly how and in what manner." The acts of gazing and glimpsing had not led Bremer to the understanding she wished for; whether further staring at the human objects offered to her gaze would have allowed her to arrive at such understanding was a question that for Bremer had no answer.[3]

Travelers who on their own came upon very small groups of Indians were dissatisfied to see so few. Charles Fenno Hoffman, traveling alone in the winter of 1835 through Michigan and Wisconsin, fell in again and again with "straggling parties and broken bands of different tribes," and though he continually heard rumors about "considerable numbers" of Indians elsewhere in the interior, he could find no guide to lead him to them. Hoffman was further thwarted by his desire to locate Indians who had "preserved enough of their original habits to make them fair specimens"; he wanted, in other words, to contact precontact tribes and thus cast himself in the flattering position of the discoverer of something that he could call authentic. He failed at that project but he did learn during his search through Illinois, Michigan, and Wisconsin that old settlers continued to represent entirely vanished tribes as "hereditary enemies" of whites and that even though a tribe had been broken and driven away its name was used by locals to keep rancor alive in the absence of any Indian population whatever.[4]

Unwilling to accept such local views, other travelers struggled to produce other constructs. At Silver Lake, Wisconsin, in 1843, Margaret Fuller and her party, overtaken by a thunderstorm, sought shelter with an encampment of Pottawattami who, Fuller learned later, had returned out of homesickness to visit their former home ground. In their small traveling lodges, many of the Pottawattami lay sick, and as a whole the group was utterly destitute. To Fuller and her friends, however, the Pottawattami displayed only "gentle courtesy"—a quality non-Indians liked to see Indians exhibit. Fuller remarked that "they seemed to think we would not like to touch them: a sick girl in the lodge where I was persisted in moving so as to give me the dry place; a woman with the sweet melancholy eye of the race, kept off the children and wet dogs from even the hem of my garment." Who did not want to touch whom, however, is not as sharply clear to the reader as it is to Fuller. In the presence of a loss and poverty beyond anything she had ever seen before, Fuller struggled to rewrite the human scene by characterizing an elderly Pottawattami man first as "theatrical looking" and then as "French-Roman, that is, more romanesque than Roman." Her language suggests that the elderly man was merely acting the part of a sufferer, and even if her hairsplitting art-historical terminology operated to make his situation bearable to her, such niceties did nothing for him. Fuller's final gesture at the Pottawattami removed them altogether from their situation: "At last we got off, well wetted," she wrote, "but with a picturesque scene for memory." Once she had transformed the Pottawattami into art and then appropriated them as a memory, she had truly "at last got off" the terrible hook of considering them as real sufferers.[5]

Freezing the Indian into art was popular among travel writers, but the tactic emerges as no more than an expression of culture-bound attitudes that illuminate nothing of Indian life. Travelers showed off their knowledge of and past experience with painting and sculpture, and dropped those experiences over actuality like a veil. Those who endeavored to marbleize Indians into Greek statues also sought to romanticize them into the fictional Indians they had come to love, and to view them through their favorite literary lens. Margaret Fuller, who insisted that "the Indian cannot be looked at truly except by a poetic eye," continually hoped for Walter Scott to arrive and limn the "gypsy charm and variety" of Indian life—but her wish for the literary ministrations of Scott also expressed a covert desire to resituate North American Indians in a distant British past, where they could be only literature. In 1824 the English traveler William Blane complained that every American had read Walter Scott while Blane had read James Fenimore Cooper and, like other international travelers, was looking for Cooper's Indians. Across the language barrier Blane could not hear the elevated metaphors Cooper had made him desire, and nothing he saw in the interior resembled Glens Falls—indeed even Glens Falls itself, when Cooper-loving travelers visited it, no longer resembled Glens Falls. In their disappointment, travelers such as George Featherstonhaugh judged that Cooper "had never been among the Indians."[6]

Travelers who continually represented Indians as excellent potential subjects for the artist rarely represented Indians themselves as either interested in or productive of anything that travelers were prepared to call art. In 1819, members of the Long expedition were simply astonished when Ioways they met on their way up the Missouri took delight in studying books of engravings shown to them and were "not soon fatigued when employed in this way"; apparently the Ioways studied the engravings longer than the whites wanted them to. Most travelers, however, simply denied art to contemporaneous tribes, denied that they had designed the mounds, denied even that mounds were the products of art, and denied that art objects discovered in those mounds were "like anything of the Indian kind ever found in this country." Travelers complained that even in their removal Indians left behind "no obelisks crumbling away—no sculptured marble broken—no granite walls tumbling down—no relic of dome, turret, or spire," but at the same time noted, as did Miriam Colt, that white attempts to imitate Indian art failed utterly: the hoax objects that locals tried to market to travelers as Indian art were pathetically bad and obviously false. Travelers favored just one relationship between Indians and art: they required that Indians transform themselves into art. "Indians without paint are poor coots," said a man to Margaret Fuller in Wisconsin, and she agreed that she "liked the effect of the paint on them; it reminds one of the gay fantasies of nature." Nonetheless travelers who desired to see body paint on Indians refused meaning to that art: an Indian agent firmly told Aleksandr Lakier that "originally a large number of the markings did have meaning, that they portrayed the whole history of the man and his tribe," but that all those meanings had been "distorted" and lost. This repeated claim served both to deny history to Indians and to deny understanding of Indian art, history, and culture to white observers. Drab nineteenth-century whites, covered head to toe in what Jessie Benton Frémont called "a pall of black alpaca," scorned color in dress, assigned color only to nature and steamboats, and stared in fascination at colorfully dressed Indians. Americans, wrote Aleksandr Lakier, "pay no attention at all to dress, so long as it is not Indian dress," a matter in which he found them "obviously interested."[7]

White travelers who never spoke of other white bodies paid close attention not only to the clothes but also to the bodies of Indians. They dwelled on the physical composure of the Indians they saw, but rather than contrasting that composure to the rocking, whittling, jiggling, twitching whites of the interior, they instead employed the Indians' claimed immobility to push them out of humanity and into nature. In Minnesota in 1848, Fredrika Bremer described a "tall Indian who was standing with his arms crossed, wrapped in his blanket, under a large tree. He stood as immovable as if he had grown into the tree against the boll of which he leaned." But if that immobile Indian became dignified nature in travelers' descriptions, the Indian who sat or lay down did not: if he was male and he was not standing, he was represented as lazy, lounging, and indolent. If he was on the move, he was said to be a "nomad," or, according to Charles Dickens, "like the meaner sort of gypsies . . . wandering and restless." Furthermore, if an Indian's personal physical immobility was represented as stately and dignified, Indian group mobility and immobility were both represented as either threatening or contemptible. Travelers who had discussed white mobility in the interior as a plain fact always represented Indian mobility, in contrast, as troublesome and mysterious. Because white movers never backtrailed to homesteads they had abandoned, locals in conversation with travelers represented as trespassers Indians who returned from the West to visit their former homes in the interior. Repeatedly, Indian styles of seasonal and periodic mobility were represented as incompatible with white styles of mobility; at the same time the stabilities of Indian life emerged as incompatible with ongoing white demands for new and larger pieces of land.[8]

Even though some travelers dreamed of the notably servant-free interior as a place where "beautiful Indians might rise up to wait on them," and even though such travelers as Margaret Fuller were regaled by locals with fantastic tales of Indians subdued into servility by the power of the white man's gaze, in fact no traveler managed to make a servant of an Indian. David Macrae engaged an Indian guide without fully understanding that he had hired not a servant but a companion on the trail; when one evening Macrae asked the guide to clean his boots, the guide "declined without any indication of being offended," but the next morning he was gone. "If you do or say anything to offend their pride, and make them think they are regarded as menials, they will leave without a word, and without the slightest regard to the difficulties of your position," complained Macrae.[9]

Travelers were trapped not only by their cross-cultural ignorance but also by their tendency to represent "the Indian" as always and everywhere the same, and most of all by the conflicting demands they made of Indians. They insisted that Indians were too inconsistent to be understandable but also too proud to be malleable; they required that Indians should neither be mobile nor stay put; they desired to see both spirit and docility in the same person; they criticized Indians' hunting but wanted to be shown by Indians the best places to hunt; and they wished to feel threatened by a population that they insisted must not threaten them.

Some travelers, employing an established method of denying land ownership, asserted that Indians had no agriculture; meanwhile others were busy scorning Indians for eating from nature. In 1821, Henry Schoolcraft was so "surprised" to encounter cultivated fields of squashes, beans, and melons along the Turkey River in Wisconsin that he at once denied such evidence by pointing out that the fields were "without any enclosures" and thus not properly owned; when he came upon an asparagus patch, Schoolcraft hastened to assert that it was not evidence of cultivation: "the seeds," he wrote, "had probably been dropped by some former traveler." For a traveler to assign to another traveler's casual loss more evidence of cultivation than he would assign to the Indian population constituted an extreme effort at erasing visual facts. The ease, propriety, and delicacy of Indian table manners were ignored in favor of the assertion that Indians did not say thank-you when whites gave them food, and Indian concern that all should share equally in the food available was transformed into tales of guests forced to eat anything set before them. If one traveler claimed that Indians were forced to "eat their dogs when other food fails," later travelers escalated that detail into claims that dog meat was an Indian idea of the "greatest delicacy to set before a guest" and that identifiable whole roasted puppies had been set before them by Indians.

Because the Indian pharmacopoeia, even when glimpsed, was outside white understanding, sick Indians were presumed by travelers to be either untreated or treated inappropriately. Fredrika Bremer was one of the few who glimpsed that Indian women were the physicians; other travelers were more likely to assert that Indians used their herb collections in the production of "intoxicating liquor," and to tell stories of instant death resulting from ingestion of Indian medicine. Suicide rates among Indian women, travelers asserted, were astronomical, and yet there seemed to be enough Indian women available to support travelers' further assertion that all Indian men were polygamous. Under such a weight of conflict, travelers collapsed as observers and abandoned the possibility of falling into a direct relationship with the

Indians they wanted to write about. The point of collapse is clearly available in many travel accounts; after it occurred, the traveler often turned to making utterly culture-bound and even vicious assessments of Indian art, looks, and food as observed or rumored, and not infrequently turned also to efforts to appropriate Indian-owned goods.[10]

In the interior non-Indians regularly scorned Indians who, they claimed, selected from the range of non-Indian artifacts available to them only "light, showy, and fantastic articles"; meanwhile, however, those same scornful persons coveted Indians' goods and missed no opportunity to "annex" them, in the vocabulary of the time. If travelers had approached the moundscape of the interior in the spirit of the international treasure hunt, they often approached Indians in the spirit of the international bazaar or the great rummage sale whose attendants are momentarily absent—and then at times they displaced the nature of their own appropriative activities onto an Indian population that, they claimed, had stolen from them. Travelers cast the sharp eye of the international shopper on the products of Indian hands, drove sharp bargains for those goods despite the sellers' obvious poverty, and on occasion bought what they wanted directly from the bodies of the sellers. On many sad occasions they troubled the cross-cultural marketplace by rejecting what an Indian offered for sale and instead demanding an object or a garment that was obviously too significant or essential to be up for sale. When travelers came upon an Indian settlement whose occupants were temporarily absent, they ransacked it, stole from it, and destroyed anything they did not carry away. Travelers who vigorously disapproved of government policies that stripped Indians of their land were the same travelers who required any Indian to relinquish an object that a non-Indian wanted to buy and who apparently did not believe ownership to be a serious matter among people who owned so little. Travelers seemed to operate on the theory that the fewer the possessions the less was a person's right to keep them; only non-Indian possessors of many objects could insist upon ownership and value. Although travelers were not in a position to seize land from Indians, their seizing of Indian goods mirrors that larger phenomenon.

Many travelers first acquired on the East Coast their view of Indians as marketers of handmade souvenirs; in the East, however, travelers' shopping opportunities among Indians were organized and convenient. At Niagara in 1841, on her daily path to the dining room in her hotel, Eliza Steele shopped before a row of Tuscarora women who were "sitting upright upon the settees in the halls, enveloped in cloaks of scarlet or black, richly embroidered with beads or adorned by pieces of tin cut in flowers and tacked on. Their eyes," Steele wrote, "are fixed upon the ground, their long hair falls over their faces, and an expression of profound melancholy sits upon every countenance. You stand before them and gaze upon them, but silent, grave, and motionless they sit. You at last ask, 'Have you any moccasins?' With a dignified motion they throw open their cloaks, and their laps are filled with articles for sale. You ask the price—a low musical voice tells you the amount in a very foreign accent." Steele desired some conversation to accompany her shopping, but failed to get it: a statement of the price of the goods was the most she "could ever obtain from an Indian woman although [she] made many efforts while at Niagara, and they can both speak and understand English." Outside the hotels of the East, shopping was similarly organized: Clara Bromley and her party drove to Chipewa, a shoppers' village near Niagara "where the Indians bring the specimens of their handiwork for exhibition and sale to the numerous visitors constantly passing to and fro" and where she made "several purchases" from a display of shoes, card cases, boxes, fans, and screens.[11]

Shopping in the interior, in contrast, was rarely so organized, but travelers' desire for Indian goods did not abate. In 1868 George Rose covered his disappointment at finding no Indian goods for sale in Chicago by displacing his desire and claiming that Indians—not one of whom he had encountered—were ready at all times to "attack and scalp a friend if he should happen to possess that which they covet." Eliza Steele and Godfrey Vigne both directed shoppers to Mackinac Island as an "excellent market" for travelers wishing to "lay up a store of Indian articles . . . made by these poor people." In St. Paul in 1855, Laurence Oliphant represented himself as a smart shopper who had bought his Indian "curiosities" only in stores kept by Indian agents who sold only goods acquired "from famous chiefs" and thereby guaranteed them to be status purchases. That non-Indians wanted Indian goods was something they knew about each other, though they rarely articulated it and even more rarely articulated their awareness that such covetousness made an uneasy partner to their elevated sentiments about sympathy with the Indians' situation. On 29 December 1833, Charles Fenno Hoffman shared a room in a small log-house inn with two other travelers, an Illinois farmer and an experienced trader for Indian goods. The three men discussed recent federal treaty negotiations held at Chicago and Hoffman wrote that "the anecdotes told of meanness, rapacity, and highway robbery (in cheating, stealing, and forcibly taking away) from the Indians exasperated me so that I expressed my indignation and disgust in unmeasured terms." The trader, a quiet and mannerly fellow, had seemed sympathetic to Hoffman's critique but had, while Hoffman was voicing it, climbed under the bedclothes in search of warmth. When Hoffman, implying that he might have run the negotiations differently had he been in charge, said, "I should have liked to have been at Chicago a year ago," the trader's head emerged from under the blankets and he said, "Ah, sir, if you had, the way in which you'd have hooked an Indian blanket by this time would be curious." All three men laughed, but even while Hoffman laughed he realized that the "whole current" of his feelings had been unmasked by the trader's remark: he had to admit that he did want an Indian blanket, and that his desire was incompatible with his critique. Furthermore, some of the most fanatic vilifiers of Indians were the most indefatigable shoppers among them: at Mankato, Minnesota, in 1856, Harriet Bishop, who throughout her book assigned to the Indians of southern Minnesota every low quality she knew of, nonetheless bought "several valuable trinkets of their own manufacture and worn by them" directly off the bodies of Indians, both male and female, that she met; then she criticized the unsuccessful vendors among them for looking "sad and displeased" as Bishop and her party left the scene.[12]

Other travelers desecrated or stole whatever they found of Indian goods whose owners were absent. In 1837, Francesco Arese and his companions ransacked a temporarily deserted Omaha village: Arese found a collection of eagle and swan feathers and contemptuously used them to clean his pipe; he and his companions gorged themselves with as much food as they could hold, filled every sack they had with the rest, "allowed the horses to stuff themselves out of shape," and then ran. Arese enjoyed the escapade but his attempt to repeat it backfired. He next approached a very quiet Sioux village on the Des Moines River. In sight there was but one resident, a man who "had stuck an arrow into the ground, hung his mirror on it, and was busy painting his face red and black and putting feathers on his head: that is, he was completing his toilet for presenting himself worthily to the enemy." Longing for a fight and a pillage, Arese and company dismounted, started on foot through the tall grass, and circled the village so as to enter at a distance from the solitary warrior. They were approaching the nearest dwelling when "a cloud of crows and birds of prey, and a few wolves came out of it." On looking into the tent, Arese discovered its occupants all dead of the smallpox, "nothing left of them but what the wolves and birds of prey had not yet eaten ... men's bones and horses' mixed together, a few remnants of clothing and weapons." On this occasion Arese took nothing, ate nothing, used nothing, and chose not to do battle with the Sioux warrior who was apparently the sole survivor; instead he "fled the awful spectacle," he wrote, and "all the rest of that day we met wolves."[13]

When not frightened off by death, however, many non-Indians shopped their way through Indian possessions left untended, and when there was no one present to sell, travelers simply took. In Kansas in 1862, Miriam Colt and her mother sorted through every object in a large and temporarily deserted Indian village: "buffalo horns, buffalo skins and mats, tin pans, plates, tin sieves, knives, spoons, wooden bowls, camp pails, brass kettles, clam shells, and Indian trinkets. We made a selection," wrote Colt in the language of the shopper. The two women returned home with a wagon full of their "plunder," as they called it, but while they scoured up the items for use, they comfortably reclassified them as "thrown-away Indian utensils." Sometimes shopping took on the cast of the rummage sale. At a Cheyenne camp fifty miles from Fort Larned, Kansas, in 1867, Henry Morton Stanley watched some "boys in blue," who had just scored a bloodless victory over the deserted camp, wander through it in search of goods about to be reclassified as "mementos"—calumets, tomahawks, war clubs, beadwork, moccasins, arrows, knives, puppies, and dolls. As Stanley watched the soldiers, each rummaged about, picked up something, carried it a few yards, and threw it away; then another soldier picked up the discarded item, carried it for a few yards, and again threw it away. Nothing, apparently, was quite what the soldiers wanted, but all the goods were thoroughly rummaged through and scattered. Dissatisfied, the soldiers later burned the village. The rummaging gesture appeared so regularly as to constitute non-Indians' most characteristic motion toward Indian goods: shoppers, half interested and half contemptuous, searched for something desirable among others' possessions; next they temporarily appropriated it and then perhaps discarded it for someone else to appropriate; and finally they reclassified the item of choice as "thrown away," as a memento, as a souvenir, as theirs. Among Indian-fighters, Indian-haters, and ordinary folk who had never met an Indian, according to Charles Fenno Hoffman, "the rights and privileges, the property, the life of an Indian, do not weigh a feather."[14]

Travelers accompanied their intense desire for Indian goods with ferocious rejection of the looks of the Indians who made, wore, used, and sold those goods. Nineteenth-century whites were accustomed to making openly critical judgments of looks: the drab uniformity of white Western-style dress throughout much of the century acted to focus the gaze intensely on facial features, hair, and posture. Even travelers sensitized to operative American racial divisions and given to lamenting how much those divisions mattered gave no quarter on looks; they enforced a single unquestioned standard of physical beauty, and anyone who failed to meet it was ugly. Anna Jameson, for example, recognized that "nations differ . . . on the subject of beauty," but she insisted typically that "there exists luckily a standard in reference to which we cannot err . . . for the type of physical beauty we go to Greece." Travelers' regular and unsparing use of "ugly" acted as the very vortex of judgment, sucking down and out of human consideration any person to whom it was applied. Upholding a single standard of Greek beauty meant banishing from consideration all blacks, all Indians except for a few young males, and most white women. The standard was applied heartlessly to any white woman who either assumed or was thrust into a public role, especially women married to politicians; the higher the politician's office, the more his wife was castigated for her ugliness, and presidents' wives were judged ugliest of all. White men escaped the looks judgment unless their public manners were notably disgusting; children were exempt unless they were black children; a white woman with a baby in her arms was usually exempt; an elderly male Indian could escape judgment if he maintained an upright posture and never lay down; no woman of any race who was past forty could escape negative judgment on her looks.[15]

Influential travelers much read by others, such as Henry Schoolcraft, insisted not only that all Indian women were unbeautiful but also that their lack of culturally desirable looks was a "universally accepted" fact. When Schoolcraft was presented with a reported exception, he asserted that a supposedly "comely" Indian woman, one whose "regularity of feature would be acknowledged by the more civilized people of Europe," must certainly be unchaste and therefore could not contend in the nationwide cross-cultural beauty contest. When a traveler saw an Indian woman he considered undeniably beautiful by his European standard, he usually dealt with the sight by pushing the woman into future ugliness and asserting that she would certainly "lose her beauty very soon [and] when faded, exhibit a harshness of feature which is almost forbidding." It was this claimed early fading that, according to Charles Fenno Hoffman, caused Indian husbands to desert their wives early in marriage. Hoffman's quite intricate argument assumed that an Indian woman whose looks *he* valued would soon lose them; that any Indian husband valued his wife *only* for her possession of the same looks that Hoffman valued; and that a man's looks—whatever his race—figured into the equation not at all.[16]

Women travelers were drawn into the discussion of looks when they applied nineteenth-century European standards of taste to Indian use of body paint and Indian needlework. Fredrika Bremer found Indian needlework excellent—and bought plenty of it—while simulta-

neously judging it "deficient in taste and knowledge of design."
Moreover, with the eye of a person who wore only black, Bremer
lamented Indian taste for "fine colors." Judgments about color and
workmanship, however, were not easily separated from culture-bound
judgments of looks. In 1848 Bremer was escorted on her Minnesota
visit by Governor and Mrs. Alexander Ramsey; on meeting the official couple, Bremer had judged Mrs. Ramsey to be "very pretty" but
had not remarked on the governor's looks. When the Ramseys took
Bremer to visit an Indian village near St. Paul, Bremer was introduced
to a young Indian woman named Feather-cloud who was attired for
the occasion in "her wedding dress of embroidered scarlet woolen
stuff." Bremer judged Feather-cloud to be beautiful, "remarkably
light-complexioned," and the owner of a perfect profile. Bremer asked
to sketch her, and did so; but later, while Bremer was occupied with a
second sketch of a man denominated "the old chief," both Feather-
cloud and Mrs. Ramsey slipped out of the wigwam without Bremer's
noticing. When the two women returned, Ramsey was wearing
Feather-cloud's scarlet wedding dress; there had been, however, no exchange, for Feather-cloud was wearing not Ramsey's dress but a plain
garment of her own. To Bremer, Mrs. Ramsey was no longer pretty
but somehow all wrong: the dress, Bremer complained, was "too
showy" for Mrs. Ramsey, who lacked the "mystic beauty" needed to
carry it off. Moreover it was vaguely offensive to Bremer that
Feather-cloud was so openly amused by the effect of the dress on
Mrs. Ramsey; the possibility that Feather-cloud might have been
judging Mrs. Ramsey's looks was intolerable. Feather-cloud's identity,
which was attached to the dress, seemed unsuitable to Mrs. Ramsey,
Mrs. Ramsey's identity was not available for Feather-cloud to try on,
and Bremer did not wish to sketch Mrs. Ramsey. The cultural division
that had encouraged Bremer to view Feather-cloud as an exotic objet
d'art had been encroached upon, and Feather-cloud found the switch
funny while Bremer did not. Feather-cloud's culturally desirable looks
qualified her as an appropriate subject for a European sketch artist but
for nothing beyond. The incident had other uncomfortable implications for Bremer: she had chosen to view Feather-cloud as a European in Indian dress, but Mrs. Ramsey actually was a European in
Indian dress, and as such she posed a challenge to Bremer's fantasy,
which promptly collapsed. Bremer seemed also to have felt excluded
from something going on between Mrs. Ramsey and Feather-cloud.
Bremer's sketching was a version of shopping: she might not have
been buying but she did want to appropriate a keepsake; Mrs. Ramsey, however, had bested Bremer by entering that stage of shopping
known as "trying on," while Bremer remained in the stage called "just

looking" and in the sketch-taker's position of quintessential out-siderism. It rarely occurred to travelers that their looks or indeed the looks of any white person could be submitted to judgment by any Indian; they assumed that Indians must wish to look like white Europeans just as they assumed that Indians must want the goods of white Europeans.[17]

Engulfed in a great shadow cast over them by culture-bound white notions of beauty and status, the daily lives of Indian women slid into obscurity.[18] Travelers who raided the books of eighteenth-century French travelers for cues repeated their assertions about matters of women's lives—childbearing, for example—that not one of them had ever observed. Pierre Charlevoix was a favorite source for travelers wanting to write about Indian women. In 1721, Charlevoix had claimed that in childbirth "Indian women are generally delivered without pain, and without any assistance; there are some, however, who are a long time in labor and suffer severely." Later travelers re-peating Charlevoix usually dropped the second clause in favor of elaborating on the first. They claimed that Indian women felt no labor pains but casually dropped infants while working in the fields or while out on the trail. Charlevoix had also asserted that all Indians were polygamous, that all despised women, and that "to call an Indian a woman is the highest affront that can be offered him." That final as-sertion stuck like glue, even though such later travelers as Henry Schoolcraft and Charles Fenno Hoffman repeatedly denied that there was any truth in it: they observed instead that if an Indian male be-haved like neither a white American male nor a stereotypical "brave" he was then defined *by white males* as behaving like a woman, a child, or a Frenchman. Charlevoix, who had been forced to notice that the Indian societies he contacted were matrilineal, had been unable to reconcile the fact that women became tribal chiefs with the observed fact that these same women cooked; later travelers ignored him on the subject and simply assumed that all tribal chiefs were male. Charlevoix had also asserted that Indian women were "no more than the slaves of their husbands" while at the same time they exercised full authority over their children and over all daily and domestic matters; later trav-elers repeated the enslavement assertion but excised the material on domestic authority.[19]

White travelers both male and female measured Indian life not against their actual experience and knowledge of white society but against a passel of social assertions, some of which were merely wishes: that men were superior to women, that all whites married for love and practiced lifelong marital fidelity, that no white man ever abandoned wife and family, that no marriage foundered, that domestic duties were to be performed by women only and were also contemptible, that men held authority in the family and passed it to their sons, that no white woman performed hard physical work, and that such gender divisions were natural and right while other styles of gender division were wrong. Through these fogged lenses little was observable. In order to bring Indian life into line with standard white views, Thomas McKenney proposed "a project for organizing the Indians under a patriarchal government," but more typically travelers merely repeated judgments that obviously conflicted with observable details. In 1843, Margaret Fuller represented Indian women as beasts of burden "coming home from the woods, stooping under great loads of cedar boughs" but recorded that these same women were singing and laughing; she further represented Indian women as slovenly only to wonder at their decorum, their delicacy, and the precision and care with which they handled objects. Only Anna Jameson saw that in Indian societies "there is no class of women privileged to sit still while others work," thus bringing to the surface a concept unacceptable to bearers of white cultural myths about disoccupied feminine refinement. Very rarely did any woman traveler put on paper the degrading term *squaw;* but all male travelers used that term, and all, while swearing that Indian women's lives bore no resemblance to white women's lives, at the same time displaced onto Indian women the worst elements of white domestic life and gender asymmetry. Having heaped such white cultural baggage onto Indian women, travelers then rejected both the baggage and its bearers.[20]

Travelers who had entered the interior complacent in their views of the Indians they expected to meet emerged bearing a bewildering mix of observation, bloody local tales, and material drawn from old travel books. They ceased offering solutions to what had been defined for them as a problem and instead many resorted to the replacement stance that Indians were "mysterious" and that it was their "fate" to perish before the white onslaught on the interior. In effect, that fallback position was indistinguishable from the call for extermination that travelers had rejected. The more travelers disliked what they had seen of white activities in the interior, the more they sympathized with the Indian situation; but these sympathetic travelers also fell into speaking of Indians in the vocabulary of fate and inevitable destiny. Travelers who were critical of white treatment of Indians could not logically favor assimilation, and few entertained amalgamation as an answer; instead most repeated the claim that amalgamation "as a general rule" weakened both races by perpetuating the worst characteristics of each.

Some travelers drew solace from meeting any Indian who expressed awareness of his imperiled situation. Aboard a steamboat from Cincinnati to Louisville, Charles Dickens met the Choctaw Pitchlynn, who wore a suit, introduced himself with an engraved card, was perfectly bilingual, and had read the novels of Walter Scott. Dickens, however, did not want Pitchlynn to cross cultures; he wanted him to be a "real" Indian, and thus said to the man that he "regretted not to see him in his own attire." Pitchlynn responded that "his race was losing many things besides their dress, and would soon be seen upon the earth no more." If the shopper's stance was the foremost comfort point for travelers meeting Indians, a statement like Pitchlynn's came in a close second: an Indian's expressed awareness of his imperiled situation could be at once transformed, in the mind of the traveler, into the Indian's acceptance of that situation. Furthermore, if the Indian seemed both aware of his situation and passive in the face of it, he could even be read as accepting a policy of extermination as fate. Once Dickens and Pitchlynn got past the hard part of the conversation, they joked about buffaloes and then shook hands. Dickens invited Pitchlynn to visit England and assured him of good treatment there, but Pitchlynn shook off the invitation with the remark that "the English used to be very fond of the Red Men when they wanted their help, but had not cared for them much since." Then he left, and Dickens, watching Pitchlynn move away across the deck, characterized him as "another kind of being," thus preserving him as different from the common humanity milling about the deck. Whether aestheticized into Greek and Roman statuary, immobilized in the past, or exoticized, Indians could not attain in these reports a simple survival position, and as long as they were seen as validating their own imperiled position simply by being aware of it, they had no chance of entering travelers' psyches as anything but incomprehensible beings. Many travelers who found themselves opting to go along with policies of extermination toward Indians nonetheless continued to express deep regret over those policies, to severely criticize both the United States government and Americans who supported such policies, and to sign off on the issue once they located an Indian who validated their view by admitting recognition of its inevitability. They did not see their own position as incomprehensible.[21]

In a search for pleasant and understandable Indian material to distract them from contemporaneous conditions too painful to dwell on, numerous travelers turned to retailing legends—not tribal legends but white-concocted legends about Indians, sentimental European-style legends about thwarted romance and star-crossed lovers and death leaps. Because so much of the fakelore is about death, it can be read as a series of approaches to a culture under siege; furthermore, the legends are most unstable whenever they concern those matters of Indian life that travelers least comprehended—family structure, authority, and the position of women. The travel writer's favorite among made-up legends was the story of Winona, which had a conveniently visible geographical location—a high bluff on the upper Mississippi—that travelers could easily view from a comfortable position aboard a steamboat or train.

In Henry Schoolcraft's 1821 telling, the Sioux Winona loves a "young chief" but her parents wish her to marry an "old chief." Winona apparently accedes to their wishes, but while the wedding feast is in preparation, she exits "her father's cabin," makes a run for the cliff, throws herself off, and is "instantly dashed to a thousand pieces" on the rocks below. Schoolcraft's tale is about both romantic love and European-style male authority over women's lives; in his framing, a woman's sole route of resistance to male authority is suicide. Schoolcraft kept his story contained within tribal society and admired it as an "instance of sentiment" that, in his view, elevated Sioux culture.

When Fredrika Bremer, aboard a steamboat up the Mississippi in 1848, retold the Winona story, the arranged marriage with the old chief vanished and Winona, no longer in love with anyone, was made to choose between death and "marriage with a young man whom she did not love." In Bremer's version, Winona makes no athletic dash to the cliff but instead warbles a "death-song" to unknown auditors. The bloody death on the rocks is also gone; Winona merely throws herself into the water below. Since Bremer's Winona has no rival preference to the man chosen for her, the focus of the tale shifts over to parental authority, self-extermination, and death as preferable to marriage without romantic love.

In 1853, before Mary Eastman began her retelling, she not only made the standard claims about Indian women's domestic enslavement and their physical ugliness but also firmly established as inevitable the extermination of the Sioux and their culture. Only then did she begin her "tale of sorrow and passion," in which the beautiful fourteen-year-old Winona, dressed by Eastman in a lovingly detailed catalog of all the goods that travelers coveted, is happily married to an unobjectionable man but fails to reproduce. Her husband turns to drink, beats her, and eventually brings home a second wife who bears many children and laughs scornfully at the sad and barren Winona. Although traces of earlier versions are evident in Eastman's title— "The Lover's Leap"—there is no leaping in Eastman's tale: it closes on a Winona relegated to the position of faithful nurse to her often ailing husband. Eastman's version banishes both death and parental authority from the tale in order to center on womanhood ennobled by suffering. In no version of the tale does Winona reproduce, and only in Eastman's version does another Indian woman, in that polygamous situation that white writers loved to linger over in horror, reproduce for her.[22]

Eastman's version was without influence on later tellers who, in the mid-1850s, performed cross-cultural moves on the tale. In Ida Pfeiffer's version, Winona is betrothed to "one of her own people" but by chance becomes "warmly attached to a white man who, having lost his way, had come into her wigwam." On her wedding day, Winona throws herself into the river, and her bridegroom has restored to him "only her inanimate corpse." Pfeiffer's is the first version to record no tribal identification for Winona and to posit the cultural superiority of the white male as husband.

The Winona story was further malleable, however, and travelers of many persuasions made it serve their ends. In 1857, Harriet Bishop, a missionary traveler, restored the tension of parental authority to the story but narrowed that authority to the father's alone. In Bishop's version, Winona's "chieftain father" is so misguided in his fondness for her as to "pledge her to a favorite brave of his band" even though she loves another. "The father was incorrigible!" exclaimed Bishop, and compared his cruelty to that of "thousands in civilized lands." Although Winona, according to Bishop, feigns compliance with her father's wish, and even displays a certain forced cheerfulness, her spirits are crushed. On her wedding day Winona, attired in a snowy-white blanket, detaches herself from a party of berry-gatherers, bounds with a wild cry toward the precipice, pauses upon the brink to fling up her arms, and throws herself into the river below. A few weeks later her father dies of grief, while the equally grief-stricken object of her true love wanders aimlessly until he comes upon a missionary who not only converts him but returns him to his tribe to convert others. Bishop's lengthy retelling is replete with moonbeams, whippoorwills, and whispering zephyrs, but it is no longer a romantic tragedy. Bishop's story says that authoritarian men will see the light after causing a woman's death, but also posits male religious conversion as an end so important that a woman's life is not too great a sacrifice for it.[23]

Later retellings were often no more than capsule versions. Aleksandr Lakier's 1859 version was about simple parental authority: Winona throws herself into the water because "her parents did not want to give her to her favorite warrior." Visiting the town of Winona, Minnesota, in 1855, Laurence Oliphant mocked the Winona legend but employed it in his ruminations on the claim that "a few years will suffice to obliterate all traces of the [Indian] nations who once inhabited these shores." Oliphant chose to understand the Winona story as a covert discussion of extermination, and of self-extermination at that. The story absolved whites of responsibility while representing Indians as engaged in a spectacular suicide disconnected from any white activities. By 1865, under the pen of George Borrett, the Winona story made a nearly final racial shift when "the Indian maiden flung herself [from the crag] in despair at the persecutions wreaked on her by her tribe for her wilful love of the paleface." Borrett's capsule version not only denied amalgamation but also represented Indians as a culture under internal siege over the issue of race-mixing. In all versions of the Winona story, Indian sexuality, a subject that troubled and frightened travelers and of which all palefaces were fully ignorant, was both expressed and denied. The story, in typical white style, first offered sexuality as the province of pretty young people surrounded and pressed on by forbidding authoritarian adults, and then canceled the subject when it forbade both sexual experience and reproduction by killing off the woman involved. The story refused Indians access to the supposed fulfillment of youthful non-Indian romantic love while allowing the teller to linger over an apparently enjoyable coalition of sex, desire, and death.[24]

In 1883, in *Life on the Mississippi,* Mark Twain burlesqued the Winona story by putting it in the mouth of an old gentleman who had once traveled the interior with a panorama and a lectern but who was, when he met Twain, employed in "helping to work up the materials for a Tourists' Guide which the St. Louis and St. Paul Packet Company are going to issue this summer for the benefit of travelers." Twain represented himself to the man as a collector of Indian tales and to his readers as egging on the man until the old fellow moved into "his lecture gait" and offered the going commercial version of the legend: in it, the Sioux are no longer residents of southern Minnesota but merely in the area on a fishing trip. Winona has engaged herself to one lover while her "stern parents" have promised her to "a famous warrior." At this point in the tale, however, the old gentleman encountered pronoun trouble. According to him, Winona, perching on the very edge of the bluff, began to "upbraid her parents, who were below, for their cruelty, and then, singing a death-dirge, threw herself from the precipice and dashed them in pieces on the rock below." Twain was eminently satisfied that it was indeed the cruel parents who had been, in this version, dashed to pieces when their daughter fell on them; he remarked that of the fifty lover's leap stories he had collected, this was "the only jump in the lot that turned out in the right and satisfactory way." Winona, though "a good deal jarred up and jolted . . . got herself together and disappeared before the coroner reached the fatal spot; and 'tis said she sought and married her true love, and wandered with him to some distant clime, where she lived happy ever after, her gentle spirit mellow and chastened by the romantic incident which had so early deprived her of the sweet guidance of a mother's love and a father's protecting arm, and thrown her, all unfriended, upon the cold charity of a censorious world." Twain's legendary version of the legendary old gentleman's version he characterized as "an admirable story"; it is certainly more inspired nonsense than the solemn and didactic versions, also nonsense, that preceded it and that functioned as tools in a continuing and covert white effort to frame Indian culture and society in some way pleasing and comfortable to the teller.[25]

Barriers—some erected for travelers and some by them—of language, fakelore, and ridicule stood between travelers and the cultural life of Indian tribes. In the interior both meaning and interest were continually denied to Indian utterance. In 1827, the *Western Magazine and Review* complained of a volume of Indian materials collected by Henry Schoolcraft that "nothing can be more tedious, and palling, than collections of Indian orations"; the magazine's reviewer selected for notice from the volume a single "amusing anecdote which illustrates Indians' reckless fondness for ardent spirits." Many English-speaking travelers refused to consider Indian languages and speech as acceptable communication. In 1819 Stephen Harriman Long described his chosen westward route to Indians he met near Council Bluffs and became infuriated when they laughed at his itinerary; he rejected the "representations of the country" that they offered in favor of his own disastrous choice, and went off to become scandalously lost in the West. Fredrika Bremer complained of the "nasal tones" of Indian languages, which she did not understand, and Frederick von Raumer described a Seminole on an Ohio riverboat delivering a long and fluent speech to the passengers but, claimed von Raumer, *not caring* whether his auditors understood him and "not in the least disturbed by the fact that his audience did not know a word of what he was saying."[26]

The French traveler Ernest Duvergier de Hauranne, a socially sensitive and observant traveler, was out of the ordinary because he reported not only his own responses but also his fellow travelers' responses both to him and to events they all witnessed. In contrast, most travelers, no matter how large their party, suppressed its size and nature in order to represent themselves as solitary and intrepid. De Hauranne, like all French travelers, was fascinated with Indian life and after arriving in America had also become interested in the national insistence on bestowing identities: he meticulously reported on each mistaken identity

Americans had given him during his travels—that of a French count, a correspondent from the London *Times,* a Swede, a novelist, an Iowan, a wounded Union officer. He was unprepared, however, for the identity that Americans insisted on bestowing on Indians.

In 1865, on the strength of a newspaper advertisement, de Hauranne bought a ticket for a Great Lakes excursion aboard the *Algona.* His excursion party constituted only one segment of the passenger list, but it was the most boisterous segment. At various stops along the shores of the lakes, de Hauranne watched his fellow travelers gape at working Indian women, laugh loudly at them, and "annoy them with their jokes," while simultaneously buying the items the women were producing—"small wares which curious whites can buy at low prices . . . articles that require much time and patience, the trifling profit of which would be disdained by the busy European." The Indian women uttered not a sound to the excursionists. "One would have said," wrote de Hauranne, "that they considered us unworthy of a word." Shamed by the behavior of his fellow travelers, de Hauranne tried taking refuge in the position of the sketch artist, just as Fredrika Bremer had done in Minnesota. Unlike Bremer, however, de Hauranne had no access to the domestic interiors of Indian life. Instead he sat outside a wigwam while children who had fled inside appeared repeatedly at the window and door of the dwelling to display to him domestic objects—now a bowl, then a knife—and while adult Indians who had remained outside the dwelling smiled and laughed at him. De Hauranne had been pained when his fellow excursionists laughed at Indian women but was discomfited when the laughter went into reverse and the Indians "amused themselves" over his desire to fall into some relation with them through artistic appropriation. Only his sketch was under his control: he could not shut his ears to "the sounds of scoffers" emanating from his fellow passengers' "assault" on the Indians' dignity and he could not comprehend his own position.

While he sketched, however, he awaited the event promised by the excursion company—"a gathering of Indian tribes climaxed by a war dance." Hearing some shouts and cries in the distance, de Hauranne presumed the dance was about to begin and hastened to the shore, where he discovered "a handful of children and old men dressed in rags and tatters" plus a number of hands from the *Algona* who had donned horsehair wigs and splotched their faces with paint, all together performing a "clownish parody" of a tribal dance. De Hauranne's fellow passengers had again positioned themselves as laughers: "Their sides splitting with laughter," he wrote, "they urged on the performers as though they had been trained dogs, and even joined in the dance themselves wearing foolish grins on their faces" while "the

had been meaningful, and that he could on his own produce an equally effective display of unmeaning. To the end of the century, similar dramas of cultural superiority were played out for observers in similar settings of mockery wherein, however, similar responses carried greatly divergent meanings that no traveler was capable of explaining.[30]

Even the best observers among the travelers described highly organized Indian societies and social practices and then regularly branded them *not civilized;* at other times, as on the editors' excursion observed by John White, travelers pulled tribal groups into their own society in order to examine them and require them to perform. Then they pushed them away and departed. In 1839, the French traveler Michel Chevalier wrote, "In the United States the democratic spirit is infused into all the national habits and all the customs of society; it bests and startles at every step the foreigner who, before landing in the country, had no suspicion to what a degree his every nerve and fiber had been steeped in aristocracy by a European education. It has effaced all distinctions except that of color; for here a shade in the hue of the skin separates men more widely than in any other country in the world." Travelers who had suffered agonies in the racial climate of the interior, especially when they found themselves complicit in behavior they abhorred, turned with relief to the examination of white customs in the all-white arenas of travel in the interior.[31]

Chapter 6

A Table Set for Hundreds

In antebellum Cincinnati, locals were making fortunes in hog slaughtering and meat packing, and escapees from their operations roamed the streets. In 1851, Emmeline Stuart-Wortley designated Cincinnati "The Empire City of Pigs," and thought its residents "fortunate that the pigs condescendingly allow human beings to share that truly magnificent location with them." Stuart-Wortley found her view of the pigs' social dominance corroborated in the local newspaper, which admitted that "the pigs are becoming masters of the place: they push the two-legged citizens into the streets, and they occupy the sidewalks. So things begin to look serious here, and we are prepared any day for a *pronunciamento* of the pigs, they carry their snouts so high already, and seem so bristling with importance." In 1856, Cincinnati pigs struck Isabella Bird as "lean, gaunt, and vicious-looking"; even after shopping in the most splendid stores, Bird stumbled over pigs—"disgusting intruders," she called them—on her way out the door. Charles Weld, who claimed that Ohio farmers calculated their pigs by the acre, visited no Cincinnati street that did not hold at least a dozen pigs "poking their noses into the dirt-heaps, or acting as dams to the gutters, in which they repose during the heat of the day."

Weld pointed out that the pigs, however, "performed an important duty in the social economy of the city, as scavengers," and relieved residents of the burden of paying for garbage collection. Pigs were correspondingly repaid by social protection: Aleksandr Lakier stepped off the boat at Cincinnati to confront a "huge sow with a full litter of suckling pigs," and learned that she was not to be disturbed by humans: "No one drove her away; on the contrary, everyone stepped around her," wrote Lakier.[1]

Not only did pigs, a major food source, have the run of Cincinnati's streets, but they dominated other arenas also. Some travelers found pigs entertaining everywhere, "a constant source of amusement," as Charles Dickens did when, along the Ohio, he traveled "a road that was perfectly alive with pigs of all ages; lying about in every direction, fast asleep; or grunting along in quest of hidden dainties." Furthermore, pigs announced their presence to travelers on the rivers of the interior. Stuart-Wortley characterized an Ohio River steamboat as "part palace and part pigstye," for directly beneath the "gilded bowers with rose-colored hangings" of the ladies' staterooms traveled hundreds of pigs in "state-styes" that Stuart-Wortley guessed might also be gilded and rose-colored. Never before had Stuart-Wortley encountered such "chatty porkers" as these; they grunted and squeaked so incessantly that, she claimed, all the other livestock aboard were forced to "listen in respectful silence." After her third sleepless night aboard the pork ship, Stuart-Wortley became so accustomed to the pigs' noise and odor that, she wrote, "had the parting porkers afterwards held out the trotter of friendship," she might have accepted it. In 1870, David Macrae reported that after westward-rushing humans abandoned the town of New Philadelphia, in Missouri, pigs took it over, and not only occupied its empty stores and churches but roamed at will through the grounds of its onetime college, "preparing to graduate in pork." Porcine behavior that entertained some frightened others; in 1842, at an Upper Sandusky, Ohio, inn, a Bostonian with whom Charles Dickens had struck up an acquaintance found the snoring and mosquitoes inside the inn so unbearable that he fled for shelter and sleep to the coach "which was airing itself in front of the house. This was not a very politic step as it turned out, for the pigs scenting him, and looking upon the coach as a kind of pie with some manner of meat inside, grunted round so hideously, that he was afraid to come out again, and lay there shivering till morning."[2]

Food ran in the streets of the interior, it might be said, effectively recycling whatever food the human residents of the interior had left uneaten. The pigs made a picture of plenty ready-to-hand, of plenty on the move, of plenty to be respected and not interfered with by its potential consumers. The interior's great plenty of meat and poultry was not wild, not seasonally connected or seasonally scarce, and not lamb or veal. It was the pig that made its presence most fully felt, it was pork that was available even when no other meat was, and it was perhaps pork's availability that kept other foods off the table. In 1847 George Featherstonhaugh hoped that the numerous lakes near Madison, Wisconsin, meant that fish might appear on the table at the tavern where he stopped to eat, but only the familiar salt pork appeared. "So to the old business we went," wrote Featherstonhaugh, "of bolting square pieces of fat pork, an amusement I had so often indulged in that I sometimes felt as if I ought to be ashamed to look a live pig in the face." In the antebellum interior, however, a traveler did have to look pigs in the face, and because the street pigs were nobody's pigs in particular, their presence seems intimately connected to indigenous views of animal food and of eating whose remarkable dietary consequences emerge from the material recorded by travelers.[3]

"Before I went to America," wrote Godfrey Vigne in 1832, "I had no idea in how short a time a meal could be dispatched." Like other travelers in the interior, Vigne had to adapt at once to the public dining rituals of the interior or risk going hungry amid plenty; there was no other choice. The essence of dining was time, and a successful diner had to display speed, agility, shrewdness, determination, and a good eye, for no traveler ever found a way to make individual adjustments in the dining rituals or use them toward individual dining ends. In 1827, William Bullock estimated that in the hotels and inns and on the steamboats, "twenty minutes only" were allowed for the principal meal. In 1839 Michel Chevalier noted that of the average three hundred persons admitted en masse to a steamboat or hotel dining room, two hundred left the table after fifteen minutes, "and in ten minutes more not an individual was to be seen." All Americans ate rapidly, but as travelers moved from the East Coast deeper into the interior, they often noted, as did Basil Hall in 1829, "a gradual acceleration in the speed at which the people swallowed their meals." Speed-eating was a feature of life in the interior that could be explained neither by the press of other activities nor by the time allotted for a meal at any given eating establishment. Diners, in fact, allotted more time to waiting for a meal than they did to consuming it. Aboard a Mississippi River steamboat to St. Paul in 1857, Christopher Columbus Andrews found it "amusing to see gentlemen seat themselves in range of the plates as soon as they were laid, an hour before the table was ready," only to bolt the meal itself in ten minutes and rush off. These passengers had, after the meal, nowhere to go and nothing special to do but wait for the next meal. On a Missouri River steamboat in 1867,

Henry Morton Stanley watched male passengers "dragging out a miserable existence and constantly smoking, or indulging in agonizing yawns" while "contriving to pass the intervals between meals. At the first welcome sound of the bell, all unite in a grand rush to the table and gorge themselves with two dozen different viands, from fish, fowl, flesh, to pudding, cake, and molasses, and in ten minutes and five seconds, they will be found around the stove, smoking away as energetically as ever." At railroad dining stops—a feature of travel before the invention of the dining car—eating practices far outrushed the time allotted: on a rail trip from Chicago to Cincinnati in 1855, Charles Weld characterized dinner as "a wonderful scramble; though fully half an hour was allowed for the meal, it was bolted in five minutes."[4]

The ritualized speed of dining in the interior bore an intimate relation to conditions of public dining that obtained for many decades. Inns, hotels, and steamboats served three meals a day at fixed hours, and, because the cost of the meals was included in the ticket price or hotel charge, travelers paid for the meals whether they ate them or not. On long tables in the hotel dining rooms and steamboat saloons, waiters set out all elements of the meal, every dish available, and enough of each dish to feed as many as three hundred eaters. Only after all the food was on the tables did the waiters ring the dinner gong and open the doors to the dining room, whereupon travelers rushed in, seated themselves, and served themselves. Rarely was there any passing of dishes from one diner to another; diners ate the foods nearest them, the foods they could reach, or the foods before which they had battled to position themselves. There were no printed menus and next to no opportunity to make individual requests or have them honored. In most public dining situations, women were seated first, or men waited until women sat down; once the men sat down, however, no other special considerations were available to any diner.

Public dining had its rules, diners knew them or learned them soon enough, and some diners developed strategies for using the rules to their advantage. Aboard a Mississippi River steamboat, Godfrey Vigne watched the behavior of both his fellow travelers and the stewards who were acting as

guards at the top of the staircase to prevent any gentleman from walking in before the bell rings. As the hour draws near, conversation is gradually suspended, and the company look as if they were all thinking of the same subject. Groups of lank thin-jawed personages may be seen "progressing" towards the door, and "locating" themselves around it, in expectation of the approaching rush, listening to the repeated assurance of the black stewards within, that no gentleman can by any possibility be admitted before the time. At length the bell rings, and the guards escape as they can; if they were not brisk in their motions, they stand a chance of being sent headlong down stairs, or jammed in between the wall and the opened doors. In less than a quarter of a minute, 150 or 200 persons have seated themselves at table, and an excellent breakfast of tea, coffee, eggs, beefsteaks, hot rolls, corn cakes, salted mackerel, mush, molasses, etc. is demolished in an incredibly short space of time. The crowd then slowly re-ascends the staircase—and three-quarters of them are quite surprised that they should be afflicted with dyspepsia![5]

No matter how much individual travelers might have disliked adapting to them, the rituals of speed-eating were not individually re-sistible; travelers who determined to eat at their own pace, or a pace they considered to be more refined, failed in unexpected ways. In 1864, on his first day aboard a Mississippi River steamboat, Milton Mackie observed with disapproval that "there was much fast eating on board" but determined that he at least would "dine methodically." When his eating method brought him to the point of wanting some roast beef on his plate, Mackie looked about and saw none; a waiter told him that the beef "was all paid out." Rather than be "put on short allowance," at his next meal Mackie abandoned method and picked up his speed so as to compete with the other diners. Public meals had a highly disciplined and sharply announced beginning that then dis-solved abruptly into individual choice when diners departed the table immediately upon ingesting their foods of choice, and travelers unfa-miliar with the ritual learned quickly. Admitted with 150 other eaters to a great hotel dining room in 1834, Henry Tudor finished his soup, helped himself to some fish, and, he wrote, "was comfortably settling myself in my chair for a couple of hours to come, when, casting my eye along the line of the table, I was immediately startled to find that half the chairs in various portions of its length, and which but a few moments before were fully occupied, had been deserted; and in five minutes afterwards I was left in a state of solitary abandonment, with the exception of three others." Tudor's surprise turned to alarm, how-ever, when he saw "the dishes all leaving the table along with the guests." When a waiter reached for the remaining dishes in Tudor's immediate vicinity, he "laid an embargo on two of them" in order to salvage for himself some semblance of a complete dinner. He began to feel awkward. "At length," he wrote, "perceiving that I was a lonely unit out of 150 well-dined and departed persons, shame got the better of my appetite, and I sprung up and departed too, fully resolved the next day to imitate my neighbors, by devouring my repast in double-quick time and in solemn silence. The least communication with your neighbors is entirely out of the question."[6]

To the Russian traveler Aleksandr Lakier, the gong-controlled long-table dining system seemed amazingly loose and potentially open, especially in the hotels, to any nonpaying persons who might join the crowd and rush into the dining room at the crash of the gong. "How is it all controlled?" Lakier asked. "Who is a hotel guest and who is a stranger? To sort them out would be difficult and would require that documents be shown and questions asked. Therefore whoever wants to take advantage of the hotel's largesse would find nothing simpler, though I was assured that this seldom happens." All other travelers who wrote on the public dining rituals, however, felt heavily controlled, and felt that eating itself was seriously modified when expressed in terms of time and speed. Moreover, they observed that speed-eating became a free-floating cultural phenomenon in the interior. Locals ate fast even when away from the long tables, when ordering à la carte, when paying by the piece for the food, when the food was free, and when their eating was unconstrained by considerations of time, money, or scarcity. They ate fast at home and they ate fast when away from home.[7]

A notable social consequence of speed-eating was that the diners chewed and swallowed in silence, or at least without speaking words to each other, for in 1842 Mrs. Felton noted with disgust that in her steamboat dining experience "few words were spoken, but it was by no means a silent repast." It was as if the silence of the great prairie landscape, a silence oppressive to so many travelers, had reappeared on the foodscape where its oppressive quality created new discomforts for travelers. If the press of time dictated silence, the conditions of mobility enhanced it: Hugh Tremenheere thought that the absence of conversation at the long tables was a feature of a society whose members were all strangers to one another. To some travelers the silence at meals was a genuine torture. On an Ohio River steamboat Charles Dickens came to dread the crash of the dinner gong: "I never in my life did see," he wrote, "such listless, heavy dulness as brooded over these meals: the very recollection of it weighs me down and makes me, for the moment, wretched . . . I really dreaded the coming of the hour that summoned us to table; and was as glad to escape from it again as if it had been a penance or a punishment." Mulling over his experiences in the interior in 1865, George Borrett felt he could arrive at no understanding of why dinner had to be "a solemn feed" or of how "human nature had been able to scrape itself so bare" of the social arts that he connected with refined dining. Silence at meals dominated the various men-only milieux of the century: in the lumber camps of Minnesota, total silence at meals was an enforced rule, and in the men's bars and men-only public restaurants of the interior, a heightened self-imposed speed requirement put conversation out of the question. As George Holyoake wrote in 1881, "I liked to watch businessmen eating, though I cannot say I ever saw it done. All I observed was that a gentleman enters, reads the bill of fare, speaks to the waiter, pays the cashier, and departs. He has, doubtless, taken his dinner; but the operation is so rapid that I cannot say properly that I witnessed it."[8]

In the dinner-table silence there was nothing uncivil. Travelers oppressed by mealtime silence were simultaneously amazed by the level of uncomplaining civility that accompanied it. In 1835 in Ohio, Patrick Shirreff observed that waiters were "generally addressed in a whisper, and a loud tone is never heard at table. The conduct of some people in Britain, who command attention by oaths and noise, does not suit this region of America, where the mild and unassuming are never neglected." To Michel Chevalier, the interior's high level of civility signaled, on the one hand, an extraordinary self-discipline, a silent and polite social order created in the absence of powerful authorities over behavior; on the other hand, Chevalier identified the innkeeper, the steamboat captain, and the coach driver as authorities, as the leaders and organizers of the "flying camp" that constituted society in the interior; they were "the generals of the great migration," and their views—unlike those of elected officials—were never questioned. "All rise," wrote Chevalier, "breakfast, dine, sup, when the landlord or his lieutenant general, the barkeeper, thinks fit to ring the bell or beat the gong; it is just as it is in a camp. They eat what is placed before them without showing the least symptom of impatience; they allow themselves to be overturned and their ribs to be broken by the one, they suffer themselves to be drowned or burnt up by the other, without uttering a complaint or a reproach. The life of founders of empires consists of a mixture of absolute independence and passive obedience."[9]

The absence of complaint about the food, whether required by the informal power of innkeepers or by a culturally demanded level of civility toward everyone, seriously affected the dining ritual. Diners in the interior might signal dislike of the food by leaving it uneaten but not by demanding replacement or registering complaint—at least not until they had left the dining scene and were no longer under the control of the innkeeper. Frances Trollope, traveling by coach through the interior, thought that the practice of impromptu stops for meals resulted in "abominably bad" food; she was at a loss to understand "the patient manner in which our American fellow-travelers ate whatever was set before them, without uttering a word of complaint, or making any effort to improve it." Their silence, however, did not mean that they thought the food was good; it meant that they were holding their complaints in reserve and would express them later to the strangers to whom they had not spoken during the meal itself. No sooner had the travelers returned to their seats in the stage than they began to complain about the meal that they had just silently consumed: "'Twas a shame'—'twas a robbery'—'twas poisoning folks'— and the like." When Trollope asked why they had not voiced their complaints to the innkeeper, her fellow stage passengers assured her that innkeepers and hotelkeepers couldn't "bear to be found fault with." The situation suggests that the public civility displayed by travelers resulted both in private resentments against "the generals" and in the acceptance and silent ingestion of meals that were inexpressibly bad. At the long public dining tables, moreover, speed, silence, and absence of complaint all together resulted in what might be called ideological dining: a fully social situation of dining at long tables with hundreds of others was conducted asocially, without connection to the other diners. The constraints of speed forced diners to choose between eating and socializing, and in the interior everyone chose eating. Under such pressure, dining became a fully interior experience conducted in a crowd: diners transferred the foods of the interior into their private interiors while risking as few external abrasions to their social selves as possible.[10]

Among its other restrictions, the dining situation in the interior discouraged expression of class or taste difference. No one could demonstrate his membership in a superior taste culture by complaining about food that others were ingesting uncomplainingly, and no one could demonstrate social superiority by making special demands on waiters, food preparers, or dining-room managers. The dining experience was fully egalitarian—no diner had precedence, and no diner could demonstrate that he or she was a person of quality who could afford to make delicate choices, demand better service than another, spend more time over the food, have more friends to dine with, conduct a higher-quality dinner-table conversation than another, eat in privacy, or even make a choice of eateries. The enforced classlessness of public dining was, as always with class matters in the interior, a point of interest to some travelers and a source of agony to others.

Travelers divided drastically over how to read the manners of the long table. The American traveler Charles Fenno Hoffman found the manner of the eaters to be "grave and decorous at table, to a degree approaching to solemnity, though they ate with the rapidity characteristic of Americans at their meals." In contrast, class-conscious

British travelers were ideologically required to find the system revolting, and they did. The intensely class-conscious Frances Trollope found eating aboard an Ohio River steamboat an "ordeal" during which "it was impossible not to feel repugnance." Because Trollope was unable to grasp the style of manners being practiced, she judged the scene to show "a total want of all the usual courtesies of the table." For some, the democracy of the long table did not so much erase class difference as bring it into sharper focus. In 1859, John MacGregor, who claimed that few people liked better than he did "to consort with all classes," nonetheless objected to "forcing those people to an apparent equality whose habits and tastes are different, and who clearly indicate they are not at ease." MacGregor was ready to stoop to others' levels, but not to sit alongside them; he displaced his discomfort with the situation onto those whose presence had made him uncomfortable, and asserted that they would be happier and more comfortable if not forced to eat at the same table with him: "Sometimes," he confessed, "men sat next one without any coats; and more than once my next neighbor at the hotel dinner was a lad with bare feet. This futile attempt at 'equality' where both sides are uneasy, deepens that painful silence at meals, which I find almost intolerable." The Russian Aleksandr Lakier, traveling in the same year as MacGregor, reversed MacGregor's views and asserted that it was not the barefoot, coatless locals but the foreign traveler who was uneasy with the politics of dining: the fact that "all of the steamboat's conveniences were used on a basis of complete equality without any distinctions of title, rank, or status" constituted, Lakier thought, a series of shocks to a European traveler who would, as a result, express displeasure with the "local equality and would carry away a rather unfavorable notion of the society as a whole." Lakier reinforced his point by repeating the popular cautionary tale of a German prince who, not wanting to dine at the common long table on a Mississippi riverboat, asked the captain that dinner be served to him privately. Although the captain seemed to assent, at dinnertime he stopped the steamboat at an island, ordered a table set up on the island for the prince, escorted the prince off the boat to his private dining table, and then cast off, leaving the prince to dine alone on the island.[11]

If speed, silence, and social equality were at the center of the interior's dining rituals, money was on its margins. Although numerous travelers liked to assert that American society as a whole was obsessed with money, just as many travelers had experience of a broken or nonexistent connection between food and money in the interior. In 1809 in Illinois, the always cranky and complaining Fortescue Cuming found that locals would "accept no payment" for food they dispensed to him, and claimed it was "the first instance of disinterestedness we had experienced on the banks of the rivers" where all other services, he claimed, required payment. James Hall paid "reasonable prices for bread, butter, and milk" purchased at cabins during his travels in Illinois, but residents would not take payment for meals he ate in their houses, and most "seemed offended at being offered money" for food he procured from them. Harriet Martineau tried to buy wild strawberries from children who refused to sell because they could not connect berries with money; in that surprising situation, Martineau felt she had glimpsed "the end of the world; or rather, perhaps, the beginning of another and a better." In the interior, money measured the worth of food in neither private nor public situations; the money ritual and the food ritual were held one apart from the other. Money did not clarify the value of food; the fact that steamboat meals were included in the ticket price and hotel meals in the room charge further shaded money's connection to feeding. The controls placed over food in the interior were not, as elsewhere on the globe, scarcity and expense but rather time and space. The prevailing system in the interior's public dining spaces allowed large numbers of people entrance, for a restricted period of time, into the presence of a staggering abundance of food. No one paid by the dish or by the piece for what he or she ate; an eater paid not for the food directly but instead for a tightly circumscribed few moments of access to the abundance on display. Once in its presence, an eater could use the moment as he or she liked and attend to the foods of choice that were within reach. The weak connection between money and food had other effects: after the eating ritual on the steamboats was over, in a secondary display of abundance, all the leftovers were thrown into the river. On an Ohio River steamboat, James Stuart watched a steward throwing bread and meat overboard, and the steward told him that "no one in this country will make use of it."[12]

Such features of the dining situation as dinner gongs, long tables, and required speed affected not only the eating experience but the diet itself. It might be said that in the public eating spaces of the American interior, under conditions of intense mobility, there surfaced a diet and cuisine indigenous to the American interior that spread into private homes and into restaurants offering printed menus and pricing by the dish. The food culture of the interior was not a borrowed but an indigenous culture; like its refusal to assign value to imported luxury goods for the home, the antebellum interior refused to honor a borrowed food culture. This one was its own. The abundance of the diet of the interior involved neither a parade of dishes brought one by one to the table nor a succession of courses. Its abundance was simultaneously present—all elements of the meal at all their different temperatures and with all their different flavors occupying the table all together. Eating in a Cincinnati hotel in 1827, William Bullock wrote: "In no part of my travels have I seen a table spread with more profusion"—though Bullock did wish that the plates had been warmed and that he might have been granted "a little more time to enjoy the repast, twenty minutes only being allowed." Across the interior the public bounty was always on display; at the Planter's House in St. Louis in 1842, Charles Dickens counted fourteen dishes on the table at once. The food displays common in the interior were not general across the country, as those travelers who entered the Cotton South discovered. In 1833, Thomas Hamilton wrote that in his "steamboat progress down the western waters, [he] had become accustomed to a table loaded even to excess with provisions of all sorts. In the Southern States there is no such profusion. Our dinners on board the *Isabella* were scanty in quantity, and far from laudable on the score of quality." In the interior, however, food displays were taken for granted. Anthony Trollope was amazed by the spread that his fellow passengers saw as ordinary on a steamboat crossing of Lake Michigan in 1862: "A poor diet," he wrote, "never enters into any combination of circumstances contemplated by an American." The food practices of the interior had staying power: in 1889 Max O'Rell invited his readers to take a seat with him "at the *table d'hôte* of the best hotel in any second-rate town" in the interior. There would be, he claimed, no printed menu; instead a young woman would approach, "dart a look of contempt" at the diner, turn her back, and utter the following: " 'Croutaupoturbotshrimpsauceroast-beefturkeycranberrysaucepotatoestomatoesappletartmincepievanil-lacream.' Do not attempt to stop her; she is wound up, and when she is started is bound to go to the end," wrote O'Rell. "You must not hope that she will repeat the menu a second time either. If you did not hear, so much the worse for you. Unfortunately the consequences are grave; it is not one dish that you miss, it is the whole dinner. You are obliged to order all your repast at once, and the whole is brought to you from soup to cheese at one time."[13]

Besides observing no sequence of courses in a meal, the dining rituals of the interior further erased distinctions among foods appropriate to the three meals of the day and ignored imported beliefs about which foods appropriately accompanied others. Anthony Trollope found a steamboat supper of beefsteak, tea, apple jam, and hotcakes to be in no wise unusual for its mixture, and in 1855 Charles Weld ate at Cambridge, Ohio, a standard breakfast of "beefsteaks two inches thick, Indian corn-bread, molasses, and very sedimentary coffee." Charles

Dickens crossed from the East Coast into the interior on a canal boat where, at six, the long table was laid for supper with tea, coffee, bread, butter, salmon, shad, liver, steak, potatoes, pickles, ham, chops, black puddings, and sausages. The next morning at eight the long table was spread with exactly the same foods for breakfast; the noon meal was again the same spread, varied only by the absence of tea and coffee. "Some," wrote Dickens, "were fond of compounding this variety, and having it all on their plates at once." Frances Trollope noted also that ham and beefsteak appeared on the home tables of the interior at all three meals, and was astounded to see locals eat such combinations— all previously unknown to her—as eggs with oysters, ham with apple-sauce, and steak with stewed peaches. "No matter where you look," wrote Aleksandr Lakier after dining aboard a steamboat in 1859, "everything is mixed up on the plates." Observing such mixtures of food in 1884, Emily Faithfull announced that "the American stomach has been for years, generally and individually, the laboratory of the profoundest experiments in the matter of peculiar mixtures." These conditions further operated to award sugar a powerful position in the diet of the interior. A small supper offered to D. Griffiths in Ohio consisted of sliced beef, custard, and nutcakes—one meat and two sweets. Frances Trollope noted that locals in Cincinnati were "extrava-gantly fond, to use their own phrase, of puddings, pies, and all kinds of 'sweets,'" and expected them to appear at any meal. On the long din-ing tables, moreover, before the gong was beaten and the doors opened to the diners, desserts were set out alongside all the other foods comprising the meal. As a result, sweet items crept forward into the meal, available to be eaten along with rather than after the other food items. Even when the arrival of menus pushed dessert back to the end of the meal, other sweet items—especially sweet preserves—maintained their positions at earlier points in the meal. If, theoreti-cally, rapidity of eating indicated a minimal involvement with the food, the focus on sweets signaled, in contrast, a high degree of in-volvement, and a possibly conflicted set of attitudes toward eating.[14]

Meat dominated the diet of the interior; it was served three times a day on all levels of society and in circumstances both urban and prairie. D. Griffiths, who roamed Ohio during the 1830s and stopped at many private houses, found the most common breakfast offered him to be "fried pork steaks, boiled potatoes, toast saturated with cream, and coffee." At a St. Louis hotel in 1864 Milton Mackie com-plained that every time he ventured into the dining room for "a cup of tea and a bite at a biscuit, [he] never could escape the everlasting 'Have a beefsteak, sir?' of the waiters." Beefsteak was most commonly served up swimming in two inches of melted butter, a treatment that all travelers found both remarkable and constant. Meats other than pork and beef made fewer recorded public appearances; in 1822, John Woods reported that "these Americans hold mutton in the utmost contempt, and I have heard them say that people who eat it belong to the family of wolves. And many of them, who in the summer are sometimes short of meat, when their bacon is exhausted, would live on corn-bread for a month rather than eat an ounce of mutton, veal, rabbit, goose, or duck. Their dislike arises from prejudice, as many of them have never tasted these things. I have heard a few of them say they like mutton; but even if fond of it, they will never purchase it, for fear of the scoffs of their neighbors." Social pressure against the foods listed by Woods held strong in the antebellum interior; in 1843 William Oliver reported from Illinois that "mutton is never seen at table, except at the house of some person from the old country, or from the eastern states, and the natives cock their noses at it as we should do at a boiled rat." If neither pork nor beef was present at a meal, dairy products, especially cream and butter, rose to dominate in their place. At the home of Governor Chase of Ohio in 1859, Isabella Trotter and her husband were served a light supper consisting of apple compote, "a silver basket full of sweet cakes, of which the Americans are very fond," bread, fresh butter "in silver perforated dishes, and a large tureen of cream toast. This is also a common dish, being simply slices of toast soaked in cream and served hot. I thought the cream toast excellent, and a great improvement on our bread and milk in England, but papa did not like it." On most occasions, hot bread, cakes, and rolls served as carriers for the butter, and Godfrey Vigne noted that for Americans the rolls could never be "too new or too hot."[15]

Numerous travelers noted that the capricious climate exercised little effect on the habits of the locals, who continued to travel and to eat their usual diet without regard for the revolving seasons. The interior's fondness for ice, ice water, and ice cream—a fondness perhaps originally generated by the heat of the summer—came to transcend seasonal change and temperature shift. Residents of the interior, according to William Hancock, survived the summer by consuming "iced beverages in endless variety and unlimited quantity"; at a Cincinnati dinner party in 1859 the guests, according to Isabella Trotter, were served "piles of vanilla ice cream a foot and a half high" along with iced catawba champagne. And at a St. Louis hotel in 1864 Milton Mackie reported the waiters "handing about the ice cream in slices which suggested the resemblance of small prairies." The cold, the creamy, and the sweet held powerful positions in the diet, but always in combinations of cold-and-sweet or cold-and-sweet-and-creamy. Cold-and-intense-and-not-sweet was not a favored combination, as Godfrey Vigne had learned when he noted in 1832 that "nobody would touch a water ice, and in general cream ices only were to be met with." The beverage that came to dominate the long dining tables of the interior was perhaps the only beverage that could have accompanied the food mix as eaten: ice water, great pitchers of which lined the tables, their presence perhaps less related to the antebellum efforts of the temperance movement than to the fact that the interior had developed an ice-water cuisine, a thrice-daily repetition of meats and sweets that only water could stand up to, a democracy of eating that required democracy's drink, the one liquid that anyone could drink with any combination of foods.[16]

In the diet of the interior, vegetables, when they had any standing at all, occupied a shaky position. While vegetables were seasonal, the cuisine of the interior was making moves in a nonseasonal direction; furthermore, the quality of the vegetables of the interior came in for regular questioning. In 1826, Timothy Flint—a longtime resident explainer of life in the area—found it strange that "in this rich soil, and under this powerful sun," the roots and vegetables grown were relatively tasteless. "Take everything into consideration," wrote Flint, "this is not so good a country for gardens. The tender vegetables of a garden generally prefer a milder sun and cooler air." Frances Trollope, on the other hand, found the "common vegetables abundant and very fine" but noted that the harvest was very quickly over; the fruits of the interior, Trollope asserted, were miserable and sour. In the 1840s, ignoring the matter of cultivation entirely, some travelers liked to make great claims for the wild fruits and berries of the interior that, they asserted, would easily "supply the place of tame fruit"; Catherine Stewart suggested that wild berries might take the place of "those delicacies the farmer, in subduing a new soil, finds little leisure to cultivate," but the landscape cover that had produced wild berries and plums was being eradicated by the locals, and it was apparent that the uncultivated landscape could not supply the diet of the mobile population. In the meals offered by inns, hotels, and steamboats, foods that were seasonal, difficult to obtain, and in unreliable year-round supply simply did not appear unless in the form of pickles or sweet preserves.[17]

Claims that residents might eat from nature continued to appear, though moving steadily westward, into the 1860s; frequently the claims mixed the cultivated with the uncultivated. In 1856, Sara Robinson offered pages of guidebook praise for the "exceedingly lovely" Kansas climate and its abundance of melons, cantaloupes, and vegetables of all kinds, plus wild fruits and berries said to grow spontaneously there, but her experiences in the actual Kansas emerged differently. Fruits and vegetables receded from view when Robinson complained that there was "an abundance of nothing save cheese, beef, ham, and sugar." In search of greens the Robinson family took to eating not from the orchard of fantasy planted in the text but from actual Kansas nature: they ate mandrakes until warned off by the death of an entire local family poisoned by eating too many of them. Saddest of all travel books is Miriam Colt's *Went to Kansas* (1862), the narrative of a vegetarian family lured from the East Coast by the promise of joining a planned, prebuilt community in Kansas, only to find themselves in a land without vegetables. Aboard the steamboat down the Ohio, the Colts, as "plain eaters, had to pick here and there to get plain food." At dinner, out of the array of "meats and fish, cakes, pastries, nuts, and candies," only hominy was suitable to their dietary regime. Upon arrival in Kansas, the Colts learned that there was no planned vegetarian community awaiting them; they had bought a share of exactly nothing, and, without the elements of a vegetarian diet, they were forced to eat a diet of poverty in the land of abundance: "hominy, johnnycake, Graham pudding, *some* white bread, now and then stewed apple, a little rice, and tea occasionally for the old people." Refusing to eat at the top of the food chain as were others in the interior, the Colts suffered genuine deprivation.[18]

A thread of specific and indigenous food can be traced through travel literature about the interior, along with a thread of missing or rejected foods. Long-table dining favored large foods over small ones, since they were easier and quicker to transfer to one's plate. "The only difficulty," wrote Milton Mackie, "is in getting little enough of anything. Just a bite of a thing—*un morceau*—is an impossibility. A thin cut can't be had. A man, therefore, with a delicate stomach, is entirely out of place here, where the arrangements are all designed for persons who are ready to 'go the whole animal'." Foods that could be preserved, held on ice, or slaughtered on a reliable basis seized control. Pork, beef, potatoes, butter, and cream occupied the dietary center, surrounded by the equally reliable pies, puddings, and cakes and ringed by the eternal pickles and preserves. Seasonal or hard-to-obtain items dropped from sight, and vegetables occupied, apparently, the same dubious position in the interior as did the gardens that might have produced them. Spices, herbs, and intense flavors had no position at all; salt and pepper occupied the diminished position of seasoning. Nothing was attention-getting about the flavors of the foods; it was their abundance that seized the attention. In the absence of a printed menu, foods had to be preparable in quantity for easy visual identification by diners who were allowing themselves no more than twenty minutes to eat, and who wanted to see what they were helping themselves to. Consequently no meat was masked by a sauce; a steak swimming in two inches of clear hot butter remained perfectly identifiable as to its animal source and its cut. There were no prepared dishes—except puddings—whose contents could not be visually discerned, and plate decor was discouraged as pointless and of questionable edibility. Every food had to be not only identifiable but easily ingestible: hence all fish were beheaded and all bread was, as Isabella Trotter wrote, "alas! always cut in slices whether at the hotels or in private." Fruits that might have required peeling, coring, and special utensils were transformed into the easily eaten pie. Finally, nothing about the food was allowed to puzzle, delay, or take control over the eater, and no element of the dining ritual required the diner to express his wishes to anyone or to name foods. A diner who was going to risk eating drastically incompatible foods did not have to announce that plan to a waiter. No American in the interior was to be, at the long tables, intimidated by food, eating, preferences, taste choices, waiters, or other diners.[19]

Identifying desired foods by sight rather than by reading their names or naming them to a waiter—eating with one's eyes, in effect—had consequences: specific names of foods and dishes became blurred, or foods lost their names altogether. Travelers, whether they stopped at private houses, inns, or hotels, became familiar with "corn bread and common doings," a meal that included pork and bacon, and with "wheat bread and chicken fixings," a meal that could include ham, sausages, steaks, and more, along with the chicken. On the other hand, the broad label "relishes" could designate stewed crab apples, pickled eggs, salt-fish, steak, sausage, chicken, ham, bacon, cheese, butter, crackers, cream, bread, and sweet cakes. These generalized and overlapping codes for food made it possible to eat a great many foods without having to name them or specifically request them. When, in the 1860s, hotels in the cities of the interior attempted to import into this generalized food culture specific and named prepared dishes, the names were often confused, misspelled, or inadequate to the task of identifying the nature of the dish. In St. Louis, Milton Mackie saw on the menu of a large hotel "Lamb chop santees" and "Macaroni à la Italienare," and, like other travelers who claimed familiarity with foreign food cultures, scoffed at both the names and the preparations they referred to. "The kitchen," Mackie wrote, "is no cuisine. The cook is not 'abroad' in these parts. Both his dishes and his French are execrable." A recognizable name of a dish often failed to signal a recognizable preparation, but most diners in the interior were unbothered by such confusions because they cared little for "made dishes" and favored instead having everything about a food readily exposed to view, visually available for choice or rejection. When, at the long tables of the interior, all was set out to be eaten together or in any order desired, diners needed no specialized knowledge in order to eat and did not have to inform anyone of the nature or quantity of their food desires. Food and eating were not topics of conversation in the interior; the contents of the long tables came close to eluding entirely the confines of language and terminology.[20]

Dominant dining rituals were adjusted only to accommodate demonstrations of social inequality. The Planter's House in St. Louis, in antebellum slaveholding Missouri, was praised by many travelers for its excellent service and its "bountiful notions of providing creature comforts," but Aleksandr Lakier was appalled by the "unimaginable discipline" the hotel imposed on its black servitors: "Negroes serving at table must, at the first ring of the *maître d'hotel,* who is usually white, leave the dining room with measured steps and go to the kitchen for the food. Another ring and they change the plates. They enter and leave in step like precision soldiers; no one takes one step more or less than another. One of them sets a plate on one side of a long table; at that precise moment and with exactly the same gesture another sets a plate opposite it. Whether there is an unoccupied place or even a whole row of such places, the Negro is not flustered. He acts as if someone were sitting there and hovers about the table, all of it being done for the sake of monotonous harmony. When I saw these maneuvers by living black puppets, I did not believe my eyes." A dinner so served to numbers of phantom diners, according to Lakier, seemed "interminable" in its length; speed as a value had, at least at the Planter's House, found itself bested by a calculated display of social and racial inequality, a display that also pushed abundance out of its usual central position and onto the fringes of the dining experience.[21]

The dining ritual was also adjusted in order to define the interior's style of gender asymmetry and women's different relation to food. The adjustment took several forms: ladies first, ladies last, and no ladies. Aboard the steamboats, women passengers entered the dining room at the head of the line of diners, with the captain, and no man sat down until the women were seated; after that point the men dispatched the meal with the usual speed, scraping back their chairs from the table after ten minutes or so and individually rushing away. Sometimes the women "did not follow the general example and remained a little longer" at the table. In other dining situations women took last place. In Michigan in 1839, Caroline Kirkland watched her neighbors, a woman and her grown daughter, prepare a noon meal by setting out sliced hot bread, a plate of fried pork, and bowls of milk, yellow pickles, applesauce, and mashed potatoes. At the sound of the dinner horn, men and boys rushed into the room, filled all the seats at the table, and "fairly demolished in grave silence every eatable thing on it. Then, as each one finished, he arose and walked off." Before the dinner horn was sounded, Kirkland had watched the two women prepare their appearances for the arrival of the men by vigorously combing out their very long hair all over the food-preparation site. On that count, Kirkland wrote, she "had made sundry resolutions not to touch a mouthful," but when the men rushed in and took all the seats at table, she was mortified to be robbed of even the opportunity to refuse the food. Kirkland thought she would get nothing to eat, but, after the men had left, the two women cleared and relaid the table, and invited Kirkland to sit down with them to bread, applesauce, pickles, "a plate of small cakes and a saucer of something green cut up in vinegar. I found we had only been waiting for a more ladylike meal," wrote Kirkland. This gender-divided dining scene suggests, however, certain definitions of "ladylike." In this same Michigan society, servants were always affronted by suggestions that they might eat separately from the family, or at a later time; here, however, Kirkland's two women neighbors took on a social position that hired help always refused. Just as Kirkland was about to be seated at the ladies' reduced and postponed version of the meal, however, her husband arrived in the company of the land speculator he had been dealing with and announced that the Kirklands must depart at once. As the still-hungry Kirkland was whisked out the door by her husband, she looked back to see the land speculator slide into her seat at the table and tuck into what had been her plate of food. Throughout the complex situation, a woman's chance to eat sank lower and lower on the scale of priorities—below men's food requirements, below women's appearance requirements, below business demands, until finally it dropped off the scale altogether and Kirkland went hungry. Twice during the visit, food that Kirkland thought would be hers was eaten by men, and on both occasions she saw them eat it.[22]

Whatever the women ate at their separate meals, no man wanted to join them in eating it: at a rough hotel in Rolla, Missouri, Anthony Trollope, however unwillingly, joined the other men in a "general stampede into the eating-room" at the crash of the gong, noting that if he hesitated to join the men he would have to eat later with the women, "and your lot will be then worse." On certain social occasions women and men ate simultaneously but separately and differently. At a Washington's Birthday Ball at a hotel in Cincinnati, the men, Frances Trollope reported, left the ballroom for a sit-down dinner "spread for them in another large room of the hotel." The women remained in the ballroom, each was given a plate, and waiters appeared "bearing trays of sweetmeats, cakes, and creams. The fair creatures then sat down on a row of chairs placed around the walls, and each making a table of her knees, began eating her sweet but sad and sulky repast." When Trollope questioned the custom, she was told that "the arrangement was owing neither to economy nor want of a room large enough to accommodate the whole party, but purely because the gentlemen liked it better." Furthermore, since no table was set for the women, they could not be served the dinner; their dining situation could be described as the uncomfortable consumption of the solace of sugar. The diet of the interior was thus in many senses a white man's preserve; the dining ritual could be slowed or elaborated only by certain demonstrations of race and gender, and was apparently most comfortably engaged in by men on a gender-separated basis. Women's eating could be a partial shadow of men's eating, or an eruption of sugar. The dining rituals exerted pressure on women by emphasizing gender difference and feeding it differently, and the food situation in effect dramatized the social structure of the interior. When eating could be used as a performance of matters of race and gender, it was.[23]

Even in small-scale and isolated dining situations, the dining rituals of the interior held steadily to their focus on speed, silence, repetition, and gestures of gender differentiation. In 1857, Thomas Gladstone stayed at an isolated inn in Kansas; washing facilities behind the inn consisted of two tin basins "filled with the muddy water of the Missouri," a square foot of mirror, and a comb and brush suspended on a string. Gladstone's room held two beds, two shuck mattresses, and three other occupants besides himself. The inn was unpainted, unchinked, and uncarpeted, but its dining was ritualized, and the movements of the diners were as practiced and precise as those of dancers. The table was laid for breakfast at six with the usual fare: meats, cakes, apple preserves, applesauce, fat bacon cooked in grease, corn bread, molasses, tea, and coffee. When Gladstone entered the dining room, "the crowd," as the innkeeper referred to the guests in general, was already stationed around the table. Each man stood with one hand upon the back of his chair. The ritual began. The women seated themselves, the innkeeper gave a signal, "and a simultaneous action ensued," wrote Gladstone of the men's movements. "The movement of the chair with one hand, the seizure of the nearest small dish with the other, the sudden sitting down, and the commencement of a vigorous eating, were the work of a moment. In five minutes the company had left the table for the gallery or the street front," there to await the next meal. Dinner at half past noon was the same, the same foods in the same quantities ingested with the same ritual; supper at six was the same. And, wrote Gladstone, "the next day the same."[24]

Though every traveler might have observed scenes of eating identical to those Gladstone saw, they noticed these scenes differently, depending on the traveler's gender. In 1838, James Logan focused on the eaters and saw a meal in the interior as an "every man for himself, and none for his neighbor" proposition, whereas in contrast Ida Pfeiffer attended in 1856 to the preparers and noted that the sameness of every meal in the day or week "spared the ladies much trouble in contriving a variety of dishes." These and many other seemingly small divisions in viewpoint and experience become, when added up, the great gulf that in the nineteenth-century interior constituted the gender divide and signaled not only difference in attitudes but separation in space. The spatial gender divisions of the nineteenth-century interior, no matter whether as gestures or as strictly enforced realities, constricted the behavior of both men and women and rendered them to each other as mysterious.[25]

Chapter 7

Strangers

Aboard the gorgeous white-and-gold steamboats that churned the rivers of the antebellum interior, a traveler strolling the deck fore to aft took a walk that began in squalor and ended in luxury. The fore compartment was a men-only area where gathered "the tobacco chewers, the smokers, and the card players" and where, according to numerous male travelers, a man might well find himself among low life and hard cases in a "dim, close atmosphere, reeking with tobacco and rum all day and all night, crowded with dirty, vulgar, swearing men." The men-only barroom came next, and was equally foul; in the center of the cabin deck was the dining room which, though often ringed with shelflike berths for men, was used by both genders and was therefore cleaner. Its rear doors opened into the Ladies' Cabin, a glittering paradise of gilt and plush luxury. Emmeline Stuart-Wortley, among others, lingered in description of its "sumptuous upholstery— the flowery devices of the many-colored carpets—the sweeping curtains—the profusion of ornaments." A man afforded even a passing glance into the Ladies' Cabin was often sufficiently stunned by its "magnificent and luxurious appointments" as to say, as Aleksandr

Lakier did, that he "did not know if it were possible to wish for a better dwelling on *terra firma*."[1]

The Ladies' Cabin had, however, another feature never observed by passing men. Amid its blue and white and gold splendor stood an ironing board on which, according to Eliza Steele, "all the ironing of the boat, and crew, and often of the passengers, is done . . . the steam and perfume of the wet clothes, charcoal furnace, and of the ironer is extremely disagreeable. In one instance I knew this to be the case all night, the girls taking it by turns." In all of her steamboat travels on the Illinois, the Mississippi, and the Ohio rivers, Steele claimed, she "suffered from this annoyance" and finally demanded to know "why may there not be a room in some other part of the deck" where the ship's ironing could be done. But in the insistently gender-divided space of nineteenth-century America, ironing was not among the few activities classified as gender-neutral: it was a domestic activity, and women who occupied the upholstered pastel splendor of the Ladies' Cabin were reminded that it was to their part of the world that housework, with its heat and odors, was assigned, and that even if they themselves were not ironing, ironing was theirs to live with.[2]

The American gender divide that travelers experienced and studied in detail assigned specific behaviors and activities to either one gender or the other, resulting in a world sharply and asymmetrically split. The Ladies' Cabin was designed to contain a form of being that, throughout most of the nineteenth century, was defined as distinct from the form of being that smoked and swore in the forward quarters reserved for men. Anything one gender could do the other must not do, and each had to avoid the behaviors and activities of the other or risk censure, loss of identity, isolation, and scorn. Men and women did different work, had different access to money and amusement, spoke in groups about different subjects, wore different clothes, ate different food at different rates, were subject to different judgments on their looks, were required to manage their bodies differently, practiced different manners and different addictions, had different access to both space and information, worked within different limits imposed on looking at and speaking of the other gender, and were subject to different degrees of definability. Among the few gender-neutral activities available, however, were traveling, writing, and getting oneself published. Anyone, regardless of age or gender, could be a travel writer and, sitting in gender-divided space, perform the gender-neutral activity of writing about gendered space.

Travelers observed physical gender division most fully on the steamboats and trains, at the large hotels, and at certain large social events. Few analyzed the ideological underpinnings of observable attempts at gender separation: they neither rehearsed theories of gender superiority nor discussed then-current notions about physiology and gender. But they did describe and often groan over gender division, and they had a great plenty to say about daily life in the gender divide: about what it meant to work, eat, sleep, wash up, and travel in it, and about how it was maintained and where it broke down. They noticed that divisions strictly maintained in the cities of the East tended in the interior to wobble and occasionally crumble altogether. Travel itself exposed the weakest points in the gender divide: it was class-based, it created asymmetrical inconvenience, and it could not govern the world of work and movement. Division between men and women operated no more clearly in the interior than did divisions between public and private, indoor and outdoor. As a series of gestures, however, the gender divide made itself known to every antebellum traveler, and some of those gestures persisted far beyond midcentury.

Not all women traveling on the steamboats of the interior were lodged in the Ladies' Cabin: it was reserved for those who could buy into its vision and pay for its splendor. On the open deck below, passengers who had bought the cheap tickets traveled en masse in a space defined by no gender division but what they might have chosen to create. The life they lived on the lower deck was partially visible but not understood from the deck above; no traveler saw across the class divide, and most cabin passengers stepped on the lower deck only on embarking and disembarking. It cannot be known whether men who booked deck passage controlled their behavior in the presence of women, while male cabin passengers could in the men's area engage in unrestrained and unpoliced behavior. It is, however, clear that cabin passengers belonged to no single identifiable social class, since a mixture of classes continued to torment international travelers: in 1859 Aleksandr Lakier complained that first class was so "awful a mixture of classes and levels of education" as to silence male passengers who could not imagine "what to talk about or with whom"; on the other side of the gender divide, the Swedish novelist Fredrika Bremer in the Ladies' Cabin took care to avoid all but those "few upper-class passengers who are not of the catechising order."[3]

Such remarks raise the question of who was being kept apart from whom aboard the steamboats. Although men's behavior in the presence of other men was construed as unrestrained, and although many male travelers found other men's behavior disgusting, no traveler seems to have thought that physical division of men and women was about protecting women travelers from danger, since dominant social attitudes toward women already cocooned them in protections. If the division protected women from exposure to the behaviors practiced by men in their own space, it also stowed women away in a space where men did not have to think about them. Physical separation of the two genders aboard the boats and elsewhere can be read as a purchasable class status, as recognition of the necessity to offer women refuge from men's uncontrollably bad behavior, as allotting space for men to engage in behavior that women were not supposed to see, and as an effort to prevent sexual contact that was nonetheless never spoken of.

All travelers agreed that women, even women alone, could travel anywhere in America in perfect safety; some women travelers were warned of certain dangers of travel, but they neither articulated these dangers nor experienced them. Women traveling in groups or alone moved through the interior so "protected by public opinion and every honest man" that by midcentury travel had become, according to Thomas Mooney, "a mania with the ladies." Clara Bromley asserted that in her position as "a woman and a stranger," she "met with no word or act of annoyance from first to last" in her travels, and such famous women travelers as Fredrika Bremer, Harriet Martineau, and Emily Faithfull were ushered from hand to hand, as it were, and escorted by a kind of relay team of governors, railroad officials, and first citizens. Sometimes women were perceived as so automatically protected by their very gender that they were abandoned to dangers that their local escorts refused to face. In 1856 at Springfield, Illinois, Isabella Bird was left to travel alone when her American escorts refused to go on with her to Cincinnati: "There were lions in the streets; cholera and yellow fever, they said, were raging; in short, they left me at Springfield, to find my way in a strange country as best I might." Furthermore, when traveling alone, men and women experienced different kinds of solitude. While many men travelers who undertook solitary journeys spoke of the terrors of physical solitude on the landscape of the interior, lone women's journeys were socially solitary. Traveling in Michigan, Anna Jameson found herself utterly alone, the solitary occupant of the ladies' parlor in a hotel "swarming with dirty, lazy, smoking men." Across the divide no man could speak to her and she could speak to none of them; though she rejected them, in fact it was she who, while in place in the ladies' parlor, was painfully out of place in the scene itself.[4]

A woman moving alone through the interior could always, however, count on one thing: a seat on any conveyance with wheels. The rule that all men were to give up their seats on all transport to any and all women held firm at the center of the gender divide, the only rule that never lurched or wavered. Conformity with the rule was policed by other men. Aboard a crowded train in central Michigan, the English traveler Isabella Bird watched one man after another give up his seat as women entered the car. The women, Bird wrote,

> took possession of them in a very ungracious manner. The gentlemen stood in the passage down the center. At last all but one had given up their seats, and while stopping at a station another lady entered. 'A seat for a lady,' said the conductor, when he saw the crowded state of the car. The one gentleman did not stir. 'A seat for a lady,' repeated the man in a more imperious tone. Still no movement on the part of the gentleman appealed to. 'A seat for a lady; don't you see there's a lady wanting one?' now vociferated several voices at once, but without producing any effect. 'Get up for this lady,' said one bolder than the rest, giving the stranger a sharp admonition on the shoulder. He pulled his traveling cap over his eyes, and doggedly refused to stir. There was now a regular hubbub in the car; American blood was up, and several gentlemen tried to induce the offender to move. 'I'm an Englishman, and I tell you I won't be browbeat by you beastly Yankees. I've paid for my seat, and I mean to keep it,' savagely shouted the offender, thus verifying my worst suspicions. 'I thought so!—I knew it!—a regular John Bull trick! just like them!' were some of the observations made, and very mild they were, considering the aggravated circumstances. Two men took the culprit by his shoulders, and the other, pressing behind, impelled him to the door, amid a chorus of groans and hisses, disposing of him finally by placing him in the emigrant-car, installing the lady in the vacated seat. I could almost fancy that the shade of the departed Judge Lynch stood by with an approving smile. I was so thoroughly ashamed of my countryman, and so afraid of my nationality being discovered, that, if anyone spoke to me, I adopted every Americanism which I could think of in reply.

The seats-for-ladies rule was enforced without regard to class, a fact that astonished and even appalled male travelers from abroad. Aleksandr Lakier, to his own disbelief, reported that he had "been a witness as a man got off a public omnibus in order to give his seat to his housemaid, only because she was a woman." A lone woman traveler might well occupy two seats even on a crowded conveyance; the French traveler Max O'Rell claimed that on the trains an American man of any social level would "seek a place from one end of the train to the other before he will go and seat himself by the side of a young girl" or even choose to stand "rather than run the risk of incommoding a young girl by sharing a seat with her." Even though men in the interior, according to report, never said thank-you for anything whatever, international travelers of both genders were nonetheless irritated when women for whom they gave up their seats did not thank them. Francis Lieber thought that American women accepted seat-sacrifice and other politenesses from men so nonchalantly that they "deprived their social life of much of its charm," but others simply labeled the women rude and complained about their failure to be grateful for signals of "general respect." When a man's giving up his seat to a woman is read as a "general" offering from any social superior to any social inferior, it is clear why *every* man offered it to *every* woman, and every woman's failure to be grateful emerges as a visible note of resistance to a limited social position granted her by men. Nowhere, travelers insisted, were women more generally respected than in America; respect so general, however, marked women as a group of indistinguishable beings carefully seated for the ride but disconnected from the mainstream of personal achievement and individual identity. If all seats constituted women's special preserve in public, the rest of the arena was marked out for men.[5]

Nothing else about women's lives approached the complete clarity of their having to sit down. On every other count gender ideology lurched, often wildly, but nowhere did ideology and reality crack heads more resoundingly than in the area of work. In the cities of the East, many travelers had been shown for their admiration certain delicate flowers of womanhood notable for their disoccupation. Some were not bothered by that vision of pampered womanhood until they reached the interior, whose working landscape challenged the gender fiction that women did not, could not, and should not work. The vision looked terrifyingly inappropriate to life in the interior, and it seemed that someone would suffer for trying to import it. Margaret Fuller worried about transplanted women who, with no household help and seven full days a week of tasks to perform, tried nonetheless to maintain "refined neatness" in the home and to see themselves as "ornaments of society." Eliza Farnham blamed the "artificial and pernicious" education these women had received in the East for having "thoroughly distorted" their minds and made unendurable the change their life underwent in the interior. When Fredrika Bremer met at St. Louis young women who struck her as "rare hot-house plants" and "articles of luxury" lodged in expensive hotel suites, she wondered how they might function when exposed to the open air: Bremer's exposure to the interior had brought her to condemn both the "life of twilight in comfortable rooms" led by such women and the "physical weakness" that accompanied it as utterly inappropriate to their geographical location. Neither Farnham nor Bremer, however, was unconflicted on the subject. Farnham cherished a life of domestic refinement for herself and in Illinois maintained it whenever possible;

and when Bremer met young women who were not delicate, who were accustomed to work, and who were unafraid of the out-of-doors, she was appalled at their lack of refined manners and their blunt and open approach to her. "I did not scruple to cut them rather short," she wrote. "I regard these girls as belonging to—the mythological monsters of the Great West, as daughters of its giants." Although no one required refinement of men in the interior and everyone saw that delicate refinement was an unsuitable goal for women, strong and hearty women without refinement were nonetheless often found terrifying and unacceptable by both men and women travelers.[6]

While all travelers struggled with locating a socially acceptable vision of a working woman, on the subject of paid work for women they divided sharply on gender lines. Male travelers praised Americans for "never burdening women with public employment," and required women who worked as teachers and nurses to display to them "sweet faces . . . and genuinely concerned attention" as if to prove that earning had not destroyed the qualities society admired in them. Male travelers further read the fact that women rarely worked in public as a kind of pampering of women; because they did not see or gauge the time and effort consumed by unpaid work, they judged it to be no kind of work at all. These same travelers were fully aware that in American society doing paid work validated a person; because women had little access to such work, they were classed, as Michel Chevalier pointed out, with "children, minors, and idiots." From the other side of the gender divide, Harriet Martineau, Marianne Finch, and Emily Faithfull were openly critical of restrictions on work for women. In 1853 Finch wrote bitterly of the asymmetrical work situation at Oberlin College in Ohio, where all students worked but the women were so poorly paid that they had to work nine hours to earn what a man could earn in three, and thus had that much less time to read and study.[7]

Because such paid work as was available to women in the cities of the East was rarely available in the interior, the visible division in work that came to travelers' attention on the landscape of the interior was that between fieldwork and domestic work. This is not an indoor-outdoor division because a good deal of domestic work was carried on out of doors; an accurate division might be between fieldwork—done by men—and nonfieldwork, done by women. All travelers, men and women, approved of this division. Michel Chevalier claimed it to be a universal American rule that "the woman . . . is never seen taking part in the labors of the field," and when travelers saw women working in the fields, they blamed it on the unmelted Old World practices of "some German and Dutch farmers" and called it "barbarous." Harriet Martineau insisted that "German women are the only women seen in the fields and gardens in America, except a very few Dutch, and the slaves in the south." The actual division between fieldwork and nonfieldwork was less than clear. In 1853 Fredrika Bremer insisted that "it is the men in this country who milk the cows, as well as attend to all kinds of out-of-door business," but in 1856 Ida Pfeiffer sliced up the work differently; she insisted that American women never "dragged home fodder for the cattle" but did "perform the domestic employments, milk the cows, and make butter, etc." The interior's always weak distinction between indoors and outdoors made it difficult to distinguish fieldwork from domestic work, and made it unclear on which side of the work divide cow-milking should be lodged. In contrast, who could hire help was utterly clear. "The farmers with their men" and "the men's assistants in field labor" drew regular mention from travelers—all of whom admitted that women in the interior were without domestic assistance except from their daughters.[8]

Most of the assessments of women's work issued not from women travelers who had seen and done it themselves but from male travelers who, while staying at private homes and small inns in the interior, saw perhaps for the first time in their lives what kind of work and how much of it women did. They were not comfortable with what they saw; their ideas about class and work told them that someone else—some woman they could not see—should be doing such work. In 1823 William Faux was appalled that the "ladies" of the families he visited in the interior worked; he represented them as forced to work because they could hire no servants. In 1824 William Blane thought the women of the interior "the most industrious females I have ever seen in any country"; Blane did not frame the subject with a lament about absent servants. In 1829 Gottfried Duden renewed the class-based view of women's work: servants, he complained, demanded such unaffordable wages that wives and daughters of innkeepers were left to "perform the most menial household tasks" themselves while an unassisted innkeeper had to "care personally for the horses." When travelers connected women's work to servants, they operated on class assumptions alien to the interior, and were forced to suggest that some women should work so that others need not, or insinuate that work for women was temporary, and would end when—by some magical intervention that never did occur—brigades of potential servants appeared in the interior. By 1832 Simon O'Ferrall cut the subject of women's work free of class and servants when he straightforwardly described women who cooked all day in order to serve up to men three large hot meals and called their life "no sinecure." When travelers ceased thinking that women should not work, or would soon be relieved of work when servants arrived, they had to face the fact that women did work. In 1867 William Dixon watched the women of the house "whipping away plates" while the men sat by, and found the sight "trying to the nerves. The evidence of inequality," he wrote, "meets you at every turn." How it felt to be the plate-whipper at an inn or a home where strangers continually stopped was described by Eliza Farnham's sister in Illinois as "a severe burden to us females." A life of feeding and putting up movers was most fully described by Sara Robinson in Kansas in 1856; her book is punctuated by its notation: "The house is at all hours full of company . . . there is seldom a meal that we have only our own family of five . . . the house now is full in every corner. I give up my room again, and make two extra beds on the floor . . . several more strangers were in in the evening. A gentleman, just arrived from Massachusetts, is very ill . . . a part of our guests left a few days since, and on the next day, on a short half hour's notice, we had six gentlemen and a lady to dine . . . four more strangers were in, in the afternoon . . . I took a short ride on horseback, to get away from care . . . found other company on return . . . the house was full all day, and nearly all night. . . ." Robinson's husband seemed to be always away, and when he came home he brought with him still more strangers to be fed and housed. Any picture of husband and wife working side by side at home is difficult to retrieve from the travel-literature archive wherein the more usual picture is division—the husband off here and there, the wife at home, or both racing off in different directions.[9]

Travelers who wished to describe a working life in the interior but also wished to conceal the gender of the workers resorted to composing sentences free of human actors: "For most of the harder work of housekeeping," according to Gottfried Duden, "there are ways of making the labor easier. If, for instance, laundry is to be done, a fire is lighted next to a nearby brook and a kettle is hung over it." Women also employed this sentence-composing tactic when describing work done by another woman, as when Juliette Magill Kinzie noted: "Biscuits were baked, a ham, some tongues, and sundry pieces of salt-pork were boiled, coffee roasted and ground, sugar cracked. . . ." Eliza Farnham used the tactic to list chores a man may have been performing: "The tenants of the farm-yard are now astir; the cows are milked; the generous oxen are summoned to the yoke." Other travelers, when they could not ignore or deny women's work, tried to identify various distractions or rewards. In 1835 Charles Fenno Hoffman noted that "the females indeed will sometimes murmur" but indicated that their labor would surely be rewarded when they saw the prairie flowers bloom in the spring. In 1839 Francis Grund's local informants assured him that women in the interior were "obliged to work" but were "infinitely happier than your New York or Philadelphia ladies" and that absence of household help in the interior constituted "a great corrective to our vulgar aristocracy of money." Catherine Stewart claimed that numerous women whose "domestic duties were arduous" solaced themselves by thinking of "the prospects this new country held out to their children." Ida Pfeiffer denied that heavy domestic work could be thought burdensome when the women who did it were "always well dressed; indeed, that matter the good ladies carry somewhat to excess, and make their appearance on Sundays in grand state with gold watches, rings, and chains." In antebellum America, only residence in the hotels of the interior offered relief from domestic work; travelers unfamiliar with the phenomenon remarked continually on the number of families evading the problem of the unaided domestic workload by taking up residence in the huge hotels that dotted the interior. Sometimes only a segment of the family substituted the hotel for the home: in Cincinnati many married men, according to Frances Trollope, went off to eat turkey and venison dinners at the long tables of the hotels while their wives "regaled themselves on mush and milk at home." In these cases a woman who did not cook also did not eat.[10]

Travelers were quite certain that a woman's primary relationship to food was as its producer. Cookery, though highly valued, was not recompensed; however, the more food a woman could prepare, the more highly she was esteemed. A lucky stranger, Catherine Stewart claimed, who stopped at the ideal cook's house and sat down to "bacon and eggs, perhaps prairie hens, fresh butter, mealy, pink-eyed potatoes, and the refreshing beverage of tea or coffee" could not help but feel "complacency"—and, added Stewart, might also "derive a charm from the easy intelligent conversation" of the cook herself. In the interior, a man's relationship to food was solely one of consuming a lot of it rapidly, but a woman's relationship to it, beyond production, was less clear. The rushed eating atmosphere of the interior rarely allowed women to put on the displays of delicate eating that would differentiate them from the ravening, gobbling men; to try for such an effect could mean doing without a meal. Corn, ubiquitous on the tables of the interior, often furnished a test case for delicate eaters. Aboard a steamboat the English traveler Mary Duffus Hardy mistook corn on the cob for "a stuffed delicacy" and asked for "a small piece." Her fellow passengers smiled, and the captain dropped a whole cob on her plate. Although Hardy watched the other eaters for cues on how to eat the thing, in the end she could not bring herself to pick up the cob and go at it. "I don't think it is worth the trouble of eating," she announced. Not to eat at all was a choice available to women, though it was never approved for men, on whose part a refusal to eat was construed as illness or insult. Men not wishing to consume something that appeared on their plates had to resort to stratagems to get rid of the food item; they could not leave it on the plate uneaten. For women, however, not to eat was a socially approved choice, and it had in the nineteenth-century interior no connection to body weight: thin women were neither valued nor approved of. Both genders connected women's eating to judgments about delicacy and grossness. Eliza Steele thought that the food served aboard the steamboats of the interior was of high quality and might satisfy "the most fastidious palate . . . were it not for one thing—our western brethren are so fond of fat. Almost every dish of animal food is swimming in a greasy liquor." The delicate Steele, however, made no noise about the indelicate food: "I make it a point," she wrote, "of taking things as quietly as if I had ordered everything." By declining the gravy, she managed to obtain "a tolerably dry" piece of meat, and otherwise "secured a pleasant and healthful repast" for herself by choosing only vegetables, Indian bread, and "nice stewed dried peaches" at every meal.

Steele disciplined her own diet apparently unaware that anyone might be watching her, but some were always watching, and their eye was on red meat. In 1829 Gottfried Duden asserted that "the too frequent eating of meat produces unpleasant results among members of the feminine sex" and defined those results as "a number of prevalent ailments." He exhorted women to "restrict themselves to coffee, bread, and butter during the morning." Duden's view was dominant by 1850, when women were regularly told to consider avoiding meat altogether, and most certainly to avoid being seen in proximity to meat that was not well done; the influential food writer Eliza Leslie claimed that "ladies" found "any red or bloody-looking food disgusting." One attempted solution to the perceived gender split over red meat was to serve meat only in the privacy of gendered groups: at parties, men might eat steak in a separate room, whereas aboard steamboats cold beef might be served and eaten in the privacy of the Ladies' Cabin. Gendered attitudes toward eating, however, were too complex and extensive to be so easily handled: Anna Jameson, who recorded more conversation with men than did many women travelers, reported hearing "some men declare that they cannot endure to see women eat," and others "speak of brilliant health and strength in young girls as being rude and vulgar, with various notions of the same kind too grossly absurd and perverted even for ridicule." Women travelers' accounts make it clear that in an all-female setting, women ate more slowly than did men, ate—if any—less meat than men did, and filled out the meal with sweet items that were not served to men. Occasionally, however, women ate riotously when alone with each other: aboard a steamboat on Lake Pepin, Ida Pfeiffer recorded a scene of a group of women eating corn on the cob in quantity and then "pelting each other with the gnawed cobs." It seems that corn on the cob, which inhibited some eaters, released others into food behavior never otherwise observed.[11]

Both genders restrained their behavior in the presence of the other, but the restraints were asymmetrical. Men restrained their speech even to the point of total silence, and never in the presence of women engaged in any of the cursing and swearing said by male travelers to be constant in men-only compartments. Isabella Bird said that no matter what the mixture of persons she traveled with in the interior, she "never heard any of that language which so offends the ear in England. I suppose that there is no country in the world where the presence of a lady is such a restraint upon manners and conversation." Bird reported that she "never heard an oath" until she crossed into Canada, and Richard Burton claimed that restraints broke down only on the other side of the Missouri, where coach drivers were "not to be deterred from evil talking even by the dread presence of a 'lady'."[12]

Men were not required to control their limbs in the presence of women; in fact, the interior had no rules whatever on limb discipline for men. Men sprawled, flung their legs about, and put up their feet on everything; when they sat they propped their feet on every railing or item of furniture available, and when they stood they put one foot up on anything nearby. Women, on the other hand, observed strict limb discipline and abandoned it only when among other women and even then only when seated in the rocking chairs favored by nineteenth-century America. Alone with each other in a Ladies' Cabin or Ladies' Parlor, women seated in rocking chairs put up their feet on ottomans or low tables and rocked vigorously. Watching them "vibrating in different directions and at various velocities" gave Harriet Martineau a headache; aboard a Mississippi River steamboat Ida Pfeiffer claimed to have seen ten women pull ten rocking chairs into a circle, sit down, fling their hands over their heads and stick their feet out. Then "away they went full swing," wrote Pfeiffer. "There was certainly nothing very delicate or feminine in their appearance while they were engaged in this exercise." No man recorded ever having glimpsed such a scene. Ida Pfeiffer, despite her prissy disapproval, correctly called vigorous rocking "exercise," because it exhibited each characteristic of what passed as exercise for women: it was sedentary, it went on indoors, and it was unseen by men. Outdoor exercise in the interior belonged to men; women were excluded from it by the asymmetrical rules governing limb discipline, by the cumbersome clothing whose necessity only the rarest among them ever questioned, and by their lack of opportunity to acquire physical aptitudes that they might have put to use in the interior. The landscape of the interior, whether cultivated or natural, seemed closed to women: Margaret Fuller pointed out that most women in the interior had learned neither to ride, to drive, nor to row, and their satin-and-paper shoes put both walking and climbing out of the question. As a result, Fuller wrote, "their resources for pleasure were fewer." To some travelers, women seemed utterly disconnected from the landscape: in 1838 Harriet Martineau observed aboard a steamboat women locals who, she asserted, did not care even to look upon nature; they never went on deck but sat all day in the Ladies' Cabin "working collars, netting purses or doing nothing." Three years later, Eliza Steele wanted to argue with Martineau's claim, but when Steele wrote that women "knew the scene by heart, and need not brave heat and storm to see it, as a stranger would," she indirectly admitted the truth of Martineau's observation.[13]

If a woman took a risk on the landscape, men acted pleased about it. In 1831 Hannah Backhouse's ability to drive a coach-and-four was in great demand on the muddy stump-littered roads of the interior, Anna Jameson was congratulated for shooting the rapids at Sault Ste. Marie, and Jessie Benton Frémont was well thought of for undertaking a two-day mule ride without "complaints, or tears, or visible breakdown." Women, however, rarely remarked on other women's physical efforts, and only Harriet Martineau recorded a scene of apparently general approval of a woman's activity. On a hot day along the Mississippi, at a brief steamboat stop to take on bread and vegetables, a passenger named Mr. B insisted that Mrs. B, though "stout and elderly," should disembark with him and undertake to climb a river bluff. A panorama of observers—the passengers on deck, the workers on shore, a man on horseback atop the bluff—all froze in place enthralled by the spectacle of the Bs' climb. "The husband lent his best assistance," wrote Martineau, "and dragged his poor lady about one-third of the way up: when she suddenly found that she could not go a step forward or back: she stuck, in a most finished attitude of panic, with her face to the cliff, and her back to us, her husband holding her up by one arm, and utterly at a loss what to do next." At that point, a "stout boatman" rushed to their assistance and helped Mrs. B to turn around, whereupon she descended the bluff easily. It is interesting that though Martineau described both the rescued Mrs. B and the rescuing boatman as "stout," the man's stoutness had not disabled him from

activity as Mrs. B's parallel condition had. Even more important, however, was Mrs. B's reaction to the climb: "She won everybody's esteem
by her perfect good humor . . . she was perfectly contented with having tried to oblige her husband. This was her object, and she gained it;
and more—more than she was aware of, unless indeed she found that
her fellow-passengers were more eager to give her pleasure after this
adventure than before." Martineau's narrative suggests that access to
nature and movement in it need not have been gendered as they
were; everyone was pleased with Mrs. B's attempt on nature but Mrs.
B herself who, hampered by her clothing and her lack of conditioning, was pleased only to have obliged her husband. The story suggests
that women complied with gendered attitudes that men both regretted and tried to alter.[14]

Women in their turn, accompanied by a chorus of international travelers, regretted a specific behavior on the part of American men: their
spitting. The end result of the tobacco-chewing that was nearly universal among nineteenth-century American men, spitting drew more
commentary from and caused more social agony and personal revul-
sion to travelers across the century than any other American behavior.
Although most international travelers, before coming to America, had
read reports of Americans' chewing and spitting, all claimed that experiencing the practice firsthand surpassed their every expectation of
its awfulness. Tobacco-chewing's effects were kept somewhat out of
sight in New England, but travelers who visited chewing's main arenas—Congress in Washington and everywhere west of the Alleghenies—learned what it meant to live in its presence. Spittoons were
ubiquitous; travelers described seeing "the national piece of china . . .
in all parts of all houses," beside seats on trains, under the table in
restaurants, "standing sentinel" outside every hotel room, forming a
line up the stairs in public buildings, in courts where judge, crier, witness, prisoner, jurymen, and spectators were individually provided for,
in hospitals, in churches, and in pulpits. Neither spittoons nor boxes of
sand, however, could contain the flood of tobacco juice. There could
not be enough receptacles for it; the entire landscape became its re-
ceptacle. Streets, walkways, boat decks, the floors of trains and hotel
lobbies, all were described by travelers as coated with brown slime.
Frances Trollope claimed it to be impossible for women to protect
their dresses from it, Charles Weld said that after an hour's travel on
any train the floor was flooded with it, and Newman Hall could see
"not a dry spot remaining" in the American interior. Carpets were
soaked with tobacco juice: William Blane "heard it alleged, by way of

excuse, that it did the carpets good, and killed the moths," but Blane thought he "would rather have all the moths in America at work on his carpets than have them spit upon by tobacco-chewers." Chewing and spitting became the full occupation of the occasionally disoccupied: aboard a Missouri River steamboat, John MacGregor noted that the men did not "read or even pace the deck, but consumed the whole day in spitting," and William Baxter, on an Ohio River steamboat, timed a tobacco-chewer who "squirted with remarkable regularity, according to my watch, seven times per minute, or 5040 times in the twelve hours." In 1842, Charles Dickens was watching a sunset from his train window when his "attention was attracted to a remarkable appearance issuing from the windows of the gentlemen's car immediately in front of us, which I supposed for some time was occasioned by a number of industrious persons inside ripping open feather beds, and giving the feathers to the wind. At length it occurred to me that they were only spitting, which was indeed the case; though how any number of passengers which it was possible for that car to contain could have maintained such a playful and incessant shower of expectoration, I am still at a loss to understand." Both Charles Dickens and Thomas Hamilton claimed that American men spat in their sleep, or perhaps never slept at all because they were too busy spitting.[15]

Some male travelers tried to frame chewing and spitting as either a skill, an art, or a competition, but none of those compartments could either contain it or make it tolerable to them, and no prizes were awarded; even the most humorous among the travelers felt their humor failing them in the presence of spitters. Charles Dickens "was surprised to observe that even steady old chewers of great experience are not always good marksmen. Several gentlemen called upon me who, in the course of conversation, frequently missed the spittoon at five paces; and one (but he was certainly short-sighted) mistook the closed sash for the open window at three." In 1855, in the lobby of the Burnet House in Cincinnati, Charles Weld observed that local marksmen ignored the spittoons and "preferred filling the concavities" of the lobby's fluted pillars. In 1865, George Borrett framed spitting as a trial of nerves for the noncompetitor: "Enter into conversation with two or three of them," he wrote, "and you will have to keep it up under a crossfire of murky jets squirted across your face, over your shoulder, between your legs, over your hat—everywhere, in fact, within a bare inch of your person, as if you were standing up to a performance of the Chinese juggler's impalement." Who did the work of cleaning up the mess was suppressed, though it was most certainly never cleaned up by those who put it there. Although Charles Weld noted that each morning at the Burnet House "a lavatory process

[was] effected by a hose discharging a powerful and copious stream of water, which caused a brown cataract to rush down the hotel steps," he did not note the identity of the hose-holder.[16]

In the literature of travel and description, men from abroad wrote extensive commentary on chewing and spitting, but no traveling American men ever mentioned the subject. All women travelers wrote of it, even those too refined to name the practice they were criticizing. Women travelers from abroad sometimes tangled themselves in inoperative class distinctions when they wrote of spitting: Clara Bromley said that on *her* side of the Atlantic she had never seen "peasants or artisans so offensive in their personal actions as those who call themselves American *gentlemen*," and Mrs. Felton concluded that spitters had dropped off the social ladder altogether and were "unfit for the society even of those females who have the lowest claims to respectability." Such efforts at class distinction did not function in an arena where all men spat and where men refused to connect spitting to manners. There was no etiquette of spitting: Emily Faithfull said that she could not "resist a smile at the national politeness which compels an American to lift his hat and remain bareheaded if a lady enters the hotel elevator, and yet permits him to spit in front of her before they reach the next landing."[17]

Although many women felt their class level lowered when men spat in their presence, gender division over tobacco use was enforced only in regard to smoking. "On the boats," Fernando de Zavala noted, "smoking is not allowed except in a place designated for it, in order to avoid the discomfort that the ladies have from the smoke." The distinction is nice: women were protected from smoke, about which not one of them ever complained, but had no protection from the spitting which each and every one of them found loathsome. The niceties that men had chosen to observe were not the niceties the women might have chosen had they been making the rules. Men's chewing and spitting made Margaret Fuller wish that men would follow Indian example and take up the pipe, but in the interior it was women who smoked pipes, though rarely in public. Several months into his Missouri residence in 1829, Gottfried Duden realized that there were in his neighborhood "some fairly well educated women who smoke," and Caroline Kirkland claimed that "a large proportion of the married women in the interior of Michigan use tobacco in some form, usually that of the odious pipe." Women's use of tobacco was, however, kept covert, even among other women. Eliza Steele did not know that she was among women who smoked until her steamboat hit a log and the wheelhouse was smashed to pieces; out of their staterooms popped ladies, their pipes still in their mouths, to see what all the noise was about. Other uses women might have made of tobacco are not clear. Aboard a Lake Michigan steamboat that Isabella Bird described as "a fairy scene, an eastern palace, a vision of Arabian nights" decorated with flowered velvet-pile carpet, carved walnut furniture cushioned with green velvet, marble tables on gilded pedestals, massive vases of exotic flowers, and eight chandeliers, there was a porcelain spittoon in the Ladies' Saloon, and, wrote Bird obliquely, its "office was by no means a sinecure" there.[18]

Gender-divided confusion over tobacco was intense: women did not chew, spit, or smoke in public; men chewed and spat everywhere, regardless of women's presence; men never smoked in the presence of women, who smoked in private. In her consideration of such bodily refuse as saliva, the anthropologist Mary Douglas argues that all matter issuing from bodily orifices is "marginal stuff of the most obvious kind" and should be considered not in isolation but in connection with other social relations. From this angle several possibilities emerge. The spitting men were managing their social relations by creating their own rules; they gave up their seats to women, doffed their hats, curbed their profanity, and spat. At Niagara, Margaret Fuller watched a man take his first look at the falls and then spit into the waters, but on the steamboats of the interior men chose to spit on the deck rather than into the river. If by spitting on something a man "best appropriates it to his own use," as Margaret Fuller wrote of the man who spat into Niagara, then spitting American men were claiming as distinctly and absolutely *theirs* every space they spat on, including spaces occupied by women. Spitting was a power-laden gesture expressive of contempt, disdain, domination, and repugnance. When men spat everywhere, they took for their use the landscape, built or natural, whether at home, at work, at meals, or in travel, no matter who was present, who was sickened or inconvenienced, or who was made to clean up after them, and they never spoke about what they were doing.[19]

A silence not gendered but national prevailed over another difficult subject—the bodies of both women and men. Male travelers whose country of origin was anything but the United States looked openly at American women's breasts, hands, feet, hair, eyes, and any other part that they could glimpse. Edouard de Montule had been thinking that American women rarely had "truly lovely breasts" until, he wrote, some glimpses he stole in Missouri changed his mind. Fernando de Zavala thought American women had "very good color, large bright eyes, and well-shaped hands and feet" but lacked the "elegance and voluptuous manner of walking of our Mexican women." Friedrich Ratzel disliked white American women's "narrow little heads with thin hair and pale faces" and preferred the "healthy natural beauty" of women of color; and Max O'Rell spent his time in America admiring "the daintiest little hands and feet in the world" and judged the women of the interior to be too thin for his taste but prettier than women in the East. To a man, these same international travelers believed that American men were not looking at women: "A Frenchman," Max O'Rell wrote, "will always stand back to let a lady pass, but he will profit by the occasion to take a good look at her. The American, in similar circumstance, will respectfully lower his eyes." Although Edouard de Montule sought to get on an intimate footing with a woman at each stop on his itinerary, American men were never suspected of such travel activity. "Intrigue," wrote Francis Grund, "is unknown in America." So little did nineteenth-century Americans speak of each other as physical entities that a reader might page through hundreds of volumes of travel and description and believe with Max O'Rell that American men did not look at—much less desire— American women, were it not for an extraordinary narrative written by the Scots traveler James Logan. Logan's narrative is remarkable in the scattershot practice of nineteenth-century travel writing for its sustained length; it is most unusual, however, in offering a view from the lower deck of the steamboat and a moment-by-moment detailing of how it felt to join the working underclass usually ignored by the cabin passengers who rode above it.[20]

In October of 1837, James Logan had reached Chicago, the halfway point on his planned tour of the interior, when he ran short of money. Rather than write to his brother in Ontario for more money and have to wait about in Chicago for its arrival, he determined to continue on his planned itinerary to Joliet, Peoria, and St. Louis, and then eastward up the Ohio. Once that decision was made, however, Logan became exquisitely sensitive to everything he paid for: a Mississippi River steamboat operator, he wrote, "contrived to cheat him" of both the supper and the bed included in the twelve-dollar fare by departing three hours behind schedule and crushing forty cabin passengers into a twenty-berth boat. Logan also began to worry about confidence games: a speculator who befriended him on the crowded boat asked Logan "as a favor" to exchange his remaining three gold sovereigns for the speculator's silver, and Logan did so but privately felt uncertain about the evenness of the exchange. Logan began to practice small economies: he shared a bed with the speculator and thereby compromised his previous insistence on having a bed to himself. As his cash dwindled, Logan decided to take deck passage just once, just to get from Peoria to St. Louis; and because deck passengers were supplied with none of the food laid out for cabin passengers, he supplied himself with some bread and cheese. Then he plunged on to a level of travel that no other travel writer ever described.

Deck passage was just that—a deck; furnished with just one stove for heat, the open space was not only cold but too crowded to allow Logan either to lie or to sit. He stood throughout the three-hour trip. Despite his travel economies, Logan discovered at St. Louis that he could not afford cabin passage on the *Cuba* from St. Louis to Pittsburgh: he had but fifteen dollars remaining and cabin fare cost twenty. For eight dollars he bought deck passage again, spent another three dollars for a store of bread, cheese, and apples, and boarded the lower deck. "I should have done so from choice for part of the way," he wrote, "in order to see a little of the habits of those who travel in this manner; but certainly would not have willingly gone such a distance as 1200 miles, and encountered the hardships to which one must submit in traveling in this manner."

During the first days of his deck journey he worked to keep up his traveler's voice by describing Ohio River scenery and offering such facts as came his way. Because the *Cuba*'s deck was open to the elements, it allowed him to see plenty, but because there was no partition around the machinery of the boat, the deck was very dirty, and there was no place to sit. When, four days later, the *Cuba* arrived at Louisville, Logan's store of food was exhausted; he bought coffee, ham, bread, and apples from another passenger, leaving him with two dollars in his pocket and three hundred miles to go. Still unwilling to write to his brother for money, Logan instead signed on to "wood for the boat," which meant that he was roused every two hours around the clock to carry or throw wood onto the deck. He earned one dollar total for wooding and later earned another dollar by loading pig iron for twenty-five cents an hour. He reduced his meals to two a day, and also cooked for other deck passengers who had stores of food but were "not so good" at cooking as he was. As his stomach emptied, his politics sharpened; he ceased remarking on scenery, and instead began to dilate negatively on "aristocratic feeling in America," class division, slavery, and rich people who "ape European manners and expect obsequiousness from the poor."

When Logan signed on as a deck worker, he gained access to a set of berths in the stern, partitioned off from the open deck, and from that vantage point he observed phenomena not visible to nonworking deck passengers. One day he saw several male cabin passengers grouped "at the stern of the boat, where there is a small space to walk in, enclosed by a railing, looking up through some holes cut through the flooring above, and by laughter expressing their gratification. The object of their merriment did not strike me at the moment; but one of them let it out that he had seen something exceedingly interesting." After a moment's thought, Logan realized that the holes through which the men were peering had been drilled in the "only part of the deck where ladies can sit or walk in the open air." Throughout the journey to Pittsburgh, Logan watched a stream of male cabin passengers descend to the lower deck to look up through the holes in hopes of seeing under a woman's skirts. What these men might have seen in 1837 is unquestionable: women at the time wore multiple petticoats but no underpants, since in gender-divided America such garments were considered unacceptably similar in cut to men's clothing.

Logan considered warning the ladies above but was constrained by the "inevitable indelicacy in doing so"; he considered speaking to the captain but did not want to be laughed at. Furthermore, when he learned from other boatmen that the peepholes were a "pretty general" feature of steamboats, Logan felt certain that the captain already knew of the parade of voyeurs. When Logan put his below-deck observations together with the "numerous gross remarks" he heard aboard the *Cuba* from men of all classes, he judged that American men, though they had "not yet attained the acme of vice boasted of by France, are fast verging toward it." Logan's narrative provided a revelatory moment in nineteenth-century travel literature. His narrative recast the Ladies' Cabin from protected private space to space wherein women were clustered to furnish a peep show to men. Max O'Rell's assertion that American men did not look at women in public was rewritten by Logan: American men did not look at women in public because they preferred to gather in private, snickering groups to spy on them. It was, however, also obvious to Logan that some male cabin passengers preferred spying solo; these men descended to the deck but departed when they saw other men already at the peep show. Meanwhile, the surface delicacy to be observed in antebellum America, the impossibility of speaking to women of matters sexual, prevented Logan and indeed any man from telling the women above how they were being used.[21]

Throughout the century, men and women spoke differently about sex and spoke of different sexual events. The genders divided on the signals they used for reading loose morals among women, and had no parallel set of signals that indicated loose morals among men. Ernest Duvergier de Hauranne saw American women whose appearance "upset all [his] ideas of propriety and which can cause a foreigner to draw many false conclusions. But, whatever one may say about them, I have yet to see one of them sit down in an omnibus on a man's lap."

West of the interior, however, Henry Morton Stanley felt secure in judging the probable morals of women "carrying fancy derringers slung to their waists." No woman read the same signs men read, nor did international women travelers read the same signs that American women read. Aboard a Lake Superior steamer, the Austrian traveler Ida Pfeiffer was mystified when American women performed a public ostracism of a woman "about thirty . . . rather too youthfully dressed" who had "long ringlets falling on her shoulder, and a round straw hat." Scarcely had this woman boarded the boat when another woman passenger warned Pfeiffer not to speak to her, "as it was thought she did not look like a person of good character." The sector of virtue that these women were policing never revealed itself to Pfeiffer. Occasionally a male traveler spoke callously of rape, as Francesco Arese did when he told in a jokey tone the story of a woman being "passed around on the prairie," but women travelers never spoke of rape. Only one woman traveler ever described the effects of a bungled home attempt at an abortion, and that was Caroline Kirkland, who wrote a detailed description of a young woman, previously a live-in helper of hers, dying at home in convulsions and so "swollen and discolored" as to be unrecognizable. Kirkland protected herself as a reporter by claiming she was "entirely unable to understand" the cause of the young woman's death, but nonetheless went on to murmur of knowing others who had assured her "that this was but one fatal instance out of the *many cases,* wherein life was periled in the desperate effort to elude . . . public scorn" and then to whisper further that she had since learned of "more than one instance of a similar kind."[22]

Although Kirkland might cautiously and without risking censure lift the veil over the effects of attempted home abortion, no woman could without raising public outcry speak of men's bodies. Only the risk-taker Anna Brownell Jameson, who traveled alone through the northernmost interior, took the chance. Even though some male writers such as Francis Lieber claimed that "many very respectable females, of course not ladies of the higher circles, travel alone in the United States," Anna Jameson, in 1838, knew that she might be "exposing [herself] to misapprehension, if not even to severe criticism" when she set out alone. Her prediction was correct: she was ostracized, "branded with notoriety," and unable to "break or thaw the social frost" that other women directed at her. Only, however, when she described a meal she ate in the "company of two back-woodsmen, who appeared to me perfect specimens of their class—tall and strong, and bronzed and brawny, and shaggy and unshaven—very much like two bears set on their hind legs," did she court total "misapprehension." Jameson described both herself and the two men as much "too busy" with the food to express any curiosity about one another, and made it clear that after the silent meal she went on her way alone. However, other women travelers, notably Eliza Steele in 1841, read Jameson's *Winter Studies and Summer Rambles* and lingered in examination of her diction—*bronzed, brawny,* and *unshaven*—and of her bear metaphor. Out of another context in Jameson's book, Steele pulled Jameson's description of herself as "a poor, lonely, shivering woman," combined it with the vision of upright bears, and thereby saw something intolerable. Steele condemned Jameson for her "errors" without naming them, and warned any woman thinking of emulating Jameson to write a book of "voyages around my own room" instead. When a woman described the body of a male Indian, she invariably immobilized him with references to Greek statues and allowed her description to be construed as an interest in art; but when a woman described mobile white males with references to bears, she was read as publicly expressing an interest in male sexuality. The bears not only failed to shield Jameson's true subject, but actually functioned as a giveaway.[23]

In antebellum America, all women—women traveling with companions, eminent women with international reputations escorted by celebrities and officials—took a chance when they put themselves in the public eye. Writing, however, was differentiated from speaking; a woman speaking in public was a disgrace, but a woman could write and not necessarily be disgraced. Furthermore, feminists and outspoken writers might be extended private courtesy but delivered up to public jeers: "The consideration paid to ladies by an American gentleman in his private capacity," wrote Emily Faithfull, "is not always accorded to them in the exercise of his journalistic capacity." Frances Trollope was skewered for her looks and her voice, Fredrika Bremer for her age, looks, and single status, and Harriet Martineau for being without "delicacy of feeling." In a society that required women to be ornamental, women travelers such as Trollope, Martineau, and Bremer were viewed as answering to some other requirement; if they were not controlled within the category of ornament, they threatened the very existence of that category, and thereby risked being pitched into another publicly available category for women: the coarse, the ugly, even the monstrous. In the 1820s when Frances Wright lectured publicly on sexuality she violated two taboos at once, provoked public violence, and was labeled by the male traveler Andrew Bell "a venomous vixen." Other male travelers repeated stories that pictured Wright's lying on a sofa for days at a time, paying little or no attention to others around her, and occasionally producing such utterances as "I believe that bears are of more value than men." That statement, which was perfectly clear and perfectly unacceptable culturàlly, men represented as delphic. Women stepped on dangerous ground when they spoke of bears and men in the same sentence.[24]

All that could not be spoken of caused enormous trouble and a grand confusion of arrangements in the mobile nineteenth-century interior; within the gender divide as elsewhere, a comfortable position was elusive. The gender divide was elucidated less in words than in spatial arrangements whose nature and operation had to be visually intuited by travelers. When gender arrangements were violated, no one was able to address the violations on the scene, though travelers often ruminated over them later. James Logan did not know how to speak about the peepholes in the deck of the *Cuba* to either the ship's captain or the women being peeped at, and he never considered speaking to the voyeurs themselves. Aboard the steamboats, apparently clear divisions of space between men and women were violated not only vertically, by men peeping at women from below, but also horizontally, by married men who had physical access to their wives—and thereby also to other women traveling in the Ladies' Cabin. Married men surprised a number of women travelers who had thought the Ladies' Cabin offered spatial privacy and learned that it did not.

Frances Trollope found the interior's gender divide always "remarkable," if not silly and antisocial. She was appalled by its rigid enforcement aboard a steamboat in 1828 that allowed no man to enter the Ladies' Cabin and offered no alternative space undivided by gender. Trollope watched a couple "who really appeared to suffer from the arrangement. She was an invalid, and he was extremely attentive to her, as far, at least, as the regulations permitted. When the steward opened the door of communication between the cabins, to permit our approaching the table, her husband was always stationed close to it, to hand her to her place; and when he accompanied her again to the door, he always lingered for a moment or two on the forbidden threshold, nor left his station, till the last female had passed through. Once or twice he ventured, when all but his wife were on the balcony, to sit down beside her for a moment in our cabin, but the instant either of us entered, he started like a guilty thing and vanished." Such a rigorous policing of the divide did not last. Because the steamboats were crowded, and many male travelers found the accommodations reserved for them to be miserable, men appropriated women's accommodations when they could. In 1833, aboard an Ohio River steamboat, Thomas Hamilton and friend were able to appropriate the Ladies' Cabin simply because there were no women aboard. Such a situation was, however, very rare: more frequently the Ladies' Cabin was converted to split uses, or men were split on the basis of marital status, and those attached to a woman invaded the Ladies' Cabin. The gender divide was blurred and became a spatial battleground for the always slim rations of privacy and comfort; women had themselves hustled from one spot to another in order that men might be accommodated. On a Lake Michigan steamboat in 1837, Harriet Martineau and the other women aboard had to pile into their berths as early as seven in the evening so the packet company could put up male passengers for the night on the floor of the Ladies' Cabin. The movement required of the women was not verbalized: "The men simply began to troop into the cabin and lie down," Martineau wrote, "without troubling themselves to give us five minutes' notice, or to wait till we could put up our needles or wipe our pens." On an Ohio River steamboat in 1853, Marianne Finch was summoned from the deck by the stewardess and requested to retire, "as the gentlemen wished to go to bed. I followed her, wondering how my retirement was connected with the gentlemen going to bed. On reaching the cabin, I found the ladies had disappeared behind a red curtain that was drawn across the upper end of it; the remainder was converted into a dormitory for the gentlemen, by having three rows of shelves put up, each furnished with a mattress and coverlet. I had been hastily summoned that I might not witness the occupation of the shelves by the gentlemen, whom I found in various stages of preparation."[25]

These invasions occurring on short notice, these broken and ineffective gestures at gender separation, took place in a world not of language but of space. In other situations, however, speech bore no reference point in behavior. On the next—and much more crowded—steamboat she boarded, Finch observed the extreme delicacy of a woman who expressed public shock at hearing "an Englishwoman announce the birth of a nephew by saying that her sister 'was confined,' which she thought a very indelicate way of communicating that interesting fact." At bedtime, Finch and seventeen other women, none accompanied by a man, learned that they would have to sleep on the floor of the Ladies' Cabin, and the woman of delicate sensibilities turned out to be Finch's mattress-mate. As the two women began to undress, Finch spotted a man's face peeking at them through the open transom of one of the staterooms ringing the Ladies' Cabin. Only at this point did Finch learn of still another nonverbalized gender policy: on many steamboats married men, though not allowed in the Ladies' Cabin during the day, were allowed at night to enter their wives' staterooms, and thus have their needs for comfort, privacy, and sex answered to. Finch pointed out the voyeur to her delicate mattress-mate, who "coolly continued her disrobement, saying, 'What a shame for him to look out there.'" A moment later, reported Finch, two more men entered the Ladies' Cabin and walked around it in search of their wives' staterooms; meanwhile the delicate lady had, according to Finch, undressed down to "garments that doubtless she would have fainted to have heard *named* before ears masculine. However, she did not lose her consciousness at *appearing* in them before eyes of that gender." Finch found incomprehensible such gender arrangements and attitudes. Finch's mattress-mate had been trained to express public horror at the mention of bodily matters, but in a gendered group of seventeen women she became available for public view by men, and displayed the body that she would not allow to be spoken of in her presence. In a further confusion, women were to pretend that the Ladies' Cabin was their private space when it obviously offered little or no privacy. When attempts at sharp spatial gender separation failed, married men gained not only physical access to their wives but also visual access to a large group of unaccompanied women. The gender divide was at its shakiest in the interior, where life was so public as to allow delicacy to be maintained only in speech. Fernando de Zavala thought that "among the notable things in the domestic society of the United States, especially in the interior, should be listed the false modesty that degenerates into hypocrisy in conversation"; meanwhile numerous travelers noticed that nonverbal behavior went on in a world unpoliced by the standards that policed verbal delicacy, and that American women never seemed embarrassed by anything.[26]

In the nineteenth-century interior, Americans had agreed to act out but not to speak of a hierarchy of spatial arrangements. White married men had access to spaces assigned to both men and women; white married women and white single women had equal access to spaces reserved for ladies; and single white men were confined to men-only spaces. Indian men traveled among white men on the boats and trains, but no traveler ever reported the presence of Indian women among the non-Indian women; an occasional traveler reported the presence of an Indian family on the deck, but never in the boat's cabins. On the interior's travel scene black men appeared only as costumed servitors, and black women were rarely mentioned. At a Cincinnati boarding-house in 1838, Harriet Martineau reported seeing at table "a better thing than I saw at any other table in the United States, a lady of color breakfasting in the midst of us," but such a detail is extremely rare in travel literature about the interior. In an America divided by race, gender, class, and marital status, white married men had the best of it in terms of access to space, and they were often described as somewhat happy. Within the class of white persons most fully observed by travel writers, the most difficult experiences of gender and mobility were had by two groups who rarely met each other—single men and married women.[27]

Lone male travelers from abroad, accustomed to being thought of as desirable and interesting fellows, felt their position sharply reduced in the interior, on whose social scene they were kept entirely apart. In contrast, no male American traveler ever found the situation worthy of remark: from their point of view a man alone had the advantage of being free to do as he pleased in any arena of activity or endeavor. No lone man, however, could of his own volition greet or speak to a woman without its being regarded as a sexual solicitation. A woman might enlist him as her servitor or he might offer himself as such, but in neither case could he expect a reward, thanks, or further acquaintance. The special treatment of women that allowed men to pay no attention to them also prevented men from paying attention to them, prevented men and women from understanding each other's lives and attitudes, closed off exchange of information, and left the lone man at the very bottom of the white social ladder. For some it was a social agony such as they had never experienced before.

In 1859, John MacGregor studied from afar a group of women and their male companions occupying one end of the steamboat saloon: "The remarkable exclusiveness of American society (a feature I was quite unprepared for) makes it impossible for a bachelor to speak to these fair passengers," he wrote, and complained bitterly of being "driven to the other end" of the boat, into "a dim, close atmosphere, reeking with tobacco and rum all day and all night, crowded with dirty, vulgar, swearing men, who are all civil when the ice is broken, but then the ice is so very thick. With these companions I slept on the floor . . . I think there is scarcely any means of traveling made so abominable, or that might be made so pleasant." In 1866, on a ferryboat on the Mississippi, the French traveler Ernest Duvergier de Hauranne, who had no female companion or protector, was made at mealtime to wait with "the humble crowd of single men" at the back of the dining room until everyone else was seated. At a signal, these men were "crowded around the table at the lower end, and obliged to wait through three or four services before capturing a morsel of half-spoiled beefsteak or a piece of ham as tough as wood." To de Hauranne, the "rigid laws" that kept him apart from women—and indeed from any social contact except that with other lone men—served as proof that Americans "feared the contrary excess." There were more humiliations in store for de Hauranne. On a night train from St. Paul to LaCrosse, no sooner did he choose a seat than he had to give it up. He was shuttled from seat to seat and from car to car as everyone else claimed social precedence over him; in despair he left the train altogether, went out to the platform, and "sat down by the door to the toilet" to await the train's departure. He had a long wait, and turned his attention to the "splendid moonlight," the green countryside, the puddles left by a recent rain. He leaned his head against the wall of the toilet and dozed until a conductor noticed him and, after questioning him with a superior air, patted him on the shoulder and let him into the ladies' car. De Hauranne's status rose thereby, and his very nature changed; on American railroads, a conductor's authority was unquestioned, and if he admitted de Hauranne to the ladies' car, he had certified him as safe. No sooner, however, did de Hauranne take a seat than a woman passenger entered the car and fixed her eye on him. Nudged to action by his seatmate, he was forced to rise and once again lost his seat. The conductor who allowed de Hauranne into the ladies' car had apparently classified him as too pathetic to be a threat to the ladies, but he did not become a lady by entering the car, nor was he admitted to ladies' society or status; he became invisible until his seat was needed. He was still, after all, garbed in trousers, and had no claim on a seat if someone in skirts wanted it.[28]

Men were not dummies, and many of them made their way through the mobile world of the interior by attaching themselves to women—any women—who, they believed, had greater access to comfort than men did. Any traveling man could see that a married man could either cross the gender divide and occupy the women's quarters or, if he liked, stay in the men's quarters. So men took action, and without making any verbal claims whatsoever, mimicked the behavior of married men in order to achieve more comfortable accommodations for themselves; married men's travel privileges, it seemed, could be exercised by any man who could publicly mime attachment to any woman. In 1865 George Borrett explained to his European audience a crucial difference between European and American travel: in Europe a woman companion was seen as a drawback to comfortable travel, whereas in America a woman companion constituted a man's sole access to even a hope of comfort. As a result, Borrett complained, a bachelor in America had "a hard time of it" unless he was "not particular to a T" and was willing to resort to "any low artifice" in order to convince railroad conductors or steamboat stewards that he was attached to a woman, whereupon they would admit him to the ladies' compartment. En route from Cleveland to Chicago, Borrett practiced till he succeeded. "With some officials," he wrote, "the doing of a little light porterage in the way of a shawl or a dressing-case I have found to be quite sufficient to identify me as 'belonging to that lady.' With one it was necessary to do some heavier work and carry a very dirty disagreeable baby for an ugly ill-dressed mother before I could induce him to give me a berth as 'one of the party.'" As was usual in gender matters, it was not language but a public performance that had effects: since no conductor or steward could possibly have said to Borrett, "Sir, are you married to this woman?" or "Sir, did you father this baby?" a convincing performance of toting a woman's stuff sufficed to put Borrett in better traveling conditions. When a woman chose to call on male helpfulness, however, the man so used did not gain a place in the ladies' quarters. In 1856, aboard the *Thomas P. Roy* on the Mississippi, Ida Pfeiffer saw a young woman summon a passing man into the Ladies' Cabin and "without ceremony ask him to fasten her dress, though there was a female attendant and plenty of women present who could have rendered this service." The woman's action had no effects: try as she might, Pfeiffer could observe no further connection between the two.[29]

Gender-divided conditions of mobility in the interior operated to close off from social connection not only lone men but also married women. Across the century all travel writers defined the married man as the instigator of continual family mobility and the married woman as the unhappy follower: men were discontented when not moving or planning a move, and women were socially isolated by the results of continual movement. Travelers, however, divided by gender in their readings of women's resultant condition in the interior and on what might compensate them for their loneliness.

Women travelers actually spoke to local women about their lives, whereas male travelers constructed their theories from a distance. Frances Trollope thought that the women she met in the interior were the true "slaves of the soil," prematurely aged by "hardship, privation, and labor." Women told Harriet Martineau stories of men who, regardless of success in one place, moved on to another, and became in each new location "a man of business, a man of consequence, with brightening prospects." Meanwhile the woman found herself, as Eliza Steele wrote, a thousand miles from her sisters, mother, and friends, five hundred miles from a good stove, two hundred miles from an unspoiled cake of yeast. "Surrounded by difficulties or vexed with hardships at home, provided with no compensation for what she has left behind, she pines away, and wonders that her husband can be so happy when she is so miserable." Caroline Kirkland failed to find any compensation for women in constant removals, but claimed that because a woman usually hid her unhappiness from the man who had made the decision to move, the man then "made his wife a drudge without compunction" and considered her unfulfilled desires and lack of enjoyments "a trifle." Frances Trollope noted "no periodical merry-making, no village fête" that might cheer a woman, and one woman traveler after another remarked on the absence of social connection, amusement, and the intellectual life. Women in the interior usually displayed to Mary Elizabeth Blake a mood she characterized as "apathetic dejection"; Ida Pfeiffer saw the mood rise occasionally to "calm resignation." Among women travelers, only Fredrika Bremer offered, as compensation for social losses, worship of the gods of neatness and cleanliness. "No neater nor more excellent home can be found on the face of the earth than that of the American women, even of the poorest," she wrote, but she went on at once to pinpoint who benefited from such excellent neatness: "No wonder that the husband is happy within it." The bliss was his alone.[30]

Men travelers who saw in women the same loneliness and social disconnection sometimes dismissed them as phenomena lasting no more than "a few weeks." Furthermore, while noting that mobile married men were often driven onward by the lure of wealth, male travelers simultaneously condemned any woman's display of personal benefit from that increased wealth in the form of personal decoration, and strongly advised prospective emigrants to take care that their profits did not fall into the hands of their wives and daughters to be spent on "tawdry finery." A society that both required women to be decorative and condemned them for decorating themselves left them little place to stand. Michel Chevalier characterized the interior as determined to "nail women to the kitchen and the nursery from the day of their marriage to the day of their death," and he saw in it no compensation for women.[31]

In the antebellum interior, married women called upon to furnish comfort neither defined it nor experienced it: if comfort existed, it was experienced by men, whose desires created discomfort for women; if comfort was absent, women took the blame. From early on in the interior, travelers noticed the custom, foreign to them, "of the wife not sitting down to table until her husband and the strangers have finished their meal," as Fortescue Cuming observed in 1809. In the 1830s, Caroline Kirkland saw women working while their husbands sat, watched, and "complained if things were not just so," and Margaret Fuller met women "struggling under every disadvantage to keep up the necessary routine of small arrangements. While their husbands and brothers enjoyed the country in hunting or fishing, they found themselves confined to a comfortless and laborious indoor life." When the "small arrangements" of comfort broke down under illness, isolation, and overwork, travelers both male and female moved to blame women. James Stuart criticized the "indolence and inactivity" of a woman who, he claimed, "has probably broken her husband into her way of thinking, that they can live as well without as with the ordinary comforts of life." Stuart's assertion is remarkable for its candor about who demanded and who supplied comfort. In 1846, Eliza Farnham likewise claimed that sloppy homes were related not to poverty and lack of resources but to women's incapacity "to appreciate a better condition or help to create one." Farnham's charge fails to identify who it is the woman would be helping in the project of betterment. All discussion of married women's difficulties in the interior avoided cross-racial comparisons. The unending white critique of the white construct of Indian marriage—the Indian husband hunting, fishing, and carrying nothing while his Indian wife "sank at every step under a heavy burden"—was always firmly represented as utterly unlike white marital work arrangements.[32]

The wedding, meanwhile, was elaborately celebrated on the interior's greatest icon of mobility, the steamboat, whose bridal apartments were claimed by both men and women to be the most lavish sight ever to strike the eye of a traveler. Aboard the *Bostona* in 1853, Emmeline Stuart-Wortley described the bridal apartment as "a complete mass of elaborate gilding and painting, and of satin, velvet, ribands, and lace in a thousand festoons, and fringes, and loops, and tassels. The force of upholstery and haberdashery could no further go." Men were equally dazzled: in 1855 Charles Weld marveled over "beds covered with white satin, trimmed with gold lace; painted cupids suspended from the ceiling," toilet facilities of ivory and the finest china, velvet upholstery, soft pile carpets, and floral designs covering every wall and door. When the heyday of the steamboat was past, however, Mark Twain recalled without fondness the Bridal Chamber "whose pretentious flummery was necessarily overawing to the now tottering intellect of that hosannahing citizen," and regretted that "the animal that invented that idea was still alive and unhanged." If the steamboat celebrated the wedding, the other icon of mobility, the train, handled the end of the relationship: by the 1880s Indiana in particular was the land of easy divorce, and Emily Faithfull reported that when the train stopped at Indiana depots, the conductor called out, "Ten minutes for refreshment and five for divorces."[33]

The steamboat's Ladies' Cabin, a space violated from below by peepholes, invaded by the ship's domestic work, and besieged on every side by married men, by single men miming marriage, and by general overcrowding, emerges as a special locus of decorated discontent filled with women traveling in pretend luxury toward a comfortless life, as a shuttle of confinement moving toward disappointment. On a gusty lightning-lit evening in 1834, aboard a Mississippi River steamboat, Harriet Martineau and her companions in the Ladies' Cabin determined together on seeing the confluence of the Ohio and the Mississippi, which sight the boat was scheduled to pass at about two in the morning. Because the Ladies' Cabin had no attendant of its own, Martineau vigorously impressed upon a male traveler of her acquaintance that he must have her summoned by the ship's steward in time for her to see the sight; another woman passenger, Mrs. B—the same stout woman who had earlier become wedged on a river bluff during a climb undertaken to please her husband—"would not trust to being called, but sat up, telling her husband that it was now his turn to gratify her, and he must come for her in good time to see the spectacle."

Both Martineau and Mrs. B were in for a disappointment. Martineau's acquaintance fell asleep and awakened, he claimed, "just a minute too late" to have her summoned. Mr. B, on the other hand, remained awake, and at 2:00 A.M. stuck his head into Mrs. B's room to tell her that the floor of the Ladies' Cabin was so covered with sleepers that she could not possibly make her way over them to the deck. How he had stepped over the sleepers to reach her room is not recorded. After delivering his message, Mr. B shut the door before Mrs. B "could open her lips to reply." Mrs. B's spirits were crushed. The confluence of the great rivers had been, for her, a planned-for and ready-to-be-cherished high point of her journey. She had missed it, and she lamented her loss throughout the following day: "The three great rivers meeting and all: and the little place on the point called Trinity and all: and I having sat up for it and all! It is a bad thing on some accounts to be married. If I had been a single woman, I could have managed it all for myself, I know."

From such negatives and losses emerges a suggestive picture of women—especially of married women—in the mobile universe of the interior. In attempting to climb the river bluff, Mrs. B had undergone physical stress and had risked public humiliation to gratify Mr. B; in return, Mr. B had gestured at fulfilling her wish, but the very mode of his gesture ensured that it would not be fulfilled. She couldn't say he hadn't tried, but he had tried only to let her know she was not to be gratified. The very nature of the Ladies' Cabin contributed to her disappointment, and the fact that at night sleeping male bodies covered the floor of the Ladies' Cabin ensured it. Together the protective arrangement of space and the violation of that same arrangement spelled loss.[34]

When travelers turned from their examination of gender-divided space to the great space of the interior itself and attempted to imagine its future, they did not consider rearranging the social constrictions that pressed so hard on both genders, and they did not imagine a future cleansed of tobacco juice. Instead they saw space divided into profitable rectangles from which dreams like bubbles rose.

Chapter 8

Yesterday's Future

O n 26 December 1841, the English traveler William Oliver
  booked passage on a Mississippi River steamboat for a spot he
had long dreamed of visiting—Kaskaskia, Illinois. Founded in 1685,
Kaskaskia was one of the oldest French towns in the interior, in its
time famous enough to have "sent its name far over the world." In
1841, however, Kaskaskia was not a regular stop for a steamboat, and
among the passengers only Oliver and his companion had selected it
as a destination. There was no landing at Kaskaskia; instead, at an apparently unmarked spot, the steamboat simply ran in against the riverbank. The workers shot out a plank and tumbled Oliver's luggage
ashore, Oliver and his companion followed, and the order was given
for the steamboat to go on. Oliver had expected to see on arrival "at
least a few houses and an inn at the landing of a place so old as
Kaskaskia," and was troubled to find nothing there but himself and his
companion, standing below the bank and watching the sun set over
the Missouri woods to the west. He clambered along the shore
through knee-deep clay until he found a way up the steep bank; then
he beat his way through "a complete smash of huge logs, broken
limbs, and brush" toward a roofless hut he spotted in the distance.

There he found a wretchedly ill family whose intended passage across the Mississippi had been blocked by ice on the river; he engaged two men of the family to transport him and his luggage through the frosty night to the town.

In 1841, Kaskaskia held a population of perhaps a thousand, down from a reported seven thousand a century earlier; surviving buildings included a courthouse, a church, a nunnery, a land office, and a hotel. Daybreak told Oliver that there was nothing to be seen in Kaskaskia but decay, and that his desired experience of the interior's French past was not to be had at that spot. The town's sole source of amusement for Oliver was on display above the bar in the hotel, where hung "a splendid plan of an extensive city of the name of Downingville, with churches, public buildings, squares, etc., complete." When Oliver inquired after the location of Downingville, he learned that he was in it: Downingville was "no other than an imaginary city at that wretched place, Kaskaskia landing." In search of a brush with the interior's past, Oliver had got chilled, scraped by twigs, and plastered to the knees with clay only to stumble into the future. His route to the future was that frequently taken by such journeys in the nineteenth-century interior: contemplation of a wall poster showing a gorgeously detailed and precisely gridded dream. The saloon paintings of imaginary cities that hung above bars and decorated hotel lobbies were without doubt the foremost indigenous art form produced by the interior in the nineteenth century: some were transformations in paint of the very spot where they hung, but just as regularly the paintings advertised the planned geometric beauty of a town hundreds of miles distant. Such town plans, according to numerous travelers, were "magnificent in appearance," filled with "handsome squares, avenues, and streets, and pictures of the noble edifices with which, in the imagination of the artist, they are ornamented." All were, nonetheless, projections into the future, for on the advertised spot itself a traveler was likely to find no more than "a wooden shed in the midst of stumps." The grid itself, with its geometric regularity, its section lines, its numbered streets running east and west, its north–south avenues named for trees, made it possible to transform the landscape and create the future. The grid firmed up dreams, located them in space, and gave them exact dimensions.[1]

Land speculators were roaming the interior well before the township and range survey of 1804 imposed the grid over the landscape, but pre-grid speculators, however expansive their visions, dreamed shapelessly. In 1767 Jonathan Carver claimed to have gained from the Sioux in Minnesota a vast and unmeasured Naudowessie Land Grant encompassing most of east central Minnesota, but it was without any boundary more specific than Carver might choose to draw around it; and in 1797 Gilbert Imlay, in a prospectus for the North American Land Company, contemplated the real estate available in the interior and felt "the mind grow almost wild, and become lost in the magnitude of the object, and the astonishing accumulation of wealth, which arises from this species of investment." The grid, however, disciplined the speculative mind and shaped dreams in rectangles; the survey established townships of exactly six square miles, and, with lines crossing each other at right angles, subdivided each township into thirty-six equal sections of 640 acres each, further subdivided those into quarter-sections of 160 acres each, and then into half-quarters, and then into 40-acre parcels, the smallest division sold by the federal goverment. Within these beautifully regular divisions and subdivisions, speculators produced miracles of art and imagination so infectious that many travelers who had never before considered land ownership were seized by speculation fever. All around them were American movers so serene and confident in their occupancy of the gridded future that to debunk seemed downright dumb.[2]

In 1855 Lawrence Oliphant was so impressed by "the blind confidence which induces crowds of utterly destitute people to emigrate to comparatively unknown regions" and "the cool presumption with which crowded steamers start for cities which do not exist, and disgorge their living freights upon lonesome and desolate shores, to shift for themselves," that he, too, at Superior, Wisconsin, visited the land office. He put himself in the hands of an impressive land agent, "a very communicative and civilized young man, evidently imported from New York or Boston for puffing purposes." While studying an artistically rendered city plan, Oliphant became fascinated by some lots available just two doors from the bank, around the corner from the grand hotel, and fronting on the central square. Oliphant and the agent set out onto the grid and entered the art-town to eyeball the lots of his choice. Armed with billhooks, they cut their way through a dense forest that the agent called Third Avenue and described as "the fashionable quarter." Third Avenue ended in a small streambed named West Street. Through tangled underbrush the two men hacked their way along West Street "until it lost itself in a bog, which was the principal square, upon the other side of which," wrote Oliphant, "covered with almost impenetrable brush, was the site of our lots. We did not think it worth our while cutting our way through them to the business quarter." The able agent offered a "glowing eulogy" to the wisdom of Oliphant's choice of lots, but Oliphant himself confessed to some skepticism. In most cases, seeing a section on the actual landscape was not the correct approach to take to the cities of the future.

David Macrae, at each steamboat fuel stop along the Mississippi, saw in a clearing a wooden house and "a large board stuck across two poles" informing visitors that they had arrived at "Bowden City" or "New Babylon." Macrae found these sights suggestive: the locals, he wrote, were "walking by faith, not by sight" through "a world of preparation." Eventually such dreams left the interior littered with desolate sites that never sprang into the future—unoccupied and un-painted buildings with unglazed windows, abandoned when the fu-ture popped to life elsewhere—but meanwhile many travelers came to feel that while in the interior they were actually touring the future. Drawn into the futurist mood of the moment, travelers not only de-tailed the look of the future but also offered suggestions about how to make it materialize more quickly. Some built their predictions on all that the interior most obviously lacked at the moment they visited it, and others built theirs by erasing existent qualities that they found an-noying or unpleasant. Over half a century the location of the future wandered westward down the Ohio River, then north across Michi-gan, then westward and up the Mississippi into Minnesota and Wis-consin: as its location shifted, the qualities travelers assigned to the future shifted also, congealed at times, and then shifted again.[3]

Of the many dreams and predictions of the future voiced through-out the literature of travel, the dominant and longest-running of those dreams blossomed out of the fertility of the soil and was played out in a discussion of how much work would be required to make the soil produce what they guessed it was capable of. For some time, travelers argued over how much in the way of crops, cattle, and profits could be elicited from the landscape without anyone's actually engaging in the labor of cultivation. Early travelers unaware of the depth and density of the root system that underlay the prairie association predicted that a cultivator would need only to strip the landscape of its trees before commencing successful farming. To them, treeless areas looked most favorable for cultivation, and the treeless future looked like the best future. In 1698 Louis Hennepin asserted that "there are vast forests to be rid up" in the Mississippi Valley and that a settler might better choose treeless spots where, he thought, "the ground is ready for the plow." In the opening decade of the nineteenth century, travelers re-peated Hennepin's claim. In 1805, when Thaddeus Mason Harris saw the banks of the Ohio being "cleared of those enormous trees with which they were overgrown," he praised the treeless future; in 1809 Fortescue Cuming enjoyed imagining the forested area around Zanesville, Ohio, as eventually "divested of its trees" and thereby im-proved. After 1810, however, travelers were too shocked by the look of the stump-littered landscape to ever again praise treelessness. By

1836, so major a shift in attitude had occurred that James Hall represented treeless prairie as uninhabitable and efforts to clear woodland as productive of "disastrous consequences." Hall asserted that "bankruptcy, disease, disappointment, and death have traced the footsteps" of the emigrant farmer who attempted such clearing.[4]

Throughout the first half of the century, travelers with sweeping visions of the future ignored all obstacles in order to represent the interior as a virtually work-free landscape of spontaneous fertility. Farming they represented as "a mere pastime," and crops as "springing up almost spontaneously." A farmer had to do no more to get a corn crop, they claimed, than drill holes in the ground and drop in the seeds. Even more effortless farming could occur where helpful gophers "had plowed up the prairies" so effectively that a farmer needed only to drop seed on land already worked for him by those little rodents. The soil of the interior was so rich, travelers repeated, "it would do it injury to give it manure." Meanwhile, forest—if any remained—and native grasses, they claimed, served to nourish the cattle and swine "without the expenditure of a cent." Farming in the interior was tabbed "child's play" and even an "ecstasy in the life of nature." Many of these observations travelers made from the deck of a steamboat.[5]

Standing between their dream and its fulfillment was the dense and tangled prairie association that covered many parts of the landscape under discussion; as a result, on the ground the dreams were shaded by facts. There, farmers told ignorant travelers of the difficulties of eradicating the prairie association, while knowledgeable traveling farmers who took a look at the situation began to write about steam power, about the cost of hiring persons to break up the prairie, and about prairie grasses too hardened by midsummer for free-ranging cattle to eat. Travelers who attempted farming in the interior engaged in bitter parody of the claims that had lured them to the work-free landscape. In 1839 Walter Wilkey was emphatic in his critique of how Illinois had been sold to him for its "pure air—sweet water—healthy climate—(mark that, fellow traveler)—fertile and easy cultivation of the prairies—extensive and *self-sown* wheat fields!—and, what was wonderful indeed, always free and accessible to innumerable droves of well-fatted *wild Hogs!* ripe for the slaughter, and so exceedingly kind and accommodating to Maine emigrants, as to approach their barnyards once a week not to be *fed,* but to be *butchered!*" On those rare occasions when travelers used the phrase *garden of the world,* they surrounded it with the quotation marks of doubt, or lodged it, as John Stillman Wright did in 1819, in ominous discussions of such phenomena as *sick wheat.* Shortly thereafter the phrase *garden of the world* passed into the literature of speculation and promotion and stayed there, expressive neither of the landscape nor of its produce, but of profits only.[6]

Other dreams for the interior, though none so long-lasting as that of work-free cultivation, rose like bubbles from one or another travel book, were kept aloft for a time by others, and then allowed to drift out of sight, faded but unbroken. One such dream represented the interior as a global center of trade, wealth, and political power; that vision travelers based on their belief that the interior's waterways would forever retain their dominance as routes of travel and transport. Antebellum French, German, and even English travelers predicted that the states of the interior—especially Missouri, Illinois, and Iowa—would not only become the power center of the United States but also conduct their own foreign policy. No American travelers engaged in any like visions; they predicted instead great population density and even an urban future for the interior. In their dreams one city after another in the interior rose to displace New York City from its position. While international travelers' vision of population density brought with it predictions of "vice erecting its power" and even "the complete dissolution of the union," Americans envisioned "moral greatness" arising from a dense population. For a relatively brief moment—between 1815 and 1824—travelers envisioned refinement and the life of the mind arriving in the interior: in 1819 David Thomas imagined seeing the valley of the Mississippi "filled with intellect, and with elegance," and both Adlard Welby and William Blane imagined "letters and refined manners," along with other civilized luxuries, "abounding" in the interior. Other voices, however, sounded other notes: in 1815 Daniel Drake, a longtime resident and observer, regretted being unable to predict when the interior might be "prepared for the reception and permanent residence of learning and philosophy," and John Melish noted that local efforts along the Ohio to counteract gaming and drinking with public libraries had failed. Fredrika Bremer in 1848 was one of the last travelers to use the interior to visit the future—and not only the future but the millennium itself, which, until she herself arrived on the scene, she had believed was due to appear in the interior. Bremer had imagined the interior as "a giant sunflower" and suffered genuine pain at the loss of her dream: at Chicago she saw "thousands of shops and thousands of traders but no Temple of the Sun, and only a few worshipers of the sun and of eternal beauty. I no longer have any faith in it," she wrote of her vision. "It is gone!" In its place she glimpsed "a popular life of a totally new kind," so new in fact that she could not describe it.[7]

The moment of Bremer's visit to the interior was also the moment of the gold rush to the Far West, and consequently the moment when the interior ceased to be, for travelers, the future. Silence descended over the subject until the mid-1850s brought outbursts of loss. Along the Ohio River, John Oldmixon and Charles Lanman mourned the disappearance of trees, flowers, fish, deer, clear skies, and the native population, which left behind a world where "man jostles man, ruts disfigure the earth, and stenches fill interminable streets, where a dense population drink whiskey, feed pigs, and higgle over European frippery." Thus ended, without resolution, a half century of conversation over the interior's future; visible contrasts between the cities of the interior and their natural surroundings continued to seem pleasant and exciting to some but depressing to others; travelers dropped the subject of spontaneous fertility and instead described machines they saw working the landscape; increasing population density failed to seem meaningful; and treelessness lost all its earlier appeal. In 1828, longtime observer Timothy Flint had peered into the future and seen only the present: when he tried to look ahead a hundred generations into the life of the interior, he could glimpse only "the same harvests . . . the same flowers . . . the same rivers . . . the same valleys" offering themselves to the eye. Travelers who claimed for half a century that the interior's present was in itself the future implied that present and future were identical, and that the future would be indistinguishable from the present. The present, however, threw some obstacles in the path of visionary delight, primary among which was the matter of human health and threats posed to it by the very activity of creating, on the landscape, the future.[8]

In the nineteenth century many believed health to be a by-product of travel. The search for health served as a potent justification for any journey; once a traveler asserted health to be the purpose for travel, he or she was released from any further explanations of the length of the trip, the style of travel, the behavior of the traveler, or the itinerary chosen. Health as a motive for travel swept all before it and erased all behind it. Health-seeking travelers kept their privacy intact; they were required neither to divulge the nature of their debility nor to discuss how their travels affected it, and when a health-seeking traveler noted any complex and difficult social phenomena requiring explanation, the traveler could avert the challenge by asserting that he or she was "traveling for health, and not to enlighten the people with my wisdom," as Eliza Steele did in 1841. Travelers whose personal health was not at stake, however, paid close attention to assessing the relative healthiness of the areas they traveled through. In their assessment they were joined by locals roaming the interior in search of a "healthy" spot to settle. Together they argued over which landscape markers spoke of disease and which of health. At the center of the discussion was malaria, *the* disease of the interior for most of the century, and a disease intricately connected to ongoing landscape alteration. From one angle, travel literature constitutes a running record of guesswork about which landscape activities gave rise to malarial conditions and about how malaria was transmitted.[9]

From early in the century onward, travelers noticed that in some locales everyone they met seemed to suffer from agues, fever and chills, and intermittent fever, whereas in other areas no one so suffered. In 1818 in Ohio, Henry Fearon observed that "a man's being sick is as common in this country as being in distress is in England," so common that work continued regardless and Fearon met persons suffering from fever and chills "even during their most active occupations." To most observers such phenomena meant that it was the locale, not the locals themselves, that was unhealthy; once travelers observed a number of ailing locals, they went to work defining landscape features that might be the markers of disease. Between 1808 and 1858 travelers guessed that unhealthy spots were marked by low ground, shoddy agriculture, the mosquito population, the interior's "prodigious power of vegetation," riverbank occupancy, dog-days weather, "evening damp," the vicinities of mill dams and marshes, wet prairie, bad water, and even the presence of prehistoric mounds. Not until malaria had vanished from the interior did anyone come to understand which of these observed factors had conjoined to produce malarial conditions.[10]

Malaria is transmitted by the *Anopheles* mosquito, which breeds in water under sunlit conditions and, if there are few cattle about to bite, resorts to biting humans. If a mosquito bites a human who is already infected with malaria, the mosquito then transmits the agent of malaria to the next humans it bites. Common conditions of life in the antebellum interior encouraged the transmission of malaria. When locals felled trees and thus exposed rivers and small streams to sunlight, they created breeding grounds for *Anopheles;* they further exacerbated the situation by clearing land that they did not at once cultivate. Because relatively few cattle were available to be bitten, the mosquitoes went for the humans. Travelers themselves contributed to the situation: intense mobility meant a continual passage through the interior of infected persons who were there bitten by *Anopheles;* although the travelers moved on, the mosquitoes remained to transmit the disease to the uninfected. Just as travelers noticed, malaria did indeed appear in selected localities, and an area where everyone was infected might be relatively near an area where no one was infected. Gradually, as cultivation became more general, numbers of cattle increased, travel left the rivers for the roads and rails, marshes were drained, and windows were screened, malaria receded from the interior and disappeared well before its mode of transmission came to be understood. While it lasted, however, malaria ruled the lives of the infected, many of whom learned to plan their activities around attacks that in most cases occurred every third day and entirely drained their strength. Babies and children suffered the most, though their conditions were less visible to travelers and rarely described. Malaria caused entire settlements to be abandoned, caused some settlers to backtrail, and encouraged others to flee westward. Rumors of abandoned areas in the interior spread around the globe in curious and wishful form; Ole Rynning reported that in Norway, rumor had it that emigrants to the interior would on arrival find "cultivated farms, houses, clothes, and furniture ready for them, everything in the condition in which it was left by the former owners."[11]

Individual flight from malaria was also common: some desperate sufferers lit out alone in hopes of finding relief elsewhere. In 1849 Amasa Delano of Ottawa, Illinois, was so weakened by malaria that his doctor told him to change his residence and somehow resume physical activity if he hoped to survive. Gold-rush news tempted Delano to try California for his recuperation, so he said good-bye to his family and set out with three companions for St. Joseph, Missouri, where he planned to rendezvous with a large party leaving for California. Everywhere, however, lay further danger to survival. On the first leg of his trip, from St. Louis to St. Joseph, a fellow passenger aboard the *Embassy* died of cholera; at St. Joseph one of Delano's companions was also stricken and within hours died horribly. Terrified by these events and exhausted by the preparations to be made at St. Joseph for the overland trek, Delano experienced a malarial attack:

> The day was very warm, and being unaccustomed to labor, when night came, I went early to bed, at a house where I had obtained lodgings, exhausted by the fatigues of the last few days. Before I got to sleep, I felt strangely. Was there a change in the weather? I could not get warm. I piled on more clothes. I felt as if I was in an ice-house. Ugh! the cold chills were creeping along my back. I involuntarily drew up my knees, and put my head under the bedclothes, but to no purpose—I was shivering, freezing, and then so thirsty!—I wanted a stream of ice-water running down my throat. At length I began to grow warm, warmer; then hot, hotter, hottest. I felt like a mass of living fire—a perfect engine, without the steam and smoke. There seemed to be wood enough from some source, but I poured

in water till I thought my boiler would burst, without allaying the raging thirst which consumed me. At last the fever ceased, and then, indeed, the steam burst in a condensed form through the pores of my burning skin.[12]

Delano chose to medicate himself with mercury. At a time when futures both personal and communal were in jeopardy from malaria, many theories of treatment were advanced and a long debate over how infected locals might treat themselves wove through travel literature. Travelers argued over the effectiveness of quinine, and recorded observing both heavy use of it and "violent local prejudice" against it. Sufferers among the travelers medicated themselves with not only mercury but calomel and opium. Some argued the efficacy of huge doses, of "going resolutely into drugs and medicines" for several days, while others argued for minute doses on the theory that "it is impossible to give (or take) doses too small." Some treated themselves with brandy and whiskey, tippling continually from small bottles they carried on their persons, while others insisted that malaria was more prevalent among drinkers. Some of Caroline Kirkland's Michigan neighbors advanced the theory that pork cured malaria. From 1850 onward, many set out for Minnesota, whose climate was said to exert "a tonic influence," and where, it was claimed, even the swamps were pure and wholesome.[13]

Some of the ailing tried the curative powers of exercise and the outdoor life that were generally—though no more generally than cathartics and purgatives—prescribed for men who were malarial, consumptive, or just plain sickly. Unlike the cathartics, however, the outdoor-life prescription was strictly gendered; there existed no concept of outdoor exercise for women, who were conceived of as getting their exercise elsewhere. According to Francis Grund, women in the interior "scrub their own floors, clean the door-handles, wash the windows, sweep the rooms, make themselves busy in the kitchen, and walk about with children in their arms" for exercise. If women did not attain health from such indoor exercise, censorious male travelers put their failure down to "sweets, pie-crust, and iced water immoderately indulged in from the cradle to the grave." No man, however, was about to try women's exercise of his own volition; he was offered instead, and he chose, icons of the hunter and the sportsman as representative of masculine health. Outdoor life for men was connected to neither cultivation nor contemplation, and was to be found in neither walking, thinking, botanizing, nor studying scenery. Instead it defined itself in such risky activities as rapids-shooting and killing large animals. The outdoor-life prescription coincided in time with a bubble lofted by international travelers: their dream that the interior could serve as a fabulous hunting ground for sportsmen from around the globe.[14]

Travelers who wrote of hunting in the interior drew, within the single activity of killing animals, some careful distinctions among practitioners. The sportsman they distinguished from the white male hunter who had arrived early in the interior, who had lived to hunt, and who, reportedly, had bought no land; although that hunter was often admired and even romanticized into an "unaffected child of nature," he was simultaneously delivered an emphatic shove into the past. He was not approved of as a sportsman; nor were locals who in the spring released entire herds of pigs to range over the countryside and munch their way to fatness on acorns so that the locals could then in the fall hunt those same pigs. Pig-hunting was never considered by travelers to be a sporting proposition. Sportsmen were also careful to distinguish their activities from those of Indians; it is worthy of note that the literature of the traveling sportshooter is frequently also a literature of Indian-hating, and it is the sportsmen who clung tenaciously to the term *redskin* even when no one else used it. Throughout the first half of the century, travelers repeated a confusion of claims about how Indians hunted. Indians, they said, fired the prairie in order to lure large animals to the burned areas where they could be easily slaughtered, or fired the prairie so as to lure herbivorous animals to the new growth said to spring up immediately after burning, or fired the prairie in order to "bewilder the game" or "compel the deer to assemble," whereupon, depending on the writer's view, they either slaughtered great numbers or engaged in selective killing and careful conservation. Travelers' assertions that Indian hunters "destroyed the chase" and "drove away the white man's game" existed side by side with their stories about Indian abilities to track animal prints "through pathless forests . . . straight forward in the most direct line." All sporting travelers agreed, however, that not only did Indians eat and use what they killed, but they *needed* to eat and use it, and it was on that exact point that Indians failed to be sportsmen. A sportsman, in nineteenth-century terms, might use the animal or bird he shot by eating it or making a trophy of it, but he might just as well leave it lying in a bloody heap on the landscape. Either way, he did not *need* it, and on that point he rearranged himself from a hunter into a sportsman and even from there into a naturalist.[15]

Around 1840, sporting travelers began to offer readers specific advice on equipping themselves for hunting on the prairies. The advice literature opened in unpretentious discussions about the value of a Scotsman's plaid as armor against mosquitoes; Charles Augustus Murray explained how at night he continued to breathe but warded off bites by rolling his entire body, head, and face in his plaid. As subsequent travelers discussed the need for a double-barreled rifle, and suggested carrying a zither for entertainment, the advice escalated in detail until it reached a high point in George Charles Grantley Fitzhardinge Berkeley's account of his preparations for prairie sport. Berkeley transported across the Atlantic his weapons, his dogs, named Brutus and David, and one unnamed servant, but he outfitted his "prairie chest," as he called it, in New York City, with "choice provisions" to fall back on should weather, sickness, or "savage and treacherous people" interfere with his hunting. Berkeley stocked up on hermetically sealed cans of beef and gravy, mutton, potted chicken, potatoes, cherries, and apples. Since he personally "hardly ever drank anything but sherry," he supplied himself with three dozen bottles of same, plus a few bottles of port and "a certain amount of good brandy," and set out for the interior, where he hired nine more servants to complete his entourage. In the subsequent catalog of his disappointments, the interior's trees appeared first; either the trees were not where Berkeley wanted them or they were entirely absent. This landscape failing Berkeley bizarrely blamed on "the reckless hands of the red men" who, he said, "set fire to the plains and woods for the mere purpose of enjoying the passing glare, or of dancing by a fire," and who had thereby destroyed the hunt for him. The interior, however, had more disappointments in store for Berkeley than merely its ill-placed trees. The sporting life in the interior did not confer health. When the foods in the hermetically sealed cans proved too rich and heavy to taste good to Berkeley, he placed the blame on the "fickle climate" of the interior. He regretted the brandy and sherry and port; the landscape, he claimed, had affected his liver and convinced him that liquor was "the worst thing that can be taken" on a sporting foray into the prairies. Worse yet, his hired American bearers, rather than answer to his demands or tolerate his overbearing treatment, regularly deserted him. Mystified by their refusal to display the habits of servitude, Berkeley blamed their desertion on poor physical conditioning, and judged them to be "most indifferent walkers and very easily tired." In the end, his enterprise a failure, Berkeley fled to Canada where, he observed fiercely, "fields were much better laid out and fenced, all things wore a more cheerful appearance, and as to sheep, the superiority of breed was at once observable." Up to that point in his journey, neither fields, fences, nor sheep had been at issue, but by the time Berkeley reached Canada, he was an angry and disappointed sportsman, and his dream of the American interior as a field of play was shattered.[16]

The sportsman's dream of a vast hunting ground in the interior collapsed in many ways, not all as individually spectacular as Berkeley's sherry-propelled fiasco, but all generally disappointing. Whether they came from abroad or from America's East Coast, avid sporting travelers were astonished to learn how few large animals actually occupied the interior. In 1797 Gilbert Imlay, puffing land sales, had populated his version of Illinois with immense herds of deer, elk, and buffalo "grazing in enchanting natural meadows," but none of Imlay's later readers saw anything to approach that sight. In 1804 when Constantin Volney toured the area between Vincennes and Kaskaskia that Imlay had described he saw only horseflies. Volney, however, chose to believe that Imlay's herds had been there until, annoyed by clanking cowbells, they all departed and swam westward across the Mississippi. In 1825 Henry Schoolcraft found Illinois to be "desolate of animated nature," though bones of elk and bison told him that those animals had once been there. Not a single buffalo, claimed Schoolcraft, remained east of the Mississippi, nor did much else; even in the northern interior Schoolcraft recorded seeing only wolves, owls, gophers, bears, squirrels, and mosquitoes. In 1851 Arthur Cunynghame found no game on the landscape of northern Illinois, but insisted on its marvelous resemblance to a vast game preserve even as he himself decamped to Iowa to shoot grouse.[17]

The presence of buffalo—along with the dream of hunting them—on the prairies of the interior was too appealing for some antebellum sportsmen to abandon, so they adjusted fact into suggestion. When John Bradbury claimed to have seen large herds of buffalo he did not locate the sighting; Charles Lanman claimed to have seen buffalo but only from the height of "a lofty bluff" and even then only with the aid of a spyglass. When locals confidentially told sportsmen that there were buffalo remaining in the interior, they always located the noble animals at exactly the distance the interior had settled on for the unattainable: sixty miles. Buffalo were sixty miles from St. Louis when Godfrey Vigne heard about them in 1832, and they were sixty miles from Fort Ripley in Wisconsin when Lawrence Oliphant heard about them in 1855. Since sixty miles constituted two days' travel, Oliphant settled for bagging a badger. That so large an area could be free of large animals was so inexplicable to travelers as to cast doubt on any and all animal stories set in the interior. Many travelers refused to believe in the reported existence of gophers, and merely repeated without comment bits of fantastic zoology they heard concerning deer: that deer always died of heart failure before being brought down by a pursuing wolf; that deer had been captured bodily by barehanded women in the backyards of Illinois.[18]

Deer, which could be hunted in many parts of the globe, were of less interest to most traveling sportsmen than were fauna peculiar to North America, and in the absence of buffalo they turned to the wild turkey—with equal lack of success. Bénédict Révoil hunted east of the Missouri for eight years but "never got within gun-shot of a turkey," and William Oliver was too fidgety to succeed; he complained that at his slightest movement his turkey prey set off "at a speed which defies pursuit." Travelers discovered new ways to be humiliated at sport: Charles Lanman thought to chase gray wolves but they turned on him and became the pursuers; wolves at which John Benwell fired returned at night to snatch his pet terrier. In 1835, at Prairie du Chien, Wisconsin, Charles Fenno Hoffman mistook *Canis familiaris* for *Canis lupus* and chased a hunting dog for a mile before his experienced horse realized his rider's mistake and simply came to a halt. In 1855 in Minnesota, Lawrence Oliphant could not catch a fish with either fly, bait, or troll lines; at St. Anthony, as fish leaped from the water around their canoe, Oliphant's desperate fishing companion "destroyed his own peace of mind, and kept continually hooking his friends, in unsuccessful attempts to delude his prey with gaudy-colored flies; but he could only boast of one rise, and that was known to himself alone." In 1839 in Michigan, Caroline Kirkland rescued a deeply embarrassed British hunter who had marked his cache of dead birds with his cap and then lost sight of it; he had, he complained, wandered the unmarked prairie for two hours in search of the cap and birds but could "see nothing but grass everywhere . . . these prairies of yours—one might as well be on the ocean in a cock-boat . . . it is really excessively awkward." In 1832, Godfrey Vigne failed in his every sporting endeavor in every recommended spot until he hired, near Detroit, two Chippewa guides, under whose careful tutelage he successfully shot and retrieved a wild fowl.[19]

Some sporting travelers who had seen nothing to shoot resorted to listing wildlife once native to an area or to describing long-vanished elk and cougar. Lawrence Oliphant wrote of drifting off to sleep at night in dreams of the comparatively certain pleasures of the English fox hunt. These, however, were not hunters' delights but writers' pleasures. When travelers' frustration and desire were, on the one hand, compounded by the tantalizing tales of locals, but were on the other hand uncontrolled by licensing requirements or enforced game laws, they lost their balance and began to kill what was not game, to kill it by methods they themselves disapproved of, and to kill it out of all season. They forgot about asserting the health-giving properties of their activity. Near Mansfield, Ohio, Godfrey Vigne became so frustrated at getting off not a single sporting shot during an entire morning that he began to shoot at robins, and William Oliver's companion, after a failed day of deer-hunting, shot a skunk and suffered double consequences: upon his return to the inn, several local loafers set up a howl: "'Ah, you've been killing a skunk! you've been killing a skunk!' For a while he put on an enquiring and much-injured look, requesting, with some hesitation, to know what they meant; but the truth was only too palpable, and he made a merit of necessity by joining in the laugh against him." In Minnesota in 1855, Lawrence Oliphant, disapproving of himself as he did it, fired at swimming wild geese, managed to wing one, and then had to chase it down on land. Other travelers resorted to watching locals engage in dubious activities: Charles Augustus Murray watched bored soldiers, in the absence of game, hunt bees and then cut down each bee-tree they located; the bored soldiers that Charlotte Van Cleve watched in Minnesota engaged in the hunt by trapping a wolf in a box-trap, muzzling it, and then "letting it loose for a race for its life over the prairies, with hounds and hunters in full pursuit. All the blue coats and brass buttons of the hunters," wrote Van Cleve, "did not make that a brave thing to do"; and in Missouri Gottfried Duden watched locals, under the guise of training their hunting dogs, torture a wolf in extremity. In the hunting atmospherics of the interior, English writers sniffed at French and American methods, and Americans snickered at overequipped English hunters; the less successful the hunters were, the less likely they were to speak of how healthy a pastime sportshooting was.[20]

Where hunters in the interior found game plentiful, they killed as much of it as they could. It is as if only the relative absence of animal life controlled them; their sporting life was otherwise uncontrolled by licenses, game laws, seasons, or need; they made a distinct contribution to erasing the future for indigenous birds. For a time they found in abundance the prairie chicken, a highly specialized bird dependent for its food on the original prairie cover of grasses and forbs, for its courtship ritual on a shortgrass prairie, and for its roosting on a tallgrass prairie. In 1833 James Stuart found the Illinois prairie filled with prairie chickens, and west of Chicago in 1855 Charles Weld had "excellent shooting" of prairie chickens, but in 1859 seven sportsmen spent a full day near Vincennes trying to bag prairie chickens for Isabella Trotter's dinner and got nothing. In 1864, John Francis Campbell predicted extinction for the prairie chicken: "There are no game-laws in America," he wrote. "Therefore sporting poulterers overrun the country, and the race of prairie-hens will soon be eaten." In an atmosphere where "all is game," as he put it, he thought that little could avoid extinction. By 1870, prairie chickens were scarce even in Iowa, and agents of New York City restaurants were buying all that professional hunters could bag. "That mighty Babylon of America," wrote David Macrae, "stretches out its hand even to the western prairie to pick up delicacies for its epicurean taste." Menus on Pullman Hotel Cars running from Chicago to Omaha in the 1860s and 1870s listed such items as Prairie Chicken, Pheasant, Snipe on Toast, Quail on Toast, Golden Plover on Toast, Blue Winged Teal, Woodcock on Toast, and Broiled Pigeon; a dozen years later the game birds were gone and such menus offered steaks, chops, and fried chicken. As they crossed the country, travelers complained that menus showed so little regional difference.[21]

Some sporting travelers ate game, but rarely wrote of eating anything they themselves had killed; they were more likely to describe eating an animal shot by an unidentified other. Charles Fenno Hoffman hunted regularly in Wisconsin in 1835 but only once mentioned eating game—a bear shot by a troop of soldiers who went out hunting in one of those moments, he wrote, "when the resources of the library are exhausted." Parker Gillmore advised his sporting audience that squirrels were a delicacy, but he did not consume one in view of his readers. William Blane resolved several times to taste possum, having been assured that it was as tasty as young pig, but every time he was about to pop a morsel into his mouth, he envisioned the possum's "long, naked, prehensile tail" and could not eat. In the view of many sportsmen, to take for food only a certain cut of a large animal and leave the rest behind certified one as a sportsman, not a wanton killer; on the western plains, hunters who slaughtered entire herds of buffalo took only their tongues for food, thus attempting to certify their taste level and lack of need and at the same time validating the slaughter by taking a single consumable away from a bloody scene whose truest intent was to prevent use of the animal as a food source. Hunting was for many of them a display of not searching for food; at the same time, however, cultivation that made hunting for food unnecessary interfered seriously with hunting for sport.[22]

Women travelers made late entry into the landscape of game and sport: they ate game, they listened to hunters' stories, they looked at and occasionally acquired samples of taxidermy, and they mentioned no connection between any of these activities and health. Anna Jameson hated the continual hunting carried on by the company of men she traveled with; she required of the men that at the least "the fish should gasp to death out of my sight, and the pigeons and wild ducks be put out of pain instantly." She was, however, far more candid than were traveling sportshooting men about the pleasures of eating the fish and game, wherein she forgot all her "sentimental pity for the victims." Only Margaret Fuller loved to hear sportsmen's stories: "How pleasant it was," she wrote, "to sit and hear rough men tell pieces out of their own common lives." She could not, however, remember any of the stories "well enough . . . to write them down." In Wisconsin, Fuller met a local hunter who displayed to her a rack and told her in detail about its original owner: "the prettiest, the most graceful" deer he ever beheld. "I chose him at once," he told Fuller, "took aim, and shot him dead. You see the antlers are not very large; it was young, but the prettiest creature!" That hunter fired not at meat but at beauty; his attitudes are interestingly complicated by the behavior of George Armstrong Custer who, during his residence on the shortgrass prairies just west of the interior, filled his spare time with gardening, kept a large menagerie of pets, deeply admired the looks or fine coat of a large ruminant before killing it, gave its meat to the men of his garrison to eat, practiced taxidermy on the remains, and decorated his house with the results. Custer, according to Elizabeth Bacon Custer, thought it cruel to make a captive of a field mouse and found no lack of fit between his love of animals and his love of hunting.[23]

While some travelers who hunted their way through the interior kept a running record of random shooting at birds and mammals they neither needed nor even attempted to retrieve, it is a rare traveler who spoke directly against the activity. In 1855 John Oldmixon, on his way down the Ohio, prepared himself as many travelers did by reading travel books: a book by a "clever, gentlemanly fellow" particularly disturbed Oldmixon, for the gentleman "took a run into the interior chiefly to kill all the unfortunate birds he could bring his dog and double-barrels to bear on, in pure wanton amusement." Oldmixon, who thought the hunt a detestable slaughter, was arriving in the interior just as market hunters were stripping the prairie landscape of game to be shipped to the cities. Meanwhile the sportsmen, after having struggled to dissociate their doings from those of Indians, wandering buckskin-clad locals, and market hunters, found little to shoot at on an unfamiliar terrain where they knew neither the habitats nor the habits of local fauna. Some sportsmen, angered, shot the feathered songsters. Eventually the claim that the sportsman was a health-seeker wavered and died in the face of the slaughter about to commence on the plains to the west of the interior.[24]

Some travelers looked to glimpse the future of the interior not in visions of a golden grid, a sanitarium, or a shooting gallery, but in its children, and in the remarkable difference between them and urban children of the East Coast. To Harriet Martineau, eastern children of apparent privilege looked "pallid and dried" from being shut up throughout the winter in houses heated to eighty-five degrees; they promptly caught cold when released into the out-of-doors. In contrast, children in the interior lived outdoors and looked anything but fragile to Martineau. Although she was at first fearful for "mere babies playing on broken wooden bridges" and small boys climbing trees and piloting canoes through rapids, she came to admire the "dexterity, fearlessness, and presence of mind" that children gained from so living. To other travelers, however, these same children were both astonishing and terrifying: awed travelers observed social tyrants in bibs and diapers, children who ordered their own meals in eating-places, sought and gave directions, conducted their own businesses, shepherded older family members through unfamiliar situations, and explained technologies to their parents. Useful as such functions might be, international travelers had never before seen children performing them, and their settled notions of who controlled whom, and who had access to knowledge, were challenged by the behavior of these children. Some male travelers, especially those from abroad, could not bring themselves to ask directions or information of a child, even when they knew the child had the information. Travelers gloomily suggested that they were looking at a filiarchy.[25]

Aboard a Mississippi River steamboat on Lake Pepin in 1860, Anthony Trollope, accustomed to seeing English children "banished, snubbed, and kept in the background," watched with horror the unfamiliar sight of children settling in for their evening meal along with the adults: "The care-laden mothers would tuck the bibs under the chins of their tyrant children, and some embryo senator of four years old would listen with concentrated attention, while the Negro servant recapitulated to him the delicacies of the supper-table, in order that he might make his choice with due consideration. 'Beefsteak,' the embryo four-year-old senator would lisp, 'and stewed potato, and buttered toast, and corn cake, and coffee—and—and—and—mother, mind you get me the pickles.'" Such children, Trollope insisted, were wretched and uncomfortable, deprived of the happiness of being "made to obey orders" and go to bed at six. Ida Pfeiffer dismissed all such children as "ill brought up," but from another point of view they were not being brought up at all; they were running their own world and attempting, sometimes unsuccessfully, to train their parents to immediate compliance to its conditions. Pfeiffer noted that when children "screamed and roared" for something aboard the steamboats, their parents at first refused, only to comply later. Pfeiffer thought this the "very worst plan they could have adopted," but then she herself favored steadfast refusal over compliance in all cases.[26]

Travelers who disliked seeing children boss their elders were also uncomfortable when children emulated their elders too closely. Some said that they were not children at all. In Illinois on the Fourth of July in 1841, William Oliver watched a group of boys who were overseeing the local festivities and judged them to be not boys but "rather little men"; in 1865 George Borrett flatly asserted that "there are no children in the States, no girls or boys as in merry England, but only immatured young men and women." When Borrett thrashed about for a comparison illuminating to his readers, he settled on comparing American children to French children, but the Russian traveler Aleksandr Lakier considered the same comparison and then rejected it: "The world," he wrote, "does not produce any youngsters more independent than the American." In 1859, Lakier got lost while walking the banks of the Ohio and sought to hire the guide services of a group of boys whose path he crossed. The boys stepped aside to hold a colloquy, and then the oldest, who looked about twelve, notified Lakier that they had decided to help him. Lakier, in a gesture of equality and comradeship, offered the twelve-year-old a cigar, which he lit up at once and "smoked no worse than an adult." Along their walk together, the boy told Lakier of his plans to start up his own business two years hence; its nature he had not yet settled on, but he indicated to Lakier that the nature of the business mattered less to him than its profitability. When Lakier parted from the boys, he paid them all in silver and "they took it with pleasure, as befits true Americans whatever age they might be." Like Lakier, Harriet Martineau was much amused by "the businesslike air of the children," but others failed to be amused. When Frances Trollope stopped at a house in Cincinnati to buy a chicken, the woman of the house called on her ten-year-old son, Nick, to handle the transaction. Trollope had previously seen Nick in the street, "playing marbles in the dust and swearing lustily," but had not known him to be a businessman. Nick the chicken merchant informed her that he bought, from local farmers, eggs by the hundred and lean chickens by the score, fattened the chickens in coops of his own making, and sold them at double his cost. When he made change for her out of a deep pocket full of bills and coins, Trollope asked him if he gave his earnings to his mother, who appeared to be living in desperate squalor. Nick answered, "I expect not . . . I takes care of it." Trollope claimed that Nick was not extraordinary, that his was but one story out of a thousand she might tell, and that his character was "hard, dry, and calculating." Arthur

Cunynghame, who also met with businessboys in the interior, asserted them to be so independent of their parents as to forget that they owed "any filial duties" whatever to them.[27]

Travelers who disliked certain habits and attitudes prevalent among men in the interior were especially shocked to see these same habits and attitudes evinced by boys. Like the adult men of the interior, the boys of the interior chewed and spat everywhere, they cursed and swore—and unlike their elders, did so in the presence of women—and they practiced no limb discipline: upon entering a railroad car, they at once sprawled over the seats and put up their boots on the Utrecht velvet upholstery. They cherished violence; when, aboard a Mississippi River steamboat in 1856, one worker killed another, Ida Pfeiffer reported that "boys of nine or ten years old went to look at the dead body, and came back as gaily as possible to tell what they had seen. I knew," wrote Pfeiffer, "that human life was held rather lightly in America, but I did not expect to find the feelings of the young people blunted at so early an age as this." Some travelers were simply helpless before the boys of the interior: aboard a Lake Michigan steamboat, Ernest Duvergier de Hauranne tried grimly to write while a swarm of boys played ball against his back; occasionally one delivered a headbutt to de Hauranne while others snatched items from his writing desk. He could think of nothing to say to them. Charles Dickens, however, felt a "glow of delight" when aboard a steamboat a boy engaged in a prebreakfast tobacco-spitting contest became obviously ill, his face turning pale while "the ball of tobacco in his left cheek quivered with his suppressed agony." Such boys, as many travelers discovered, refused to transform themselves into helpful scouts on demand. In 1885 a male companion of Emily Pfeiffer's did the distinctly non-American thing of getting lost on Chicago's numbered grid; he looked to a passing boy for help. "I want to go to a Hundred and Twenty-Seventh Street," he said to the boy. The boy looked sharply into his face for a moment before responding, "Then why the hell don't you go?"[28]

Travelers' astonished and terrified commentary on American boys rarely extended to American girls, but if the boys of the interior seemed to predict a future populated by cursing, spitting, cigar-chomping, violence-loving commodities traders utterly beyond anyone's control, the girls engendered in some travelers a delicious fantasy of a vast future servant pool. Frances Trollope mourned elaborately over the sad fates in store for American girls whose belief in "the fable of equality" had denied them lives in domestic service, which she represented as "that sure and most comfortable resource of decent English girls." Trollope failed to press any of these girls into service for her, and Harriet Martineau reported that women in the interior who took eleven-year-old girls to train in seven-year domestic apprenticeships always lost them around the age of fourteen, just when they were becoming "really serviceable," because the girls' friends talked to them about the advantages of being free. If the boys of the interior had already entered their future, the girls were refusing the future to which some travelers imagined tying them. What other future might await these girls was unglimpsed: travelers noted that, in their teens, girls were not timid; they traveled in pairs and groups, and laughed too loudly for the tastes of some; and two of them who disembarked from a steamer at Galena, Illinois, in 1856, horrified Ida Pfeiffer by clapping her on the shoulder and "bawling" in her ear that she was just like their grandmother. At Rolla, Missouri, in 1862, Anthony Trollope observed at length a group of young women—whom of course he could not approach for conversation—and concluded that they were intelligent, beautiful, "sharp as nails . . . and tyrants to their parents. They have faith in the destiny of their country . . . but they believe that destiny is to be worked out by the spirit and talent of the young women." Since the behavior of these young women tied them to no past that observers were familiar with, the observers tied them to the future; in the case of the young women, however, the future, unlike that so clearly acted out by the boys, remained misty.[29]

In 1797 the enthusiastic French land speculator Gilbert Imlay urged his audience to view the interior as "a creation bursting from a chaos of heterogeneous matter and exhibiting the shining tissue with which it abounds." The nature of that creation was still under contest when there occurred a development predicted in none of the forays into the future attempted by travelers, a development that ensured that travelers would never settle—nor even finish sketching—the nature of life in the interior: the great decades of detailed observation and critique of the interior ended when travel itself shifted from the roads and waterways, from foot, horseback, stage, and steamboat, to the rails.[30]

Chapter 9

Sunset

In April of 1894, at Harrisburg, Pennsylvania, the English traveler Theodora Guest and her husband launched themselves on a ten-thousand-mile, six-week-long tour of the United States. As travelers of status, they rode in the luxury of *Wildwood,* a private railroad car belonging to Frank Thomson, president of the Pennsylvania Railroad. The sixty-two-foot-long *Wildwood* held a sitting room, bedroom, bath, dining room, kitchen, and servants' room, and was staffed with a cook and a waiter. Guest's personal maid traveled with her, and the Pennsylvania Railroad also supplied the Guests with a Mr. S "to organize everything" for them and "in short, to show them America." Throughout the trip, Mr. S slept on a sofa in the dining room of the car. Because the *Wildwood* brought up the rear of each train that pulled the Guests across America, the finest scenic views from their rear platform were all theirs except when, now and again, another private car was attached for a time behind theirs. That annoyed them, and they were always relieved to regain their observation position. Mr. S saw to it that the Guests were carefully protected from America: at each of their stops, a private conveyance waited to whisk them from their private car to other private arrangements.

On her tour, Theodora Guest exercised five interests: sketching scenery—a selection of these sketches appears in her book; writing up her impressions and judgments of America; shopping; bird-watching; and collecting and pressing wildflowers. The latter two of these interests, which had been exercised by foot travelers and horseback travelers throughout a century's travel in the interior, posed certain difficulties for a traveler enclosed in private varnish. Crossing Pennsylvania, Guest became so excited over a white flower that she saw in "royal profusion" on the landscape—profusion being the only feature that could have brought a flower to a train traveler's attention—and became so anxious to ascertain its perhaps exotic nature that the train halted while the conductor "went running back along the track, followed by the brakeman with a flag; both men disappeared up a bank, and in less than four minutes," wrote Guest, "I was in possession of a large bunch of beautiful white flowers." On examination, the flowers turned out to be rather ordinary trillium, but Guest exclaimed that "it was real sport that a train should stop to pick a flower!" The birds that she liked to spot from the train were so much more difficult to acquire than the flowers that at Niagara, near the end of their tour, Guest's husband ventured out and bought her a stuffed Baltimore oriole as solace. Even when Guest stepped out of the *Wildwood,* its cocoon surrounded her. Everywhere across America human guides interposed themselves between the Guests and the selected sites they visited, filtered the experience for them, and occasionally hustled them back to the train if something unexpected presented itself. As a result, Guest characterized the American landscape as "moving panoramas of wonder and beauty," though occasionally the panorama had a flaw: the Mississippi, for example, "left her," she wrote, before she had seen quite enough of it. All in all, it is as if America moved while Guest herself sat still in the private car, the American landscape unrolling itself past her window.[1]

Unlike the travelers of the first seven decades of the nineteenth century, Guest had not a word to say of Americans, American manners, or American society, because she saw nothing of them and because the profusion of guidebooks and maps laid out in the *Wildwood* did not operate to raise her level of information. Occasionally the Guests stepped off the train for exercise while the passengers on the forward cars, who were without access to a dining car, rushed into the depot diner for a thirty-minute feed, but at such times the Guests stayed very near the train for fear of its departing without them, and they saw nothing of their surround. Neither on their way west nor on their return did much in the interior catch their eye, and if it did they were confused about it. Ohio, Guest announced, was "very pretty cul-

tivated country, with enormous cornfields, a few cows, fewer sheep
. . . but no large rivers"; for her this was truth, since the great river
that constitutes Ohio's southern boundary, the river whose scenery
furnished a first long view of the interior to decades of foot, horse,
coach, and boat travelers, was not on the itinerary of a train traveler.
At a St. Louis hotel, Guest ordered "roast sage hen" in the belief that it
was the indigenous prairie chicken—by 1894 hunted so close to extinction that no one was eating it—and complained that it "tasted like
grouse," which it probably was. The Guests decided "to omit Kansas
City altogether, one large town being very like another," and to speed
on to Colorado instead; on their return east through Minnesota, they
missed Minnehaha Falls, which Guest, a devoted reader of Longfel-
low, had wanted to see; short of time in Chicago, they took an elevator to the top of the auditorium tower to see the city, but "the lake
was misty and the town smoky," wrote Guest. "Otherwise the view
would have been very fine." Having missed Lake Michigan, Guest determined to substitute Lake Erie on her way out of the interior, but
that was not to be: "During the night we skirted Lake Erie," she
wrote, "which I never could see, though I got up three times and
looked everywhere for it."

In sum, Guest wrote of the interior, "there were no special features
in the scenery," and in sum she characterized her experience of not
seeing it as "profound repose" except for a single terrible moment
when a threat from the outside pierced the side of the *Wildwood* and
reached the Guests within. In the spring of 1894, America was in the
depths of depression, and here and there in the interior, contingents of
unemployed men, segments of Jacob Coxey's Army of the Unemployed, were rumored to be threatening to disrupt rail service. In
southwestern Wisconsin, the conductor "strolled" into the *Wildwood*
to tell the Guests that "the next station was in the possession of
Coxey's Army, and that it was quite possible that they would make an
attempt to capture the train." Guest had heard of Coxey's Army: during a visit to the White House at the start of her travels, Mrs. Grover
Cleveland had mentioned the phenomenon but had assured Guest
that "none of the big people were alarmed about it, though of course
they did not like the disaffected feeling which it exhibited." The conductor was also reassuring; he speculated that the penalty for halting a
mail train would deter the men from taking any action. Guest was,
nonetheless, jarred from her "profound repose" by the potential for
personal harm in the situation. Approaching the station where the
men of Coxey's Army were gathered, the train ran in "pretty fast and
pulled up very short" to drop off the mail, but the stop was long
enough for Theodora Guest and the crowds filling the platforms on

both sides of the train to take a good look at each other, and long enough for the men on the platforms to recognize the level of privilege that had pulled up in front of them, and long enough for them to yell angrily at the frightened occupants of Frank Thomson's *Wildwood*. As soon as the train pulled away and the confrontation was past, Guest turned to studying pretty birds that, she wrote, "sat on the telegraph wires for us to admire them" as if exhibiting an appropriate response to the *Wildwood*'s passing through their territory. By the end of Guest's trip, her moment of class confrontation in the interior had been long since forgotten; she pronounced the entire tour "lovely . . . no *contretemps* of any kind . . . universal kindness and courtesy . . . nowhere but in America can one experience such luxury." When she expressed this last sentiment to Lawrence, the waiter who had not only answered to but anticipated her every requirement throughout six weeks in the *Wildwood,* he replied, "The Americans just idolize this kind of traveling."[2]

Lawrence's oblique response to Guest was full of truth, though not all the truth was in it. By 1894, when Guest traveled and Lawrence waited on her, it had been nearly twenty-five years since any traveler had moved through the interior on any vehicle but a train. In 1870, moments after the opening of the transcontinental railroad, it was as if travelers threw away their walking shoes, jumped off their horses, tumbled out of coaches, leaped from canoes, dove from steamboats, and dashed for the nearest depot to board a train. Toting with them into the cars certain longings as yet unsatisfied by America—longings to see dramatic scenery, to be waited on, to experience the safety and relief of sharpened class division—they sat down on the velvet upholstery under the looming overhang of the upper berth, and pulled down the tapestry window shade. Everything about travel changed, and the interior—without itself undergoing sudden change—was transformed.

By 1870, when travel writers rushed en masse for the trains, nearly all the major innovations that caused them to choose, value, and at times "idolize" American railroad passenger cars were in place, and though the cars exhibited innumerable variations in detail and decor, the basic floor plans and central features of both day coaches and sleeping cars remained essentially stable through the end of the century. A day coach held two rows of double seats divided by an aisle, and seated fifty to sixty passengers; because Americans simply refused to ride facing backward, most passenger cars featured the walkover seat, a bench seat with a reversible back, so that all seats could be snapped into forward-facing positions no matter how the car was coupled to the consist. Layout of the sleeping cars, for which a traveler paid an extra charge, was dominated by the twelve-and-one open-section design favored by George Mortimer Pullman. A *section* was Pullman's term for a combined upper and lower berth; each car held twelve such sections plus one private compartment, a washroom at one or both ends, and a linen locker. What was a chair car by day became a sleeping car at night, when the berths were made up: the lower berth was composed by reversing seatbacks and sliding the seats together to form a bed frame, and the upper berth was swung down on brass hinges from the ceiling of the car. Curtains divided the berths from each other and from the aisle. All internal innovations in washing facilities, gas lighting, and steam heating appeared on the extra-charge sleeping cars well before appearing on others, but the most notable internal changes, over the last three decades of the century, were all in the car's decor, in an elaboration of decorative wood, fabric, and upholstery that was meant to speak of luxury. One external innovation altered the travel experience for both day-coach and sleeping-car passengers: the Sessions Vestibule of 1887 linked all cars in the consist into one rolling unit. No longer did passengers have to leap platforms to cross from one car to another, from the coach to the dining car to the smoking car; the vestibule made all cars easily accessible to a traveler no matter what the exterior conditions. Because the very existence of the sleeping car promoted the idea of night travel over long distances, travel writers had much less to say about inns and hotels than they once had and much more to say about the internal arrangements of their conveyance.[3]

The long aisles and forward-facing seats of American passenger cars were so different from the compartmentalized first-class carriages of British and European railways that international travelers were simply astonished by them, and often judged them, as the English traveler Henry Lucy did in 1884, "vastly superior" because they allowed travelers free movement through a train filled with pleasurable possibilities. In 1889, the French traveler Max O'Rell pronounced them "perfection. In point of comfort," he wrote, "the American trains are to the French and English trains what these latter are to the stagecoach of bygone days. Nothing can surpass the comfort and luxury of the Pullman cars, unless it be the perfected Pullman that is called the vestibule train. Six or seven carriages, connecting with one another, allow of your moving about freely over a length of some hundred yards. Dining-room, sleeping-car, drawing-room car, smoking-room, library, bathroom, lavatory, the whole fitted up in the most luxurious style. What can one desire more? . . . Everything has been thought out, everything has been carried out that could conduce to the comfort of travelers."[4]

In the American interior a nineteenth-century traveler experienced at the time the best trains in the world. While American East Coast railroads, without distance to consider, were rather resistant to innovation, and while railroads running west out of Omaha put up a group resistance to the dining car and clung to the practice of brief eating stops at selected stations, the mood of the interior was fully receptive to all innovations in travel technology. Furthermore, the Pullman Palace Car Company was based in Illinois and conducted its experiments on railroads in that state. As a result, travelers both international and American noticed a sharp uptick in the quality of the accommodations when they steamed into the interior. The British traveler W. F. Rae, who had found travel "very fatiguing" on the East Coast, thought that railroads in the states of the interior could teach easterners how to better carry him in comfort. The American Samuel Bowles marveled at the interior's trains and found it truly "strange" that in a region where comfort and luxury seemed to count for so little, a traveler experienced "more comfortable and luxurious accommodations for railway travel than anywhere else in the world."

And so a certain order of comfort, a tangible definition of it, encased travelers as they moved across a landscape on which comfort had been deranged or unavailable for over half a century. Some travelers, especially the English among them, called it classless comfort. Because no one asked them to specify a class of travel when they purchased tickets, and because the open-plan coaches held what looked to them like a great variety of passengers compared to the four or five they might have stared at in a British railway compartment, they could infer only that American railroad travel was classless. The subtleties of social class in America remained, as they had always been, closed to the English. The steamboats had offered just two classes—cabin and deck—and a gender divide on the cabin level; the trains, however, exhibited nearly a dozen layers and divisions—the private car, the chartered train or car, the excursion, the sleeping cars, ladies' cars, gents' cars, day coaches, emigrants' cars, cars designated for blacks only and for Chinese only, and the positions atop and beneath the cars' exterior. No traveler ever saw all these divisions on any single train, and because the intricacies of American class division on the rails were neither spelled out in print nor rendered orally to travelers unfamiliar with them, perhaps no one traveler ever became aware that so many divisions existed.

When in 1857 the Russian traveler Aleksandr Lakier stepped up to the ticket window to buy his first American day-coach ticket, he was dazzled by the number of routes and lines displayed on the railroad map and "amazed that the schedule showed but one price for everyone." Disbelieving, he handed over his money and "stammered something about a class," but the agent without reply simply thrust a ticket at him. Lakier, fearing the impatience of the Americans in line behind him, abandoned his effort to be informed and rushed with the crowds to claim a seat in the classless car. After examining the novelty of the walkover seat, testing the velvet upholstery, and noting the subjects of the car's three wall paintings—a girl with a tambourine, a landscape, and George Washington—he looked around at his fellow passengers and realization dawned: "Where are the common people?" he asked. "Where are the rich and powerful of this world? Where are the ladies?" At that moment it was clear to Lakier that there had to be other classes and divisions of travel, but his vantage point did not allow him either to know what they were or to see what their arrangements were like. The railroads, it could be said, constituted an ideal setup for at once dividing the clientele by class and keeping the divisions hidden from those being divided.

Atop the mostly invisible class ladder of the railroad was the private car like the one in which Theodora Guest traveled, a privilege for which travelers had to qualify but for which they did not pay; the other nonpaying rider was the hobo at the bottom of the class ladder who rode atop or beneath the car. Neither of these classes wished to be seen by other passengers in other divisions of the train. At a stop on Robert Louis Stevenson's cross-country rail trip, he once saw "two men whip suddenly from underneath the cars." Stevenson "should have liked dearly to become acquainted with them" but they, holding no corresponding desires, vanished at a run into the surround. M. M. Shaw, recorder for the Pennsylvania Railroad Conductors nine-thousand-mile excursion in 1897, and his fellows one day discovered a hobo who had wedged himself into a sixteen-inch-wide space between two ice chests mounted on the underside of the dining car. The man, John Bell of Alabama by name, was so immobilized and caked with dust that the conductors at first guessed him to be dead, but when a waiter from the dining car extended to him a sandwich and a can of water, he reached out for it; like his counterpart Theodora Guest riding in the private varnish, he was fed at the railroad's expense and like her he declined to budge for fear of losing his place. Eventually John Bell vanished and the conductors estimated that he had traveled 782 miles in his position beneath the car.[5]

Like John Bell the hobo, travelers at the top of the class ladder hated being required to give up their places. Isabella Trotter and her husband toured the East Coast in private varnish as guests of the line, but when they set out for the interior they were made, to Trotter's displeasure, to "endure all the tortures of the common cars" and hated it. Ethel Abbott and her family rode in a private car from New York to Chicago and were transported from Chicago to Pullman's company town near Calumet, Illinois, on George Pullman's own private car. Disappointingly, the Abbotts were left to return to Chicago on "one of the ordinary cars . . . among a lot of nasty common men" and from there eastward on similar "hot and dirty cars. We missed our special car very much," wrote Abbott.

Indeed, not until Omaha, just as they were about to depart the interior for the West, did many travelers become aware of other divisions on the train and experience the shock of being mixed with them. Because of the immense difficulties of bridging the Missouri's shifting riverbed, and because of a general change to other lines at Omaha, passengers were transferred from Council Bluffs across the Missouri to Omaha in heterogeneous groups from which all the railroad's class divisions had been erased. W. F. Rae, seduced by his reading of promotional literature, had envisioned a luxurious through train zipping him undisturbed from New York to San Francisco; crossing the Missouri in a crowd of undiscriminated travelers made him miserable, and he warned no one to "underrate the discomforts to be faced and borne" at Omaha. Those discomforts were not physical but social. Sleeping-car passengers like Rae and Mary Duffus Hardy suffered through being "crammed into a long, comfortless, wagon-like car with a host of nondescript folk, some bearing babies, bundles, or baskets of fish or vegetables, some tattered and torn, some unshaven, unshorn, all mixed up higglety pigglety." To discover that there were some phenomena of rail travel—the Missouri River being one of them—that George Pullman had not brought under his control was "unsavory" to Hardy: she looked about her wondering how "the genteel element had been wholly eliminated . . . from the motley assemblage." Such abrupt slides down the class ladder could present themselves whenever travelers left the mainline routes. Emily Faithfull had been pleased to discover in America that "though the Great Republic acknowledges no first or second class," she could for a few extra dollars buy a seat in a parlor car and, from New York to Chicago, enjoy space, fresh air, upholstery, mirrors, and the company of "ladies and gentlemen." When she bought a ticket out of Chicago into Wisconsin on a short line that carried no parlor cars, the contrast in travel conditions was so great that she claimed to have personally glimpsed the abyss: she was forced to ride in what looked to her like a baggage car among "fellow-travelers who, not to put too fine a point upon it, stand in terrible need of the national piece of china known as a spittoon."[6]

If antebellum travelers had expected and desired to meet Americans, converse with them, and study their habits, many post–Civil War travelers wanted mostly to avoid them, and the railroads offered them modes of avoidance that had never before been available. In his 1872 guidebook of delicate hints to wealthy travelers, Charles Nordhoff suggested that at Chicago his readers charter a Pullman car through to San Francisco so as to avoid the otherwise inevitable meeting with the masses at Omaha. The charter was another step in travelers' process of buying their way upward and inward into isolation aboard the trains and riding, as Samuel Bowles recommended, from Boston to the Golden Gate in "a degree of comfort and luxury unequalled heretofore in all the dreams of travel, and without necessarily leaving the car from the beginning to the end of the three-thousand-mile ride." Travelers whose purses were lighter and who lacked the connections to maneuver themselves into someone's private car could buy a shadow of such private arrangements on an excursion. In 1883 Mary Elizabeth Blake recommended the excursion for its services and protections, and for the security of its class level as contrasted to independent travelers' risk of meeting a "haphazard arrangement of neighbors" in their car. Blake's money bought her not only "little courtesies and personal attendance" but also the service of having the United States rearranged and its "prominent points of interest . . . grouped together and brought to your notice." Excursion travelers, however, generally saw little that was not brought to their notice: when William Hardman's excursion director had nothing on the docket for the day, no meeting with local dignitaries, no protected formal tour of a stop on their route, Hardman, who characterized himself as "a pioneer," simply returned to the sidetracked excursion train and sat there through the hot summer day, "melting helplessly," rather than set out on his own. Those who did not care for the group nature of an excursion could find other new ways to separate themselves from the ordinary run of travelers. For a brief time in the late 1860s, before the dining car became an institution, Pullman marketed the hotel car, a parlor and sleeping car that carried a cook and held a small kitchen designed to feed only those who had bought seats in that car. English travelers' long agony of class-mixing in the interior began to diminish rapidly with the arrival of such accommodations: many became almost comfortable. The consist to which one of these hotel cars was attached still made its dining stops for passengers in the day coaches to rush out and gulp a quick meal in the depot—but meanwhile the hotel-car passengers ate in splendid isolation while watching those others dash for food. W. F. Rae bought a seat on a hotel car and confided that "an additional zest was given to the good things [on the menu] by the thought that the passengers in the other cars must rush out when the refreshment station is reached, and hastily swallow an ill-cooked meal." Moreover, as Rae sat in the hotel car watching the others scramble on the platform, he imagined himself to be Queen Victoria; his class level shot up with his opportunity to observe others doing what he needed not do, and his enjoyment of his situation was heightened by his view of those who did not share it.[7]

Catherine Bates was at times one of those day-coach passengers, seated among persons who might well be carrying sack lunches—a practice sternly proscribed for parlor-car travelers by Charles Nordhoff—and who sat up all night. Three times a day Bates rushed off the train, as she put it, "to gobble up whatever tough messes of food happen to be within reach during the very short time allowed for meals. On these occasions everything is heaped up on one plate. Eggs and bacon, tough mutton or stringy beef, potatoes, tomatoes, Indian corn, and squash pies must be eaten alike, off the one platter, or left alone. At first you feel you would rather perish than degrade yourself to the level of a pig and its trough, but hunger is a strong argument in the long run." The three meals of the day, for such a traveler, might well be identical, with elements of breakfast, lunch, and dinner reappearing at each stop. Earlier travelers in the interior, those going from inn to inn and those eating on the steamboats, had been familiar with such eating experiences—all meals alike, all eaten in a great hurry. Steamboat travelers had on their own volition bolted the food, only to retreat to the boat deck and do nothing, but railroad travel enforced the rush to eat; travelers could choose to eat fast, or be left behind, or go hungry. When steamboat travelers wanting to avoid the common long table had asked to be served privately, they had been refused, mocked, and even put off the boat, but W. F. Rae could buy in the hotel car the private meal to which no steamboat traveler ever had access: 127 different items and preparations—although still no "made dishes" except Pork and Beans Yankee Style, Beef Pot Pie Family Style, and Chicken Croquettes—might appear on the hotel-car menu for him to choose among. Thus railroad travel slid a new level of travel eating—in privacy, at leisure, and by choice—into the previously unoccupied space above the democratic long table.[8]

Below the day coach were travel divisions that travelers did not choose but were ordered to take: cars set aside for Chinese travelers only and for black travelers only. In the nineteenth-century North after the Civil War, no black traveler was ever permitted to buy a regular coach ticket; blacks were made to ride either in the baggage car at half price or at times in cars emblazoned with the words *Second Class*—the only such appearance of this term in travel literature about the American interior. In 1889 the French traveler Max O'Rell, finding that two of the three day coaches on the train he was boarding were full, stepped into the empty third car and took a seat. Almost at once a conductor appeared and shooed O'Rell out, repeating, "Come out, you can't travel in that car . . . it is the colored people's car . . . I tell you you can't travel in this car." O'Rell is the only traveler to record such an experience, and, in an altered travel atmosphere that encouraged travelers to attend to calibrating their own comfort at the expense of general observation, he is one of a tiny number of travelers even to note the existence of such cars. And because deliberately traveling poor—roughing it—was not the style of post–Civil War America, Robert Louis Stevenson is the only travel writer to record a trip on another utterly distinct division of travel—the emigrants' car.[9]

Emigrants' cars, from the 1840s onward, offered both American movers and recent immigrants a cheap ride to the Far West. On these cars the railroads preserved familiar hierarchies of nineteenth-century travel by first dividing all passengers by race, and then subdividing the white passengers by gender and marital status. Of the three emigrant cars Robert Louis Stevenson saw attached to the consist at Council Bluffs, the first was reserved for white women, men married to those women, and their children; the second carried all Chinese travelers; the third held white men traveling alone. Unlike the steamboats, however, where differences in decor and comfort marked the gender divisions, all three of the emigrant cars were identical, utterly plain converted wooden boxcars, fitted with rows of plain wooden seats, a few ineffective lamps, a stove at one end of the car, and a toilet at the other.

Only on the level of emigrant travel were rail travelers required to cooperate with strangers. After a railroad official had sorted the emigrants into their respective cars, that same official entered the cars to sell to the emigrants straw-filled cushions and boards that could be laid from bench to bench to form beds. Because each potential bed would take up two seats, the men in Stevenson's car had to be encouraged to chum up in the purchase of the boards. Reinstating the old interior's practice of forcing men to bunk with strangers if they wanted a bed at all, the official went through the car "introducing likely couples" and matching bedmates. Although his first efforts to match Stevenson met rejection not from Stevenson but from the potential bed-chums selected for him by the official, eventually a young Pennsylvanian whose naval service had "trained [him] in desperate resolves" accepted Stevenson as his bed-partner, and together the two paid the "white-haired swindler" two dollars and fifty cents for the board and cushions. When the number of eager takers began to dwindle, the official cut his price to a dollar and a half, and at evening of that same day, when the train stopped at North Platte, Nebraska, locals in their nightclothes rushed aboard the emigrant cars to sell identical straw cushions first for twenty-five cents each and then for fifteen cents with the bedboard thrown in gratis. Stevenson's resentment grew.

Stevenson kept himself apart from the other emigrants in the only way he could—he refused to reveal to them his name—and at times he alleviated the physical misery of his travels by thinking over American place names: "There is no part of the world," he wrote, "where nomenclature is so rich, poetical, humorous, and picturesque as the United States of America . . . the names of the states and territories themselves form a chorus of sweet and most romantic vocables: Delaware, Ohio, Indiana, Florida, Dakota, Iowa, Wyoming, Minnesota, and the Carolinas. . . ." He needed poetic solace because the line had reserved not only special cars but also special treatment for the emigrants: the conductor, for example, refused either to communicate with them or to answer their direct questions, "for one answer led to many other questions, as, what o'clock it was; or, how soon should we be there? and he could not afford to be eternally worried." On his own, a newsboy working the train assumed the performance of duties withheld by the line: he notified the emigrants when and for how long they would stop for food, stood lookout so that none of them should be left behind at a stop, and made a grateful Stevenson consider "how easily a good man may become the benefactor of his kind."[10]

No matter the class in which travelers moved through the interior, train travel focused all of them on time itself, at the expense of space. When time took top priority for all travelers, no longer could international travelers draw lines as they once had between their own supposedly leisurely style of travel and the hasty scramble practiced by Americans. English travelers understood why the station platforms at Chicago were occupied by watch salesmen, and all travelers expressed relief when, in 1889, the railroads adopted four standard time zones for the country and thus banished the profusion of clocks, each featuring the local time according to a different railroad, that had covered depot walls and confused travelers. Furthermore, the half-century-long conversation about American mobility carried on by travelers in the interior ended: rail travel melded all styles of mobility into one, and no traveler could any longer draw distinctions between his or her style of mobility and the style of the traveler in the seat ahead or the berth above. Most important of all for the interior, railroad travel asserted a powerful definition of the term most contested throughout the literature of travel in the interior—*comfort*. Railroad travel, in effect, inhaled the subject of comfort, removed it from its location on the landscape, and instead of allowing travelers to discover its shape, told them what comfort was: access to class division and personal service inside a confined gadget-filled space whose every inch was decorated. Thus railroads answered to certain longtime travelers' desires that the landscape, which answered only to itself, had refused to accommodate. For travelers at all levels—from the hobo wedged between two ice chests beneath the car, to the emigrant confined in a stinking boxcar, to the day-coach passenger attempting to sleep sitting up, to the Pullman passenger struggling to undress for the night while prone in a berth—personal physical comfort and discomfort became the compelling content of travel. The traveler's world turned inward and shrank to a small personal mix of desires, dislikes, and disappointments.

First-class travelers fell into absorption with the vehicle itself. Pullman Palace Car travelers busied themselves for hours in examining the decor, trying out the gadgets, testing the ride, listening to the conductor explain how it was smoothed by such marvels of American engineering as the Allen Paper Car Wheel, calculating the class level of the other passengers, and enumerating potential comforts. In 1860, Anthony Trollope admitted that "the great glory of Americans is in their wondrous contrivances"; foremost among these was the sleeping berth, which was to Trollope a "delight" and worth the extra dollar's fare just to watch it made up. In a Silver Palace Drawing-Room and Sleeping Car in 1874, John Boddam-Whetham, who found "not much outside to claim his attention," occupied himself for several hours of his trip between Niagara and Chicago with admiring the car's contrivances; he lost his enthusiasm when he attempted to undress and sleep in the berth. "The horrors of that first night in a Pullman car," he wrote later, "are indelibly impressed on my mind." Across the seventy-year history of the open-section sleeping car, few travelers solved the problems it posed of how far to carry one's undressing in the public space of the train aisle, how to finish undressing in the berth itself, and in what posture to attempt unassisted ascent into the upper berth. M. M. Shaw, despite a career as a conductor on the

Pennsylvania Railroad, had never attempted to use a berth until the first night of his nine-thousand-mile excursion in 1897. He stayed up late socializing, and was one of the last to turn in. He wrote:

> It is a new and strange experience to me, but I go at it to win. There is nobody in sight, but the presence of a carload of people is felt. The long, narrow aisle of the car is deserted, but I hesitate to exercise the privilege its deserted condition would seem to warrant. I desire to undress, but I wish to hide to do it, and with this end in view I crawl under the curtains that inclose our berth. As I do so the train starts on its way again. Mrs. S has retired some time ago, and I think is asleep. There is not much room for me, but I determine to make the best of it. Balancing myself on the edge of the berth, I make a few changes in my apparel, and come very near being precipitated into the aisle while so doing by a sudden lurch of the car as the train struck a curve. In regaining my equilibrium I stepped upon the madam, who quietly inquired what I was trying to do. "Only coming to bed, my dear," I answered. "Is that all," she replied, "I have been watching you for some time and thought you either had a fit or else was practicing gymnastics and using the curtain pole for a horizontal bar." I made no reply, I didn't blame her, and lay down thankful that she was the only witness to the performance.

Unlike those antebellum travelers who had either criticized or outright hated conveyances in the interior, many rail travelers wanted to like sleeping-car travel. Some travelers, such as John Erastus Lester, claimed a traveler "could not fail to sleep soundly" in a berth, and others were convinced that they ought to be sleeping comfortably even when they couldn't manage it. When sleep would not come to Mary Elizabeth Blake on her 1883 excursion, she was able to persuade herself that she was getting "so much more for her money" by staying awake.[11]

Whether the walkover seat was any more comfortable a contrivance than the berth is arguable. The seat's very reversibility allowed of no contouring in the chair pad, and the mohair upholstery used in day coaches was intended to repel dirt and to hold the passenger in place, not to be pleasant to the touch. The very activity of assessing the degrees of personal comfort afforded by such matters was, however, absorbing in itself, and the decor surrounding the gadgets, a decor that multiplied and spread and elaborated itself until by the end of the century no inch of a sleeping car was left untouched, tended to numb any critique travelers might have mounted of the version of comfort that encased them.

Nineteenth-century wooden passenger cars, susceptible to full decoration as only wood could be, were decked out in a design vocabulary of cut velvet, plush, velours, tooled leather, carved and inlaid wood, gilded rosettes, lions, and torches, figured carpets and fringed portières, mirrored recesses for ferns and flowers, etched and frosted glass, frescoed toilet bowls, and silver-plated taps. Unlike the spacious gold, white, and blue style of the steamboats, the ensuing riot of decor in railroad cars designated as Greek Reading Rooms and Italian Renaissance Dining Cars and Napoleonic Sleeping Cars ran parallel to urban domestic interiors of the late years of the century; like that style, railroad decor aimed to shut out nature. Although nothing about the elaborately ornamented and festooned cars—with their oppressive overhead weight from both the cherubed ceilings and the carved mahogany overhang of the upper berth—suggested looking outside the car, perhaps the car's most telling feature was its window coverings: wooden slat blinds further draped with damask, tapestry, or ball-fringed velvet that actually obstructed a view of the landscape. *Luxury* was the dominant term applied by the railroads to the overall effect, and although Emily Faithfull sniffed that "a great deal has been written about the luxury of American railroad traveling. It did not strike me as luxurious," and though W. F. Rae rewrote it to "luxury tempered by accidents," that overall effect was nonetheless pronounced "magnificent" by many travelers.[12]

Just as compelling to travelers as the gadgets and the decor was the experience of being expertly served aboard the trains, an experience previously alien to both travel and life in the American interior. Some antebellum travelers who visited the South had much enjoyed being waited on in plantation style, but had felt pangs of guilt over the enslavement of those who waited on them; on the postwar Pullman cars, they enjoyed without a pang the services of the black men, almost all former slaves, whom George Pullman recruited in Georgia and the Carolinas to work as waiters and porters. No traveler remarked on the absence of black passengers in the cars served by the black porters; a nearly complete silence had fallen over the subject of race. Some travelers described the porters with a vocabulary of race and attitude—"a good-humored negro," "the brightest of mulatto boys," "a colored gentleman," "a young African"—but others banished the servitors from the syntax and described their excellent dinner as provided by "the gods" or wrote in the passive voice: "You have cooked and served for you a dinner," and "The housekeeping is done for you." The Pennsylvania Railroad Conductors took on their excursion George H. Anderson, the janitor of their conductors' room in Philadelphia, and though they trusted him rather than themselves with their "thirty-two cases of nourishment" and the artillery they carried for fending off desperadoes in the Far West, they also renamed Anderson, very early in their tour, "Alfalfa." Travelers like Mary Duncan, who mistook the emergency air cord for a bell rope to summon the porter, thought they were in a more commanding position than they actually occupied, but in fact the porter was always on call and travelers unaccustomed to being served seized the opportunity and made extravagant use of the porters and waiters. Only Mary Elizabeth Blake, after using the porter throughout the day to bring pillows, brush her clothes, and pick up her orange peels and peanut shells from the carpeting, noticed that he was tired.[13]

Every traveler, however, noticed the sharp divergence between the wonderful cleanliness of the Pullman car and the dusty condition of their own persons after even a single day of travel. Travelers' persons were filmed with the flying residue of the landscape they barely saw, while the cars themselves were kept fastidiously clean; on many cars, all linen was changed daily and no towel was used more than once. An unnamed porter told M. M. Shaw that "cleanliness is an important rule in the Pullman service, and we are obliged to strictly enforce it." One enforcement was subtle: passengers' boots and shoes were kept from soiling the berths by the porters' cleaning them during the night. But the toilet facilities on the trains were so minimal and so cramped that travelers found them "woefully inadequate to the number of aspirants for cleanliness." Mary Duffus Hardy loved rail travel but found it miserable to stand in line with an "army of dishevelled females . . . besieging one four-foot space" in the daily effort to wash up. Culturally desirable looks were difficult for women to produce in the confines of a train, and the elaborations of women's clothing were unsuited to the miniaturization of services, unsuited to sleeping in a berth, and unsuited to dressing in an aisle. Catherine Bates asserted that the railroads' operative definition of comfort on a sleeping car was a man's notion: "The accommodation for them is more ample and their style of dress makes comfort more attainable." Bates wearied of being required to say that she had never in her life been so comfortable as she was on the train when, from her point of view, "every condition of feminine comfort was conspicuous by its absence." Women travelers were certain that men's toilet facilities were larger and better than theirs, but men also "chafed at the common corner and washbowl and single looking-glass, however elegant and cleanly." Everyone, from John Bell of Alabama who rode beneath the car, to Samuel Bowles of Massachusetts who rode in a private charter, was dirty; the cars were clean.[14]

Women's complaints about unequally apportioned gendered space were but one element in the gender tug-of-war over space that occurred on the trains and that further focused travelers' attention on internal arrangements. Although no women worked for the Pullman company—or indeed for any of the roads at any level—and no women had any role in the design or placement of the rolling stock, gender had a history in travel, and gendered arrangements of space in steamboats, hotels, and inns had gained enough power through repetition that in the early years of rail travel—immediately before and after the Civil War—gender arrangements on the trains echoed the old divisions by offering ladies-only cars and reserving the best arrangements for women. But by the late 1860s rapid change occurred as men traveling alone made their move toward spatial primacy. For most of the century, lone men had been made, in the interior, to share beds with other lone men, they had been expected to relinquish their seats to any and all women travelers, they had been crowded out of stages and made to ride on the top in the rain, and they had been seated last at meals and served last once seated, but in the sleeping cars for the first time in the history of travel in the interior, a man traveling alone could buy a space that could not be taken away from him. The advantage of traveling with "a lady" and thus gaining access to comfort through her presence was erased.

In 1869, W. F. Rae found "good reason to rejoice in his loneliness, and to pity those who are accompanied by ladies." With "no incumbrances to whom he must be polite and attentive . . . the traveler who has engaged and paid the extra charge for a seat in a palace car takes possession of it," wrote Rae exultantly. "This seat he retains throughout the journey. It is absolutely reserved for him." The palace car and the reservation system thus reclassified women—previously defined as a ticket to comfort—as encumbrances. No matter that such lone women travelers as Mary Duffus Hardy continued to put men traveling alone into the same category as conductors and porters—all, to her, potential servitors—and required them to fetch coffee and ices, tote luggage, and fend off beggars at depots; after all, wrote Hardy of the population of her car, "there was plenty of him and only four of *us*." At least a man like Rae now had a seat, and only one specific display of bad behavior could cause him to lose it. At Creston, Iowa, Robert Louis Stevenson, observing a drunken man who had entered the car, classified the man as "aggressively friendly, but, according to English notions, not at all unpresentable upon a train." To American eyes the man looked otherwise. At the next stop, Cromwell by name, the conductor came by, spoke a few words to the man, and then "had him by the shoulders, twitched him from his seat, marched him through the car, and sent him flying onto the track. It was done in three motions, as exact as a piece of drill," and when it was done, the passengers laughed. "They were speaking English all about me," wrote Stevenson, "but I knew I was in a foreign land."[15]

Aside from such publicly performed exclusions, however, men were no longer kept apart from women in travel; the sleeping cars especially brought about an abrupt revolution in older ideas of gendered space and privacy. Utterly changed, along with the status of lone men, were the spatial divisions that had once, on the steamboats, gestured at keeping men and women apart while they slept. The railroads used all their space, and avoided the difficulty of calculating how many men and how many women might be traveling by making no gender divisions whatever in the sleeping cars. Man, woman, married, single—when reserving a berth all were the same.

The genders, however, were not expert at mixing with each other, and often failed to read each other's behavior accurately. In 1875 Martha Summerhayes, on a train west out of Chicago, fell into conversation with the man who shared her section. Trying at first to read him through the dubious orange color of his boots, she worried that he was an anarchist, but later, when he told her that he was a widower with a young son, she decided that he must be a gentleman. As their acquaintance advanced, however, he confided in her that he had danced on the grave of his dead wife and then, looking steadily at Summerhayes, he said to her "very deferentially, 'Madame, the spirit of my dead wife is looking at me from out your eyes.'" Frozen into silence, Summerhayes waited for the man to depart for the smoking car, whereon she changed sections and sat with another woman until the man left the train. Women travelers like Emily Faithfull, who were accustomed to such features of American gender division as separate hotel entrances for ladies, found "distasteful" the idea of a male stranger occupying the berth above hers and being enclosed behind the same curtain, and Catherine Bates dreaded taking the path to the women's lavatory in the morning and on her way "running up against men in various stages of undeveloped toilette; whilst the shaking of the train may precipitate you into the lap of some unfortunate man sitting on the side of his berth, trying to button his boots." Anthony Trollope averred that even when he had the opportunity he would never dream of speaking to an American woman in a railroad car. James Hogan, nevertheless, much enjoyed eavesdropping on "vivacious young lady passengers" exchanging confidences in loud whispers behind the curtains.[16]

Moreover, men traveling alone who had finally gained their own reserved spots in the sleeping cars were not limited to those cars as were women travelers; they were, however, still at a distance from the men's travel occupations that were defined on the trains exactly as they had been defined on the steamboats—as smoking, drinking, and gambling. These men's amusements were lodged in a head-end car on the train—parallel in space to their positioning in the fore section of the steamboat. While the antebellum men's car had been no more than a baggage car where men might go to smoke, after the war the baggage section of the car was partitioned off, and the remainder spruced up to offer not only smoking and card playing but also "refreshments." Throughout the 1870s and 1880s the combined car picked up additional features for men: a barbershop, a bath, a library, and, significantly, a valet—an addition that brought into the men's quarters the ironing board previously lodged in the ladies' cabin on the steamboats. Simultaneously, however, the new practice of posting stock quotations in the combined car began effectively to recast as businessmen those persons who had been, on the steamboats, lowlifes; and once the business definition arrived, paneling and plush seats appeared in the previously unadorned combined car. A man holding a reserved seat in a sleeping car, however, was still at some distance from his habits until the 1880s, when he was physically reunited with them; card playing spread everywhere throughout the train, and smoking lounges for men began to appear in every sleeping car. In 1881, Thomas Holyoake, on a trip from Ottawa to Chicago, made it his "custom to spend a part of every day in the cozy smoking saloon of the car, with its red velvet seats, and bright spacious-mouthed braziers for receiving lights or ashes." Holyoake claimed that his "object was to study in detail the strange passengers who joined us," but his masking excuse was unnecessary; the railroads were in the business not of exiling men to distant hideaways but of awarding travel space in general to them.[17]

Even while smoking remained compartmentalized in lounges, spitting continued unconstrained in all spaces. When in 1853 Alfred Bunn complained of the absence of luggage space in day coaches, he noted that he could not deposit his packages on the floor because, if he did, "they would be spit upon to a certainty; indeed, even in the event of dropping money on the floor, no decent person could venture to wade through the stream of saliva floating thereon, unless he put on an old glove." In 1882, Ethel Abbott, spoiled by traveling in George Mortimer Pullman's private car, was appalled when forced to ride back to Chicago on an ordinary day coach "among a lot of nasty common men, who all had the detestable habit of spitting," and in 1885 Emily Pfeiffer, traveling to Chicago, felt less than honored by an in-car visit from a railroad official who spat throughout his conversation with her. The boasted presence of Brussels, Turkey, and Axminster carpeting in the cars did not reduce spitting but did produce more spittoons: a china spittoon sat next to each seat in the coaches and next to each table in the dining cars; in the men's lounge cars, where facing rows of single seats lined the car, brass spittoons sat in trios in the broad center aisle.[18]

Meanwhile the special ladies' car began rapidly to vanish from trains in the interior, and special in-car refuges for women travelers shrank in size. By the 1880s women's space was no more than two chairs in the same small compartment that held the sinks and boxed-in toilet, and no woman traveler remarked on finding these arrangements either useful or comfortable. If a train pulled an observation car at the rear of the consist, "ladies" were imagined, in railroad promotional literature, to be occupying it, but more usually the railroads failed to imagine any specific gender-defined activities for women, and thus assigned no special space to their doing nothing. A reader watches Mary Elizabeth Blake in her 1883 *On the Wing* claiming space for herself in the car by "disposing her wraps in graceful negligence" and then progressively enlarging that space by dipping into others' stuff: "You can," she wrote, "read your neighbor's books; or, if you want anything under the sun, from a cambric needle to a French bonbon, from a postage stamp to an encyclopedia, there are a score of valises besides your own to choose from." Charles Nordhoff, looking to occupy buyers of his guidebook while their train crawled across the interior toward the desired mountain scenery, advised the male traveler to read, write, and study photographs, but relegated women travelers to sitting at the window and sewing. These disoccupied ladies who were imagined looking out the window were engaging in a travel activity that not only had sunk to a low priority but was also difficult to perform through windows covered with slat blinds and drapes, and impossible to do from ladies' lounge areas whose sofas were fixed with their backs to the windows. Women's space on the trains continued to diminish throughout the 1880s, and in the last decade of the century it disappeared: when the barbershop, the library, the smoking lounge, and the card rooms took over most of the space in the observation car, men's special spaces completed their leap from the head-end combined car to the choice position at the rear of the consist. The only further outbursts of gender exclusivity on the rails were such men-only features as the Chicago & Alton's "stag sleeper" on the nonstop all-Pullman Midnight Special from Chicago to St. Louis.[19]

By the early 1880s the trains had triumphed completely as the vehicle of choice for travel writers, and travelers' attitudes toward both other vehicles and other travelers thereby changed significantly. In 1883 Mark Twain remarked sourly that Mississippi steamboating was "not absolutely dead; neither is a crippled octogenarian who could once jump twenty-two feet on level ground; but as contrasted with what it was in its prime vigor, Mississippi steamboating may be called dead." Travelers who had employed a variety of modes of travel noticed that the dominance of train travel entailed losses: in 1839 Frederick Marryat thought that scenery viewed from a train became "invariably uninteresting." Only a few later travelers desired at times to try modes of travel other than the train. In 1874, on a train in western Iowa, Joseph Alexander envied two horsemen he spotted galloping across the landscape, and at St. Louis in 1894, Theodora Guest wished for but did not take a trip on a steamboat that looked like "a living illustration of Mark Twain's books." Most travelers, however, did not even care to change trains, much less shift to another type of conveyance entirely. They advised each other on which was the most direct of competing east-to-west routes, and became impatient when a site of choice was not reachable by rail.

Train travel also altered travelers' fears: they began to fear Americans as they had not feared them since 1815. Inside the cars they feared pickpockets, swindlers, luggage thieves, and gamblers, and outside they feared desperadoes. Some women travelers became suspicious of men who were too helpful in regard to their baggage. Men in men's groups—such as the newspaper editors' excursion John White traveled with in 1870 or the railway conductors' excursion M. M. Shaw recorded in 1897—traveled "armed to the teeth," and although many travelers thought that Americans were more sociable on trains than they had been on the steamboats, they suspected that very sociability of "conveying a false impression." Rail travelers' overwhelming fear, however, was of missing the moment of the train's departure from a stop and being left behind in space. Travelers writing in anxious tones warned that American conductors seemed unconcerned whether or not ticket holders were in their seats when the train departed; no one called out or signaled, and no bell or whistle sounded. Some swore that the conductor spoke no word to signal departure; others thought they heard the conductor "confidentially observe to himself, 'All aboard'" just before the train glided out of the station. In 1884, two seconds before the train began to chuff away from a stop in Illinois, a conductor said softly to Henry Lucy, who had disboarded to stroll the platform, "Don't get yourself left." Over this behavior, claimed to be typical, Lucy fumed: "That way of putting it exactly represents the situation. If a train over an hour or two late pulls up at a roadside station and, presently moving off without a warning note, leaves a passenger behind, he has 'got himself left'."[20]

The space in which Henry Lucy would have been left, had the train departed without him, travelers also feared, because in the final two decades of the century, the landscape of the interior had come once again to be experienced as sheer undifferentiated space. International travelers reverted to seeing space in the interior as travelers had a century before them—as "unlimited" and "inconceivable"—while American travelers like Richard Harding Davis, who in 1892 could scarcely keep track of where he was in the interior, felt "mixed sensations of pride at the size of his country and shame at his ignorance concerning it." The interior's space at century's end differed, however, from the space glimpsed by early travelers: rail travelers knew less about the interior's space, and were less capable of learning anything about it, than any travelers who had preceded them. In his ignorance Richard Harding Davis had a great deal of company, but he had fewer companions in his shame: by the end of the century, travelers displayed their ignorance with confidence, and announced their confusions with serenity.

Before the rails, travel in the interior was specially marked by a circling motion on the landscape, and by continual changes of conveyance as a traveler took a stage here and a horse there and a boat somewhere else. The interior had no center, and travel in it had no one specific itinerary. Train travel, however, standardized itineraries and, for the first time, defined destinations. When almost all travelers rode the same rails into and through the interior—from New York to Chicago to Omaha with minor variations of Chicago-to–St. Louis or Chicago-to–St. Paul—many of the old paths of interest were forgotten, and wandering came to an end. In the style of travel created by the railroads, the interior, which lacked both specific notable destinations and dramatic scenery, was in trouble. Once rail travel came to dominate, the Ohio River was never again seen or mentioned by a travel writer; no one traveling the interior reported on elegant old Cincinnati or praised its bookstores, and its longtime title of "Queen City of the West" travelers shifted first to Chicago in 1869 and then to Denver in 1889. No traveler ever again mentioned the interior's prehistoric mounds and earthworks, or saw Galena or Cairo; Indiana and often Iowa also were blotted from travelers' view because most travelers crossed them at night. Chicago was proclaimed the center of a landscape that had previously made do uncentered. Every westward-rushing traveler, however, had to cross the Mississippi River, the sight of which antebellum travelers had awaited with excitement and on which they had traveled for hundreds of miles. To cross the Mississippi on a railroad bridge, however, was not to travel the Mississippi: mere crossing reduced the great river to its width and depth, erasing both its length and the nature of its banks. Those few travelers who crossed the Mississippi at St. Louis were especially disappointed with the river; Henry Lucy said it was "simply a solution of yellow mud" and Henry Vivian called it nothing but "a stream—the most disappointing first-class river I ever saw." Although eastbound travelers usually crossed the Mississippi at Burlington, Iowa, during the night, westbound travelers sometimes caught a glimpse of the river just as night came on. James Hogan, however, noticed only the bridge and missed the river; John Lester instructed the porter to rouse him to see the river, but he too became preoccupied with the bridge; and W. F. Rae was so frightened by the creaking and swaying of the bridge that his life—rather than the Mississippi—began to flash before his eyes and he missed the view entirely.[21]

Travelers so disengaged themselves from the landscape that when they did notice something, they settled for offering a wild guess about it. Sealed in the Pullman cars and feeling no wind around their ears, travelers wondered idly why farmers in the interior planted rows of poplars, pronounced the climate of northern Illinois to be very dry, reported dimly on the rumored existence of *chipmucks,* classified skunks as felines and claimed that they danced on their hind paws—instead of balancing on their forepaws—before spraying, and empty-headedly wondered, as they looked out at the interior, "where all the people came from, and where all the grain and hay they grow goes to." Misunderstanding the nature of cultivation in the interior, they hatched schemes to import Chinese labor to grow cotton in Nebraska. They guessed that cities must have preceded agriculture in the interior, forgot about the honeybee and thus anointed the train itself "the true harbinger of civilization," and discussed how odd it was that the least valuable land in the interior had been, they had heard, the first settled. Simultaneous with these idle confusions, they began to inflate the interior's very recent past, paint it as heroic, and relay tales of "great battles between the whites and the Indians" only forty years past, of once constant attacks by ferocious large animals, and of struggles and perils that had left the locals "ennobled" by their victories.[22]

In travelers' end-of-the-century rewriting of the history of settlement, such terms as *pioneer* and *frontier* made their first appearances in travel literature about the interior. This new version required in the telling a hostile view of the indigenous Indian population, and travelers, not one of whom after 1870 ever visited Indian life on the ground, were ready to supply it. Indian-hating, in the closing decades of the century, became dogma among travelers and produced bizarre assertions that Indians had driven the game out of the interior and cut down its trees—thus shifting over to Indians blame for some of the greater landscape excesses committed by white men. No rail traveler even glimpsed an Indian until he or she reached the westernmost border of the interior. Instead travelers heard about Indians.

Immediately upon leaving Omaha for the West, travelers on the first transcontinental trains had their fears excited by hearing from other passengers tales of torture and of the brutality that defenseless travelers might be expected to encounter at the hands of Indians in the vicinity. Although some travelers noticed that these horrific tales combined poorly with the visible landscape of farmhouses and cultivated fields that lined both sides of the right-of-way, the threatening atmosphere that the rumormongers sought to create became more real when an agent of a railway insurance company moved through the cars and "vigorously canvassed the passengers" to buy insurance against the perils just ahead. Then, about a hundred miles west of Omaha, travelers were afforded a ritual glimpse, a ceremonial view made to seem unplanned, of a group of Pawnees posed in various attitudes about the station platform. Passengers were informed that the Pawnees, though "friendly," were armed and bloodthirsty, that they lived by hunting and "gloried in getting scalps." Travelers had their attention called to "wisps of hair" fluttering from a group of not-too-distant lodge poles. Then, in the next step in a complex orchestration of attitudes, frightened travelers were reassured that the Pawnees on view were not "wild Indians"—a usage that only Robert Louis Stevenson pierced through to its meaning of *independent*—since Indians of that description usually made a point of "avoiding the neighborhood of the train." Some passengers disboarded to "dance and jest around" the display group of Pawnees, not one of whom ever moved during the process; other travelers cowered in the train, and when they peeked out at the Pawnees they saw them exactly as they had been coached to see them and exactly as what they had insured themselves against. In extreme contrast, contemporaneous guidebook writers who were selling not insurance but the idea of family tourism liked to represent the Indians arrayed at prearranged stops as there to "delight the children," but those travelers who risked no more than a peep out the window at the human display invariably pronounced the

Indians assembled for their viewing to be dirty, ugly, and lazy, thus expressing standard nineteenth-century imperial views. Those same travelers, however, took pleasure in Indian place names and believed them "far better than the modern ones," and they still wanted and attempted to procure the Indians' goods. Theodora Guest, glancing at "some of those miserable dirty Indians with papooses" from her vantage point in a private car, wrote, "Why the latter live (or indeed why they *should* live) I cannot conceive"; her personal travel agent, however, was later dispatched to buy an Indian blanket for her. In 1884, the excursion train on which William Hardman was traveling to Yellowstone came upon, at Gladstone, North Dakota, a party of Gros Ventre seeking a ride westward to a powwow at a Crow reservation. The excursion director, displaying his greatheartedness to his customers, allowed the men onto the observation platform of the excursion train, whereon the excursionists crowded at the end of the car to stare at the Indians and to shop directly from their bodies. Once having bought every bag, bracelet, and pipe available, the excursionists abruptly redefined the Gros Ventre as "hideous, dirty, sly-looking imbeciles" and, only 53 miles down the track from Gladstone, forced them off the train even though the Gros Ventre were still 250 miles from their destination. Hardman complained that the Gros Ventre "did not show any gratitude for the service we had already rendered them. I feel sure," he wrote, "they would have enjoyed nothing so much, if they had the chance, as scalping our whole party." The pattern of Hardman's narrative—staring in fascination at Indians, seeking to acquire all their visible desirable goods directly, if necessary, off their bodies, and then expressing loathing and fear of them once they had been stripped of their goods—obtains throughout all travelers' narratives of contact until the end of the century.[23]

However rare the glimpses train travelers had of the Indian population, they saw very little more of the non-Indian population that had supplanted them. Sitting in reserved seats in Pullman sleeping cars on through trains, travelers spotted locals either at a great distance or in quick attempts to peer into depots as the train roared on through. Miriam Follin Leslie peeped out once into a depot and judged that the women of the interior looked "tired and sad," but because travelers' experience of gender and gendered attitudes had moved entirely inside the train environment, Leslie had no information to offer about women's lives. Grace Greenwood spotted a few children on a station platform in western Illinois and judged them to be "not always well behaved, not always cleanly, but merry and wide-awake." Furthermore, because no local informants were available to them, cross-country travelers took the plunge into landscape assessment unaided by either current information or any experience on the ground. Many travelers, tired of guidebooks that described every scene as "one of the most stupendous in nature and well worth a voyage across the Atlantic to witness," had already abandoned those guidebooks as useless well before they arrived in the interior, and their East Coast informants had turned out to know so little of the rest of the country that their advice too was discarded as soon as travelers crossed the Alleghenies. Travelers fell to issuing reports not only about what they themselves failed to see but also about scenes that could no longer be seen anywhere in the interior. Some travelers, thumbing through books by earlier travelers, appropriated from them descriptions of things that no one had seen for decades: these travelers reported on prairie conflagrations sweeping in their path a landscape cover no longer there to be swept, and gushed over the fragrant far-wafting perfumes of gorgeous prairie flowers that they did not see and whose odors could, in any case, never have penetrated Pullman's double-glass windows.[24]

Most travelers, however, knew nothing of such unseeable features of the interior's past, and while train travel in and of itself obliterated distinctive features of the interior that persisted, travelers rewrote and transformed other features. Because most travelers recorded the interior on the east-to-west axis of their tour, they traveled toward the setting sun and thus never experienced the abrupt sunset of such unusual interest to antebellum travelers. Many gave up the effort to comprehend the scale of the interior: William Hardman labeled Illinois and Iowa "a previously inconceivable expanse of level country . . . very strange," and Catherine Bates rejected the scale of the "general run of huge American lakes" in the interior and opted for Lake George instead. Furthermore, since the interior's landscape became, from the train window, either a running side view or a rolling-over experience, scarcely a single travel writer experienced the distinctive prairie-bowl all-around raised horizon that set apart the experience of movement in the interior from both the East and the Far West; instead they experienced a one-sided view of the bowl that translated into nothing more than limited vision or a short fetch. In 1878 in northern Illinois, Henry Vivian was genuinely puzzled when he encountered a vestige of the prairie-bowl effect: he was on the lookout for a prospect, but instead, he wrote, "Again and again I asked myself whether I could see a mile from the train, and, with one or two exceptions, I was forced to return a negative answer." In the East, railroad cars were regularly emplaced so that passengers who had bought the most expensive accommodations faced the best scenery, but westward through the interior no such stratagems were called for; the interior was no more about to give itself to the eye than it ever had, no matter how much the eye had paid for the view. The extraordinary physical effects of experiencing the interior as a surround were no longer available when train travel converted both the interior's splendidly dense and various insect population and its astounding weather into mere noise, and even then only the biggest bugs and the loudest thunderclaps could make themselves known to train travelers. In 1856 near Decatur, Illinois, William Ferguson was frightened when the song of a swarm of locusts penetrated the car. Unable to imagine what insect activity could produce such a roar, he could only note balefully: "They were not eating." The weather was likewise converted into noise, and thunder that boomed loud enough to be heard over the rumble of the train was still capable of terrifying travelers. On a train crossing Iowa, Grace Greenwood and other passengers sought to aid an English traveler who, "used only to moderate insular thunder, was utterly prostrated and appalled, and thrown into violent nervous spasms" by the noise. Guidebooks began to suggest in the 1870s certain categories of sights—such as Chicago—that a traveler might leave the train to see only if the weather was "fine enough" to warrant it, and thus to require of the climate certain pleasant and undramatic qualities whose appearance in the interior remained as unpredictable as ever. Most travelers' focus was on not the climate of the interior but the interior climate of the train, of whose "atrocious ventilation" every traveler complained. To the old fresh-air travel experience of open coaches, unchinked walls, and steamboat decks, the trains presented a complete contrast. All women travelers and many international travelers claimed to be "gasping" in cars heated to eighty degrees while the conductor saw to it that both windows and ventilators were kept tight shut. "I guess we can't afford to warm the prairies as we pass," a conductor remarked to Emily Faithfull as he reached across her to close the window she had just opened. As a result, travelers' concerns about both weather and health shifted off the landscape and into the car itself, where they wrote of their battles against the deleterious effects of "second-hand breath."[25]

The pig—the interior's notable animal, whose command of the urban streets and whose rural frolics antebellum travelers had enjoyed observing—was in the closing decades of the century seen only at the point of death, during travelers' obligatory visit to the Union Stockyards in Chicago. Antebellum travelers had visited or avoided the stockyards just as they chose, but every east–west rail traveler had a layover in Chicago of just the right length for a tour of the stockyards. Henry Lucy, told that nine out of any ten travelers who passed through Chicago visited the stockyards, refused to go and wrote: "Unless people have a fancy for seeing pigs killed, there is nothing in

Chicago to keep a traveler." Isabella Trotter also refused, and waited in the carriage while her husband took the tour, and Theodora Guest, though a guide assured her that "ladies went the rounds" and saw within forty-five minutes the pig caught, killed, and transformed into roasts and chops, took only ten steps before she turned back. James Hogan thought that there must be a more "attractive or refining spectacle" available in Chicago and did not go; but Catherine Bates went, in part because she was not accompanied by a man who could go for her, and in part because she refused to fall in with the "curious notion that in some way cruel sights are less degrading to men than to women." She was appalled by the experience. She and her companion spent an hour on the streetcars to get to the stockyards, and then walked a long way through them to Hutchinson's Pig-Killing Yard. During the walk, Bates eyed the parallel "forced procession of the miserable pigs" along covered wooden bridges toward death. Then she watched them, one by one, "pass through a door into a building where a large iron hook is fastened on to one of their legs and they are hauled down some steps on one of which stands a man with a carving knife. He makes a hasty slash at the throat, but the wretched animal is not killed, only slung on, to be caught by another man who unhooks it, throws it into boiling water to loosen the hair, and it is then passed on to a cruel machine with jagged iron teeth where it is thrown ruthlessly backwards and forwards until all the hair of the skin is removed. I saw," she wrote, "pigs kicking, struggling, and most evidently in torture *after all three of these fiendish performances.*" Bates's guide assured her that she was observing nothing but "muscular movement after death," but he did not make a believer of her. She called him "glib" and asserted that it was impossible to believe that the pigs "were really *dead* when they were shrieking and squalling, kicking their legs and rolling their eyes in agony." She came away convinced that the pigs "were capable of intense suffering and did suffer intensely long after their throats were cut." Sickened and disgusted, she inveighed against the owners of such operations who had "fattened and grown rich on this fiendish cruelty." In his guidebook for travelers on their way to California, however, the slaughter of a pig was the only tourist sight Charles Nordhoff suggested between New York and Omaha; he recommended the stockyards, in an extreme contrast to Bates's view, as an exhibition of "care for the feelings" of the livestock. William Hardman went to the stockyards because his excursion party was scheduled to go and he never questioned his excursion director's plans, but he refused to describe what he had seen: "Nothing," he wrote, "would induce me to visit it again, neither do I care to dwell any longer upon it now." Although Hardman repeated the bromides about the animals' comfort and their painless death that Catherine Bates rejected, he was nonetheless clearly desperate to get away from the scene but could not because in his party were "some strong-minded ladies . . . who lingered so fondly among the horrors of the place that the weaker sex (in this case the men) were in despair." The sorry reduction in the pig's presence from the jolly street theater and municipal garbage-removal service it had once supplied to its passivity in an efficient slaughter spectacle is notable: pigs had come under containment and could surprise a traveler only by the way they died. Beyond the standard stockyards visit, most train travelers saw no animal life, either wild or domestic, in the interior.[26]

The landscape of the interior, unlike the pigs, was not avoidable, and travelers had a long exposure to it. Until, in the 1890s, a few luxury trains tried for speed, the best postbellum trains crawled through the interior at but thirty to forty miles per hour. Even though many through trains crossed all of Indiana and all of Iowa under cover of night, there remained a lot of the interior to unroll in daylight, posing, it might be argued, the greatest challenge to travel writers of any North American landscape, denying itself to the camera and the sketch artist, and shouldering aside any writer's store of standard scenic adjectives. The interior was such a challenge that many travel writers searched out ways not to write about it: Ethel Abbott spent all her time despising the other passengers' clothes in detail, and Mary Duffus Hardy discussed the smoothness of the ride and described her meals. Travelers pretended their readers already knew too much about a landscape that the writer knew too little of to describe; Henry Lucy transported himself from New York City to Chicago during a chapter break, and John Lester avoided "re-stating many well-known facts" by opening his narrative in Chicago. Horace Greeley claimed to be in a hurry and preferred to start his narrative at the Missouri River, and W. A. Bell began his in St. Louis. Some travelers looked at photographs and dreamed ahead to the Royal Gorge in Colorado or to Yosemite. At Omaha, W. F. Rae experienced "a general feeling of relief . . . the journey was now fairly begun" and the challenge of the interior was left behind.[27]

All travelers had heard of the prairies of the interior, as had all their readers in the nineteenth century; and when travelers knew they might be in the vicinity of prairies, many made an effort to glimpse the distinctive landscape whose extraordinary character had taken its name around the globe. Train travel and the prairies, however, never made a successful match. Antebellum travelers who tried to see prairies from the train had little success in their struggle to render them in prose. William Ferguson and William Hancock both rode the antebellum Illinois Central, but neither could describe the landscape that the road took them through. Ferguson called the sight "inconceivable," and Hancock, after claiming that "it is easier to say what a prairie is not than what it is," abandoned even that tack and decided a prairie could best be described by a poet, which he was not. By 1870 Newman Hall, also on the Illinois Central, saw still less prairie, and wrote: "Very little of the primeval grass remained." Once there had been so much prairie that no one had thought it would all disappear, but two 1873 travelers, Grace Greenwood and John Lester, saw in both Illinois and Iowa nothing but cultivation, whereon both decided that cornfields must be "plowed prairies," and Greenwood even made an unconvincing stab at transforming a cornfield into "a symbol of the infinite."[28]

The cultivated landscape of the interior was no less difficult to describe than the prairie it had replaced. James Shaw fumbled with such adjectives as "oriental and tropical"; and Robert Louis Stevenson, who found the interior "not at all as [he] had pictured it," settled on awarding it "an elegance peculiar to itself." M. M. Shaw collapsed all of Illinois into "a rich agricultural region"; Catherine Bates, who was most impressed by the "really appalling" heat of the interior's summer, took only a moment to notice that Iowa looked "much more green" than had points westward. Numerous other travelers blurred three or four states of the interior into no more than "pleasant green fields" or into nothing but a color—"one superb shade of green." In contrast to the general cultivated streak of "bright verdure" that the train rolled over, remnants of the original prairie association began to draw distinctly bad reviews from travelers who dismissed them as "a rank profusion of weeds" and "a bad crop of coarse hay." At Dixon, Illinois, in 1876, Miriam Follin Leslie stepped out of her private hotel car for a moment to have a "poetic fancy" on a prairie remnant, but a few real raindrops sent her back to the car where she and her companions pronounced the scene "dismal." Finally, in 1892, Richard Harding Davis, in an unparalleled descriptive sweep, characterized the entire interior as "a very wonderful, large, unfinished, and out-of-doors portion of our country." In the flip and helpless atmosphere of such descriptive efforts, the English traveler John White stands out for his effort to contest such dismissals by forcing himself to see. Crossing the interior in October of 1869 with an excursion of 150 newspapermen who at once "resolved themselves into card-parties" from which they never looked up, White alone scrutinized the landscape of northern Illinois.

He noted that only along the railroad right-of-way did the prairie association remain. Even though reduced from an expanse to a strip, it nonetheless retained "all its wildness—prairie, untouched as though the white man had never drawn round it his fatal and narrowing circle of outposts—prairie, that looks friendless and desolate and doomed, as it heavily sways to the wind its long, rank, withered grasses." When at nightfall the train entered Iowa, White went out to stand on the train's rear platform to continue studying the landscape by moonlight and to grasp, in the process, "a new idea of space."[29]

The difficulties of approaching the interior aided by the sense of sight alone were for most observers insurmountable. If settlers had eradicated the landscape's original cover, travel writers were tempted to eradicate the replacement landscape and to define the interior's subtle repetitions and fineness of detail as mere tedium, and many succumbed to the temptation. Choosing to favor the urban and the dramatically scenic elsewhere, they abandoned the contest to understand and define the interior, and characterized what they saw of it as monotonous, wearisome, dull, uninteresting, dreary, and without either interest or "views." Frustrated and even irritated by the interior's nearly thousand-mile-long horizontal insistence on being itself, they turned to reading; they yawned; their "spirits drooped." They drew down the "dark heavy blind" and closed the "pretty gray curtains" and chose to wait it out. A nearly century-long conversation about the interior—how to live there, how to experience the landscape, and how to locate comfort on it—was ended. Whatever comfort was, the through trains that crawled across the interior had preempted the right to define it: within the train, travelers could cite and number their potential comforts, as they never could on the landscape, and buy their way onto specific class levels that had been incalculable on the landscape. Many, having left their readers a picture of almost nothing, were relieved to be out of the interior, and the only remaining conversation about what they had left behind was conducted between trains.[30]

Like Theodora Guest, whose quick confrontation with Coxey's Army on a station platform troubled her briefly, Robert Louis Stevenson also received a message by looking out of the train at people on the platform. Some potent messages about the interior were delivered to travelers not by the landscape they glanced at but by persons shouting to the train from outside it. As the emigrant train that carried Robert Louis Stevenson in a car full of men "fleeing in quest of a better land" steamed westward away from the interior and toward "the land of gold," it continually passed other emigrant trains, trains just as crowded as the one Stevenson rode, steaming eastbound into the interior. Whenever Stevenson's train met one of those eastbound trains at a station, the same eerie event occurred: the passengers from the eastbound train "ran on the platform and cried to us through the windows, in a kind of wailing chorus, to 'come back.' On the plains of Nebraska, in the mountains of Wyoming, it was still the same cry, and dismal to my heart, 'Come back! Come back!'"[31]

Notes

CHAPTER 1. SECRETS OF THE INTERIOR

1. The term *landscape* needs to be paused over here. D. W. Meinig, ed., *Interpretation of Ordinary Landscapes* (New York: Oxford University Press, 1979), differentiates landscape from nature, scenery, environment, place, region, area, and geography; he defines landscape as "expressions of cultural values, social behavior, and individual actions worked upon particular localities over a span of time. Every landscape is an accumulation and every landscape is a code" (1–6). To use the term *landscape* is to collapse the old binary distinction between *man* and *nature;* landscape, says Denis Cosgrove, *Social Formation and Symbolic Landscapes* (London: Croom Helm, 1984), "derives from the active engagement of a human subject with the material object . . . landscape is a *social* product, the consequence of a collective transformation of nature" (13).

2. The interior's boundaries have been argued over. In 1828, Timothy Flint defined the interior as the Mississippi River valley, noted that others complained of "a vagueness in this appellation" but insisted it was "a very definite and significant term" (*Condensed Geography,* 3). In 1836, James Hall spread the interior from the northern lakes to the mouth of the Ohio, a distance of about six hundred miles, and said it was "properly *the West,* the seat of what is called the western population, and the most valuable tract of country in the United States" (*Statistics,* 13). In 1867 Henry Morton Stanley was certain "after a careful investigation" that the interior ended and the West began "on the western bank of the Republican River, two miles east of Junction City" (Stanley, 140–41). For Frederick Jackson Turner, *The Significance of Sections in American History* (New York: Holt, 1932), the Middle West embraced Ohio, Indiana, Illinois, Michigan, Wisconsin, Missouri, Iowa, Minnesota, Kansas, Nebraska, North Dakota, and South Dakota. "Great as are the local differences within the Midwest," wrote Turner, "it possesses, in its physiography, in the history of its settlement, and in its economics and social life, a unity and interdependence which warrant a study of the area as an entity" (127). Edwin Fussell, *Frontier: American Literature and the American West* (Princeton, N.J.: Princeton University Press, 1965), however, sees Turner's definition as no more than an unrecognized metaphor of a "Middle Region" that is simply "not frontier" (436). For William Cronon, *Nature's Metropolis: Chicago and the Great West* (New York: W. W.

Norton, 1991), the Great West extends from the Ohio River to the Pacific (xvi). Wilbur Zelinsky, *Cultural Geography of the United States* (Englewood Cliffs, N.J.: Prentice-Hall, 1973), says, "Everyone within and outside the Middle West knows of its existence, but no one seems sure where it begins or ends," even though Zelinsky believes it is "justly regarded as the most modal, the section most nearly representative of the national average." Although Zelinsky's Midwest has no "genuine focal zone," it is surrounded by a "first-order cultural boundary." Zelinsky urges seeing the area as an "eastward-pointing equilateral triangle" that cuts a little north of the Ohio River, slices off the lower third of Missouri, and extends westward to the 100th meridian (118–19, 128–29). Zelinsky's triangle is what was experienced in the antebellum nineteenth century as the interior.

3. Tremenheere, 2; Rose, xi; Scott, vii; Kirkland, *Western Clearings,* vi.

4. Consideration of the individual motives that drove travelers does little more than distract from their observations of landscape, culture, and society, and from any conflict larger than the personal and individual. If the late twentieth century wonders whether travelers have anything more important than themselves to report on, the nineteenth century saw the matter differently. Nineteenth-century travelers prided themselves not on being selves but on being eyewitnesses, and no matter what they might have learned of themselves in their travels, they saw a journey not as a voyage of self-discovery but as an opportunity for forthright social assessment.

5. Lieber, 224–25.

6. There are, of course, great and obvious differences between nineteenth-century travel literature and late-twentieth-century tourist literature. Travel literature is by and about travelers and can employ many tones, whereas tourist literature is an offering to travelers and aims to be always celebratory; only in its silences and exclusions does tourist literature suggest a critique. Nineteenth-century travel literature relied on words and rarely used illustrations because its readers had no interest in illustrations, whereas tourist literature deploys its photographs to pull some items into view and suppress others. The congruence between the two literatures overrides their differences: both are literatures of the landscape and both speak to movers of movement. If nineteenth-century travel writers spoke for the interior, today in tourist literature the interior speaks of itself and constructs itself for travelers.

7. Stanley, 140–41.

8. In February of 1994, schoolchildren in Tipton, Iowa, organized a campaign to pressure state legislators into naming the bison the state mammal. There was concern as to how the pigs would take the news, but eventually the legislators acceded to the children's wish and designated the bison Iowa's state mammal through 1996.

9. See David Costello, *The Prairie World* (Minneapolis: University of Minnesota Press, 1969). Efforts to revive and restore prairie remnants by reintroducing plant species, regular burning, and grazing bison are ongoing here and there across the interior, but efforts to bill these restorations as tourist draws have their doubters. "I don't know how many people will come and watch the grass grow," says one local of the proposed Walnut Creek National Wildlife Refuge–Prairie Learning Center near Prairie City, Iowa (*Des Moines Register,* 11 January 1994, 3M).

10. These statues are not without their critics. In the St. Paul City Hall–Courthouse stands a fifty-five-ton onyx statue done by Carl Milles in 1936 and named "The God of Peace": according to Milles, "five Indians are sitting around a fire smoking their pipes of peace. Out of that smoke of tobacco and fire arises in their imaginations their god of peace, talking to them and all their world." The statue is

considered by members of the Winnebago tribe to be unrelated to and disrespectful of their actual religious beliefs.

11. Van Cleve, 162.

12. "Authentic reconstruction" is a term of absolute exactitude that does as much as it can with the past. A reconstruction, unlike what it reconstructs, is always authentic; its provenance is unquestionable.

13. Attacks on and rejection of Frederick Jackson Turner's Frontier Thesis issue from historians, geographers, and anthropologists. James C. Malin, *History and Ecology* (Lincoln: University of Nebraska Press, 1984), asserts that *frontier* means "the frontier of the culture of modern Europe" and consequently denies both values and rights to the cultures it displaced (106–7), and Patricia Nelson Limerick, *Trails: Toward a New Western History* (Lawrence: University Press of Kansas, 1991), asserts that the "frontier model relentlessly trivialized the West . . . rendering the nineteenth-century past irrelevant to the twentieth-century present" (69). Geographers object to the Frontier Thesis as divorced from historical facts. Wilbur Zelinsky, *Cultural Geography,* calls the Turner thesis "a great quasi-religious folk legend . . . but if we wish to discover how American culture really developed, we must turn elsewhere" (35). Zelinsky believes frontier ingenuity to be exaggerated and points out that gear associated with "frontier" life was invented in the East. The anthropologist Mary Louise Pratt, *Imperial Eyes: Studies in Travel Writing and Transculturation* (London: Routledge, 1992), rejects the term *frontier* because it is "grounded within a European expansionist perspective"; she seeks to replace *frontier* with "contact zone . . . the space in which peoples geographically and historically separated come into contact with each other and establish ongoing relations, usually involving conditions of coercion, radical inequality, and intractable conflict" (6).

14. Although frequently called "English" in tourist literature, this Christmas past has little to do with England except for the fact that English literature furnished its favorite text—Charles Dickens's *A Christmas Carol* (1843)—a text about the virtuous urban poor dependent on the chance enlightenment of the wealthy for food and medical care. On the American scene, the current vision of Christmas past is capable of vacuuming up nearly anything and reassembling it into Christmas. On December Sundays, for example, in Fort Abraham Lincoln State Park, four miles south of Mandan, North Dakota, travelers can visit the house from which George Armstrong Custer rode away in June 1876 on his way to the Little Big Horn, and there, for a fee, experience the "Custer Christmas Celebration." Travelers will be able to "step inside the white mansion, decked in holiday finery, and join the taffy pulls, Christmas carol sing-alongs, and story-telling. Tour guides in gingham frocks and velvet gowns string cranberries and popcorn around the Christmas tree. You almost expect to see the blond-haired general with a bagful of Christmas presents in tow . . . guests can top off their visit with an authentic 1800s family feast."

15. Contemporary writers on the subject of the Victorian revival and how to achieve its look struggle with a covert discussion of class, and often end up defining the style by separating it from whatever was practiced by "the strictly rural or rustic folk" (Allison Kyle Leopold, *Victorian Splendor* [New York: Stewart, Tabori, and Chang, 1986], 20–21)—that group which nineteenth-century British travelers longed to meet and graciously condescend to but could never locate in the interior. Thus *the Victorian* separates itself from what it is not; wherever those rustic folk existed, it was not in the interior, where travelers could find neither folk nor rustics nor simplicity. John Gloag's discussion of the subject of comfort in *Victorian Comfort: A Social History of Design* (London: Adam and Charles Black, 1961)

is often acidic: "The Victorians loved comfort without shame . . . the love of comfort in time debilitated the critical faculties, and the decline of taste in the 1820s and 1830s coincided with the rise of an insensitive plutocracy whose leaders unconsciously cultivated a philosophy of comfort, which was adopted by the middle classes, expounded in its material aspects by Dickens—who liked writing about cosy rooms and cosy inns and food and drink and good fellowship—and embraced by everybody who enjoyed modest, easy, or affluent circumstances . . . they closed their eyes . . . and revelling in comfort, lost their sense of sight so far as the form and color of their cities and homes were concerned" (xv).

16. Logan, 131; I. Pfeiffer, 15.

17. A traveler fully on the run from the B&B phenomenon might want to flee as far west as Montana, whose *1993 Lodging Guide* features a teepee on its cover.

CHAPTER 2. THE DERANGEMENT OF COMFORT

1. F. Trollope, 97–99.

2. Latrobe, 121; Volney, 290; Oliver, 76.

3. F. Michaux, 189; Amphlett, 173; Blane, 125; T. Flint, *Recollections,* 54; Kirkland, *Forest Life,* 43–44.

4. J. Flint, 231–32; Collins, 20; Duden, 65; Martineau, *Society* II, 93.

5. T. Hamilton, 160; Fuller, 35; Featherstonhaugh I, 91; Fuller, 21; A. Trollope, 86; Hoffman I, 222.

6. Chevalier, 302–3.

7. Baily, 219, 198; F. Michaux, 150; Melish II, 261–62; Gerstacker, 76.

8. Backhouse, 119; Scott, 155; Duden, 134; Griffiths, 90; Kinzie, 170.

9. Welby, 292; J. Flint, 265.

10. Shirreff, 315; C. A. Murray II, 77; Kirkland, *A New Home,* 73, 84, 111, 114.

11. Kirkland, *Forest Life,* 63; *Western Clearings,* 35; *A New Home,* 43; Fuller, 44–45.

12. Hall, *Statistics,* 61; Frederick Marryat, 183; Vigne II, 81; Welby-Gregory, 94–95.

13. C. A. Murray I, 260; Frederick Marryat, 212–13. In 1993, the Department of the Interior sponsored a three-day meeting in Chicago to develop a plan to recover the oak savanna, a landscape that looked like an open grove of oak trees with an understory of wildflowers and hazel bushes, and that once covered 30 million acres of the interior. According to William K. Stevens, "Restoring an Ancient Landscape," *New York Times,* 2 March 1993, B5, "less than 1 percent of high-quality oak savanna remains, in fragments that biologists say are too small and scattered for many of the species that live there to survive in the long run. Hundreds of thousands more acres exist in degraded and biologically impoverished form, their ecological character destroyed and most of the many species that once lived there long gone."

14. Hoffman I, 184; E. James I, 164.

15. Birkbeck, *Notes,* 149, 154.

16. Birkbeck, *Notes,* 9, 151, 127, 102, 102, 115, 112, 111; *Letters,* 38; *Notes,* 50.

17. Flower, 107, 133, 124; Birkbeck, *Notes,* 125, 113; Flower, 128.

18. Cobbett, *A Year's Residence,* 291, 285; Hulme, 48, 50.

19. Howitt, x; Flower, 123, 129–30; O'Ferrall, 112.

20. Faux, 255, 252, 264; Welby, 251, 254, 266; Hodgson, 26.

21. Stuart II, 242.

22. Martineau, *Society* I, 321; C. A. Murray I, 260; Frederick Marryat, 212; Newhall, 53; N. Hall, 126; Medley, 89.

23. Woods, 343; Flint, *Recollections,* 251; Stuart II, 244; Latrobe, 232.

24. A. Trollope, 187; F. Trollope, 95; Trotter, 251; T. Hamilton, 160; Fuller, 21, 35; Featherstonhaugh I, 91; A. Trollope, 86; Hoffman I, 222.

25. Montule, 129; Shirreff, 252; Lakier, 221; Vigne II, 279.

26. Welby, 283; T. Hamilton, 175; Dickens, 130; Cunynghame, 177; Dickens, 130; Levinge, 242; F. Trollope, 37.

27. Dickens, 246; Grandfort, 116; Alexander, 77; Bunn, 37.

28. Bradbury, 304; Stuart II, 266; Shirreff, 398; Cunynghame, 124; F. Trollope, 100; Weld, 13; C. A. Murray I, 218; Oliver, 31; A. Trollope, 196; E. Pfeiffer, 90. Francis J. Grund's *Aristocracy in America* (1839) is a full documentation of the effort to build class distinctions in eastern cities even while no such distinctions functioned in the interior.

29. Kirkland, *Forest Life,* 116, 64; C. Stewart, 93; Griffiths, 87; Kirkland, *A New Home,* 66; Martineau, *Retrospect* II, 50; J. Flint, 137; F. Trollope, 52; Faux, 230.

30. T. Hamilton, 178; A. Trollope, 204–5.

31. B. Hall III, 388; Cuming, 202; Blane, 146; Latrobe, 297–98; T. Hamilton, 248.

32. Paul Wilhelm, 269; de Zavala, 52; Chambers, 147; Faux, 198; A. Trollope, 198, 189.

33. Martineau, *Retrospect* I, 36; *Retrospect* II, 184; Paul Wilhelm, 269; de Zavala, 52.

34. F. Trollope, 102; von Raumer, 449; Oliphant, 279–80. Erving Goffman, *Behavior in Public Places* (Glencoe, Ill.: Free Press, 1963), discusses how a "participant in a social gathering may be obliged to sustain at least a certain minimal main involvement to avoid the appearance of being utterly disengaged," and argues that newspapers serve this social activity by "providing a portable source of involvement, which can be brought forth whenever an individual feels he ought to have an involvement but does not" (51–52).

35. J. Hall, *Letters,* 130; Hoffman II, 100; A. Trollope, 87.

36. Kirkland, *A New Home,* 192; von Raumer, 449; Kirkland, *Western Clearings,* 222.

CHAPTER 3. DREAMING ON THE RUN

1. Thomson, 89–90. David Costello, *The Prairie World* (Minneapolis: University of Minnesota Press, 1969), summarizes much that is known of the prairie landscape that once covered one-third of the North American continent and whose "universal characteristic was the dominance of grasses" (4). The prairie's real beginnings lie in the Cenozoic era some 60 million years ago, when conditions first began to favor plant and animal life. According to Costello, "in the Miocene and Pleistocene epochs, which covered a period of some 25 million years, mountains rose in western North America and created a continental climate favorable to grasslands. Ancient forests declined, grasslands became widespread, flowering plants evolved, and elephants, horses, and camels almost like our modern species flourished on the ancient prairies. The Pleistocene, which began about one million years ago, was a time of continuous change. There were four major ice advances and retreats. In the northern portion of the continent this waxing and waning of the glacial ice displaced the floras and faunas and greatly changed their areas of distribution. The fossil evidence indicates, however, that most plants of the modern prairie were present during Pleistocene time" (13–14). Around 1800,

when the earliest travelers entered the interior, "in what is now Indiana and Illinois the prairie was more or less continuous on the uplands, while the forests formed strips along the streams and rivers. West of Illinois the prairie became dominant and covered much of western Minnesota, Wisconsin, Iowa, and Missouri. Here the forest belts narrowed until they occurred mainly along stream courses and on river bottoms" (37). The root system that underlies the prairie association of dozens of grasses and broad-leaved herbs can extend to a depth of fifteen feet.

2. David Wilson, *In the Presence of Nature* (Amherst: University of Massachusetts Press, 1978), 19–20; O'Ferrall, 114; Scott, 103. It is to be remembered that no living eyes have seen or can see the landscape that nineteenth-century travelers saw: the prairie association was even then being eradicated by the plow, and the landscape of the American interior has, since 1800, been more thoroughly altered than any other landscape on the face of the globe. It is rare to find even a small remnant of deep-soil prairie; only in old graveyards or along railroad rights-of-way or in certain prairie preserves does some remain. Nonetheless, even though the prairie association of grasses and forbs has vanished, the effect of the landscape of the interior was not eradicated with it. Prairie eradication did not allow landscape variety to emerge but instead substituted the visible grid of cultivated fields for the miles of shoulder-high grass, producing not a natural landscape but what Claude Lévi-Strauss has described in *Tristes Tropiques,* trans. John Weightman and Doreen Weightman (London: Jonathon Cape, 1973), as a "vast outdoor factory." Contemporary geographers regularly point out that, then as now, many parts of the landscape of the interior tend to imprison the viewer in horizontals. The trail—or interstate—ahead is often the only source of a vertical in the landscape but it is a vertical foreshortened by the nature of the horizon. See Yi-Fu Tuan, *Topophilia* (Englewood Cliffs, N.J.: Prentice-Hall, 1974), for a full discussion of such effects.

3. Schoolcraft, *Travels in the Central Portions,* 329. From the point of view of the cultural geographer Wilbur Zelinsky, *Cultural Geography of the United States* (Englewood Cliffs, N.J.: Prentice-Hall, 1973), the North American landscape in general is "coarser than in most parts of Europe, Asia, or middle America . . . less often punctuated by minor irregularities that might catalyze and shelter local cultural peculiarity" (40).

4. T. Hamilton, 167–68; D. Griffiths, 30; Daubeny, 193; Tremenheere, 153; Oliphant, 295; Goddard, 248.

5. Fearon, 217; Borrett, 116; Macrae, 159; Dickens, 52; MacGregor, 113; Stevenson, 123–24; Wilde quoted in Peter Conrad, *Imagining America* (New York: Oxford University Press, 1980), 19.

6. Dickens, 183; Martineau, *Retrospect* II, 20, 23; T. Farnham, 63; Hall, *Statistics,* 76; Blane, 185; Beltrami II, 132; Oliver, 98; Scott, 74–75. Perhaps the interior was too large to love; the geographer Yi-Fu Tuan suggests, "just as the pretense to 'love for humanity' arouses our suspicion, so topophilia [love of place] rings false when it is claimed for a large territory. A compact size scaled down to man's biologic needs and sense-bound capacities seems necessary. In addition, people can more readily identify with an area if it appears to be a natural unit" (*Topophilia,* 101).

7. Shirreff, 7, 243–44; Hoffman II, 316–17; C. A. Murray I, 261; Bremer, 92; Buckingham, *Eastern and Western* III, 234–35; Blane, 200.

8. C. A. Murray I, 261; Arese, 112, 115; Gerstacker, 63–67; Martineau, *Society* I, 218; F. Trollope, 49–50.

9. Paul Wilhelm, 406; E. Farnham, 325; Vigne II, 1–2; Chevalier, 204.

10. Faux, 281; Schoolcraft, *Travels in the Central Portions,* 215; Flagg I, 233; B. Hall, 385; Blane, 182; Dickens, 182; Campbell, 277; Hoffman I, 226.

11. N. Hall, 160–61; Campbell, 290; Ellsworth, 137.

12. J. Flint, 51–52; Stuart II, 91; Fuller, 25; Woods, 311; Drake, *Discourse,* 11; J. Hall, *Western Monthly Magazine* 1, no. 2 (February 1833): 53; Lieber, 71; Mooney, 22.

13. Frederick Marryat, 192; Stuart II, 157; Arese, 51; T. Flint, *Recollections,* 136.

14. F. Michaux, 192; J. S. Wright, 41; Amphlett, 195; Faux, 179; Tocqueville II, 144; Chevalier, 261–62; Kirkland, *Forest Life,* 30.

15. Scott, vii; Andrews, 89; T. Flint, *Recollections,* 241–42.

16. Frederick Marryat, 102; Weld, 203; O'Ferrall, 167; C. A. Murray I, 148; Holyoake, 243; Alexander, 74; Kirkland, *Forest Life,* 29; Lakier, 150, 176; Dickens, 72; Chevalier, 270, 299. David M. Potter, *People of Plenty: Economic Abundance and the American Character* (Chicago: University of Chicago Press, 1958), observes: "In a country where the entire environment was to be transformed with the least possible delay, a man who was not prepared to undergo personal transformation was hardly an asset. Hence mobility became not merely an optional privilege but almost a mandatory obligation, and the man who failed to meet this obligation had, to a certain extent, defaulted in his duty to society" (97).

17. Kirkland, *A New Home,* 172; *Forest Life,* 27–28; T. Flint, *Recollections,* 206–7; Chevalier, 270.

18. Chastellux, 252–55; Dickens, 186; Lakier, 147; Scott, 70; Oldmixon, 167; T. Flint, *Recollections,* 76. Geographers differ over how life in the interior was affected by the grid that the township and range survey imposed over the landscape. Wilbur Zelinsky, *Cultural Geography of the United States,* maintains:

> The explanation for the prevalence of the isolated farmer lies neither in European precedent nor in economic logic. After 1787, with remorseless rectangularity and with the greatest possible disregard for the sphericity of the earth and the variable qualities of its surface, more than two million square miles of public domain were blocked off into 36-square-mile townships and these in turn, subdivided into 36 sections, each one mile square. . . . Note the lack of provision for town sites. . . . The layout of roads and, more particularly, the shape of individual properties and the placement of farmsteads within them, reveal a strong bias toward solitude.

Zelinsky further observes that "the urge toward very large, isolated, individual properties seems to go beyond any rational economic reckoning. This is most obvious in the isolated farmstead, for which no convincing argument can be made in terms of transportation systems or social utility" (46–48, 90–91). John Brinckerhoff Jackson, "The Order of Landscape: Reason and Religion in Newtonian America," in *Interpretation of Ordinary Landscapes,* ed. D. W. Meinig (New York: Oxford University Press, 1979), says he searched travel literature—whose "set pieces on American scenery" he found "all but impossible to read"—for mentions of the grid and found next to nothing. Jackson is impressed by the isolation of settlers' homes but keeps the subject of isolation disconnected from the grid (158–59). John Fraser Hart, *The Look of the Land* (Englewood Cliffs, N.J.: Prentice-Hall, 1975), on the other hand, disagrees with Zelinsky and rejects the argument that the grid ensured isolation and prevented socialization. Says Hart, "The township and range survey system is the best and simplest system of land division ever invented by the mind of mortal man. It provides an excellent frame of reference for orientation, and it conveys a sense of neatness, order, and stability. . . . It is patently ridiculous to assume that a rectangular survey system forces farmsteads to be isolated one from another" (57). There is little material in travel literature allowing consideration of the grid question; it may be, as John Brinckerhoff Jackson, "The Order of Landscape," remarks, that the "rational, mathematical aspect" of the interior "has been revealed to us only within the last generation, with the coming of commercial flying" (160). However, the astute Caroline Kirkland in *Forest Life* remarked on the grid's effect on travel and mobility: traveling a rare curving road in Michigan, "a road of Nature's laying," she noted, "We scorn to be turned aside when we are laying roads. Not that we run them in a direct line between the places we wish to connect. Nothing is further from our plan. We follow section lines most religiously, and consequently—the sections being squares—we shall in time have the pleasure of traveling zigzag at right angles from one corner of the state to another." Kirkland is also the only observer to use the checkerboard image to describe the interior—and this in 1842, well in advance of commercial flight. Kirkland, who personally wished for "a lake in every other quarter-section" of the big board, put the lie to the usual idea that no one "saw" the grid until airplane flight was possible; she saw it and its consequences in terms of travel and connection (127–28).

19. Robinson, 57, 64; Caird, 66; Martineau, *Society* I, 357; D. Griffiths, 35; Dickens, 194; F. Trollope, 198–99.

20. Ashe, *Travels in America,* 244–45; Dana, 6–7; Latrobe, 125; Flagg I, 286–87; Baxter, 242–43; von Raumer, 20–21; J. Hall, *Statistics,* 36; T. Flint, *Recollections,* 120; Baxter, 243; Lanman, *Adventures,* 10–11; Dickens, 182; C. A. Murray II, 69; Oliver, 22–23; Bird, 140; Trotter, 215.

21. Robinson, 28; F. Trollope, 197; Hulme, 53; Kirkland, *A New Home,* 120–21. From one point of view, prairie flowers might be seen as leftover food, if in fact they had once coevolved with the low-browsing dinosaurs of the Cretaceous period who were powerful plant feeders and ate enormous quantities of vegetation. From another point of view, Mary Louise Pratt, *Imperial Eyes: Studies in Travel Writing and Transculturation* (London: Routledge, 1992), suggests that descriptions of flora and fauna, longtime standard components of travel literature, after 1750 began to form a story of "urbanizing, industrializing Europeans fanning out in search of non-exploitive relations to nature, even as they were destroying such relations in their own centers of power." Botanizing travelers were thus seeking to "secure their innocence" and expressing "a great longing for a way of taking possession without subjugation and violence" when they rejected the interior's scenes of "improvement" and sought instead to glimpse a floral display on the uncultivated prairies (28, 7, 57).

22. Oliver, 27; Blane, 190; F. Michaux, 221–22; E. James II, 166–67; Blane, 182; Shirreff, 243; Parker, 70; Rusling, 27; Latrobe, 220; Welby, 287; Blane, 188; A. Mackay, 131; T. Flint, *Recollections,* 239; Paul Wilhelm, 398–99; J. Hall, *Statistics,* 81; Arese, 118. James Fenimore Cooper used the bit of lore about setting fire to a spot of grass to good effect in *The Prairie* in 1827.

23. Curtiss, 94–95; White, 241; W. M. Stewart, 31; Macrae, 180.

24. E. James I, 93; Flagg I, 79; Oliver, 68; Frederick Marryat, 52; Dickens, 37; Rose, 216.

25. Macrae, 158.

CHAPTER 4. MARVELS AND WONDERS

1. Featherstonhaugh, 142–43. Featherstonhaugh's claim that he was going to send the skull to "a learned craniologist" was credible in light of interests of the time in skulls. Stephen Jay Gould, *The Mismeasure of Man* (New York: W. W. Norton,

1981), examines the craniometry practiced by, among others, Samuel George Morton of Philadelphia, whose theories of skull size worked in service of race-based views and were extremely popular in the 1840s.

2. Steele, 229; Ashe, *Travels in America,* 35; Brown, 306; Blane, 54; Hoffman II, 110.

3. Flagg I, 155; Brown, 298; Thomas, 94; Saxe-Weimar, 148; Atwater, 47; Buckingham, *Eastern and Western,* 351; "W. P. C.," Editorial Notes, *American Antiquarian and Oriental Journal* 1, no. 1 (April 1878). In 1992, Mary Norris, traveling Ohio for Fodor's travel guides, liked Circleville but classified it under "Places that Didn't Make the Guidebook." Its contemporary sights include a pet-food factory and the Ted Lewis Museum; its annual rite is a Pumpkin Show. See *New York Times,* 3 December 1992, sec. 5, 23. Brian Fagan, *Elusive Treasures: The Story of Early Archeologists in the Americas* (New York: Scribner's, 1977), notes that "few people are interested in preserving archeological sites of alien societies, especially if they contain no treasure or valuable statuary. Today it is estimated that fewer than 25% of the river valley sites in the midwest have not been at least partially destroyed" (118).

4. Buckingham, *Eastern and Western* II, 397; Chester, 240–41; Lakier, 145. See Drake, *Picture,* for a full treatment of the Cincinnati moundsites.

5. Frederick Marryat, 222–23; Mackinnon, 147.

6. Saxe-Weimar II, 97; Lakier, 185; Stephen Williams, *Fantastic Archeology: The Wild Side of North American Prehistory* (Philadelphia: University of Pennsylvania Press, 1991), notes that "a recent survey of old collection photos at the Peabody Museum that I made showed that almost every nineteenth-century Ohio collector had an 'inscribed stone'" (175).

7. Paul Wilhelm, 201; J. Flint, 107; T. Flint, *Condensed Geography,* 196; Buckingham, *Eastern and Western* III, 332; Hoffman II, 82–83. See Stephen Williams, *Fantastic Archeology,* and Robert Silverberg, *Moundbuilders of Ancient America: The Archeology of a Myth* (Greenwich, Conn.: New York Graphic Society, 1958), for complete treatment of Moundbuilder mythology.

8. Houstoun I, 274; Beck, 43; Schoolcraft, *Travels,* 331; O. H. Marshall, "Mound Joliet," *American Antiquarian* 5, no. 1 (January 1883): 76. See also Ephraim Squier and E. H. Davis, "Ancient Monuments of the Mississippi Valley," *Smithsonian Contributions to Knowledge* 1 (1848), and Cyrus Thomas, *Report on the Mound Explorations of the Bureau of Ethnology* (Washington, D.C.: Smithsonian Institution Press, 1894). Some contemporary views, such as that Mary Louise Pratt takes in *Imperial Eyes: Studies in Travel Writing and Transculturation* (London: Routledge, 1992), do not see the arrival of archaeology as an unmixed blessing: "As with the monumentalist reinvention of Egypt in the same period, the links between the societies being archaeologized and their contemporary descendants remain absolutely obscure, indeed irrecoverable. This, of course, is part of the point. The European imagination produces archaeological subjects by splitting contemporary non-European peoples off from their pre-colonial and even their colonial pasts. To revive indigenous history and culture as archaeology is to revive them *as dead.* The gesture simultaneously rescues them from European forgetfulness and reassigns them to a departed age. . . . European discourse of landscape deterritorializes indigenous peoples, separating them off from territories they may once have dominated, and in which they continue to make their lives. The archaeological perspective is complementary. It, too, obliterates the conquered inhabitants of the contact zone as historical agents who have living continuities with pre-European pasts and historically based aspirations and claims on the present" (134–35).

9. T. Flint, *Recollections,* 169; Ferguson, 312; Ellet, 123; Brackenridge, *Journal of a Voyage,* 67; Mackenzie, 193; Beltrami, 164; Flagg I, 71; C. A. Murray II, 54; Lewis, 198; Lanman, *Adventures,* 25.

10. See Mary Campbell, *The Witness and the Other World: Exotic European Travel Writing* (Ithaca, N.Y.: Cornell University Press, 1991), for the history of the appearance of physical grotesques and monsters in early travels and voyages. See Hugh Honour, *The New Golden Land: European Images of America from the Discoveries to the Present Time* (New York: Pantheon, 1975), for discussion of visual images of the Americas.

11. Colin Clair, *Human Curiosities* (London: Abelard-Schuman, 1968), 18; Ashe, *Travels,* 91; S. H. Long, *Six-Oared Skiff,* 63–64; Brown, 88; Melish II, 133; Vigne II, 65.

12. Schoolcraft, *Travels in the Central Portions,* 177; McKenney, 122; Gerstacker, 30; Berkeley, 386–87.

13. According to Stephen Williams, *Fantastic Archeology,* early travelers had no better way of ascertaining these matters of coexistence than do contemporary investigators: "Strange anomalies persist even today; for example, there still is not a single well-documented association of artifacts with extinct fauna east of the Mississippi River. There are plenty of pleistocene fossils and plenty of carbon 14 dates to show quite clearly that a number of cultures of that age, between twelve thousand and nine thousand years ago, when most of the Megafauna became extinct, existed in the East. We have only tiny peepholes on the past, and for excavators in the East that one special opportunity still eludes us at this moment" (312).

14. Schoolcraft, *Lead Mines,* 284–94; E. James I, 115–17; Beck, 253, 273, 290; T. Flint, *Recollections,* 173; Flagg I, 105, 296–97; Buckingham, *Eastern and Western* III, 143–44.

15. J. Priest, 282; Hill, 87; Wood, 248. See Williams, *Fantastic Archeology,* for complete analysis of Josiah Priest's methods and his popular book. Among the eight states of the old interior, Missouri regularly took the prize for rumored grotesquerie. In 1883, Mark Twain made a contribution in *Life on the Mississippi* when he told of an "interesting cave a mile or two below Hannibal, among the bluffs. I would have liked to revisit it, but had not time. In my time the person who then owned it turned it into a mausoleum for his daughter, aged fourteen. The body of this poor child was put into a copper cylinder filled with alcohol, and this was suspended in one of the dismal avenues of the cave. The top of the cylinder was removable; and it was said to be a common thing for the baser order of tourists to drag the dead face into view and examine it and comment upon it" (324).

16. Duden, 43; Frederick Marryat, 222–23; Scott, 184–85; C. A. Murray I, 244–45; Daubeny, 189.

17. Drake, *Discourse,* 17; F. Michaux, 235; Latrobe, 102; Duden, 43; Blane, 97; Elisha Lewis, *American Sportsman* (Philadelphia: Lippincott, 1857), 359.

18. Blane, 239–41.

CHAPTER 5. STILL LIFE

1. Woods, 342; Robinson, 76–77. Nineteenth-century travelers were the legatees, and the repositories, of centuries of report, rumor, and image-making about the native populations of the Americas; they had in their minds and in their vocabularies complex and conflicting ideas about exoticism, nobility, primitivism, and savagery, about peoples who lived at peace with nature and about peoples who did nothing but make war on each other. To attempt to sort out, explain, or offer correctives to what they reported is outside the bounds of this study. I will focus on how travelers placed Indians on the landscape of the interior and on the attitudes they offered their readers; in other words, the local representations they made for consumption.

2. Bird, 143–47; Macrae, 179–80; Rusling, 37–38; Stanley, 138–39; Lanman, *Adventures*, 35.

3. Bremer II, 58–59.

4. Hoffman I, 155, 271; II, 21, 31.

5. Fuller, 74–75.

6. Fuller, 23, 82; Blane, 37; Featherstonhaugh, 240. See Lucy Maddox, *Removals* (New York: Oxford University Press, 1991), for a full discussion of Fuller's continual use of foreign models in spite of her insistence that American writers must not use them.

7. James I, 265–67; Schoolcraft, *Travels in the Central Portions*, 180–81; Holmes, 454; Colt, 74; Fuller, 75; Lakier, 198; Frémont, 32.

8. Bremer II, 21; Lanman, *Adventures*, 29; Birkbeck, *Notes*, 119; Stanley, xvi; Dickens, 196.

9. Alexander, 187; Fuller, 72; Macrae, 186. Not until the late decades of the century did Americans find a way to make Indians serve them. In 1887, on the East Coast, Catherine Bates visited every medium and séance available, and invariably found the medium using an Indian guide to the spirit world. "I have asked several times," Bates wrote, "why *Indians* play so large a part in mediumship here, and the answer has been that they seem to haunt the country which once belonged to them, and that being intelligences of a lower and comparatively undeveloped nature, they are more easily used as messengers by the higher grades of spirits" (226–27).

10. Schoolcraft, *Northwest Regions*, 302–3, 325–26, 330, 340–41; Bremer II, 31–32, 35, 48; Bishop, 271, 283; Stanley, 283; Francis Amasa Walker, quoted in Ronald Takaki, *Iron Cages: Race and Culture in 19th-Century America* (New York: Alfred A. Knopf, 1990), 184–85.

11. Steele, 62–63; Bromley, 51–52. Americans seemed to love brilliance, color, and glitter in steamboat and hotel interiors, but not in their own clothing. They scorned Indians for wanting to wear what whites wanted not to wear but to inhabit.

12. Rose, 231; Vigne II, 117; Steele, 110; Oliphant, 257; Hoffman I, 234–35; Bishop, 298.

13. Arese, 77–79, 97–98. Among the Indians, 1837 was the terrible smallpox year.

14. Colt, 74–76; Stanley, 40; Hoffman II, 30.

15. Jameson II, 311. No more cruelly detailed survey of the looks of Indian women can be found than in Richard Burton's *Across the Plains*, 129–30; Burton's text as a whole expresses every variety of loathing and contempt for all Indians except for the exterminated East Coast tribes that Burton claimed were noble. Numerous travelers told stories about white men who could judge desirable character in Indian men simply by looking at them: Juliette Magill Kinzie in 1855 offered a story about Henry Clay examining a lineup of Chippewa men, "looking carefully at the countenance and bearing" of each, and then announcing, without having heard any one of them speak, which one was to be "the principal orator of the nation" (100–101).

16. Schoolcraft, *Northwest Regions*, 232; Hoffman II, 20–21.

17. Bremer II, 59. In *Removals*, Lucy Maddox remarks on the treatment of Indian looks in the work of Francis Parkman: "The one completely unredeemable fact about Indians for Parkman, the feature that makes them not only exotic but killable, is that they are physically ugly . . . Parkman constantly reads these faces, seeing in their physical difference (which he perceives as ugliness) signs of their moral difference (which he perceives as inferiority). The physical differences be-

tween himself and the Indians are great enough to allow him to declare the Indians less than fully human, and therefore dispensable" (165–66).

18. Historians have found it extremely difficult to reconstruct day-to-day Indian life in the early decades of the nineteenth century. Charles E. Cleland, *Rites of Conquest: The History and Culture of Michigan's Native Americans* (Ann Arbor: University of Michigan Press, 1992), asserts that written history is so "strongly dominated by male understanding and interests" that it has obscured the life of the nineteenth-century Indian village whose activities were attached to and dominated by women (186). Glenda Riley, *Women and Indians on the Frontier, 1825–1915* (Albuquerque: University of New Mexico Press, 1984), says that "many white commentators frequently transferred their own view of white women as inferior beings to their perceptions of native societies, thus managing to ignore matrilineal Indian groups, the status granted Indian women due to their share in production, and the native women who served as warriors, shamans, healers, and religious leaders" (21). Carol Devens, *Countering Colonization: Native Americans and Great Lakes Missions, 1630–1900* (Berkeley: University of California Press, 1992), an examination of missionaries' doings among the Indians of Michigan, finds that "the Indian system of balanced yet autonomous male and female roles baffled, even horrified, the priests," who then moved deliberately to change it and to push Indian women into a subordinate—and invisible—role in the community (25).

19. Charlevoix, 52–54, 367.

20. McKenney quoted in Fuller, 144; Fuller, 150, 111; Jameson II, 305; Bremer II, 35–38.

21. Hoffman II, 27; Fuller, 121; Dickens, 165–67; Kinzie, 76–77.

22. Schoolcraft, *Northwest Regions,* 330–31; Bremer II, 20–21; Eastman, 187–90.

23. I. Pfeiffer, 433; Bishop, 219–20.

24. Lakier, 197; Oliphant, 289–90; Borrett, 145. In his collection of Indian legends, Stith Thompson, *Tales of North American Indians* (Bloomington: Indiana University Press, 1966), records no romantic suicide stories, no lovers' tales at all. Contemporary tourist literature from Winona, Minnesota, no longer retells the legend but does contain a small photograph of a white woman who attained local fame in the 1920s by acting in beaded buckskin the part of Winona in the town's annual pageant. It is more thought-provoking to note in John Williamson's *English-Dakota Dictionary* (St. Paul, Minn.: Minnesota Historical Society Press, 1992) that the Dakota Sioux words for *girl* are *wicinyanna, wicincana,* and *wicincal;* the words for *woman* are *winohinea* and *win yan.*

25. Twain, 343–45.

26. *Western Magazine and Review* 1, no. 1 (May 1827): 43–51; James II, 192; Bremer II, 41; von Raumer, 441.

27. De Hauranne I, 139, 235, 287, 206–10, 231, 216–23, 252.

28. Ibid., 274, 289.

29. White, 250–53. In 1870 just about everyone knew George Francis Train (1829–1904), who had made a fortune in shipping, railroading, and street railways. A relentless self-promoter, public eccentric, attention-seeker, and anglophobe, Train forced himself to public notice in America and elsewhere between 1862 and 1872 with continual spectacular activity and bizarre speech-making in connection with the most attention-getting events and causes he could locate. In 1869 he announced himself as a candidate for the presidency and over the next three years regularly thrust himself to the center of any public gathering. Numerous travelers met him: in 1862 Ernest Duvergier de Hauranne had Train pointed

out to him in New York City as "the theatrical and eccentric George Francis Train . . . perennial gladiator and *enfant terrible* of the [Democratic] party" (140); in the same year Edward P. Hingston heard Train lecture in Henry Ward Beecher's church in Brooklyn. According to Hingston, Train invented every story he told about himself, and included astonishing statistics along the way, "outrivalling a dozen Baron Munchausens." When a member of the audience asked to know how many guns were in the possession of the Chinese army that Train had been talking about, Train replied "with charming accuracy, so many thousand, so many hundred, *and five; but two of them are cracked*" (Hingston, *The Genial Showman* [New York: Harper and Brothers, 1870], 82). The audience cheered, laughed, and applauded throughout the uproarious lecture. In 1872, after Train had been declared legally insane but was still on the loose promoting himself, Emily Faithfull met him on an Atlantic crossing. Train introduced himself to her "by exclaiming, as he struck his heart with his hand, 'Madam, you have seen a Republican and a Democrat, but in me behold an American citizen.'" He then presented Faithfull with his photograph, beneath which was printed "Future President of the United States," and told her that as soon as he was installed in the White House, he intended to have the English ambassador hanged from a lamppost. Faithfull "ascertained with some relief that Mr. Train's ambitious pretensions received no support from his countrymen" (Faithfull, 5–6). In his later years, Train dropped into anonymity in New York City, socializing with children only. His autobiography, *My Life in Many States and in Foreign Lands* (1902), however, is said to be a demonstration of his continued willingness to seize all credit for the success of any enterprise with which he had any connection.

30. White, 250–53.

31. Chevalier, 183.

CHAPTER 6. A TABLE SET FOR HUNDREDS

1. Stuart-Wortley, *Travels* I, 169, 194; Bird, 125; Weld, 54; Lakier, 148.

2. Dickens, 168, 195; Stuart-Wortley, *&C.,* 9–10; Macrae, 176–77. In *Life on the Mississippi,* Mark Twain discussed his reading in antebellum travel literature and remarked that "it is a most strange world that these touring foreigners—all now dead and gone—take us into; a most strange and unreal-seeming world. We rub our eyes and say, *Is* this America? For, in it there is a New York with hogs prowling in the business streets—hogs which did not give the road, but took it; and bemired or tripped up people who got too slowly out of the way" (402).

3. Featherstonhaugh, 95. The pigs formed a "pork aristocracy" that in 1845 Charles Lyell was careful to distinguish from the other pork aristocracy, the human one—"the class of rich merchants who have made their fortunes by killing, salting, and exporting about 200,000 swine annually" (Lyell II, 72). In *The Hog in America, Past and Present* (1886; rpt. Wilmington, Del.: Scholarly Resources, 1974), Silas M. Shepard offers a sharp and amusing discussion of the pig's "easy adaptation" to the North American climate, though it was no native beast; he also offers pig figures from the 1840 census, the first to report numbers of domestic animals, and he offers many excellent line drawings of nineteenth-century pigs. "There is money, *and lots of it,*" says Shepard, "in raising hogs for pork" (3, 10, 78). R. O. Cummings, *The American and His Food* (Chicago: University of Chicago Press, 1941), reports that "it is conservatively estimated that per capita meat consumption during the decade 1830–1839 was 178 pounds annually, which is 48 pounds more than was eaten in 1930" (15).

4. Vigne II, 266; Bullock, xvi; Chevalier, 270; B. Hall, 138; Andrews, 31; Stanley, 103; Weld, 197.

5. Vigne II, 266–67.

6. Mackie, 54; Tudor, 37–39.

7. Lakier, 22; Mary Douglas, *Purity and Danger: An Analysis of Concepts of Pollution and Taboo* (New York: Praeger, 1966), 64.

8. Felton, 82–83; Tremenheere, 151; Dickens, 170; Borrett, 114; Holyoake, 33.

9. Shirreff, 288; Chevalier, 217.

10. F. Trollope, 395.

11. Hoffman I, 92; Dickens, 158; F. Trollope, 19; MacGregor, 95, 104–5; Lakier, 223. David Potter, in a passage that seems to bear on these matters from *People of Plenty: Economic Abundance and the American Character* (Chicago: University of Chicago Press, 1958), suggests that in antebellum America, "equality came to mean, in a major sense, parity in competition. Its value was as a means to advancement rather than as an asset in itself. Like an option in the world of business, it had no intrinsic value but only a value when used. Since the potential value could be realized only by actual movement to a higher level, the term 'equality' acquired for most Americans exactly the same connotations which the term 'upward mobility' has for the social scientist" (92).

12. Cuming, 292; J. Hall, *Letters,* 123; Martineau, *Society* II, 327; Stuart II, 168. Margaret Visser, *Much Depends on Dinner* (Toronto: McClelland and Stewart, 1986), contains considerable interesting discussion of garbage and leftovers.

13. Bullock, xvi; Dickens, 174; T. Hamilton II, 248; A. Trollope, 84; O'Rell, 290–91.

14. Weld, 231; A. Trollope, 85; Dickens, 145–49; F. Trollope, 297; Lakier, 61; Faithfull, 50–51; Griffiths, 90; F. Trollope, 298. On the theory of involvement with food, see Erving Goffman, *Behavior in Public Places* (Glencoe, Ill.: Free Press, 1963), 62.

15. Griffiths, 90; Mackie, 194; Dickens, 59; Woods, 284; Oliver, 52–53; Trotter, 192; Vigne II, 279.

16. Hancock, 307; Trotter, 204; Mackie, 193–94; Vigne II, 281.

17. T. Flint, *Recollections,* 246–47; F. Trollope, 36; C. Stewart, 135.

18. Robinson, 4, 40, 75; Colt, 34, 50.

19. Mackie, 193–94; Trotter, 192. In *The American and His Food,* R. O. Cummings reports that in the 1830s, newspapers and health journals branded fresh fruit and vegetables dangerous, a potential source of cholera, and "affirmed as a general principle that no person, whether gentleman or farmer or tradesman, woman or child, could eat to advantage, or even with impunity, vegetable matter which had not been softened and changed by culinary processes" (43).

20. Scott, 31, 62; W. Priest, 33; Mackie, 194.

21. Dickens, 174; Lakier, 212–33.

22. Lakier, 61–62; Kirkland, *A New Home,* 33–34. Sally Cline, *Just Desserts: Women and Food* (London: Deutsch, 1990), asserts that the "sexual dynamic" in contemporary Western society continues to be manifested through food: "By looking at food we can get at the kernel of the political relationship between the sexes. . . . Women's subordination is locked into food. . . . We are socialized to win men's love and approval with our meals and our shape, to reflect male values with what we serve and how we serve it, and to retain this affection and respect by eating less and behaving differently ourselves" (3–5).

23. Borrett, 90; A. Trollope, 197–98; F. Trollope, 154.

24. Gladstone, 156.

25. Logan, 103–4; I. Pfeiffer, 428–29.

CHAPTER 7. STRANGERS

1. Ratzel, 217; MacGregor, 102; Stuart-Wortley, &C., 257; Lakier, 61.

2. Steele, 211–22. In 1834 on a Mississippi River steamboat, Harriet Martineau apparently took ironing in the Ladies' Cabin so for granted that she noted it only when it failed to occur on a Sunday (*Retrospect* I, 185).

3. Lakier, 192; Bremer II, 22.

4. Lakier, 58; Mooney, 22; Bromley, preface; Bird, 100; Jameson II, 82.

5. Bird, 160–61, 107–9; Lakier, 64; O'Rell, 70; Lieber, 18.

6. Fuller, 38–39; Farnham, 127; Bremer II, 23, 84–85.

7. Lakier, 38; de Hauranne, 94; O'Rell, 68; Chevalier, 300; Martineau, *Society* II, 118; Finch, 357–58; Faithfull, 242. Cynthia Eagle Russett, *Sexual Science: The Victorian Construction of Womanhood* (Cambridge, Mass.: Harvard University Press, 1989), conducts a complete investigation of the contributions made to notions of the physiological division of labor by Malthus, Adam Smith, Saint-Simon, Comte, Milne-Edwards, and Herbert Spencer—notions to which Marx, Engels, and Veblen took strong exception (138–51). How travelers divided on the subject cannot be glimpsed in those gendered discussions of travel literature that treat only books by women and only books by men. It is notable that while women critics and historians tend to write books about women travelers, men write books represented to be about "travel" or "travelers" that consider men's experience only. Neither Dennis Porter in *Haunted Journeys* (Princeton, N.J.: Princeton University Press, 1991) nor Eric Leed in *The Mind of the Traveler: From Gilgamesh to Global Tourism* (New York: Basic Books, 1991) deals with women travelers contemporaneous with the men they focus on; they justify the exclusion by asserting that women travelers have a different sensibility, and a mysterious one at that, or, as does Leed, by casting travel in a father-son framework that blots out women. All assertions about "travel" that follow on such exclusions are equally dubious. Shirley Foster, *Across New Worlds: 19th-Century Women Travellers and Their Writing* (New York: Harvester Wheatshear, 1990), spends several pages analyzing the standard disclaimer-of-intent-to-write-a-book that prefaces nearly every nineteenth-century travel book I have seen; she reads it as a specific feature of women's writing and decodes it as "self-belittlement" (19). Had she attended to travel books by both genders she would have seen the disclaimer of intent in each and every text by each and every traveler and might have demystified it on other and less psychological terms. Sara Mills, *Discourses of Difference: An Analysis of Women's Travel Writing and Colonialism* (London: Routledge, 1991), discusses the modes of denigration exercised on women travel writers not so much by men (who tend to ignore them) as by women, who label them spinsters, old maids, adventuresses, and tomboys, condescend to them by adopting a first-name basis in writing of them, and generally represent them as freaks and oddities. The gender scene is complex. It is certain, however, that exclusionary gender practices in work on travel literature distort both the text and the scenes of travel, and weaken the analysis.

8. Chevalier, 330–31; Lieber, 67; Schoolcraft, *Travels in the Central Portions,* 167; Martineau, *Society* II, 39; Bremer I, 624; I. Pfeiffer, 428.

9. Faux II, 17; Blane, 258; Duden, 48; O'Ferrall, 63; W. H. Dixon, *New America* II, 21–23; Farnham, 111; Robinson, 49, 53, 54, 72, 77, 86, 93.

10. Duden, 72; Kinzie, 140–41; Hoffman I, 222; Grund, 43; C. Stewart, 135; I.

Pfeiffer, 428; F. Trollope, 25. The communal solution that Charlotte Perkins Gilman proposed in *Women and Economics* (1898) of trained household specialists each focusing on just one task—cooking, cleaning, laundering, nursing—is essentially an urban solution to the housework problem and cannot be adjusted to life on the grid of the interior.

11. C. Stewart, 135; Hardy, 37; Steele, 254–55; Duden, 134; Leslie quoted in Richard J. Hooker, *Food and Drink in America: A History* (Indianapolis: Bobbs Merrill, 1981), 113; F. Trollope, 32; Martineau, *Society* II, 197; Jameson II, 154; I. Pfeiffer, 432.

12. Bird, 151–53; Burton, 6.

13. I am indebted to Erving Goffman, *Behavior in Public Places* (Glencoe, Ill.: Free Press, 1963), 27, for the phrase "limb discipline." Steele, 210; Martineau, *Retrospect* I, 108–9, 172; I. Pfeiffer, 432; Fuller, 38; Steele, 210.

14. Backhouse, 107; Jameson II, 234; Frémont, 56; Martineau, *Retrospect* I, 189–90.

15. Bunn, 267–68; O'Rell, 52–53; Dickens, 97, 113, 148; Faithfull, 119; F. Trollope, 19; Weld, 197; N. Hall, 118; Tudor II, 421; Blane, 28; MacGregor, 104; Baxter, 105; Dickens, 114; T. Hamilton II, 164. Compton Mackenzie, *Sublime Tobacco* (Gloucester, England: Alan Sutton, 1984), points out that *spitting,* the word I use here, is the word to use: "The genteel use of *expectoration* for spitting is much less genteel, really, because expectoration means getting rid of phlegm in the chest or in the bronchial tubes, whereas spitting merely means getting rid of superfluous saliva"; Mackenzie also notes that *cuspidor,* from the Portuguese, "won the day in the United States as a genteel substitute for spittoon, in the same way as casket has displaced coffin" (35).

16. Dickens, 122; Weld, 214; Borrett, 81.

17. Bromley, 26; Felton, 75; Faithfull, 324.

18. De Zavala, 35; Fuller, 5; Duden, 184; Kirkland, *A New Home,* 89; Steele, 212; Bird, 169–70. For a woman to spit in the nineteenth century was a matter of incalculable seriousness in a country where all men spat all the time. When Benjamin Butler arrived in New Orleans during the Civil War, the women there expressed their resistance in a variety of ways: according to Mary Ryan, *Women in Public* (Baltimore: Johns Hopkins University Press, 1991), some pinned Confederate flags to their dresses while "others greeted Union soldiers by crossing the street, turning around, or raising their skirts in a gesture of repugnance. The most brazen daughters of the Confederacy launched a barrage of saliva at their conquerors." This last was too much to suffer and drew complaint from the soldiers that they "could not walk the streets without being outraged and spit upon by young girls" (143). No tobacco tinge excused their saliva, and no trousers made their actions acceptable.

19. Mary Douglas, *Purity and Danger: An Analysis of Concepts of Pollution and Taboo* (New York: Praeger, 1966), 120–21; Fuller, 5. It is worthy of note that most men who have written of nineteenth-century manners have avoided the subject of spitting almost as thoroughly as the spitters did. Gerald Carson, *The Polite Americans* (New York: William Morrow, 1966), gives the subject several deprecating pages, but John Gloag, *Victorian Comfort: A Social History of Design* (London: Adam and Charles Black, 1961), remarks only that "by the 1890s the spittoon was on its way out; either because it was condemned as an unhygienic nuisance, or because more men were smoking cigarettes and spat less than cigar and pipe smokers" (80). Gloag's avoidance is an interesting one: the spittoon was most certainly not invented for cigar and pipe smokers, but for users of the chewing tobacco that he prefers not to mention. Kenneth Ames, *Death in the Dining Room and Other Tales of Victorian Culture* (Philadelphia: Temple University Press, 1992), announces his de-

termination to take up matters he claims are usually ignored in discussions of the nineteenth century, but then he never mentions the spittoon in his discussion of the furnishings of the nineteenth-century house. John Burnham, *Bad Habits: Drinking, Smoking, Taking Drugs, Gambling, Sexual Misbehavior and Swearing in American History* (New York: New York University Press, 1993), races past the subject of chewing to focus his discussion entirely on smoking. His strategies of avoidance are so complete that he misses the fact of women's pipe-smoking throughout the nineteenth century. John Kasson, *Rudeness and Civility: Manners in Nineteenth-Century Urban America* (New York: Noonday, 1991), also chooses to miss the subject by looking beyond it: "Etiquette authorities helped turn the face of respectability against tobacco chewing, limiting its scope by the late 19th century." It is characteristic to choose to talk of the habit's gradual disappearance instead of speaking of the habit itself. Kasson also, oddly enough, says: "In the mid-19th-century, tobacco spit flew without restraint in places frequented by men" and then he lists those places as railroad cars, stages, steamers, hotels, churches, hospitals, shops, offices, and private houses. Every one of these places was also frequented by women; Kasson's list is a tacit admission that men spat everywhere and in front of anyone (125–26). For a man's discussion of spitting, one must turn in the twentieth century as in the nineteenth to men from countries other than America. In *Being and Nothingness* (trans. Hazel E. Barnes [New York: Philosophical Library, 1956]), to which I was led by Mary Douglas, Jean-Paul Sartre did an extended spin on matters of viscosity and sliminess that seems distinctly apropos of the saliva that bathed the landscape of the interior. In his effort to "compel the *slimy* to reveal its being," Sartre proposed that "so long as the contact with the slimy endures, everything takes place for us as if sliminess were the meaning of the entire world. . . . The slimy manifests a certain relation of being with itself . . . it is a possible meaning of being" (604–12).

20. Montule, 112; de Zavala, 98; Ratzel, 214; O'Rell, 18–19; Grund, 69; O'Rell, 70.

21. Logan, 103–21. Alison Lurie, *The Language of Clothes* (New York: Random House, 1981), notes:

> Although she was so heavily armored against a frontal assault, the mid-Victorian woman was often readily accessible in another direction, since she had no underpants in the modern sense. She might if she chose wear what were called "drawers"—loose, wide-legged undershorts made in two separate sections, joined only at the waist and otherwise completely open—but these conferred status rather than protection. Though this left the Victorian lady embarrassingly exposed in case of accidents, closed underpants were considered immodest because they imitated male garments. Victorian feminists later drew attention to this contradiction: Dr. Mary Walker, for instance, remarked that "if men were really what they profess to be they would not compel women to dress so that the facilities for vice would always be so easy." (219)

22. Arese, 137; de Hauranne, 27; I. Pfeiffer, 448–49; Stanley, 88; Jameson II, 307; Kirkland, *A New Home,* 160. Mid-nineteenth-century caution on sexual subjects was preceded by eighteenth-century exuberance and followed by late-nineteenth-century candor. Late in the century, when all travelers took to taking "peeps" at Mormon life in Utah just as they had earlier "peeped" at Indian life in the interior, an enormous gender divide opened up on the subject of men's and women's sexuality. There is no greater contrast than that between Emily Faithfull (1884) and Richard Burton (1862) on the subject of polygamy as a sexual prac-

tice; their two books are as divided as if they had toured two entirely different Utahs.

23. Jameson I, vii; II, 137; Lieber, 69; Steele, 112.

24. Faithfull, 324; review of Martineau's *Retrospect of Western Travel, The Western Messenger* 5, no. 2 (May 1838): 135; A. Bell, 239; Saxe-Weimar II, 91. It is worth noting that the 1848 Women's Rights Convention at Seneca Falls, New York, did not come out in favor of public speaking for women. Frances Wright, among others, had put sexuality on the agenda: Mary Ryan, *Women in Public,* notes that "from the 1830s onward into our own time, women were open and increasingly vociferous participants in political debates about sexuality" (95), but Carroll Smith-Rosenberg does not see things opening up readily for this discussion: "At no other period in American history has such a sexually repressive belief system been so elaborately delineated," writes Smith-Rosenberg. "Appearing suddenly in the 1830s and 1840s, it contrasts sharply with the sexual permissiveness of either the 18th or the 20th century. What we choose to delineate as 'Puritanism' began in America during the last stages of preindustrial commercial capitalism" ("Sex as Symbol," *Prospects* 5 [1980]: 51–52). Mary Louise Pratt, *Imperial Eyes: Studies in Travel Writing and Transculturation* (London: Routledge, 1992), suggests that the complaints and critiques about women travel writers began to intensify around 1828 because by then "there were enough European women travel writers in print to form a category for men to complain about" (170).

25. F. Trollope, 183; T. Hamilton II, 248; Martineau, *Society* II, 2–3; Finch, 314.

26. Finch, 355; de Zavala, 55; Lieber, 78; Pickering, 19. Late in the twentieth century, it is still standard to hear nineteenth-century women as a gender described as "prim and proper," a particularly repellent formulation that operates to keep those women eternally in their cages, restrained by that label as if they alone created and perpetuated it. In the nineteenth century, a flirtation could be seriously constructed; only the twentieth century is so vulgar as to claim that "nothing happened" unless sex occurred; and even likely sexual adventurers such as Elizabeth Custer worked in the 1870s to preserve a conventional surface. Facile repetitions of formulae about propriety do not allow investigation of actions and behaviors beyond the surface.

27. Martineau, *Retrospect* II, 38.

28. MacGregor, 102; de Hauranne, 236–38, 247–48.

29. Borrett, 83; I. Pfeiffer, 416–17.

30. F. Trollope, 117; Martineau, *Retrospect* II, 39–40; Steele, 151–52; Kirkland, *Forest Life,* 27–28, 38, 210; Blake, 215–16; I. Pfeiffer, 429–30; Bremer II, 429.

31. E. James I, 169; Hoffman I, 222; O'Rell, 102–3; Buckingham, *America* I, 3; Duden, 69–70; Chevalier, 303. Stow Persons, *The Decline of American Gentility* (New York: Columbia University Press, 1973), notes that antebellum America attached "great importance . . . to home and family life as the principal props of civilization and order," but his analysis does not make any separations between persons benefiting or not benefiting from this social phenomenon (74). John Mack Faragher, *Women and Men on the Overland Trail* (New Haven, Conn.: Yale University Press, 1979), works to reconstruct "the relationship between men and women in marriage in the mid-nineteenth-century Midwest," and concludes that westward movement did not significantly change family or gender roles (3). The more interesting question may be how the roles were acted out in a different organization of space; the interior appears to have expanded some roles and compressed others into different shapes from those they held on the landscape of the East Coast.

32. Cuming, 134; Kirkland, *Forest Life,* 184; Fuller, 62–63; Stuart II, 237; E. Farnham, 68; Griffiths, 151.

33. Stuart-Wortley, *&C.,* 265; Weld, 184; Twain, 231; Faithfull, 49.

34. Martineau, *Retrospect* II, 195–96.

CHAPTER 8. YESTERDAY'S FUTURE

1. Oliver, 19–21; Oliphant, 154–55, 207. Both the date of Kaskaskia's founding and the high-water mark of its population are matters of debate throughout travel literature.

2. Imlay, 556.

3. Oliphant, 159–60; Macrae, 164–65.

4. Hennepin II, 555, 623–34; T. M. Harris, 352; Cuming, 227; J. Hall, *Statistics,* 98, 107.

5. Latrobe, 113; Ellsworth, vi; Buckingham, *Eastern and Western,* III, 216–17; Stuart II, 221; Bremer I, 600–603.

6. Stuart II, 217; Shirreff, 463–64; Scott, 101–2; J. S. Wright, 23, 37; Wilkey, 85; C. W. Dana's title, *Garden of the World.* In the 1850s, attempts to transport the landscape of spontaneous fertility west of the Missouri to Kansas failed utterly and resulted in narratives about food scarcity—see especially Sara Robinson, Miriam Colt, and Dixon's *New America.*

7. See Imlay, Paul Wilhelm, and T. H. James; Kirkland, *A New Home,* 55; J. Hall, *Letters,* 176; Ashe, *Travels,* 250; T. H. James, 172; Thomas, 187; Welby, 187–88; Blane, 194; Drake, *Picture of Cincinnati,* inscription; Melish II, 182; Bremer I, 208, 606, 613–14; II, 137, 145.

8. Oldmixon, 128; Lanman, *Adventures,* 214; Oliphant, 185; Alexander, 68; Flint, *Condensed Geography,* 14.

9. Steele, 188; Hoffman II, 57; Abel, 1; Paul Wilhelm, 306; Cuming, 206. Sheila Rothman, *Living in the Shadow of Death* (New York: Basic Books, 1994), discusses fully the advice given to consumptives on the matter of traveling for health, and notes that "it was up to [the invalids] to select the destination and devise the regimen most suitable for their particular constitutions" (7). Charles Rosenberg, *Explaining Epidemics* (New York: Cambridge University Press, 1992), points out that at the beginning of the nineteenth century "the body was seen metaphorically as a system of dynamic interactions with its environment. Health or disease resulted from a cumulative interaction between constitutional endowment and environmental circumstance" (12). That attitude is exactly the one many travelers carried.

10. Fearon, 219; Ashe, 105; Montule, 106; Flint, *Recollections,* 28, 84; F. Trollope, 177; Hoffman I, 154; Kirkland, *A New Home,* 237; Dickens, 171; Bremer II, 98; Robinson, 98–99; Pidgeon, 195.

11. Rynning, 75. For my understanding of malaria, I am indebted to Daniel Drake, *Malaria in the Interior Valley of North America* (1850; rpt. Urbana: University of Illinois Press, 1964); to Erwin Ackerknecht, *Malaria in the Upper Mississippi Valley 1760–1900* (Baltimore: Johns Hopkins University Press, 1945) and *History and Geography of the Most Important Diseases* (New York: Hafner, 1965); to Charles H. Rosenberg, *Explaining Epidemics;* and to Melinda S. Meade et al., *Medical Geography* (New York: Guilford, 1988). Unlike yellow fever, which was an urban disease, malaria was a distinctively rural disease.

12. Delano, 19–20.

13. Kirkland, *A New Home,* 203; *Forest Life,* 67, 72, 102; Delano, 13–14; Frank

Marryat, 379–81; Logan, 112; Bishop, 145. Erwin Ackerknecht points out that "quinine is an excellent remedy, but it has limited value in prophylaxis because it is capable of attacking the plasmodia in their asexual stages only. Quinine does not avoid infection; quinine does not sterilize the carrier . . . but quinine does have one quality which nobody denies and which may be decisive in certain historical situations: it stops the clinical attack, it makes people fit to fight and to work, when without quinine they would not be able to do so" (*Malaria in the Upper Mississippi Valley 1760–1900,* 126–27). Ackerknecht also points out that malaria was endemic for twenty years during settlement in Minnesota; in the 1890s it declined and disappeared everywhere in the interior except Missouri. Charles H. Rosenberg is interesting to read on the "extraordinary vogue of mercury" as a treatment: "If employed for a sufficient length of time and in sufficient quantity, mercury induced a series of progressively severe and cumulative physiological effects: First, diarrhea, and ultimately, full-blown symptoms of mercury poisoning. The copious involuntary salivation characteristic of this toxic state was seen as proof that the drug was exerting an 'alterative' effect." By 1862, "mercury still figured in the practice of most physicians; even infants and small children endured the discomfort of mercury poisoning until well after the Civil War" (*Explaining Epidemics,* 16–17, 27).

14. Grund, 142; Borrett, 90. In *Living in the Shadow of Death,* Sheila Rothman discusses the gendered nature of health-giving activities prescribed in the nineteenth century and points out that, in the case of consumptives especially, "it took bacteriology to override gender," whereon all were sent to the sanatorium (7).

15. Oliver, 81; E. James IV, 31–32; Hulme, 46; Carver, 283–86; F. A. Michaux, 221–22; E. James II, 166–67; Abel, 1; Fuller, 72; Bremer II, 62; Oliphant, 211.

16. C. A. Murray II, 39; Gerstacker, 124–25; Berkeley, 2, 46–47, 98, 390.

17. Imlay, 45; Volney, 378–79; Schoolcraft, *Travel in the Central Portions,* 205–6, 296–97; *Northwest Regions,* 281–82; Cunynghame, 2, 53–55.

18. Bradbury, 135; Lanman, *Adventures,* 36–37; Sullivan, 132–33; Vigne II, 66; Oliphant, 221–23; Ashe, *Travels,* 4; Fuller, 41; C. A. Murray II, 121, 130, 149. James Hall, though a longtime resident of Illinois, refused to believe in the existence of the gopher. In 1821 at St. Peter, Minnesota, Henry Schoolcraft desired so to see a gopher that a certain Colonel Leavenworth "directed a couple of soldiers to exert themselves in procuring one." They brought back something that looked mighty like a rat to Schoolcraft, and perhaps it was (*Northwest Regions,* 83). As to the buffalo, the only large grazing animal that survived the Ice Age in North America: in 1750 about 40 million buffaloes grazed on the North American prairies; in 1830 the last buffaloes east of the Mississippi were killed in Indiana and Wisconsin; in 1889 only 285 buffaloes remained alive in the United States. See Erich Hobusch, *Fair Game: A History of Hunting, Shooting, and Animal Conservation* (New York: Arco, 1980), George Laycock, *America's Endangered Wildlife* (New York: W. W. Norton, 1971), and Robert McClung, *Lost Wild America* (New York: William Morrow, 1969), for more on the subject. Elisha Lewis's *American Sportsman* (Philadelphia: Lippincott, 1857) reproduces numerous newspaper articles of the 1850s that record how the interior was swept clean of animals and birds to satisfy the rage for eating game in the cities.

19. Révoil, 28; Oliver, 74; Lanman, *Adventures,* 47; Benwell, 135; Hoffman II, 12–13; Oliphant, 177, 247; Kirkland, *A New Home,* 272–73; Vigne II, 62–63, 97. Wolves kill in packs and are currently the foremost predator in the United States even though only 3 percent of the gray wolf's original range remains. In Minnesota's Boundary Waters area—where no motorized vehicles are allowed—there are 1,700 wolves, the largest number in the lower forty-eight.

20. Oliphant, 201, 239; Vigne II, 86; Oliver, 71; C. A. Murray II, 121; Van Cleve, 62; Duden, 78–79; Révoil, preface; Cunynghame, 56.

21. Stuart II, 195; Weld, 188–89; Trotter, 217; Campbell, 293; Macrae, 180–81; Arthur Dubin, *More Classic Trains* (Milwaukee: Kalmbach, 1974), 40; Robert J. Casey and W. A. S. Douglas, *Pioneer Railroad: The Story of the CNW System* (New York: McGraw-Hill, 1948), 189; Blake, 29–30. Many nineteenth-century hunters to the contrary, there were indeed game laws, and Elisha Lewis, in *The American Sportsman* (1857), wrote of them: "By the game-laws of Illinois and others of the Western States, every person is liable to a fine of fifteen dollars who shall kill, ensnare, or trap any deer, fawn, wild turkey, grouse, prairie-chickens, or partridges, between the 15th of January and the 1st of August" (93). Lewis, however, was also fully aware that these laws were not being observed, and that the rage for eating game in the cities of the East overrode any protective laws. In *America's Endangered Wildlife*, George Laycock reports that "guns, traps, and nests played devastating roles in the plunge the prairie chickens took in the late 1800s. The wild chickens were collected by the barrelful and the boxful. They were hauled off in market wagons and trains for sale in the cities. In 1871, in Chicago alone . . . meat markets sold more than half a million prairie chickens. In New York, in 1878, one large market sold more than two thousand a day during the Christmas season" (32). A small population of prairie chickens survives today in Wisconsin.

22. Hoffman II, 7–8; Gillmore II, 132; Blane, 134.

23. Jameson II, 317; Fuller, 72, 152; Faithfull, 300; Custer, 201–3, 144. Kenneth Ames, *Death in the Dining Room and Other Tales of Victorian Culture* (Philadelphia: Temple University Press, 1992), analyzes the nineteenth-century dining-room furniture decorated with carved images of the hunt and its effects.

24. Oldmixon, 129. John Bradbury is a notable example of the running-hunt traveler.

25. Martineau, *Society* II, 155, 173–74; Woods, 247; Greeley, 249. Over the half century from 1810 to 1855, the number of children per family in the United States dropped from 5.8 to 3.6—a very sharp decrease.

26. A. Trollope, 93; I. Pfeiffer, 420, 432.

27. Oliver, 61; Borrett, 114; Lakier, 160; Martineau, *Retrospect* I, 38; F. Trollope, 122–24; Cunynghame, 108.

28. J. Flint, 171; E. Pfeiffer, 86; I. Pfeiffer, 416; de Hauranne, 230; Dickens, 113; E. Pfeiffer, 103.

29. F. Trollope, 117–18; Martineau, *Society* II, 137–38; I. Pfeiffer, 432; A. Trollope, 199–200.

30. Imlay, 44.

CHAPTER 9. SUNSET

1. Guest, 44, 256. Lucius Beebe, *Mr. Pullman's Elegant Palace Car* (New York: Doubleday, 1961), discusses the private-car craze that escalated rapidly between 1865 and 1895, by which time "the list of private car owners embraced almost every top-ranking industrialist and banker and a good many at some remove from the upper brackets of finance. All railroaders from the rank of division superintendent upward had their own cars, which were not known in the strict latter-day terminology as 'business cars' but explicitly as private cars . . . it was the grandest property to which any American could aspire . . . it became imperative for the wives and families of the socially exalted to travel by private car" (352–53).

2. Guest, 47–48, 51, 53, 179, 186–87, 101, 181–82, 257. In 1917, A-No.1, the fa-

mous tramp, claimed that twenty-three years earlier, he and Jack London, aboard a moving train, had entered a private car from the observation platform and slept all night in its sitting room until discovered by the porter, who made them leave before "his folks" awoke. See A-No.1, *From Coast to Coast with Jack London* (Grand Rapids, Mich.: Black Letter Press, 1917), 126–30. In 1907, London himself began *The Road* (New York: Macmillan, 1907) with a story about forcing his way into the private varnish in 1892 and confronting the resident millionaire with a demand for two bits. No private-car traveler whose narrative I have read demonstrated any awareness of hobo life. Major strikes against American railroads in 1887 and 1894 registered little with travelers no matter what their nationality; the subject surfaced with a distinctly antiunion bias only in an occasional parlor-car conversation. Catherine Bates saw, on arrival in St. Louis in 1887, a "miniature Aldershot Camp on the line," but her efforts to learn the identity of the campers were brushed aside with the terse answer "Soldiers to guard the property and lives of the employers" (II, 16).

3. Beebe, *Mr. Pullman's Elegant Palace Car,* 138; Arthur Dubin, *Some Classic Trains* (Milwaukee: Kalmbach, 1964), 40; John H. White, *The American Railroad Passenger Car* (Baltimore: Johns Hopkins University Press, 1978), 266–73. Railroad construction, which began in the interior in Illinois in 1833, advanced at a stunning rate. Throughout the decade of the 1840s, in five states of the old interior—Illinois, Missouri, Iowa, Wisconsin, and Minnesota—97 miles of rails were laid. Across the following four decades these numbers rose to 4,607 miles, 4,410 miles, 13,331 miles, and, between 1880 and 1890, 74,100 miles.

4. Lucy, 152; O'Rell, 269–70.

5. Rae, 376; Bowles, *Parks and Mountains,* 39; Lakier, 57; Stevenson, 144; M. M. Shaw, 138–39, 144–48.

6. Trotter, 163; Abbott, 24–25, 37; Rae, 66–67; Hardy, 83; Faithfull, 45–46, 119–20.

7. Nordhoff, 20; Bowles, *Parks and Mountains,* 41; Blake, 222–26; Hardman, 113, 147; Rae, 29–30. Hardman went so far as to dedicate his book to his excursion director, "Uncle Rufus" Hatch, whose persona is imposed over everything Hardman saw in America. Catherine Bates, who liked to characterize herself as a "Female Columbus," looked into the Raymond Excursions, said to be "rather more expensive and decidedly more exclusive" than Cook's tours, which Blake so enthusiastically recommended. Bates rejected the excursion on the grounds that "the very fact of feeling that you *must* keep up and on for a certain number of weeks would be enough to make some of us ill from sheer nervousness" (II, 317, 77–79).

8. Bates II, 6–7; Robert J. Casey and W. A. S. Douglas, *Pioneer Railroad: The Story of the CNW System* (New York: McGraw-Hill, 1948), 189–90.

9. O'Rell, 278.

10. Stevenson, 115–18, 106–7, 120–21. John H. White, *The American Railroad Passenger Car,* explains that

> although emigrants were usually carried in broken-down coaches, some lines built special cars for emigrant traffic . . . as the tempo of Western settlement increased, the need for equipment that was adapted to the lowest possible fares became evident. A happy solution was found in specially outfitted boxcars. The Illinois Central ordered twenty in 1855 at just $200 above the normal boxcar unit price. Windows were placed on either side of the center doors, end doors were cut in, and seats were installed. In the same year the Michigan Central reported that it had fifty cars on the same general plan. End platforms were added and the seats were removable, so that emigrants could be carried west and freight east. (466)

In 1873 John Erastus Lester rode the Michigan Central and remarked that the emigrant trains were "run at a lower rate of speed, and at much lower fares, than those used for general travel" (6). See Walter Licht, *Working for the Railroad* (Princeton, N.J.: Princeton University Press, 1983), for a discussion of the employment of children as newsbutchers on the railroads.

11. A. Trollope, 73–74; Boddam-Whetham, 27, 30; M. M. Shaw, 30–31; Lester, 21; Blake, 2–3. Peter T. Maiken's *Night Trains* (Chicago: Lakme, 1989) is a full exposition of Pullman's attachment to the open-section sleeping car and of how he destroyed competing designs by absorbing competing companies.

12. Faithfull, 47; Rae, 31. Russell Lynes, *The Tastemakers* (New York: Grosset & Dunlap, 1954), quotes George Mortimer Pullman on the desired effect, from his point of view, of the decor: "I have always held that people are greatly influenced by their physical surroundings. Take the roughest man, a man whose lines have brought him into the coarsest and poorest surroundings, and bring him into a room elegantly carpeted and finished, and the effect upon his bearing is immediate. The more artistic and refined the external surroundings, the better and more refined the man" (95–96). I am indebted to John White, Arthur Dubin, and Lucius Beebe for the photographic views of the car interiors the travelers rode in; I note Beebe's and Dubin's enthusiasm for the decor without sharing it any more than did the travelers who wrote of these trains from personal experience. In the nineteenth century Pullman drew rapturous press notices from white men; the cars were made, designed, and decorated by white men; the entire literature of enthusiasm over them in the twentieth century has been produced by white men. This is worth noting even if meaningless. A further book about railroad travel, Wolfgang Schivelbusch's *The Railway Journey: Trains and Travel in the 19th Century*, trans. Anselm Hollo (New York: Urizen, 1977), should be noted for not illuminating American rail travel at all: Schivelbusch's contentions about upholstery and landscape apply only to European travel.

13. Hardy, 81–82; Blake, 14; Stevenson, 107–8; Nordhoff, 23–24; Lester, 21; M. M. Shaw, 14, 82, 165; Blake, 228.

14. Shaw, 18; Blake, 227; Hardy, 75; Bates II, 19–23; Bowles, *Parks and Mountains*, 39–40.

15. Rae, 53–54; Hardy, 92–93; Stevenson, 112–13.

16. Summerhayes, 194–96; Faithfull, 45–46; Bates II, 23; A. Trollope, 102; Hogan, 73.

17. Holyoake, 216.

18. Bunn, 146; Abbott, 24–25; E. Pfeiffer, 99. English travelers, who never got the hang of traveling with one or two large pieces of luggage as Americans did, customarily approached a train with ten or twelve small packages, each one of which had to have a baggage ticket written out for it, and over the profusion of which railway agents regularly grumbled.

19. Blake, 3–4, 14; Nordhoff, 25. Mary Elizabeth Blake remarks again and again in her book on the "home feeling" that she created around her, or discovered, on her excursion train. Numerous feminist critics such as Aileen Kraditor, Mary Ryan, and Linda Kerber have, over the past few decades, noted and discussed the repeated connection of women with home in terms of its posing a polarity between the home and the world. In travel literature, some women who ventured out of the home apparently felt compelled to transform the world into a version of the home.

20. Twain, 140–41; Frederick Marryat, 101; Alexander, 93–94; Guest, 52; Blake, 28; Rae, 49–50; Lester, 2; Lakier, 164, 190; Rae, 186; White, 207; M. M. Shaw, 145–46; Dickens, 61–62; Bird, 107–8; Lucy, 158–59.

21. Alexander, 93; Ferguson, 378; R. H. Davis, 4–5; Rae, 40, 62; Hogan, 66; Lucy, 43–44; Vivian, 188; Lester, 18–19.

22. Alexander, 87; Borrett, 117; Guest, 147; E. Pfeiffer, 114; Bowles, *Parks and Mountains,* 40–41; Rae, 35–36, 58–59; A. Trollope, 46–47; Stanley, 88; Lester, 12–13; Greenwood, 8. The skunk is a member of the weasel family. As to the importance of bees, John Bradbury wrote in 1819 that "bees have spread over this continent in a degree and with a celerity so nearly corresponding with that of the Anglo-Americans, that it has given rise to a belief, both among the Indians and the whites, that bees are their precursors, and that to whatever part they go the white people will follow" (34).

23. Stevenson, 141; Lester, 33; Rae, 69–81; Nordhoff, 26; Hogan, 49; M. M. Shaw, 67; Greenwood, 28; Hardy, 27–28; Guest, 140, 193; Hardman, 130–32. Ronald Takaki, *Iron Cages: Race and Culture in 19th-Century America* (New York: Alfred A. Knopf, 1990), discusses the railroads' treatment of the Indian populations from whom they had to secure right-of-way; Earl Pomeroy, *In Search of the Golden West* (New York: Alfred A. Knopf, 1957), discusses tactics used to convince tourists that the Far West was still wild. Carlton Corliss's *Trails to Rails* (Chicago, 1934) is the rare text that is candid about Indian trails on the landscape and how they were employed both by the so-called pioneers and eventually by the railroads.

24. Leslie, 39; Greenwood, 26; Rae, 62–63; Trotter, 215; M. M. Shaw, 50.

25. Vivian, 84–85; Maiken, *Night Trains,* 24–25; Ferguson, 378; Greenwood, 30–32; Bates I, 283–84; Nordhoff, 25; Bromley, 20; Blake, 227; O'Rell, 272; Faithfull, 45; White, *The American Railroad Passenger Car,* 400–406.

26. Lucy, 38; Trotter, 236; Guest, 183–84; Hogan, 68–69; Bates, 268–72; Hardman, 92–93; Nordhoff, 20–22. Pigs intruded on travelers once more in the twentieth century when, shortly after World War II, Robert R. Young, chairman of the Chesapeake and Ohio Railroad, launched an advertising campaign with the slogan "A hog can cross America without changing trains—but YOU can't."

27. Hardy, 80–82; Lucy, 34–35; Lester, 13–14; Rae, 69, 79. Frank Leslie's much-ballyhooed luxury excursion of 1877, meant to garner publicity and to produce plenty of material for *Leslie's Illustrated,* carried four artists but, according to William Taft, *Artists and Illustrators of the Old West, 1850–1900* (New York: Scribner's, 1953), produced no pictures between New York and Chicago and exactly one to illustrate the space between Chicago and Council Bluffs, Iowa: "Beginning at the latter place," according to Taft, "there are illustrations to depict almost every phase of the journey" westward (153).

28. Ferguson, 378–79; Hancock, 280–81; N. Hall, 160–61; Greenwood, 12; Lester, 19–20.

29. J. Shaw, 28–29; Stevenson, 108–9; M. M. Shaw, 208; Bates II, 233, 264–65; Hogan, 66–67; Hardy, 93; Blake, 208; Trotter, 150; Rae, 36; Rose, 217; Leslie, 37; R. H. Davis, 242; White, 207–10, 223–24, 242. John White's effort to render the landscape was so unusual that later travelers, recognizing a good thing when they saw it, stole liberally from his work to cover their own inadequacies. See especially Boddam-Whetham, 38–40.

30. Alexander, 88; Hardy, 93, 278; Bowles, *Parks and Mountains,* 44; Hardman, 140; Vivian, 100; Trotter, 145.

31. Stevenson, 137.

Bibliography

Abbott, Ethel B. *A Diary of a Tour Through Canada and the United States.* London, 1882.

Abel, Henry I. *Traveller's and Emigrant's Guide to Wisconsin and Iowa.* Philadelphia: M. I. Abel, 1838.

Adams, Emma H. *To and Fro in Southern California.* Cincinnati: WMBC Press, 1887.

Alexander, Joseph. *Promenade.* Trans. Lady Herbert. London: Macmillan, 1874.

Amphlett, William. *The Emigrant's Directory to the Western States of North America.* London: Longman, Hurst, Rees, Orme, and Brown, 1819.

Anburey, Thomas. *Travels Through the Interior Parts of America.* London: W. Lane, 1789.

Andrews, Christopher Columbus. *Minnesota and Dacotah; In Letters Descriptive of a Tour through the Northwest in the Autumn of 1856.* Washington, D.C.: R. Farnham, 1857.

Arese, Francesco. *A Trip to the Prairies and in the Interior of North America, 1837–1838.* Trans. Andrew Evans. New York: Harbor Press, 1934.

Ashe, Thomas. *Memoirs of Mammoth.* Liverpool: G. F. Harris, 1806.

———. *Travels in America.* London: R. Phillips, 1808.

Atwater, Caleb. *Writings of Caleb Atwater.* Columbus, Ohio: by the author, 1833.

Backhouse, Hannah Chapman. *Extracts from the Journal and Letters of Hannah Chapman Backhouse.* London: R. Barrett, 1858.

Baily, Francis. *Journal of a Tour in Unsettled Parts of North America, 1796–1797.* London: Baily Brothers, 1856.

Barber, John W., and Henry Howe. *Our Whole Country.* 2 vols. Cincinnati: H. Howe, 1861.

Bartram, William. *Travels.* 1791; rpt. New York: Viking Penguin, 1988.

Bates, E. Catherine. *A Year in the Great Republic.* 2 vols. London: Ward & Downey, 1887.

Baxter, William Edward. *America and the Americans.* London: Geo. Routledge, 1855.

Beauvallet, Leon C. *Rachel and the New World. A Trip to the United States and Cuba.* New York: Dix, Edwards, 1856.

Beck, Lewis C. *Gazetteer of the States of Illinois and Missouri.* Albany, N.Y.: 1823.

Bell, Andrew. *Men and Things in America: Being the Experience of a Year's Residence in the United States.* London: W. Smith, 1838.

Bell, William Abraham. *New Tracks in North America.* London: Chapman and Hall, 1869.

Bellegarrigue, A. *Les Femmes d'Amerique.* Paris: Blanchard, 1853.

Beltrami, Giacomo Constantino. *A Pilgrimage in Europe and America Leading to the Discovery of the Sources of the Mississippi and Bloody River.* London: Hunt & Clarke, 1828.

Benwell, John. *An Englishman's Travels in America.* London: Binns and Goodwin, 1853.

Berkeley, George Charles Grantley Fitzhardinge. *The English Sportsman in the Western Prairies.* London: Hurst and Blackett, 1861.

Bernard, John. *Retrospections of America, 1797–1811.* New York: Harper & Bros., 1887.

Beste, John Richard Digby. *The Wabash; or, Adventures of an English Gentleman's Family in the Interior of America.* London: Hurst and Blackett, 1855.

Bill, Ledyard. *Minnesota—Its Character and Climate, Including Copious Notes on Health, Hints to Tourists and Emigrants.* New York: Wood and Holbrook, 1871.

Bird, Isabella Lucy. *The Englishwoman in America.* 1856; rpt. Madison: University of Wisconsin Press, 1966.

Birkbeck, Morris. *Letters from Illinois.* 2nd ed. London: Taylor and Hessey, 1818.

———. *Notes on a Journey in America.* Philadelphia: Caleb Richardson, 1817.

Bishop, Harriet E. *Floral Home: or, First Years of Minnesota.* New York: Sheldon, Blakeman, 1857.

Blake, Mary Elizabeth McGrath. *On the Wing: Rambling Notes of a Trip to the Pacific.* Boston: Lee and Shepard, 1883.

Blane, William Newnham. *An Excursion Through the United States and Canada During the Years 1822–1823.* London: Baldwin, Cradock, and Joy, 1824.

Boardman, James. *America and the Americans.* London: Longman, Rees, Brown, Green and Longman, 1833.

Boddam-Whetham, John W. *Western Wanderings: A Record of Travel in the Evening Land.* London: R. Bentley, 1874.

Borrett, George T. *Letters from Canada and the United States.* London: J. E. Adlard, 1865.

Bowles, Samuel. *Across the Continent.* Springfield, Mass.: Samuel Bowles and Co., 1865.

———. *The Parks and Mountains of Colorado.* 1869; rpt. Norman: University of Oklahoma Press, 1991.

Brackenridge, Henry Marie. *Journal of a Voyage Up the River Missouri Performed in 1811.* Baltimore: Coale and Maxwell, 1816.

———. *Recollections of Persons and Places in the West.* Philadelphia: J. Kay, 1834.

Bradbury, John. *Travels in the Interior of America, 1809, 1810, 1811.* London: Sherwood, Neely, & Jones, 1819.

Bradford, William John Alden. *Notes on the Northwest, or Valley of the Upper Mississippi.* New York: Wiley and Putnam, 1846.

Bremer, Fredrika. *The Homes of the New World.* Trans. Mary Howitt. New York: Harper & Bros., 1853.

Brissot de Warville, Jacques Pierre. *New Travels in the United States of America.* Trans. Mara Soceanu Vamos and Durand Echeverria. 1788; rpt. Cambridge, Mass.: Belknap Press, 1964.

Bristed, John. *America and Her Resources.* London: Colburn, 1818.

Bromley, Clara Fitzroy Kelly. *A Woman's Wanderings in the Western World.* London: Saunders, Otley, 1861.

Brothers, Thomas. *The United States of America as They Are; Not as They are Generally Described: Being a Cure for Radicalism.* London: Longman, Orme, 1840.

Brown, Samuel R. *The Western Gazetteer.* Auburn, N.Y.: H. C. Southwick, 1817.

Bryce, James. *The American Commonwealth.* 2 vols. 3rd ed. New York: Macmillan, 1910.

Buckingham, James Silk. *America, Historical, Statistic, and Descriptive.* 3 vols. London: Fisher, Son, and Co., 1841.

———. *The Eastern and Western States of America.* 3 vols. London: Fisher, 1842.

Bullock, William. *Sketch of a Journey Through the Western States of North America.* London: J. Miller, 1827.

Bunn, Alfred. *Old England and New England, In a Series of Views Taken on the Spot.* New York: Benjamin Blom, 1853.

Burlend, Rebecca. *A True Picture of Emigration: or, Fourteen Years in the Interior of North America.* London: G. Berger, 1848.

Burnet, Jacob. *Notes on the Early Settlement of the Northwestern Territory.* New York: Appleton, 1847.

Burns, Jabez. *Notes of a Tour in the United States and Canada.* London: Houlston and Stoveman, 1848.

Burton, Richard Francis. *Across the Plains to California.* 1862; rpt. Lincoln: University of Nebraska Press, 1963.

Busey, Samuel Clagett. *Immigration: Its Evils and Consequences.* New York: DeWitt and Davenport, 1856.

Caird, James. *Prairie Farming in America.* London: Longman, 1859.

Campbell, John Francis. *A Short American Tramp in the Fall of 1864.* Edinburgh: Edmonston and Douglas, 1865.

Carver, Jonathan. *Travels Through North America in the Years 1766, 1767, and 1768.* 1778; rpt. Toronto: Coles, 1974.

Chambers, William. *Things as They Are in America.* London and Edinburgh: W. and R. Chambers, 1854.

Charlevoix, Pierre. *Journal of a Voyage to North America.* 2 vols. London: R. and J. Dodsley, 1761.

Chastellux, François Jean. *Travels in North America in the Years 1789–1792.* 1827; rpt. New York: Augustus M. Kelley, 1970.

Chateaubriand, François René. *Travels in America.* London: H. Colburn, 1828.

Chester, Greville John. *Transatlantic Sketches.* London: Smith, Elder, 1869.

Chevalier, Michel. *Society, Manners, and Politics in the United States.* 1839; rpt. New York: Augustus M. Kelley, 1966.

Child, Andrew. *Overland Route to California.* Milwaukee: C. Child, 1852.

Cobb, Joseph B. *Mississippi Scenes.* Philadelphia: A. Hart, 1851.

Cobbett, William. *The Emigrant's Guide.* London: by the author, 1829.

————. *A Year's Residence in the United States.* New York: Clayton and Kingsland, 1818.

Cobden, Richard. *American Diaries, 1835, 1859.* New York: Greenwood, 1952.

Collins, S. H. *The Emigrant's Guide to and Description of the United States.* Hull: J. Noble, 1830.

Colt, Miriam. *Went to Kansas.* Watertown, N.Y.: L. Ingalls, 1862.

Combe, George. *Notes on the United States of North America.* Edinburgh: Maclachlan and Stewart, 1841.

Cooper, Thomas. *Some Information Respecting America.* Dublin: P. Wogan, 1794.

Cramer, Zadok. *The Navigator.* 8th ed. Pittsburgh: Cramer, Spear, and Eichbaum, 1814.

Crèvecoeur, Hector Guillaume St. John de. *Letters from an American Farmer.* London: T. Davies, 1782.

Cuming, Fortescue. *Sketches of a Tour to the Western Country, 1807–1809.* Pittsburgh: Cramer, Spear, and Eichbaum, 1810.

Cumings, Samuel. *The Western Pilot.* Cincinnati: G. Conclin, 1843.

Cunynghame, Arthur Augustus Thurlow. *A Glimpse at the Great Western Republic.* London: R. Bentley, 1851.

Curtiss, Daniel S. *Western Portraiture and Emigrants' Guide: A Description of Wisconsin, Illinois, and Iowa.* New York: J. H. Colton, 1852.

Custer, Elizabeth Bacon. *"Boots and Saddles": or, Life in Dakota with General Custer.* 1885; rpt. Norman: University of Oklahoma Press, 1961.

Dana, C. S. *Garden of the World.* Boston: Wentworth, 1856.

Dana, Edmund. *A Description of the Bounty Lands in Illinois.* Cincinnati: Looker and Reynolds, 1819.

Dartt, Mary Emma. *On the Plains, and Among the Peaks; or, How Mrs. Maxwell Made Her Natural History Collection.* Philadelphia: Claxton, Remsen, Haffelfinger, 1879.

Daubeny, Charles. *Journal of a Tour Through the United States and Canada, Made During the Years 1837–1838.* Oxford: T. Combe, 1843.

Davis, John. *Travels of Four Years and a Half in the United States of America, 1798–1802.* New York: R. Edwards, 1803.

Davis, Richard Harding. *The West from a Car-Window.* New York: Harper & Brothers, 1892.

Davis, Stephen. *Notes of a Tour in America, in 1832 and 1833.* Edinburgh: Waugh and Innes, 1833.

De Hauranne, Ernest Duvergier. *A Frenchman in Lincoln's America.* 1866; rpt. Chicago: Lakeside, 1974.

Delafield, John. *An Inquiry into the Origin of the Antiquities of America.* Cincinnati: G. N. Burgess, 1839.

Delano, Alonzo. *Life on the Plains and Among the Diggings.* Auburn, N.Y.: Miller, Orton, and Mulligan, 1854.

De Ros, John Frederick Fitzgerald. *Personal Narrative of Travels in the United States and Canada in 1826.* London: W. H. Ainsworth, 1827.

Dicey, Edward. *Six Months in the Federal States.* London: Macmillan, 1863.

Dickens, Charles. *American Notes.* 1842; rpt. New York: Fromm, 1985.

Disturnell, John. *A Trip Through the Lakes of North America.* New York: J. Disturnell, 1857.

Dix, John Ross. *Transatlantic Tracings: or Sketches of Persons and Scenes in America.* London: W. Tweedie, 1853.

Dixon, James. *Personal Narrative of a Tour Through a Part of the United States and Canada.* New York: Lane and Scott, 1849.

Dixon, William Hepworth. *New America.* 2 vols. London: Hurst and Blackett, 1867.

————. *White Conquest.* London: Chatto & Windus, 1876.

Drake, Benjamin, and E. D. Mansfield. *Cincinnati in 1826.* Cincinnati: Morgan, Lodge, and Fisher, 1827.

Drake, Daniel. *Discourse on the History, Character, and Prospects of the West.* 1834; rpt. Gainesville, Fla.: Scholars Facsimiles, 1955.

————. *Picture of Cincinnati.* Cincinnati: Looker & Wallace, 1815.

Duden, Gottfried. *Report on a Journey to the Western States of North America.* Trans. George Kellner et al. 1829; rpt. Columbia: State Historical Society of Missouri and University of Missouri Press, 1980.

Duncan, Mary G. L. *America As I Found It.* London: James Nisbet, 1852.

Eastman, Mary. *Dahcotah: Or, Life and Legends of the Sioux.* New York: John Wiley, 1849.

Ellet, Elizabeth. *Summer Rambles in the West.* New York: J. C. Riker, 1853.

Ellsworth, Henry William. *Illinois in 1837.* Philadelphia: Mitchell, 1837.

Faithfull, Emily. *Three Visits to America.* Edinburgh: David Douglas, 1884.

Farkas, Alexander Boloni. *Journey in North America.* Trans. Theodore and Helen Benedek Schoenman. 1834; rpt. Philadelphia: American Philosophical Society, 1977.

Farnham, Eliza Woodson. *Life in Prairie Land.* New York: Harper & Brothers, 1846.

Farnham, Thomas. *Travels in the Great Western Prairies.* 2 vols. London: Richard Bentley, 1843.

Farrar, J. Maurice. *Five Years in Minnesota: Sketches of Life in a Western State.* London: Sampson Low, 1880.

Faux, William. *Memorable Days in America, 1818–1820.* London: W. Simpkin and Marshall, 1823.

Fearon, Henry. *Sketches of America: A Narrative of a Journey of 5000 Miles.* London: Longman, Hurst, Rees, Orme, and Brown, 1818.

Featherstonhaugh, George W. *A Canoe Voyage Up the Minnay Sotor.* 2 vols. London: R. Bentley, 1847.

Felton, the Mrs. *American Life: A Narrative of Two Years' City and Country Residence in the United States.* London: Simpkin, Marshall, 1842.

Ferguson, William. *America by River and Rail.* London: J. Nisbet, 1856.

Finch, Marianne. *An Englishwoman's Experience in America.* London: Richard Bentley, 1853.

Finiels, Nicolas de. *An Account of Upper Louisiana.* Trans. Carl J. Ekberg. Columbia: University of Missouri Press, 1989.

Flagg, Edmund. *The Far West.* New York: Harper & Brothers, 1838.

Flint, James. *Letters from America.* Edinburgh: W. and C. Tait, 1822.

Flint, Timothy. *A Condensed Geography and History of the Western States, or the Mississippi Valley.* Cincinnati: E. H. Flint, 1828.

————. *Recollections of the Last Ten Years Passed in Occasional Residences and Journeyings in the Valley of the Mississippi.* 1826; rpt. New York: Johnson Reprint Co., 1968.

Flower, Richard. *Letters from Lexington and the Illinois.* London: James Ridgway, 1822.

Fordham, Elias Pym. *Personal Narrative of Travels, 1817–1818.* Cleveland: Arthur H. Clark, 1906.

Frémont, Jessie Benton. *A Year of American Travel.* New York: Harper & Brothers, 1878.

Fuller, Margaret. *Summer on the Lakes.* 2nd ed. 1844; rpt. New York: Haskell House, 1970.

Galland, Isaac. *Galland's Iowa Emigrant.* 1840; rpt. Iowa City: Prairie Press, 1949.

Gerstacker, Friedrich. *Wild Sports in the Far West.* 1854; rpt. Durham, N.C.: Duke University Press, 1968.

Gillmore, Parker. *Prairie Farms and Prairie Folk.* London: Hurst and Blackett, 1872.

Gladstone, Thomas H. *The Englishman in Kansas.* New York: Miller, 1857.

Goddard, Frederick B. *Where to Emigrate, and Why.* New York: Frederick B. Goddard, 1869.

Grandfort, Marie Fontenay de. *The New World.* Trans. E. C. Wharton. New Orleans: Sherman, Wharton, 1855.

Grant, Anne McVickar. *Memoirs of an American Lady.* London: Longman, Hurst, Rees, Orme, 1808.

Greeley, Horace. *Recollections of a Busy Life.* 1873; rpt. New York: Chelsea House, 1983.

Greenwood, Grace. *New Life in New Lands.* New York: J. B. Ford, 1873.

Gregg, Josiah. *Commerce of the Prairies.* 2 vols. New York: Henry Langley, 1844.

Griffiths, D. *Two Years in the New Settlements of Ohio.* London: Westley and Davis, 1835.

Grund, Francis J. *Aristocracy in America.* London: R. Bentley, 1839.

Guerin, E. J. *Mountain Charley: or, The Adventures of Mrs. E. J. Guerin, Who Was Thirteen Years in Male Attire.* 1861; rpt. Norman: University of Oklahoma Press, 1968.

Guest, Theodora. *A Round Trip in North America.* London: Edward Stanford, 1895.

Haliburton, Thomas Chandler. *The Americans at Home.* London: Hurst and Blackett, 1854.

Hall, Basil. *Travels in North America in the Years 1827 and 1828.* 3 vols. Edinburgh: Cadell, 1829.

Hall, James. *Letters from the West.* 1828; rpt. Gainesville, Fla.: Scholars Facsimiles, 1967.

————. *Statistics of the West, at the Close of the Year 1836.* Cincinnati: J. A. James, 1836.

Hall, Newman. *From Liverpool to St. Louis.* London: Geo. Routledge, 1870.

Hamilton, H. W. *Rural Sketches of Minnesota, the El Dorado of the Northwest.* Milan, Ohio: C. Waggoner, 1850.

Hamilton, Thomas. *Men and Manners in America.* 2 vols. 1833; rpt. New York: Augustus M. Kelley, 1968.

Hancock, William. *An Emigrant's Five Years in the Free States of America.* London: T. Cutley Newby, 1860.

Hardman, William. *A Trip to America.* London: T. Vickers Wood, 1884.

Hardy, Mary McDowell Duffus. *Through Cities and Prairie Lands: Sketches of an American Tour.* 1881; rpt. New York: Arno Press, 1974.

Harris, Thaddeus Mason. *Journal of a Tour into the Territory Northwest of the Allegheny Mountains: Made in the Spring of the Year 1803.* Boston: Manning and Loring, 1805.

Harris, William Tell. *Remarks Made During a Tour through the United States of America, in the Years 1817, 1818, and 1819.* London: Sherwood, Neely, and Jones, 1821.

Heckewelder, John Gottlieb Ernestus. *An Account of the History, Manners, and Customs of the Indian Nations.* Philadelphia: Abraham Small, 1819.

Hennepin, Louis. *A New Discovery of a Vast Country in America.* 1698; rpt. Chicago: A. C. McClung, 1903.

Henry, Alexander. *Travels and Adventures in Canada and the Indian Territories.* New York: I. Riley, 1809.

Hewitt, Girart. *Minnesota: Its Advantages to Settlers.* St. Paul, Minn.: by the author, 1867.

Hill, Ira. *Antiquities of America Explained.* Hagerstown, Md.: William D. Bell, 1831.

Hodgson, Adam. *Remarks During a Journey Through North America.* New York: J. Seymour, 1823.

Hoffman, Charles Fenno. *A Winter in the West.* 2 vols. New York: Harper & Brothers, 1835.

Hogan, James Francis. *The Australian in London and America.* London: Ward and Downey, 1889.

Holmes, Isaac. *An Account of the United States of America.* 1823; rpt. New York: Arno, 1974.

Holyoake, George Jacob. *Among the Americans* and *A Stranger in America.* 1881; rpt. Westport, Conn.: Greenwood Press, 1970.

Houstoun, Matilda Charlotte. *Hesperos; or, Travels in the West.* 2 vols. London: John W. Parker, 1850.

Howitt, Emanuel. *Letters Written During a Tour through the United States.* Nottingham: J. Dunn, 1820.

Hull, John Simpson. *Remarks on the United States of America: Drawn Up from His own Observations and from the Observations of Other Travelers.* Dublin: William McKenzie, 1801.

Hulme, Thomas. *Journal of a Tour in the Western Countries of America, Sept. 30, 1818–Aug. 8, 1819.* 1820; rpt. Cleveland: A. H. Clark, 1904.

Imlay, Gilbert. *A Topographical Description of the Western Territory of North America.* 3rd ed. London: J. DeBrett, 1792.

Irving, Washington. *A Tour on the Prairies.* 1835; rpt. New York: Hurst, 1886.

James, Edwin, comp. *Account of an Expedition from Pittsburgh to the Rocky Mountains Performed in the Years 1819, 1820.* 4 vols. London: Longman, Hurst, Rees, and Brown, 1823.

James, Thomas Horton. *Rambles in the United States and Canada.* London: John Ollivier, 1846.

Jameson, Anna Brownell. *Winter Studies and Summer Rambles in Canada.* 3 vols. 1838; rpt. Toronto: Coles, 1972.

Jarvis, Edward. *Immigration into the United States.* Boston: J. R. Osgood, 1872.

Jones, David. *Journal of Two Visits Made to Some Nations of Indians on the West Side of the River Ohio, in the Years 1772 and 1773.* New York: Joseph Sabin, 1865.

Kalm, Peter. *Travels into North America.* Trans. John R. Forster. Warrington, England: W. Eyres, 1770.

Kelly, William. *Excursion to California Over the Prairie.* 2 vols. London: Chapman and Hall, 1857.

Kemp, Harry. *Tramping on Life: An Autobiographical Narrative.* New York: Boni and Liveright, 1923.

Ker, Henry. *Travels Through the Western Interior of the United States.* Elizabethtown, N.J.: 1816.

Kinzie, Juliette Magill. *Wau-Bun: The Early Days in the North-West.* 1855; rpt. Chicago: Lakeside, 1932.

Kirkland, Caroline. *Forest Life.* New York: G. P. Putnam, 1842.

———. *A New Home: Who'll Follow?* New York: G. P. Putnam, 1839.

———. *Western Clearings.* New York: G. P. Putnam, 1845.

Koch, Albert C. *Journey Through a Part of the United States of North America in the Years 1844–1846.* Trans. Ernst A. Stadler. Carbondale, Ill.: Southern Illinois University Press, 1972.

Lahontan, Louis Armand. *New Voyages to North America.* 1793; rpt. Chicago: A. C. McClung, 1905.

Lanman, Charles. *Adventures in the Wilds of the United States.* 2 vols. Philadelphia: J. W. Moore, 1856.

———. *Letters from a Landscape Painter.* Boston: J. Monroe, 1845.

———. *A Summer in the Wilderness.* New York: Appleton, 1847.

Latrobe, Charles Joseph. *The Rambler in North America.* 2 vols. London: Seeley and Burnside, 1835.

Lea, Albert Miller. *Notes on the Wisconsin Territory.* Philadelphia: H. S. Tanner, 1836.

Leslie, Miriam Follin. *California: A Pleasure Trip from Gotham to the Golden Gate.* New York: G. W. Carleton, 1877.

Lester, John Erastus. *The Atlantic to the Pacific: What to See and How to See It.* London: Longmans, Green, 1873.

Levinge, Richard G. A. *Echoes from the Backwoods.* London: H. Colburn, 1846.

Lewis, Henry. *The Valley of the Mississippi Illustrated.* Trans. A. Hermina Poatgieter. 1854; rpt. St. Paul, Minn.: Minnesota Historical Society, 1967.

Lewis, John Delaware. *Across the Atlantic.* London: George Earle, 1851.

Lieber, Francis. *Letters to a Gentleman in Germany.* Philadelphia: Carey, Lea, and Blanchard, 1834.

Logan, James. *Notes on a Journey Through Canada, the United States, and the West Indies.* Edinburgh: Fraser, 1838.

Long, John. *Voyages and Travels of an Indian Interpreter and Trader.* London: by the author, 1791.

Long, Robert Cary. *Ancient Architecture of America.* New York: Bartlett and Welford, 1849.

Long, Stephen Harriman. *Voyage in a Six-Oared Skiff to the Falls of St. Anthony, in 1817.* Philadelphia: H. R. Ashmead, 1860.

Look Before You Leap. London: W. Row, 1796.

Lucy, Henry W. *East by West: A Journey in the Recess.* London: Richard Bentley, 1885.

Lumsden, James. *American Memoranda, by a Mercantile Man During a Short Tour in the Summer of 1843.* Glasgow: Bell and Bain, 1844.

Lyell, Charles. *Travels in North America.* 2 vols. London: J. Murray, 1845.

McClung, J. W. *Minnesota As It Is in 1870: Its General Resources and Attractions for Immigrants, Invalids, Tourists, Capitalists, and Business Men.* St. Paul, Minn.: by the author, 1870.

MacGregor, John. *Our Brothers and Cousins: A Summer Tour in Canada and the States.* London: Seeley, Jackson, and Halliday, 1859.

Mackay, Alexander. *The Western World.* Philadelphia: Lea and Blanchard, 1849.

Mackay, Charles. *Life and Liberty in America.* 2 vols. London: Smith, Elder, 1859.

McKenney, Thomas L. *Sketches of a Tour to the Lakes.* 1827; rpt. Minneapolis: Ross and Haines, 1959.

Mackenzie, Eneas. *An Historical, Topographical, and Descriptive View of the United States.* Newcastle: Mackenzie and Dent, 1819.

Mackie, John Milton. *From Cape Cod to Dixie and the Tropics.* 1864; rpt. New York: Negro Universities Press, 1968.

Mackinnon, Lauchlan Bellingham. *Atlantic and Transatlantic Sketches.* New York: Harper & Brothers, 1852.

Macrae, David. *The Americans at Home: Pen and Ink Sketches of American Men, Manners, and Institutions.* Edinburgh: Edmonston and Douglas, 1870.

Marcy, Randolph Barnes. *The Prairie Traveler.* New York: Harper & Brothers, 1859.

Marryat, Frank. *Mountains and Molehills: or, Recollections of a Burnt Journal.* London: Longman, Brown, Green, and Longmans, 1855.

Marryat, Frederick. *A Diary in America.* Philadelphia: Carey and Hart, 1839.

Martineau, Harriet. *Retrospect of Western Travel.* 2 vols. London: Saunders and Otley, 1838.

————. *Society in America.* 3 vols. London: Saunders and Otley, 1837.

Medley, Julius. *An Autumn Tour in the United States and Canada.* London: H. S. King, 1873.

Melish, John. *Travels Through the United States of America.* 2 vols. Philadelphia: by the author, 1818.

Michaux, André. *Journal, 1793–1796.* Philadelphia: American Philosophical Society Proceedings, 1889.

Michaux, François André. *Travels to the West of the Allegheny Mountains.* 1805; rpt. Cleveland: A. H. Clark, 1904.

Montule, Edouard de. *Travels in America, 1816–1817.* Trans. Edward D. Seeber. Bloomington: Indiana University Press, 1951.

Mooney, Thomas. *Nine Years in America.* Dublin: J. McGlashan, 1850.

Morgan, Martha M. *A Trip Across the Plains in the Year 1849.* St. Paul, Minn.: Pioneer Press, 1864.

Murray, Amelia Matilda. *Letters from the United States, Cuba, and Canada.* 2 vols. New York: G. P. Putnam, 1856.

Murray, Charles Augustus. *Travels in North America, 1834–1836.* 2 vols. 1839; rpt. New York: DaCapo Press, 1974.

Newhall, John B. *The British Emigrant's Handbook and Guide*. London: T. Stutter, 1844.

Nordhoff, Charles. *California: For Health, Pleasure, and Residence*. New York: Harper & Brothers, 1872.

O'Bryan, William. *A Narrative of Travels in the United States of America*. London: by the author, 1836.

O'Ferrall, Simon Ansley. *Rambles of Six Thousand Miles Through the United States of America*. London: E. Wilson, 1832.

Oldmixon, John W. *Transatlantic Wanderings*. London: G. Routledge, 1855.

Oliphant, Lawrence. *Minnesota and the Far West*. Edinburgh: W. Blackwood, 1855.

Oliver, William. *Eight Months in Illinois*. Newcastle Upon Tyne: E. and T. Bruce, 1843.

O'Rell, Max. [Pseud. Paul Blouet.] *Jonathan and His Continent: Rambles Through American Society*. Trans. Mme. Paul Blouet. New York: Cassell, 1889.

Palliser, John. *The Solitary Hunter; or Sporting Adventures in the Prairies*. London: G. Routledge, 1856.

Parker, Amos Andrew. *A Trip to the West and Texas*. Concord, N.H.: White and Fisher, 1835.

Paul Wilhelm. *Travels in North America, 1822–1824*. Trans. W. Robert Nitske. 1835; rpt. Norman: University of Oklahoma Press, 1973.

Peyton, John Lewis. *Over the Alleghenies and Across the Prairies*. London: Simpkin, Marshall, 1869.

Pfeiffer, Emily. *Flying Leaves from East and West*. New York: Scribner and Welford, 1885.

Pfeiffer, Ida. *A Lady's Second Journey Round the World*. 2 vols. London: Longman, 1855.

Pickering, Joseph. *Emigration or No Emigration: Being the Narrative of an English Farmer*. London: E. Wilson, 1832.

Pidgeon, William. *Traditions of De-Coo-Dah*. New York: Horace Thayer, 1858.

Pittman, Philip. *The Present State of the European Settlements on the Mississippi*. London: J. Nourse, 1770.

Plumbe, John. *Sketches of Iowa and Wisconsin*. St. Louis: Chambers, Harris, and Knapp, 1839.

Power, Tyrone. *Impressions of America*. 2 vols. London: R. Bentley, 1836.

Priest, Josiah. *American Antiquities and Discoveries in the West*. 3rd ed. Albany, N.Y.: Hoffman and White, 1833.

Priest, William. *Travels in the United States of America, 1793–1797*. London: J. Johnson, 1802.

Pulszky, Francis, and Theresa Pulszky. *White, Red, Black: Sketches of Society in the United States*. London: Trubner, 1853.

Rae, William Fraser. *Westward by Rail*. New York: Appleton, 1871.

Ratzel, Friedrich. *Sketches of Urban and Cultural Life in North America*. Trans. Stewart A. Sahlin. 1876; rpt. Brunswick, N.J.: Rutgers University Press, 1988.

Raumer, Frederick Ludwig Georg von. *America and the American People*. Trans. William W. Turner. New York: J. and H. G. Langley, 1846.

Regan, John. *The Emigrant's Guide to the Western States of America; or, Backwoods and Prairies*. 2nd ed. Edinburgh: Oliver and Boyd, 1852.

Révoil, Bénédict Henry. *Shooting and Fishing in the Rivers, Prairies, and Backwoods of North America*. London: Tinsley Brothers, 1865.

Rickman, Thomas Clio. *Emigration to America Candidly Considered*. London: by the author, 1798.

Robinson, Sara Tappan Doolittle. *Kansas: Its Interior and Exterior Life*. Boston: Crosby, 1855.

Ropes, Hannah Anderson. *Six Months in Kansas*. Boston: J. P. Jewett, 1856.

Rose, George. *The Great Country*. London: Tinsley Brothers, 1868.

Rusling, James F. *Across America*. New York: Sheldon, 1875.

Rynning, Ole. *True Account of America*. Trans. Theodore C. Blegen. 1838; rpt. Minneapolis: Norwegian-American Historical Association, 1926.

Sarmiento, Domingo Faustino. *Travels in the United States in 1847*. Trans. Michael Rockland. 1847; rpt. Princeton, N.J.: Princeton University Press, 1970.

Saxe-Weimar Eisenach, Bernhard. *Travels through North America*. 2 vols. Philadelphia: Lea and Carey, 1828.

Schoolcraft, Henry Rowe. *Narrative of an Expedition through the Upper Mississippi to Itasca Lake*. New York: Harper & Bros., 1834.

————. *Narrative Journal of Travels from Detroit Northwest through the Great Chain of American Lakes to the Sources of the Mississippi River in the Year 1820*. Albany, N.Y.: E. & E. Hosford, 1821.

————. *Travels in the Central Portions of the Mississippi Valley*. New York: Collins and Hannay, 1825.

————. *A View of the Lead Mines of Missouri*. New York: Charles Wiley, 1819.

Scott, James Leander. *A Journal of a Missionary Tour*. Providence, R.I.: by the author, 1843.

Seacole, Mary. *Wonderful Adventures of Mrs. Seacole in Many Lands*. London: James Blackwood, 1857.

Sedgwick, Catherine M. "The Great Excursion to the Falls of St. Anthony." *Putnam's Monthly Magazine of American Literature, Science, and Art* 4 (September 1854): 320–25.

Seymour, E. Sanford. *Sketches of Minnesota, the New England of the West*. New York: Harper & Bros., 1850.

Shaw, James. *Twelve Years in America*. London: Hamilton, Adams, 1867.

Shaw, M. M. *Nine Thousand Miles on a Pullman Train: An Account of a Tour of Railroad Conductors from Philadelphia to the Pacific Coast and Return*. Philadelphia: Allen, Lane, and Scott, 1898.

Shirreff, Patrick. *A Tour Through North America*. Edinburgh: Oliver and Boyd, 1835.

Stanley, Henry Morton. *My Early Travels and Adventures in America*. 1895; rpt. Lincoln: University of Nebraska Press, 1982.

Steele, Eliza R. *A Summer Journey in the West*. New York: J. S. Taylor, 1841.

Stevenson, Robert Louis. *From Scotland to Silverado*. 1892; rpt. Cambridge, Mass.: Belknap Press, 1966.

Stewart, Catherine. *New Homes in the West*. Nashville, Tenn.: Cameron and Fall, 1843.

Stewart, W. M. *Eleven Years' Experience in the Western States of America*. London: Houlston, 1870.

Stuart, James. *Three Years in North America*. 2 vols. 2nd ed. New York: J. and J. Harper, 1833.

Bibliography

Stuart-Wortley, Emmeline. &C. London: Thomas Bosworth, 1853.

————. *Travels in the United States*. 3 vols. London: R. Bentley, 1851.

Sullivan, Edward Robert. *Rambles and Scrambles in North and South America*. London: R. Bentley, 1852.

Summerhayes, Martha. *Vanished Arizona*. New York: J. B. Lippincott, 1908.

Tanner, Henry S. *View of the Valley of the Mississippi*. 2nd ed. Philadelphia: by the author, 1834.

Taylor, Bayard. *Colorado: A Summer Trip*. 1876; rpt. Niwot, Colo.: University Press of Colorado, 1989.

Thomas, David. *Travels through the Western Country in the Summer of 1816*. Auburn, N.Y.: David Rumsey, 1819.

Thomson, William. *A Tradesman's Travels in the United States and Canada*. Edinburgh: Oliver and Boyd, 1842.

Tocqueville, Alexis de. *Democracy in America*. 2 vols. 1836; rpt. New York: Vintage, 1954.

Tremenheere, Hugh Seymour. *Notes on Public Subjects, Made During a Tour in the United States and Canada*. London: John Murray, 1852.

Trollope, Anthony. *North America*. 1862; rpt. New York: Penguin, 1969.

Trollope, Frances. *Domestic Manners of the Americans*. 1832; rpt. New York: Vintage, 1960.

Trotter, Isabella Strange. *First Impressions of the New World*. London: Longman, Brown, Green, Longman, and Roberts, 1859.

Tudor, Henry. *Narrative of a Tour in North America*. London: James Duncan, 1834.

Twain, Mark. *Life on the Mississippi*. 1883; rpt. New York: Heritage Press, 1944.

Van Cleve, Charlotte Ouisconsin. *Three Score Years and Ten*. Minneapolis: Harrison and Smith, 1888.

Vigne, Godfrey T. *Six Months in America*. 2 vols. London: Whittaker Treacher, 1832.

Vivian, Henry Hussey. *Notes of a Tour in America*. London: Edward Stanford, 1878.

Volney, Constantin François Chasseboeuf. *A View of the Soil and Climate of the United States of America*. London: J. Johnson, 1904.

Wakefield, Priscilla B. *Excursions in North America*. London: Darton and Harvey, 1806.

Wansey, Henry. *Journal of an Excursion to the United States of North America in the Summer of 1794*. Salisbury: J. Easton, 1796.

Warburton, George Drought. *Hochelaga; or, England in the New World*. New York: Wiley and Putnam, 1846.

Welby, Adlard. *A Visit to North America*. London: J. Drury, 1821.

Welby-Gregory, Victoria Alexandrina Maria Louisa. *A Young Traveler's Journal of a Tour in North and South America*. London: T. Bosworth, 1852.

Weld, Charles Richard. *A Vacation Tour in the United States and Canada*. London: Longman, 1855.

White, John. *Sketches from America*. London: Sampson Low, 1870.

Wied-Neuwied, Maximilian. *Travels in the Interior of North America, 1832–1834*. London: Ackerman, 1843.

Wilkey, Walter. *Western Emigration: Narrative of a Tour to and One Year's Residence in "Edensburgh," Illinois*. New York: G. Clairborne, 1829.

Wilkie, D. *Sketches of a Summer Trip to New York and the Canadas.* Edinburgh: J. Anderson, 1837.

Wood, Edward J. *Giants and Dwarfs.* London: R. Bentley, 1868.

Woods, John. *Two Years' Residence in the Settlement on the English Prairie.* London: Longman, Hurst, Rees, Orme, and Brown, 1822.

Wright, Frances. *Views of Society and Manners in America.* 1821; rpt. Cambridge, Mass.: Belknap Press, 1963.

Wright, John Stillman. *Letters from the West; or a Caution to Emigrants.* Salem, N.Y.: Dodd & Stevenson, 1819.

Zavala, Lorenzo de. *Journey to the United States of North America.* Trans. Wallace Woolsey. 1834; rpt. Austin, Tex.: Shoal Creek, 1980.

Index